INSI

# New
# Mexico

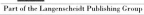

**APA** PUBLICATIONS
Part of the Langenscheidt Publishing Group

# INSIGHT GUIDE
## New Mexico

### Editorial
*Editor*
**John Gattuso**
*Principal Photography*
**Richard T. Nowitz**
*Editorial Director*
**Brian Bell**

### Distribution
*United States*
**Langenscheidt Publishers, Inc.**
36–36 33rd Street 4th Floor
Long Island City, NY 11106
Fax: 1 (718) 784 0640

*UK & Ireland*
**GeoCenter International Ltd**
Meridian House, Churchill Way West
Basingstoke, Hampshire RG21 6YR
Fax: (44) 1256 817988

*Australia*
**Universal Publishers**
1 Waterloo Road
Macquarie Park, NSW 2113
Fax: (61) 2 9888 9074

*New Zealand*
**Hema Maps New Zealand Ltd (HNZ)**
Unit D, 24 Ra ORA Drive
East Tamaki, Auckland
Fax: (64) 9 273 6479

*Worldwide*
**Apa Publications GmbH & Co.
Verlag KG (Singapore branch)**
38 Joo Koon Road, Singapore 628990
Tel: (65) 6865 1600. Fax: (65) 6861 6438

### Printing
**Insight Print Services (Pte) Ltd**
38 Joo Koon Road, Singapore 628990
Tel: (65) 6865 1600. Fax: (65) 6861 6438

©2007 **Apa Publications GmbH & Co.
Verlag KG (Singapore branch)**
*All Rights Reserved*

*First Edition 2004
Updated 2006; Reprinted 2007*

# ABOUT THIS BOOK

The first Insight Guide pioneered the use of creative full-color pho-tography in travel guides in 1970. Since then, we have expanded our range to cater for our readers' need not only for reliable information about their chosen destination but also for a real understanding of the culture and workings of that destination. Now, when the internet can supply in-exhaustible (but not always reliable) facts, our books marry text and pic-tures to provide those much more elusive qualities: knowledge and dis-cernment. To achieve this, they rely heavily on the authority of locally based writers and photographers.

## How to use this book

*Insight Guide: New Mexico* is struc-tured to convey an understanding of the state and its people as well as describe its sights and attractions:

♦ The **Features** section, indicated by a yellow bar at the top of each page, covers the natural and cultural history of the state in a series of informative essays.
♦ The main **Places** section, indi-cated by a blue bar, is a complete guide to all the sights and areas worth visiting. Places of special interest are coordinated by number with the maps.
♦ The **Travel Tips** listings section, with an orange bar, provides full information on travel, hotels, shops, restaurants and more. An easy-to-find contents list for Travel Tips is printed on the back flap, which also serves as a bookmark.

## The contributors

This book was produced by **John Gat-tuso** of Stone Creek Publications in Milford, New Jersey, a veteran of

**ABOVE:** an artist at work on Canyon Road, Santa Fe.

more than a dozen Insight Guides (including *Arizona* and *Colorado*) and editor of the Discovery Travel Adventures, a series for travelers with special interests such as bird-watching, scuba diving and astronomy. He also wrote the chapters on southwestern New Mexico and the I-70 corridor west of Albuquerque.

Gattuso's first recruit was Santa Fe writer **Nicky Leach**. The British native moved to New Mexico in 1990, after a decade working as an editor for California publishers. "I loved the feeling of space around the Las Vegas ranch house, where I first lived," she recalls. "I could watch electrical storms move across the plains into the mountains and illuminate the surround-

ing mesas all night long. Now I live in a beautiful canyon north of Santa Fe, where my companions are birds, coyotes, bears and a thousand stars every night." A frequent contributor to Insight Guides, Leach covers a host of topics, from geology and the arts to the spicy pleasures of New Mexican cuisine, then leads readers into every corner of the state, from the museums and galleries of Santa Fe and Taos to the sun-scorched expanse of the Chihuahuan Desert. The award-winning author of several guides to Southwest parks, she writes often for *Sunset* and *New Mexico* magazines.

**Larry Cheek,** author of several books and innumerable articles about the Southwest, covers New Mexico's "cultural landscape," a colorful blend of American Indian, Hispanic and Anglo influences with a quirky independent spirit.

Principal photography was undertaken by **Richard T. Nowitz**, whose vivid work is well-known to readers of Insight Guides and *National Geographic* magazine.

With more than 30 years experience as a news editor in the New York area, **Edward A. Jardim** knows how to transform a complex story into a concise narrative. Here he condenses four centuries of history into an engaging chronicle of New Mexico's development, from the exploits of Billy the Kid to the detonation of the first atomic bomb.

The indexer was **Elizabeth Cook**, and the cartography editor was **Zoë Goodwin**.

## Map Legend

| | |
|---|---|
| ▬ ▪ ▪ | International Boundary |
| ▬ ▬ ▬ | State Boundary |
| ⊖ | Border Crossing |
| ▪ | National Park/Reserve |
| ✈ ✈ | Airport: International/Regional |
| 🚌 | Bus Station |
| ❶ | Tourist Information |
| ✉ | Post Office |
| † † ☨ | Church/Ruins |
| † | Monastery |
| ☾ | Mosque |
| ✡ | Synagogue |
| 🏰 | Castle/Ruins |
| 🏠 | Mansion/Stately home |
| ∴ | Archeological Site |
| ∩ | Cave |
| 🗽 | Statue/Monument |
| ★ | Place of Interest |

The main places of interest in the Places section are coordinated by number with a full-color map (e.g. ❶), and a symbol at the top of every right-hand page tells you where to find the map.

# INSIGHT GUIDE
# New Mexico

# CONTENTS

## Maps

A hiker finds a scenic perch on a sandstone bluff in El Malpais National Monument.

## Travel Tips

## Information panels

## Places

# A LAND OF ENCHANTMENT

*New Mexico seduces with beguiling desert landscapes,
a rich cultural heritage and warm, welcoming people*

I think New Mexico was the greatest experience from the outside world that I have ever had," wrote the novelist D. H. Lawrence after coming to Taos in 1922 at the invitation of socialite and "collector of interesting people" Mabel Dodge Luhan. "[T]he moment I saw the brilliant, proud morning shine high up over the deserts of Sante Fe, something stood still in my soul, and I started to attend."

It's not an uncommon experience. Maybe it's the clear desert light, the alluring landscape, or the warmth and rootedness of the people. Whatever the case, New Mexicans have always welcomed new-comers with open arms. People land here as if by accident, or perhaps it's fate. Take, for example, Ernest Blumenschein. He and fellow New York artist Bert Geer Phillips were traveling through the West when their wagon broke down outside Taos. Blumenschein brought the broken wheel to town to be repaired and was smitten on the spot. "New Mexico had gripped me and I was not long in deciding that... the Taos valley and its surrounding magnificent country would be the end of our wagon trip." He and Phillips set down roots in New Mexico and later founded the influential Taos Society of Artists.

Like waves sculpting a sandy beach, such immigrants have altered the contours of New Mexico's cultural landscape without ever quite overwhelming it. Athabascan Indians arriving from the north in the 15th century raided Pueblo villages but couldn't eradicate them. Instead, some Athabascans – the group known today as the Navajo – learned farming from their Pueblo neighbors and were influenced by aspects of Pueblo religion. Others – the Apache – remained hunters and gatherers right up to the 20th century.

Spaniards, too, found that New Mexico was not to be easily tamed. Intending to reshape native societies in their own image, the Spanish ultimately found themselves transformed. Their colony in El Norte was a cultural hybrid. Even the Americans, with all their numbers and military might, failed to overrun New Mexico. "For once," as author Tony Hillerman observed of his home state's celebrated cultural diversity, "the American melting pot failed to operate. New Mexico produced a mosaic of cultures instead of a mixture."

And so it goes today. Newcomers to New Mexico are still touched, altered, awakened in spirit. Even the famously peripatetic Lawrence, a resident of New Mexico for less than 24 months, came back to stay, at least symbolically. His ashes were brought by his widow Frieda, who deposited them at the ranch they had shared in the mountains north of Taos, a place that Lawrence himself, enchanted by a sunset, described as "pure beauty, absolute beauty!"  ❏

**PRECEDING PAGES:** drummers at the feast day of San Ildefonso Pueblo; the proud owner of a lowrider, Española; branding cattle at the Burnt Well Ranch.
**LEFT:** traditional Mexican dancer at El Rancho de las Golondrinas, near Santa Fe.

Cow ??y, 90

# Decisive Dates

## Prehistoric cultures

**circa 10,000 BC:** Clovis hunters roam area in search of mammoth, bison and other game.
**circa 8000 BC:** Folsom people flourish throughout Southwest at the end of the last Ice Age.
**8000–500 BC:** Cochise people are first inhabitants to cultivate corn, squash and beans.
**300–1400 AD:** Mogollon culture introduces highly artistic pottery and early pit houses.
**700–1300:** Ancient Pueblo culture culminates in the highly developed Chaco civilization.

**1200–1500s:** Pueblo Indians establish villages along the Rio Grande and its tributaries.

## Europeans arrive

**1536:** Four survivors of a shipwrecked expedition, including Cabeza de Vaca, emerge from an odyssey through the Southwest with accounts that stir Spanish interest in a "new" Mexico.
**1540:** Coronado embarks on an expedition north of Mexico which, though it finds no golden cities of legend, encounters extensive Pueblo civilization.
**1598:** The first successful Spanish colony in New Mexico is founded by Juan de Oñate.
**1610:** Santa Fe, the oldest state capital in the United States, is established.

**1680:** Indian uprising known as the Pueblo Revolt forces the Spanish to withdraw from New Mexico.
**1693:** Spanish regain control of New Mexico under Diego de Vargas.
**1706:** Albuquerque founded.
**1710:** Extension of the Santa Fe Trail from Independence, Missouri, is completed.
**1776:** A mission by two Franciscan priests, Silvestre Vélez de Escalante and Francisco Atanasio Domínguez, opens a trade route to California.
**1780s:** Anglo-Americans begin infiltrating Spanish land in the Southwest.
**1804:** Copper mining begins at Santa Rita in southwestern New Mexico.
**1807:** Zebulon Pike heads the first Anglo-American expedition into New Mexico; his published account encourages American expansionism.
**1821:** Treaty of Cordoba establishes Mexico's independence from Spain. Trader William Becknell arrives at Santa Fe and quickly sells all his goods.
**1822:** Augustine Iturbide proclaims himself emperor of New Mexico.
**1828:** Gold is discovered in the Ortiz Mountains south of Santa Fe.
**1837:** Mexican authorities suppress a revolt by northern New Mexicans, mainly in the Chimayo area, over tax policy and military protection.
**1841:** A 400-man expedition from Texas surrenders to Mexican troops after invading New Mexico.
**1846:** Mexican-American War begins as Col. Stephen Watts Kearny declares New Mexico part of the United States.
**1847:** Gov. Charles Bent is assassinated at his Taos home in an Indian and Mexican uprising.
**1848:** Mexican War ends; Treaty of Guadalupe Hidalgo authorizes U.S. takeover in the Southwest.
**1850:** Congress creates Territory of New Mexico.
**1851:** Santa Fe becomes the territorial capital. Jean Baptiste Lamy arrives in Santa Fe as Roman Catholic vicar apostolic for the territory.
**1853:** For $10 million, the U.S. receives from Mexico nearly 30,000 sq miles (77,000 sq km) in New Mexico and Arizona in the Gadsden Purchase.
**1862:** Confederate troops in the Civil War suffer a defeat at Glorieta Pass.
**1864:** Navajo Indians, subdued by U.S. Army Col. Kit Carson, are forced to undergo a 300-mile (480-km) "Long Walk" to Fort Sumner.
**1868:** Eight-year-old William H. Bonney and his widowed mother, originally from New York City, resettle in Silver City, New Mexico. He becomes the notorious gunfighter known as Billy the Kid.
**1878:** President Rutherford B. Hayes, disturbed

by range wars and political corruption in New Mexico, names the Civil War general Lew Wallace as its reforming governor. While holding office in Santa Fe, Wallace works on his classic *Ben Hur* novel and meets with Billy the Kid.

**1879:** The Atchison, Topeka & Santa Fe Railroad extends into New Mexico, ending the territory's isolation and fueling Albuquerque's growth.

**1881:** Billy the Kid is gunned down by Pat Garrett.

**1885:** Geronimo leads an Apache uprising against white settlers that ends a year later with his surrender and the cessation of Indian hostilities.

**1909:** A prolonged drought causes many homesteaders to flee New Mexico.

at the invitation of art patron Mabel Dodge Luhan.

**1924:** Gila Wilderness becomes the first officially designated wilderness area in the United States.

## Modern times

**1942:** Los Alamos is chosen as a research facility as part of the top-secret Manhattan Project.

**1945:** The world's first atomic bomb is detonated at the Trinity site in a desert near Alamogordo.

**1947:** The cult of the "flying saucer" begins as the U.S. military announces the recovery of a crashed object near Roswell, New Mexico, then disclaims the announcement.

**1950:** Uranium ore is discovered in New Mexico.

**1910:** A new state constitution guarantees Hispanic children equal access to education.

**1912:** New Mexico becomes the 47th state.

**1916:** Gen. John "Black Jack" Pershing leads American troops into Mexico in search of the elusive bandit Francisco "Pancho" Villa.

**1917:** Georgia O'Keefe, at 29, returns to New York City with fond memories of New Mexico. By the time of her death decades later in Santa Fe, she is the state's most famous artist.

**1922:** Novelist D. H. Lawrence visits New Mexico

**PRECEDING PAGES:** Cowboys going to dinner, Mora County, 1897. **LEFT:** Zuni water carriers, 1903. **ABOVE:** U.S. Treasury Mine, Chloride, 1909.

**1967:** A courthouse in Tierra Amarilla is seized and hostages taken by a band of Mexican-Americans seeking to reclaim a vast section of northern New Mexico for Hispanics.

**1980:** In a rampage at the state penitentiary near Santa Fe, prisoners kill 33 of their fellow inmates.

**1991:** A federal judge prohibits the U.S. government from opening the nation's first permanent nuclear-waste disposal site in New Mexico.

**2000:** U.S. Census reports New Mexico's population at 1,819,046, a rise of 20 percent over 1990.

**2005:** New Mexico's first light rail train breaks ground in the Central Rio Grande Valley. The much-anticipated Rail Runner will eventually link Albuquerque and Santa Fe. ❏

# NATIVE HERITAGE

*From Ice Age hunters to ancient Pueblo civilizations, humans occupied New Mexico for more than 9,000 years before the arrival of Europeans*

A rhythmic drumbeat echoes across the huge plaza of Santo Domingo Pueblo. As insistent as a pounding heartbeat, the ancient sound bounces off walls, charges the air, and pulsates through the crowd of people watching from the rooftops and the doorways of the multistory pueblo.

Within minutes the central plaza begins to fill with hundreds of brightly dressed dancers. In one line are women and girls dressed in black shifts and stepped wooden *tableta* head-dresses painted with turquoise, red and black cloud and lightning motifs. In another are men and boys wreathed in evergreen boughs and dressed in leather kilts decorated with bushy coyote tails. The lines make their way up the plaza, feet shuffling in time to the beat, hands shaking gourd rattles. Even the tiniest child knows the steps.

The *tableta*, or Corn Dance, continues, off and on, all day. It is an extended prayer for a good corn harvest and the fulfillment of an ancient bargain between farming people and a pantheon of gods who control rainfall, sunshine and the natural world. These ceremonies have taken place in Rio Grande pueblos for 700 years. But their roots date to an even more ancient time, when the introduction of corn from Mexico quickened the pace of cultural change in the Southwest.

## Ancient nomads

Agriculture is a comparatively recent phenomenon in the Southwest. For hundreds of generations, people survived as nomadic hunters and gatherers, living lightly on the land, their numbers small enough to be sustained by the animals and plants within huge territories. Early visitors saw links between contemporary farming pueblos and the crumbling plastered stone buildings dotted across

---

**LEFT:** Pueblo del Arroyo, an ancient "great house" at Chaco Culture National Historical Park.
**RIGHT:** Bear shaman petroglyph, A.D. 1300–1650, at Petroglyph National Monument.

the silent sagebrush landscape at places like Chaco Canyon. Using classical civilizations like Greece, Rome and Mexico as reference points, archaeologists eagerly embraced the notion of a great lost civilization in the desert, perhaps related to the Aztecs.

It was believed then that man's arrival in

North America dated to the early Christian era. Several important discoveries in the early 1900s turned that theory inside out. In 1926, Jesse Figgins, director of the Denver Museum of Natural History, unearthed two fluted stone spearpoints and a third among the ribs of a giant extinct bison in an arroyo near Folsom in northeastern New Mexico. First discovered in 1908 by a self-educated black cowboy named George McJunkin, the Folsom site proved beyond a doubt that humans were in New Mexico 10,000 years ago, at the end of the last Ice Age, hunting now-extinct big game.

By the 1930s, it was evident that northeastern New Mexico was not the only area favored by paleo hunters. In 1931, archaeologist Edgar Howard, excavating in Burnet Cave in the Guadalupe Mountains of southern New Mexico, found spearpoints near a hearth surrounded by charred bones of Pleistocene musk-ox, caribou, camel, horse and bison. Two years later, Howard hit the jackpot at an excavation in a gravel pit at Blackwater Draw, near the town of Clovis in eastern New Mexico. Not only did he find Folsom spearpoints and bison bones but, in an older stratum immediately below, he unearthed spearpoints and mammoth bones that clearly predated those of Folsom man.

These older Clovis finds were further cor-

roborated in 1936, when Frank Hibben and Wesley Bliss of the University of New Mexico dug up shouldered spearpoints or knives, scrapers and other flaked tools mixed with bones of mammoth, mastodon and bison in Sandia Cave near Albuquerque. Folsom and Clovis Man, it seemed, had been everywhere in early New Mexico. Archaeologists now believe that Clovis hunters were among the first to arrive in North America at the end of the last Ice Age, probably via a land bridge in the Bering Strait, separating modern Alaska and Mongolia. Clovis sites in North America date to 10,000 BC, but one in Chile has proven older, pushing back settlement of the Americas even earlier.

In New Mexico, paleo hunters found perfect conditions: a warm, moist climate; plentiful big game around large glacial lakes; and a variety of rocks suitable for spear and tool making, including volcanic rock, which yielded razor-sharp obsidian. Scattered small bands of hunters roamed the region, camped wherever game was plentiful, made tools and processed kills, then moved on. Between 8000 and 5000 BC, Folsom hunters became extremely skilled at killing bison, processing up to 200 kills for just 500 hours of work per year. Family groups created the first temporary communities in the game-rich middle Rio Grande Valley, where the world's only excavated Folsom village lies in Rio Rancho, just north of Albuquerque.

## Hunting and gathering

Even as paleo hunters became more efficient at refining dart points into lethal lanceheads, environmental changes had doomed their culture. By 6,000 years ago, a warming, drying trend led to the extinction of many big-game species. A descendant of the giant bison, the buffalo, was now the game of choice on the eastern plains. Cody-era hunters stalked the large herds, using a different kind of dart, the Eden point. By 5000 BC, the buffalo herds had withdrawn to the cooler northern plains, and with them went the hunters.

A new desert culture, the Archaic, now filled the vacuum created by the disappearing hunters. Archaic people were hunter-gatherers who moved from place to place trapping small game such as deer, elk and rabbits and harvesting wild plants now proliferating in the warm desert temperatures. Archaic people were experts in the seasonal growth cycles of plants and spent the year moving from camp to camp harvesting shoots, roots, fruits, seeds and nuts as they ripened. When the climate inevitably cooled and became moister again, this intimate understanding of the land served them well.

The availability of more meat improved the health of Archaic people. Soon, their numbers were growing and family territories began to overlap. By 1000 BC, small groups of extended families were forming home bases and living in villages of semi-subterranean, oval pithouses with roofs of logs and earth. Between 15,000 and 30,000 people now lived in New Mexico, leaving behind faint traces of their passage in some 10,000 known sites.

## Mexican maize

The Cochise people who lived in the Mogollon Mountains were the first to experiment with horticulture in 2000 BC. After being given a domesticated form of wild grass called *teosinte* by neighbors to the south, they probably sowed seeds in untended plots in the highlands in the spring, went on their seasonal rounds gathering wild foods, then harvested it in the early fall along with crops of pinyon nuts. In 1948, a small-kerneled corn known as *chapalote* dating to 1500 BC was found at Bat Cave in west-central New Mexico. At the time, it was the oldest corn ever found in North America.

round. The knowledge they acquired over the next 1,000 years would take them into a world they could not imagine, where they would leave behind their pithouses and move into huge cities that reached toward the sky.

## Early agriculture

By AD 400, the Mogollon people in southern New Mexico had not only begun growing corn and squash but had added an ancient precursor to the pinto bean, which improved health by providing necessary amino acids to their diet. Population pressures pushed people to move to lowland basins that could be easily farmed.

As any gardener will confirm, growing plants require constant monitoring. A nomadic people cannot be assured of good harvests unless someone stays home to tend the fields. While the climate was moist and cool, and game and wild plants were abundant, the investment of man hours (1,000–2,000 hours a year) probably seemed too high. But when the climate again dried out and wild plant harvests diminished, early Archaic farmers were left with little choice but to incorporate agriculture into their seasonal

**LEFT:** Long House, Bandelier National Monument.
**ABOVE:** Mogollon ruins are perched on a canyon alcove at Gila Cliff Dwellings National Monument.

Although the Mogollon still favored pithouses, larger villages sprang up and included the first community meeting places, usually a larger pithouse. Southern New Mexico was densely populated, with the Western Mogollon living west of the Rio Grande and the Jornada Mogollon living to the east, in the Tularosa Basin. Increased contact among people sparked trade and innovation. The Mogollon straddled a cultural frontier between inhabitants of the Mexican highlands to the south, the Sonoran Desert and Pacific Ocean to the west, and the Colorado Plateau to the north.

Like all nomads, Archaic people wove light, portable baskets to gather, cook and store food. Ground acorns and corn were cooked by placing fire-heated stones in baskets. But the Mogollon were the first to learn pottery making, from their close ties with people in Mexico, instigating the second most important advance in prehistoric technology. Pots allowed grain to be safely stored and cooked. Early Mogollon pottery was a simple brownware coiled into basket shapes. Later it was refined into a beautiful fired redware that seemed to glow like a New Mexico sunset.

Between AD 1000 and 1150, the Mimbres branch of the Mogollon, living near Silver City, came into contact with Ancestral Pueblo people (formerly known as the Anasazi) to the north.

AD 200 and 700, the number of Basketmaker villages in New Mexico grew ninefold. Availability of land for hunting and foraging diminished, but an increase in rainfall improved crop yields, tilting the odds firmly toward farming.

Creativity is often at its greatest when people are under pressure. Such was the case in the AD 700s, in the period known as Pueblo I, when a major warming trend coupled with expanding populations and increased violence seems to have triggered a major leap forward in technology and social organization. People began banding together in larger villages in upland environments where moisture and game were

The Mimbres began making beautiful black-on-white vessels, produced by a different firing method than their redware. This Classic Mimbres pottery was prized throughout the Southwest (as it is today) for its superb quality, unusual animal motifs, and fascinating depictions of life as part of a huge trading network that included Chaco Canyon to the north and Mesoamerican cultures to the south.

## Pueblo culture

The Basketmaker period marked a major cultural shift. People were now dedicating 1,000–2,000 hours a year to crop cultivation, a huge investment of energy in a risky enterprise. Between

more abundant. Basketmakers in the north experimented with architectural styles.

Pithouses went from oval to rectangular and above-ground structures were built adjacent to them, constructed of wattle-and-daub, or *jacal*, and laid out in arcs, two rooms deep. Pottery ollas containing grain indicate the rooms were initially used for storage. But excavations of later rooms have revealed hearths, pottery, grinding stones, bone awls for weaving baskets and yucca-fiber sandals and mats, digging sticks and other tools, indicating that they were used as residences. Even more intriguing is an increase in different pottery types found at individual sites. Archaeologists believe that decorated bowls, including polychromes as well as black-on-whites, were being traded for food during uncertain times.

## The Chaco phenomenon

Just after AD 800, the first Pueblo I-style settlements were built in Chaco Canyon, forming the early core units of the later great house sites of Pueblo Bonito, Peñasco Blanco and Una Vida. Pithouses were now incorporated right into the pueblos, as circular ceremonial chambers called kivas, providing an important spiritual link with their origins that continues in pueblos today. Even as climatic uncertainty continued into the

Pueblo II period (AD 850-1000), at least 10,000 farming hamlets were founded, as young families were forced to find farmable lands wherever they could. Chaco Canyon, at the boundary of two distinct seasonal rainfall patterns, may have become increasingly important as a redistribution and ceremonial center.

Some 100 overscaled public buildings with storage facilities and room suites, known as great houses, and huge circular underground ceremonial chambers embedded in square

**ABOVE:** West Pueblo, built by Ancestral Puebloans about AD 1100, is preserved at Aztec Ruins National Monument in the Four Corners area.

rooms, known as great kivas, have been found near farming villages of this period, linked by roads across a 40,000-sq-mile area (100,000-sq-km). In a sense, Chaco's genius was to expand the small business model into a prehistoric corporate undertaking overseen by small numbers of ritual leaders at the top. If true, it was a brilliant strategy, ensuring the survival of thousands of people during a time of great uncertainty and benefiting a small but powerful elite whose burial remains indicate they lived in great privilege even as farmers struggled with malnutrition nearby.

Societies, especially those in the Southwest, that derive their power from favorable natural conditions are bound to fail, and such was the case with Chaco. Archaeologists believe that the members of its ruling elite were not just clever entrepreneurs but skilled astronomers whose most important function may have been to predict when to plant and harvest crops. The return of regular seasonal rains seems to have led to the rapid rise of Chacoan leaders, giving them unprecedented power in the San Juan Basin and beyond. The great house communities in the 11th century may have been built with labor from local farming villages whose livelihoods were tied to Chaco Canyon, the center of the culture.

While seasonal fluctuations in rainfall could be mitigated, long periods of drought could not. And it appears that Chaco's leaders did not react soon enough to the warning signs. Instead they seem to have ordered the construction of more great houses, perhaps for storage, but also, maybe, to keep up morale among starving people. They once more looked to the highlands. Between 1088 and 1090, Salmon Ruin was constructed just north of the San Juan River. In 1115, another large outlier, Aztec Ruin, was built, perhaps intended to replace Chaco Canyon as a ritual center. The end seems to have come swiftly. By 1140, Chaco's great houses were all vacant and its leaders departed.

## Migrations

The last days of Chaco Canyon saw an increase in religious activity with the construction of a large number of smaller kivas (Pueblo Bonito, alone, had 33). This suggests that society was fracturing into rival clans performing rituals to hold the Chaco world together. When people abandoned Chaco in the mid-1100s, at the start of the Pueblo III period, these clans dispersed in all directions seeking better lands. The influx of Chacoans into neighboring upland communities during troubled times frequently led to horrific episodes of violence.

Across the Four Corners, people were forced to build large walled pueblos on easily defended hilltops or secrete them under overhangs in cliffs above creeks that could be used for farming. The best known of these are the 13th-century cliff dwellings in the northern San Juan region of the Four Corners, where Cliff Palace at Mesa Verde National Park has been attracting visitors since the late 1800s. But cliff dwellings are also found at Bandelier National Monument, on the Pajarito Plateau northwest of Santa Fe; nearby Puye, ancestral to adjacent Santa Clara Pueblo; and Gila Cliff Dwellings, unique southern New Mexico cliff homes that were built by the Tularosa descendants of the Mogollon before being absorbed into the Ancestral Pueblo culture.

Finally, the Great Drought of 1276–99 emptied out the Four Corners pueblos for good.

### ANCIENT WEAVERS

In addition to being excellent potters, Ancestral Puebloans were skilled weavers, using cotton, yucca fibers and dog or human hair to produce sandals, clothing, sacks and baskets.

### FOOD FOR THOUGHT

The Southwest's most controversial archaeological debate rages around that most taboo of subjects – cannibalism. At the center of the debate is Christy Turner, who, with his late wife Jacqueline, spent 30 years researching cannibalism at Ancestral Pueblo sites after finding signs of butchering and cooking in human bones excavated in northern Arizona. In 1999, the Turners published their findings in *Man Corn*, an allusion to an Aztec word for a ritual meal of human flesh.

Though praised for its scholarship, the book's conclusions have been criticized even by supporters of the authors' work. The Turners suggest that an Aztec warrior cult from Mexico infiltrated Chaco Canyon in New Mexico about AD 900 and used ritual sacrifice to terrorize the local population into submission. The discovery of fossilized excrement containing human remains has prompted even more controversy.

Violence is an understandably sensitive issue for the Hopi and other descendants of the Ancestral Puebloans, and two new studies are only adding fuel to the fire. A survey of Pueblo excavations conducted by archaeologist Stephen Le Blanc catalogues numerous examples of violence. Similarly, Polly Schaafsma recently published the results of her study of rock art depicting warfare, which makes clear that conflict was escalating in late Pueblo times.

Some Pueblo clans walked southwest to Arizona's Hopi mesas and petitioned for entry. Others headed to the Rio Grande area, where, in the early 1300s, they returned to pithouse living in safe upland areas such as Los Alamos. By the late 1300s, they had banded together to build pueblos of up to 1,000 rooms, some 2 to 3 miles (3–5km) apart, along the Rio Grande and other waterways. Each pueblo used land from the rivers to the mountains, allowing total self-sufficiency in several ecozones.

The departure of the Pueblos from the Four Corners at the beginning of the Pueblo IV period may have been hastened by the arrival of nomadic bands of Athabascan hunter-gatherers from Canada who split culturally into the Navajo and Apache on their arrival in the Southwest. While the Apache fiercely held to their hunter-gatherer ways in the mountains, the Navajo chose to live in the northeastern portion of New Mexico known as the Dinetah. Like the Utes and Paiutes arriving from western deserts, they quickly learned corn farming, weaving and other cultural traits from their Pueblo neighbors. Their name is a corruption of *navaju*, "great planted fields," a Pueblo word that refers to the Navajos' excellent corn yields. According to their own oral histories and new scientific evidence, the Navajo may have been living in the area by 1175, far earlier than previously thought, increasing pressure on already marginal lands.

## The historic period

When Spanish conquistador Francisco Vázquez de Coronado arrived in the Southwest in 1540, he found some 150 pueblos at Zuni, Hopi and the Rio Grande area, with up to 130,000 people, by some estimates. Nearby were the remnants of large abandoned pueblos, such as Arroyo Hondo in the Galisteo Basin, which had come undone during a long drought. The people in the pueblos spoke a variety of languages: Tiwa, Tewa, Towa, Tano and Keres. They were smaller than earlier Rio Grande pueblos and built close to one another, probably to discourage raids by Apaches, Navajos and other newcomers. Each pueblo held on fiercely to its huge strips of land running from the rivers to the mountains. In this resource-rich area, people could farm, hunt, mine

turquoise, obsidian and other precious stones, and make annual treks to southern New Mexico to collect salt from dried-up lake beds. A vast trading network again linked the pueblos with other tribes across the Southwest.

Each pueblo was made up of several clans, many of which traced their ancestry to Mesa Verde or Chaco Canyon. Caciques, or village leaders, acted as spokesmen, but power was no longer concentrated among a privileged few. Rio Grande pueblos were split into moieties, each consisting of clans representing the Winter people or the Summer people. Within these, the most important leaders were the War Chiefs

and Sun Chiefs, who continued to make astronomical predictions and organize ceremonies.

One of the most powerful pueblos was Pecos, or Cicuye, just west of the Pecos River. The 650-room pueblo was a fortified, multistory city on the frontier between the Rio Grande pueblos and the eastern plains. It had been built in the 1400s as a trading pueblo and was renowned for its fierce warriors and trade goods. Apaches, Navajos, Comanches and Utes camped below its walls and bartered buffalo hides for pottery, corn, jewelry and cotton. Pecos would play a pivotal role in the coming years, as Spaniards would once more shake the foundations of the Indian world. ❏

**LEFT:** pictograph, Bandelier National Monument.
**RIGHT:** a Navajo yei dancer about 1904. The Navajo migrated into the region in the 15th century.

# THE SPANISH CONQUEST

*Along came the bold Europeans, infusing a
distinctive Iberian flair into the territory of El Norte*

The road that opened New Mexico to the outside world was of course paved by Chris Columbus, that hired-hand gentleman from Genoa who washed up on Atlantic shores thinking he must be somewhere in Asia. As we now know, he was in a Mundo Nuevo, which is what his Spanish sponsors liked to call the place. They promptly laid claim to it, giving it a distinctive Iberian flavor, a *sabor*, that's still very much there in places like the American Southwest.

On Columbus's heels came other explorers and conquistadors, like Ponce de León, first in a long line of Florida sun-seekers; Balboa and stout Cortes; Pizarro, who cut a mean swath through Peru; and somebody named Panfilo de Narváez. And here the trail to New Mexico gets warm.

## City of gold

Having helped to subdue Cuba, Narváez was instructed by Charles V to head back across the ocean, stake out Florida and open up yet another branch office for Imperial Spain. The explorer reached the Sunshine State in April 1528. Intent on finding gold, he decided to send his ships on toward Mexico and, with a 300-man force, began digging for El Dorado. Coming up empty, Narváez and his men now patched together some rough-hewn vessels and set out across the Gulf of Mexico. They didn't make it. He and all but four of his men were lost, perhaps somewhere on or off the Texas coast.

Best-known of the four survivors was Alvar Núñez Cabeza de Vaca and a black Moor named Esteban. The castaways now began an amazing eight-year odyssey among the native people of the Southwest, moving from one tribe to another as traders, healers and slaves. The ragged company finally headed south, met up with some incredulous Spanish countrymen, and arrived in Mexico City in July 1536.

Their report on the territory up north

**LEFT:** a Zuni man, about 1903. The Zuni were the first Pueblo people to encounter Coronado's 1540 expedition.
**RIGHT:** an inscription at El Morro left by a Spanish traveler in 1709.

intrigued Antonio de Mendoza, viceroy of New Spain, who, to check it out, dispatched a team headed by a Franciscan friar, Fray Marcos de Niza, and guided by Esteban. The party camped within sight of a Zuni pueblo. Esteban was sent ahead to make contact with the Indians, but, according to Zuni legend, he showed so little

respect for his hosts that the Zuni killed him and cut up his body. Terrified, Fray Marcos fled to Mexico City with exaggerated accounts of a treasure-laden civilization along the lines of the legendary Seven Cities of Cíbola.

Mendoza bought into it, knowing that Spain had her eyes out for any prospective "new" Mexicos that might be out there. He set about organizing a full-fledged expedition headed by his protégé, the dashing young Francisco Vázquez de Coronado. It went forth in January 1540 with great expectations of finding glory and material riches. Fray Marcos served as guide for what was an enormous party of more than 300 soldier-adventurers, over a thousand

Indians, six Franciscan missionaries, and a vast number of horses and livestock. Going north on old Indian trails, Coronado and his people crossed present-day Arizona and finally reached the Zuni village of Hawikuh after an exhausting journey that took months. Unhappily, Hawikuh turned out to be nothing like the shining vision suggested by Fray Marcos. He was censured by Coronado for painting such a misleading picture and sent home in disgrace. Hawikuh's inhabitants, meanwhile, took exception to this encroachment on their village, and Coronado mounted a bloody attack. It was an omen of centuries of hostilities to come.

## Settling down

After the Coronado mission, no full-fledged attempt at settlement was made for more than half a century, although various expeditions did venture forth from time to time. One such, in 1582, was headed by another Christian brother, Fray Bernardo Beltran, accompanied by the mining specialist Antonio de Espejo. Launched as an operation to rescue missionaries thought to have been menaced by Pueblo people, the expedition is credited with inspiring a new moniker for the region – la Nueva Mexico.

A chief motive for the exploratory enterprises was of course finding more of the precious

The expedition returned to Mexico City in 1542. Mission unaccomplished? Not exactly. As historians observe, this was in fact a ground-breaking venture that put one more hunk of terra incognita on the map. Coronado's people had foraged widely over what became another large appendage for New Spain. They forded broad rivers, trekked across the wide open Kansas plains, visited major Indian villages and sampled a variety of pueblo civilizations, and they marveled at the immensity of one of the world's great natural wonders – the majestic Grand Canyon. Their *entrada* had unveiled stunning new vistas but no fabulous Quivira, no El Dorado.

New World metals that were making Spain such a dominant power in the Old World order. Indeed, Espejo had found traces of gold during his foray up north. And in addition to material wealth, missionaries were intent on converting these (supposedly) spiritually misbegotten savages, noble or not, to the divine truths of the holy faith, otherwise known as *santa fé*. Most prominent among these Catholic proselytizers were the Franciscans.

Along came Juan de Oñate in 1595 as official contractor for the first colonizing enterprise in this remote northern territory. For the Spanish crown, eager to extend New Spain's outreach and, in the bargain, find gold and other precious metals, Oñate was a natural choice. His own father, Cristóbal, had assisted in the conquest of Mexico under Cortes and been lieutenant governor under Coronado. And the Oñate family had the financial resources to carry out, mostly at its own expense, such a costly mission of establishing and maintaining a colony of this magnitude.

Once again, a large contingent set forth from Mexico. The time was January 1598, the starting point Compostela, the commander Juan de Oñate. With him were nine Franciscan priests, some 200 soldier-colonists and several hundred native Indians, not to mention a vast herd of livestock. The procession moved north along the Rio Grande valley. On July 11 a stop was made at a Tewa pueblo near the juncture of the Rio Grande and the Rio Chama, in north-central New Mexico. The pueblo, just above present-day Española, was renamed San Juan de Los Caballeros. It was the first Spanish capital of New Mexico.

Some months later, the settlement was shifted to a village, Yunque, across from San Juan on the west bank of the Rio Grande. It was renamed San Gabriel; this was New Mexico's second capital. It, in turn, was followed by the third – and most enduring – capital site at a nearby location along a tributary of the Rio Grande. This was called La Villa Real de la Santa Fée – we know it simply as Santa Fe, the state's most historic community, built right atop an earlier pueblo.

## Colonial outpost

Santa Fe's beginnings as a Spanish colonial outpost date from 1607. That was the year that Oñate was replaced as governor for what his superiors regarded as an overly harsh approach in dealing with the native inhabitants. From the start, there had been instances of violent resistance, as in December 1598 when an attack by Acoma Indians cost the lives of 13 Spaniards. One of them was Oñate's nephew, Lieutenant Juan de Zaldivar. Retaliation was severe; hundreds of Indians were killed, and the pueblo was destroyed. Later, 20 Acoma men were sentenced to the amputation of one foot, and, with women and boys, 20 years of enslavement.

**LEFT:** the plaza at Zuni Pueblo.
**RIGHT:** Diego de Vargas led the reconquest of New Mexico in 1692, 12 years after the Pueblo Revolt.

Nor were Oñate's soldiers and settlers too happy with his harsh administration or with the discomforts of living on a far-flung frontier, away from the civilized amenities of New Spain proper. Lots of them took off and headed back to Mexico City, making the job of running such a remote outpost that much tougher for authorities.

It was Oñate's replacement, Don Pedro de Peralta, who had been instructed to move the capital to the more strategic site. Peralta supervised the design and construction of Santa Fe, a project completed in 1610. The second oldest European town in America after St. Augus-

tine in Florida (founded 1565), it became the base of Spanish operations in this newest region of New Spain, as several smaller settlements were strung out along the Rio Grande from south to north.

Missions were established at the pueblos, and natives introduced to European ways with varying degrees of success. It was the usual mixed bag of spiritual outreach by missionaries devoted to redeeming lost souls for Christ and, on the flip side, a closed-minded intolerance expressed in the form of disdain for Indian religious practices. Nor did it help matters that the native labor force was too often slavishly exploited. Colonial law permitted the establishment of an *encomienda* system entitling certain settlers to collect tribute from Pueblo Indians in return for protection from Comanche raids and other military threats. Tribute was supposed to be paid in the form of corn, animal skins or mantas (woven cotton cloth), but the system was widely abused, and Pueblo people were compelled to work for Spanish *encomenderos* against their will.

Despite such mistreatment, there was a great deal of cultural sharing. Intermarriage between Indians and Spaniards created a growing class of mestizos and a fruitful melding of artistic and culinary traditions. Adding variety to the

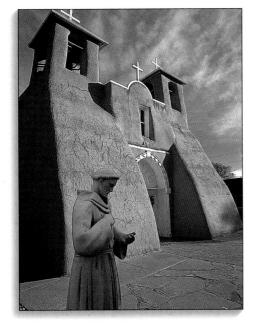

social milieu in Santa Fe were a number of French, Portuguese and black settlers as well as so-called Crypto-Jews, who were forced to conceal their Judaic heritage or face the wrath of the Spanish Inquisition.

By the 1670s, however, there was no containing the bitter resentment over attempts to suppress Pueblo dances and ceremonies. In 1675, authorities charged 47 Pueblo caciques, or priests, with resorting to sorcery in hatching plots against their Spanish overlords. Four of the religious leaders were hanged, the others whipped. But such punishment managed only to stiffen resistance by native people and stimulate a desire for retribution.

## Fighting back

They got their wish five years later, in the form of the Pueblo Revolt of August 10, 1680, a most important date in New Mexico history. In a meticulously planned operation, the territory's native inhabitants managed to strike back at their overseers, regain control of their lives, and hold onto it for a dozen years or so. It was a devastating revolt, but it came close to being aborted.

The head conspirator was Popé, a member of San Juan Pueblo, who directed his planning operation from Taos Pueblo. He was one of the caciques who were arrested and flogged in 1675, and he seems to have spent a good deal of the intervening time meeting – surreptitiously, of course – with leaders of the various Pueblos and hatching plans for retaliation. As the scheduled date for the attacks approached, runners were sent forth each day carrying lengths of rope with a sequence of knots that signified the time remaining before all hell was to break loose. The Spanish, however, captured two of the runners, so Pueblo leaders were forced to set the operation into motion ahead of schedule. And so the attacks were abruptly launched on the morning of August 10.

The lives of many Spanish settlers were saved because authorities had been tipped off to the uprising through the capture of the runners, but the results were severe all the same. Priests, settlers and whole families were massacred, missions burned, crops destroyed, religious icons and articles wrecked. Pueblo warriors from the north converged on Santa Fe, where hundreds of settlers had sought refuge.

Troop contingents, heavily armed, were sent forth to rescue groups of survivors and escort them back to the fortified capital. Also under siege was another large group of survivors, more than a thousand in all, at Isleta, 70 miles (110km) south of Santa Fe. They were under the command of Lt. Governor Alonso Garcia. Neither group was aware of the other's dire situation.

Finally, on August 21, as food and drink in the besieged city were running out, a total withdrawal from New Mexico was ordered by its governor, Antonio de Otermin. The entire region had a population of no more than 3,000 settlers. Now, a stream of nearly one-third of them, many of them widows and orphans, headed south, their long column passing smoking ruins of devastated missions and settlements. At this point, Otermin's group and Garcia's contingent were able to join for their slow, wary retreat. The Spanish burned the pueblo at Isleta and brought nearly 400 of its people with them to the south for resettlement.

The refugees, more than 1,000 in all, converged on El Paso del Norte, the southernmost settlement in the province. Here they spent the winter after an all-consuming experience. More than 400 colonists had been killed, in addition to 21 Franciscan religious.

## SAFE HAVEN

Tigua Indians from Isleta Pueblo escaped the revolt of 1680 by fleeing with the Spanish to El Paso del Norte. There they established a new village – Ysleta del Sur – Texas' only existing Indian pueblo.

finally carried out the effort to oust the insurgents and regain control of the New Mexico turf and its Pueblo society assumed office as governor in 1690. His full name: Diego de Vargas Zapata Lujan Ponce de Leon.

Vargas had instructions to take back the abandoned settlements, rebuild the devastated missions and reassert Spanish sovereignty by whatever means, including force if necessary. He went forth from his base at El Paso on August 17, 1692, with a relatively small detachment of fewer than

## The reconquest

Regaining the land was not as easy as it first appeared. It took 12 long years, in fact, for the Spanish to pull off a latter-day Reconquest. As with the Moors of old, Popé and the Pueblo leaders sought to nullify expressions of Christian belief and European lifestyle, although in fact Indians had absorbed many of the newcomers' ways with enthusiasm – taking to the donkeys and horses introduced by the Spanish like fish to water. In any event, the man who

---

**LEFT:** San Francisco de Asís Church, Ranchos de Taos.
**ABOVE:** Spanish traditions are vividly depicted in Ernest Blumenschein's 1925 *Sangre de Cristo Mountains*.

50 soldiers. They marched north along the customary Rio Grande route and arrived at the old capital of Santa Fe in early September. The city was well fortified and its occupiers determined, but Vargas managed largely through diplomatic skill (and a very large cannon) to secure the promise of a peaceful surrender.

Before the year was out, most of the territory's Pueblos followed suit and the *reconquista* – which was proving so far to be a peaceful land reclamation project, as had been the hope – was well under way. But the following year, resistance flared again when Vargas returned to Santa Fe with a host of settlers and friars prepared to carry out the recolonization of that vital community. After trying for two weeks to talk the Indians into surrendering, as the settlers and their families camped outside the city, the Spanish resorted to force.

A two-day battle was fought, with severe results. When it was over, the Spanish executed 70 Pueblo defenders and imposed conditions of servitude on others, including women and children. Some of the Pueblos adhered to the terms of the 1692 accord attained by Vargas, while others carried on protracted warfare. Altogether it was an unhappy period as, amid continuing hostilities, native inhabitants abandoned their pueblos and took to the hills. Not

until 1696 did the Spaniards succeed in regaining the upper hand over the Pueblo Indians of the Rio Grande. Little by little, normal life was restored for the European intruders and their descendants, as well as the Pueblo residents. Meanwhile, the number of immigrants was steadily increasing as the first full century of Spanish settlement drew to a close.

## New challenges

The 18th century was a largely stable and untroubled period for New Mexico. The *encomienda* system, long a cornerstone of Spanish dominance, was never revived, and the

### A RIVER RUNS THROUGH IT

It was known by other descriptives – Rio Bravo, Rio del Norte, Rio de las Palmas – but the name that stuck is what Juan de Oñate himself dubbed it: Rio Grande, the "great river." It has held center stage as New Mexico's vital waterway since early times. Pueblo Indians have drawn on its waters for irrigation since before the Europeans arrived, and it has served as a major travel corridor for both humans and wildlife. Springing to life high up in the San Juan Mountains of Colorado, it flows south for 1,885 miles (3,034km) through fertile valleys and various kinds of terrain to the Gulf of Mexico. For half its length it forms part of the U.S.–Mexico border.

Spanish clergy took a less severe attitude toward the persistence of Indian traditions. Life in Santa Fe, though difficult and isolated, was punctuated with religious festivals, fandangos, Indian trade fairs, and the arrival of caravans from Mexico City bearing finished goods and, equally precious, news of the outside world.

But there was one big headache: long-running conflict with Indian nomadic tribes – Apache, Ute, Navajo and, especially, Comanche. Also, there was an undercurrent of concern over possible encroachment with outsiders horning in on Spanish turf. French fur traders sought to do business with New Mexicans, and so did more and more English and American "gringos."

Comanche power reached its peak by mid-century, taxing the ingenuity of government administrators to seek solutions. Spanish towns and Indian pueblos were subject to constant attack. The hoped-for government goal was pacification, as civil and religious officials came to realize the necessity of a more respectful consideration for Indian customs and aspirations.

Nonetheless, in 1778, when Juan Bautista de Anza became governor of New Mexico, he determined on bringing the troublesome Comanche tribes to heel. A military effort was launched that resulted the following year in a decisive battle. A formidable and much feared Comanche leader named Cuerno Verde ("Green Horn") was killed and his band defeated.

Still, it took a formal treaty between the Spanish government and Comanche leaders, in 1786, to bring about a cessation of raids on New Mexico settlements for many years to come. Population grew as those settlements were expanded. One of them was Albuquerque, destined to become New Mexico's largest city. Founded in 1706 as the villa of San Felipe de Albuquerque, it exemplified the growth of population taking place along the middle Rio Grande.

## The Mexican interregnum

After three centuries of Spanish rule, New Mexico entered a new phase of its history in 1821. Now it was a constituent part of Mexico, whose people had decided to break with the old world and go it alone as an independent nation. The spirit of liberation was abroad in the wake of the Napoleonic wars and Spain's decline, and Mexico was not immune.

What this change in sovereignty boiled down to most significantly for New Mexico was the obvious opportunity it presented for foreign trade. Any such contact had been downplayed – in fact, outlawed – by the protectionist-minded Spanish authorities. But now, more and more caravans were plying the Santa Fe Trail, that upgraded version of the King's Highway, or El Camino Real.

The Santa Fe Trail became the chief commercial corridor connecting east and west, from Missouri to Santa Fe. The pioneering figure was William Becknell, who with 20 other men

drove a pack train from Franklin, Missouri, and arrived in Santa Fe in November 1821 with a load of goodies for sale. More merchants and fur traders of various nationalities appeared on the scene. In a region once highly isolated, they were becoming an important presence.

In 1837, dissidents in northern New Mexico denounced the administration of Governor Albino Pérez, who had been sent forth to carry out a change of government in the remote northern territory. Attempting to quell the revolt, Pérez's weak militia was defeated by the rebels, near present-day Española, and he was eventually captured and beheaded. A stronger

force came to Santa Fe in January 1838 to put down the revolt.

Inevitably, for a new crop of homegrown New Mexicans, there was an increasing remoteness vis-a-vis Mexico's far-off central region, replaced by more of an identification with the North American republic growing up close by and feeling the stirrings of Manifest Destiny. Such a rapport made it easy for homelanders to switch allegiance when the United States emerged a victor in the Mexican War that erupted in 1846 and Uncle Sam stepped in as inheritor of the long Spanish colonial legacy and the short-lived Mexican interregnum. Another chapter was now to be added to the New Mexico story. ❏

**LEFT:** Spanish soldiers depicted in Navajo rock art.
**RIGHT:** a *santero* (ca. 1935) carries on traditions brought to New Mexico by the earliest Spanish settlers.

# THE ANGLO INHERITANCE

*Gringos barged in next, adding their peculiar*
*character – and plenty of grit – to the territory's social landscape*

The next chapter in New Mexico's history was written by Anglo-Americans, representing the third of what author-historian Marc Simmons called the three "vigorous cultures" that together shaped the state's social landscape. Building on Indian-Hispanic foundations, Anglos with their materialist bent and can-do practicality barged into a backwoods province neglected first by a worn-out European power and then by an undernourished and equally remote Mexican overlord.

"*Gringos*" the intruders were called. "*Americanos.*" Whichever it was, they were brimming with energy and self-confidence. And they proceeded to blaze trade routes, build cities, mine the earth, and engineer rail lines that helped connect East and West. Reward came in 1912 when the benighted, sometimes violent territory became a full-fledged state.

Like new kids on the block, Anglos had been on the prowl since forging their new nation in the 1780s. It wasn't long before they started advancing on midwestern realms and that all-important economic and strategic artery, the Mississippi River. Spaniards became wary. They had long regarded New Mexico as a buffer zone protecting New Spain's territorial integrity, which is why they cautioned provincial officials to keep a sharp eye out for any sign of infringement.

Early on, there had been a Spanish-French rivalry over access to the virgin American interior and its opportunities. Spanish authorities had proscribed trading with foreigners, even expelling a couple of French-born brothers from Illinois named Mallet for daring to enter Santa Fe in 1739 with goods for sale. There were other trading attempts, as in the 1780s and 1790s when Frenchmen reached Santa Fe from St. Louis and San Antonio. Nor were commercial-minded Britishers welcome; Spaniards

tried to restrain them, too, from dealings with Indians in the vast Louisiana territory.

## The tipping point

Spaniards could not, however, undo the impact of the Louisiana Purchase of 1803, that $15 million blockbuster deal between Napoleon

Bonaparte and Thomas Jefferson that reconfigured the North American map and unleashed an expansionist fervor which was later to be rationalized as Manifest Destiny. Buffer zones notwithstanding, there would be no stopping the flow now as enterprising Anglos in the guise of Yankee traders and other strangers set sights on western horizons.

Tipped off to the subsequent Lewis and Clark exploration of the newly acquired territory – Jefferson had tried to keep the exploration a secret – Spanish authorities dispatched four separate expeditions in futile attempts to block it. Right after Lewis and Clark returned to St Louis from their marathon trip in 1806, another

**LEFT:** William S. Messervy, acting Territorial Governor of New Mexico, 1853.
**RIGHT:** an Atchison, Topeka & Santa Fe locomotive at the north portal of Raton Tunnel, 1881.

American sallied forth – Army Lt. Zebulon M. Pike, of Pike's Peak fame.

Pike and a 22-man detachment, charged with exploring the Louisiana Territory's southwestern geography, were arrested for trespassing and brought before Spanish authorities in Santa Fe. He wrote an account of the New Mexico territory and its Hispanic lifestyle, published in 1810, that stirred interest in the region.

At the same time, ferment started building for an end to Spanish colonial rule and an independent Mexican nation. When the break came, in 1821, it had the effect of lowering socioeconomic barriers erected by the protectionist-minded Spanish administration. The opportunity was not lost. Yankee traders and other merchandisers plied the route that became one of the West's great trading circuits: the Santa Fe Trail. What started as a trickle of wagons became in time a steady stream of "prairie schooners" as caravans rolled, mostly between Missouri and New Mexico.

Wagons from Independence, Missouri, and other starting points conveyed cheap manufactured goods that were eagerly snapped up in Santa Fe. Profits were generally handsome, as in 1824 when $35,000 worth of goods fetched a return of 300 percent. The father of the Santa

## LIFE ON THE TRAIL

"My journal tells a story tonight different from what it has ever done before. The curtain raises now with a new scene." So begins the journal of 18-year-old Susan Shelby Magoffin, who, in June 1846, became the first American woman to travel the 900-mile (1,500-km) Santa Fe Trail between Independence, Missouri, and New Mexico.

Traveling the Santa Fe Trail during one of its busiest years, Susan Magoffin and her husband of eight months, trader Samuel Magoffin, battled heat, dust, fatigue, illness, and Susan's miscarriage at Bent's Fort, Colorado, which she wrote "exactly fills my idea of an ancient castle." But the tough young Kentucky bride quickly grew accustomed to the open prairie, the mountains, meetings with Indians and soldiers, and the Hispanic people from whom she learned to speak Spanish, make tortillas, and keep an adobe house.

Magoffin's journey took place even as the United States began occupying New Mexico, and her diary brims with news of the time, including her meetings with General Zachary Taylor ("disheveled but kindly") and General Stephen Kearny ("quite a different man in every respect: small of stature, very agreeable in conversation and manners"). After a successful 15-month trip, the Magoffins returned to Kentucky in 1847. Sadly, Susan died giving birth to her third child in 1855. She was just 28.

Fe Trail was William Becknell, whose 21-man pack train broke ground in 1821 when it drove from Franklin, Missouri.

Normally isolated New Mexico began attracting merchants and "mountain men" fur traders in large numbers and Santa Fe, at the end of the trail, became a hub. Merchandise poured in, and dance halls, saloons and brothels sprang up. Some caravans pushed farther, too, heading south into Mexico proper, or west to California along the Old Spanish Trail. This intercourse had a major impact for New Mexico's history. Many of these incoming visitors, representing various nationalities, intermixed

expressed in Madrid around 1810 by a visiting Santa Fe merchant, Pedro Bautista Pino. Don Pedro had told Spanish rulers of the threat posed by American encroachment, as well as New Mexico's political corruption, economic poverty, social isolation and hostile Indians. Spain, however, had its own problems. And the Church's missionary fervor was spent.

A problem for the Mexican Republic arose in 1836 when its designee as governor of New Mexico, an outsider named Albino Perez, caused resentment by calling for higher taxes and sacking many local officials.

The result was an anti-tax revolt that erupted

with old-line Mexican families, widening social heterogeneity and breaking down old Spanish caste patterns. The mestizo element grew, and new social patterns and group identities brought shifting political alignments.

## Brief encounter

Mexico's rule over New Mexico was short-lived, lasting just 25 years, a mostly uneventful period. The new government in Mexico City did little to address concerns of a kind first

**ABOVE:** weathered adobe walls are all that remain of Fort Union, founded in 1851 to defend travelers along the Santa Fe Trail.

into a battle near present-day Española in which Perez's poorly equipped militia was defeated and he was executed. Although the uprising was eventually put down, it demonstrated a growing tendency for New Mexicans to shift allegiance from Mexico City toward the Americans and their way of life.

Mexican rule was also challenged in 1841 when a contingent of soldiers and traders was dispatched to Santa Fe in a scheme headed by Mirabeau B. Lamar, president of the new Republic of Texas and a proponent of opening a passage to the Pacific. Ostensibly a commercial mission, this Texas-Santa Fe expedition was seen by Mexican authorities as a plot to conjoin New Mexico to Texas. The invaders got lost along the way, were gathered up and thrown into jail, and New Mexico's resourceful Governor Manuel Armijo was hailed as a conquering hero.

## Another new beginning

Five years later, New Mexico embarked on a new phase of its history when another conquering hero, the American general Stephen Watts Kearny, rode into Santa Fe. The date was August 18, 1846. He declared New Mexico an American possession, and not a shot was fired in anger. The takeover was brought about by Mexico's hostility to the American annexation

of Texas in 1845, American insistence on the Rio Grande as international boundary line, and U.S. designs on California. The result was that Mexico severed relations, the U.S. Congress declared war, and the expansionist-minded President James K. Polk initiated military action.

Kearny, instructed to detach northern Mexican provinces, entered Santa Fe with 1,600 troops and formed a provisional government. No resistance was offered by the wily Armijo, who had considered it prudent to head south with his troops (he ultimately survived accusations of treason). The next year brought a plot aimed at overthrowing the province's newest

## WILLA CATHER AND THE ARCHBISHOP

Willa Cather's creative imagination and literary art made a star of Jean Baptiste Lamy with *Death Comes for the Archbishop*. Its title is misleading and it's as much biography/history as pure novel, but this acclaimed 1927 work assured the French-born priest a place on the American Catholic directory of famous names like Serra, Seton, Brownson and Cabrini – enhanced by Paul Horgan's Pulitzer Prize-winning biography *Lamy of Santa Fe.*

Cather, while visiting New Mexico, became aware of Lamy's achievement in breathing new life into a forlorn and far-flung Catholic community that Rome assigned him to oversee starting in the mid-19th century. Born in 1814

and ordained in 1838, he did 10 years of missionary work in Ohio and Kentucky before taking on the job of shepherding the faithful in New Mexico.

Lamy, depicted in the novel as "Bishop Latour," displayed the kind of moral steadfastness in the face of hardship that Cather had celebrated in *O Pioneers!* and *My Ántonia*. From her balcony at the La Fonda hotel in the 1920s, she could see the French-style St. Francis Cathedral that had been erected by Lamy over the vigorous opposition of old-line Spanish-tinged clerical antagonists. And she drew inspiration from the statue erected there in his honor in 1915. Lamy died in Santa Fe in 1888.

conquerors. The Revolt of 1847 was a northern New Mexico insurrection that was foiled. Arrests were made, but unrest persisted. Kearny's choice as governor, the fur trader Charles Bent, was assassinated and scalped by a mob of Indians and Mexicans outside his home in Taos. Other deaths occurred, and American troops fought a series of battles before the insurrection was put down. Nearly two dozen New Mexicans were hanged as a result.

In the Treaty of Guadalupe-Hidalgo, which formally ended the Mexican-American War in 1848, New Mexico was officially ceded to the United States. Geographical adjustments were made in the Compromise of 1850 (Texas gave up land claims for $10 million) and a territorial government was established in 1851. The Anglo-American version of New Mexico began to take shape, although land would be taken away to form Colorado (1861) and Arizona (1863). To create Arizona, Congress cut off the western half of New Mexico.

## Speculators and opportunists

The Territory of New Mexico began attracting merchants, land speculators, lawyers and other opportunists. There were various lures. The Gold Rush of '49 brought a wave of fortune-seekers to the region. Tradesmen and suppliers built up businesses dependent on military forts erected to protect settlers against Indian raids. Stagecoach and freight lines were inaugurated, including in 1858 twice-weekly runs through the southern part of the New Mexico Territory from St. Louis to San Francisco by John Butterfield's storied Overland Mail Company.

One newcomer whose labors left a significant imprint on New Mexico was a French-born missionary, Jean Baptiste Lamy, whose career inspired the Willa Cather novel *Death Comes for the Archbishop*. Between his arrival in Santa Fe in 1851 and his death there in 1888, the reform-minded Lamy reinvigorated missionary endeavor and built up a system of hospitals and schools even as he clashed with resistant Spanish-speaking clerics and parish leaders.

From an Anglo standpoint, New Mexico's reputation as hybrid anomaly was especially meaningful. It took straight-laced Republicans

**LEFT:** Cowboys shoot craps at the San Gabriel Ranch, south of Taos, 1923.
**RIGHT:** Archbishop Jean B. Lamy.

in Congress a long time to confer statehood on such a Democratic outpost, and Anglo residents were in no rush to yield to rule by the Hispanic majority. There was racism as well as humor in the quip by William Tecumseh Sherman, of Civil War fame, that the United States should declare war again on Mexico to make it take back New Mexico.

## Battle for the West

Although far removed from the killing fields to the east, New Mexico was a mini-battleground in the Civil War. There were few slaves, popular sentiment favored the Union cause, and

an escapade like the Texas-Santa Fe expedition cast a shadow on the Southern cause in New Mexican eyes. Nonetheless, the secessionist fervor had sympathizers in the region, while Confederates had designs on the West as a gateway to the Pacific.

In March 1861, even before shots were fired at Fort Sumter, citizens of Mesilla, in southern New Mexico, proclaimed allegiance to the Confederacy, and the town was designated capital of a "Confederate Territory of Arizona" proclaimed by Lt. Col. John R. Baylor. He had defeated a Union force at nearby Fort Fillmore. Baylor was later driven from the region by a Union force from California.

In February 1862, after a victory at Valverde near Fort Craig, Confederate Gen. Henry H. Sibley pushed on toward Albuquerque and Santa Fe but was stopped at the crucial battle of Glorieta Pass on March 27–28, 1862. This engagement, 15 miles (24km) east of Santa Fe, often called "the Gettysburg of the West," dashed Confederate hopes for a western presence.

The end of the Confederate threat enabled the Army to focus on another enemy – Indians who wrought havoc by pil-

### HANG 'EM HIGH

Criminals in Shakespeare, New Mexico, were routinely hanged from the rafters of the Grant House Dining Room, there being no suitable trees in town. The bodies were removed before breakfast.

in the 1840s, their raiding parties terrorizing homesteads and settlements along the western border. Wagon trains on New Mexico's northeastern plains bound for Santa Fe in early times were subject to raids by Comanches and Jicarilla Apaches.

One who turned to the Indian "problem" with special ferocity after the Civil War was James Henry Carleton, a Maine-born soldier who had commanded Union forces in Arizona and New Mexico. He waged total war on Mescalero Apache and

laging frontier settlements. Preoccupation with the Civil War had made such settlements vulnerable, although Indian attacks were the inevitable byproduct of a seemingly relentless advance by pioneering intruders on native grounds. As with the Spanish occupation of earlier years, attacks by hostile Indians were a serious problem in the 19th century. During the period of Mexican rule, one infamous Apache massacre wiped out a group of travelers at a spot in the Mesilla Valley on the banks of the Rio Grande, near the Mexican border, that became known (by most accounts) as Las Cruces – "the Crosses" – for the victims' graves laid out there. Navajos posed a serious threat

Navajo tribes, shunning peace councils and ordering that Indian men be killed "whenever and wherever they can be found."

## Legendary scout

A participant in the effort was Kit Carson, the legendary scout, mountain man and Indian agent. Born in Kentucky in 1809 and raised on the Missouri frontier, Carson left home as a teenager and was one of the pioneers on the Santa Fe Trail. He settled in New Mexico and later had a ranch near Taos. He became a skilled hunter and even a national legend through his guide work with the western expeditions of John C. Frémont. Carson assisted General

Kearny's force in the war with Mexico, and in the Civil War he organized Union forces from among New Mexico volunteers.

Though comparatively sympathetic to the plight of displaced Indians, Carson battled determinedly against Apache and especially Navajo forces. When the Navajo refused to be confined to a reservation, he conducted a devastating search-and-destroy mission through the heart of their land. Indian homes were burned, crops and livestock destroyed. When their traditional enemies – Pueblo, Zuni, Hopi and Ute – joined the attack on them, the Navajo presence was virtually liquidated.

the 1880s – the resourceful Geronimo was unyielding until 1886. Unlike the nomadic tribes, Pueblo people came to terms with American rule early after the 1846 takeover, but the protection promised them failed to materialize fully. It took until the early years of the 20th century for alleviation of inequities often caused by corrupt Indian agents and territorial officials.

## Billy's battle

The coming of the railroads – the Santa Fe, Southern Pacific, and Denver and Rio Grande lines – in 1880 and 1881 gave rise to a cattle boom and conflict over pasture lands between

The unhappy climax was the brutal Long Walk, which herded a Navajo remnant of 8,000 captives along a trail from Fort Defiance in Arizona to Fort Sumner in New Mexico and confinement at Bosque Redondo on the Pecos River.

Travelers along the Santa Fe Trail risked their lives under the threat of sudden attack by Comanches, Kiowas, Cheyenne and Arapaho warriors, and stray Apache bands continued to wreak havoc in southwestern New Mexico into

**LEFT:** Billy the Kid, guns blazing, narrowly escapes lawmen in a mural chronicling the Lincoln County War.
**ABOVE:** New Mexico, Arizona and Oklahoma wait for stars, signifying statehood, in a 1911 political cartoon.

sheep herders and cattle ranchers. Some businesses grew mightily – John S. Chisum, the "Cow King of New Mexico," employed as many as 100 cowboys tending 80,000 head of cattle. Range wars and cattle rustling, aggravated by political corruption and extra-legal land dealings, gave rise to a gun-toting outlaw environment that further tarnished the territory's image as a barely civilized outland.

Most infamous was the range war that erupted in the 1870s in southern New Mexico, boiling over from a rivalry between political and economic factions that resembled the vendettas of Renaissance Italy. Homesteaders and squatters made life difficult for cattlemen, and bitter disputes over land claims often involved holdings from the old Spanish families. Out of the conflict – later dubbed the Lincoln County War – arose the iconic figure of Billy the Kid, cattle rustler and gunfighter par excellence.

Ironically, that Western legend was born in seamy New York City, probably as Henry McCarty, though he was later known as William H. Bonney and Henry Antrim. Resettling with his widowed mother in Silver City, New Mexico, the youthful Billy absorbed the atmosphere of saloons and gambling halls, and may have claimed his first victim before entering his teen years. Accounts differ as to his true

character – simpatico friend or cold-blooded killer, or both.

Some say he was offered a job as a gunman by Chisum. He did, in any event, go to work for J. H. Tunstall, a popular young English-born cattleman whose murder in February 1878 inflamed his cowhands, including Billy. On April 1, on a Lincoln street, Sheriff Bill Brady and another man – both associated with the rival faction – were fatally ambushed, for which Billy later was convicted. The climax in this fierce battle between cattlemen and merchants came on July 19 when Billy, dodging bullets, fled the burning house of his associate Alexander McSween, who with others died inside.

Reports of the bloody feud reached Washington and prompted condemnation by President Rutherford B. Hayes, already concerned about western lawlessness. He chose as New Mexico's territorial governor the Civil War general Lew Wallace, who labored for three years to suppress the violence (meanwhile working at his Santa Fe residence on his classic novel *Ben Hur*, published in 1880). Wallace issued a general pardon for misdemeanors, met with Billy in Lincoln, and eventually restored order.

## End of the trail

In 1880, Billy and four companions, hiding out in a hut, were captured by a posse headed by Lincoln County Sheriff Pat Garrett. Awaiting the hangman's noose, the Kid made a spectacular escape in April 1881, killing two jail guards in the process. The end of the trail came in July when Billy the Kid, age 21, was cornered by Garrett in a darkened bedroom at a ranch house in Fort Sumner and gunned down. His last words: *"Quien es? Quien es?"* (Who is it? Who is it?)

Also reaching the end of the trail was the American frontier, and the result would be major social changes. Railroads brought increasing numbers of immigrants from the American East, and New Mexico's population increased sharply in the generation after 1880, growing to 327,301 in 1910.

A major development was the territory's emergence as a mining center yielding great reserves of mineral wealth. The first discovery of gold in the western United States had in fact been made in 1828 in the Ortiz Mountains south of Santa Fe, but it was only in the latter part of the 19th century that extensive ore deposits were located. New Mexico became known as a rich mining center whose gold, silver and other precious metals attracted investors from far and wide. As part of the railroad boom, the Southern Pacific extended its line to Silver City in 1884 and to Lake Valley, home of rich silver deposits, in 1885.

Finally, with Congress relenting, New Mexico shed its long-running territorial status on January 6, 1912, and became the 47th state of the Union. In that respect, it edged out its sister state of Arizona by six weeks.  ❑

**LEFT:** Christopher "Kit" Carson forced more than 8,000 Navajo on a "long walk" to Fort Sumner.
**RIGHT:** New Mexico rustlers, ca. 1879.

# BUILDING THE BOMB

*Here was fashioned the "terrible swift sword" that*
*terminated a great conflict while casting a shadow over humanity's future*

"**N**obody could think straight in a place like that," said physicist Leo Szilard, referring to the remote locale in northern New Mexico where a stellar cast of theoreticians and tinkerers was about to gather to build a super-bomb, beating the enemy to the punch and winning World War II for the Allies over the Axis. "Everybody who goes there will go crazy."

Szilard was talking about Los Alamos – Spanish for "the cottonwoods" – up on a stretch of mesalands about 40 miles (65km) northwest of Santa Fe. Here was to be conceived what came to be known by insiders as "the gadget," a harmless-sounding name for the deadliest invention of modern times: the atomic bomb. When finally tested in July 1945, at still another remote New Mexico location, it shook up the world and reshaped history.

## Long hairs and plumbers

Somehow, New Mexico was a likely place to try out the future-shock fantasies of such visionaries as Jules Verne and H. G. Wells, who had respectively written of moon shots and atomic bombs. Back in 1929, rocket pioneer Robert Goddard had established his testing range near Roswell. And it was near Roswell in 1947 that the reputed crash of an "unidentified flying object" – from outer space? – and the tangled sequence of government explanations gave rise to the UFO obsession. Similarly, the secret goings-on in the laboratories at Los Alamos, as World War II raged on three continents, had fueled wild speculation around the state by the time the bomb was receiving its finishing touches in the spring of 1945. But despite what Leo Szilard predicted, everybody who went there did not go crazy. If anything, the problem was boredom.

These were, after all, largely urban and Continental types, a mix of brainy European and American high-techies. (There developed

**LEFT:** J. R. Oppenheimer and General Leslie Groves at the detonation site of the world's first atomic bomb.
**RIGHT:** mushroom cloud, 6 miles from ground zero.

among them a mild rivalry pitting scientists as "long-hairs" versus engineers as "plumbers.") And here in this austere, rugged New Mexican setting, atop the Pajarito Plateau near the Sangre de Cristo mountains – and behind barbed wire at that! – they were asked to shut themselves off from the rest of the world for the

duration of a crash wartime program.

Their mission? Design and produce a weapon to be activated by the pent-up energy that is unleashed when uranium and plutonium atoms are split apart. In other words, achieve nuclear fission via a chain reaction. They did the job – only too well, some might lament – connecting the dots of sundry experimental breakthroughs achieved by such scientific luminaries as James Clerk Maxwell, Max Planck, Wilhelm Röntgen, Ernest Rutherford, Albert Einstein, Otto Hahn, Lise Meitner, James Chadwick, Marie Curie and other scientific pioneers.

It was absorbing work, part of the strictly hush-hush Manhattan Project that began taking shape in the spring and summer of 1942 and would eventually cost the taxpayers $2 billion. At Los Alamos, this massive exercise in research and development went into high gear beginning in April 1943. The birthplace of the bomb was a longtime dude ranch for well-heeled boys that was taken over by Uncle Sam and hastily transformed into a laboratory-cum-cabin complex that was a cross between army camp and mountain resort.

## Dancing with scientists

It was a talented lot. Master calculators like John von Neumann, the math genius from

Budapest. Specialists in chemistry and explosives like the Ukrainian-born anti-Bolshevik George B. Kistiakowsky. Big-name physicists and theoreticians like Denmark's Niels Bohr and England's Sir James Chadwick, both of whom had worked with Rutherford, the British nuclear pioneer; the Italians Enrico Fermi and Emilio Segrè; the Hungarian-born Edward Teller, who went on to father the hydrogen bomb; the German-born Hans Bethe and Rudolf Peierls and Otto Frisch, the man who coined the term "fission"; the Americans Luis Alvarez and Richard Feynman. Quite a few Nobel laureates emerged from among them.

During the week they mulled over such arcana as diffusion, radioactivity, metal reduction and the hydrodynamics of implosion, and on weekends they partied. To let off steam, they and their bored spouses took up such anomalous activities as square dancing, though not always gracefully – Enrico Fermi, one woman later observed, tended to dance with his brains instead of his feet.

They learned to appreciate the objects of native Indian arts and culture. They hiked and scaled the nearby mountains and rode ponies. They gave birth to a multiplicity of offspring, and played a lot of poker. They also drank and smoked a little too much, but then there was a war on and they had serious business to do.

Serious and secret. You had to be careful whom you talked to and what you said, which added to the sense of isolation. Tight security could be annoying. Soldiers guarded the gates, entry and exit were rigorously controlled, mail censored, phones virtually nonexistent. For the Europeans especially, said Laura Fermi, the Italian physicist's Jewish-born wife, Los Alamos bore a disconcerting resemblance to a concentration camp.

There were code names and nicknames for people, places and activities. Los Alamos was "Site Y," its mysterious doings the "Buck Rogers Project." Niels Bohr was "Nicholas Baker," his son Aage Bohr "James Baker." The first of the bombs was "Fat Man," followed by "Little Boy." The breakthrough test of the prototype weapon was done at a place dubbed "Trinity" by the poetic-minded J. Robert Oppenheimer ("Mr. Bradley").

Oppenheimer ran the show at Los Alamos, and ran it well, by most accounts. An academic with a commanding grasp of quantum and nuclear physics, he kept research humming along at the same time that he kept in sync his diffuse assemblage of super-smart scientists working out their dense formulae on chalkboards. He had his critics, but what counted the most was the support "Oppie" received from U.S. Army General Leslie R. Groves.

## Einstein's warning

Groves, of the Army Corps of Engineers, had been named in September 1942 to head the bomb-making effort, a cooperative civilian-military enterprise disguised by the more mundane title of "Manhattan Engineer District," today famous the world over as the Manhattan Project. It grew out of the letter of warning that Einstein, prompted by Szilard and others, addressed to President Franklin D. Roosevelt in 1939 on the threat posed by nuclear fission in the hands of a hostile power – with special reference to Hitler's Germany.

Groves sized up Oppenheimer (a "real genius") as an effective administrator capable of working smoothly with an assemblage of scientific types the general flatly labeled "prima donnas." Groves had to defend his choice in the face of criticism that Oppenheimer lacked the experience necessary for hands-on application of such engineering know-how. A more

when the married Oppenheimer paid a visit to an unhappy ex-lover and onetime Communist in San Francisco – she later took her own life – an FBI agent filed a detailed report that included mention of the kiss that was the prelude to their overnight rendezvous.

## A desert workplace

It was Oppenheimer and Groves who chose Los Alamos as one of the key Manhattan Project sites. It would receive uranium and plutonium produced for the bomb at two other huge new high-security installations – the "Clinton Engineer Works" at Oak Ridge in Tennessee and the

sensitive problem was Oppenheimer's connection with Communist-leaning relatives and intimates, including his former fiancée, his wife and his brother Frank, who was working alongside him at Los Alamos.

Such a connection horrified military intelligence officials, fearful that nuclear secrets might be betrayed. Indeed, at least one Army security officer was convinced that Oppenheimer was a Soviet spy. So he was watched like a hawk. On one occasion in June 1943,

**LEFT:** chemist at work on the Manhattan Project.
**ABOVE:** The "device" is raised to the top of the Trinity Site detonation tower.

"Hanford Engineer Works" along the Columbia River in Washington state. Oppenheimer favored a central lab where leading theoreticians could be brought together for bomb design, and Groves set specifications for the site to meet security considerations: somewhere west of the Mississippi River distant from major population centers; away from the coast and at least 200 miles (320km) from any international boundary; a tract of land set within a bowl-like surrounding. Other considerations included water supply and road access.

To scout out likely locations, Groves assigned a subordinate, who crisscrossed the country in an extensive search. A site in south-central Utah was favored, then passed up because too many resident families would have had to be evicted. Then the focus was on Jemez Springs, a deep canyon on the western slope of the Jemez Mountains in northern New Mexico. Groves and Oppenheimer and two others got into a military car and drove there from Albuquerque in November 1942.

Groves was unhappy with the lay of the land in the Jemez Springs Valley, and Oppenheimer suggested a look at a nearby site that housed the Los Alamos Ranch School. The scientist knew the territory well, having spent time here as a youth and as owner of a ranch

stoves for cooking and other camp-like amenities, and the school's Lodge and Big House became the social centers for soldiers and scientists. The place looked like a military camp except that the inhabitants were mostly civilians sporting blue jeans and casual clothes and eschewing neckties. Here, up on "the Hill," as they called their Los Alamos setting, they went to work on the gadget.

## "Shatterer of worlds"

With victory achieved in Europe by May 1945, it was becoming evident that the bomb would be looked on as the means to ending the savage

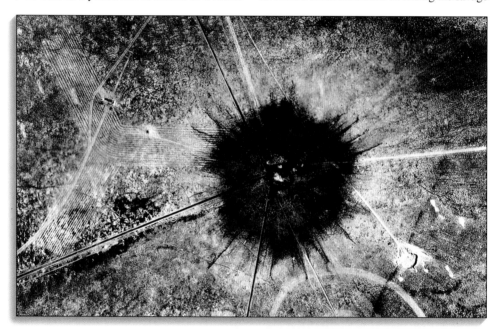

in the Sangre de Cristo range. The school property was on a 7,200-ft (2,200-km) mesa that rose 8,500 ft (2,600km) above sea level. Opened in 1917 by Ashley Pond, an outdoors enthusiast, the tract accommodated 50 log cabins set in a clearing amid pine trees and a mountainous backdrop.

The military car pulled up in front of the main log building, Groves got out and was much pleased with the location. The property was acquired, the boys sent home, and a new community arose on the mesa where once there had been a prehistoric settlement.

Army engineers constructed laboratories and barracks-like buildings, with wood-burning

war in the Pacific against a foe of do-or-die determination. By the end of that month the decision to drop it on the Japanese mainland was taking shape in the mind of President Harry S. Truman.

An actual test had to be made at some point, Oppenheimer had told Groves early on, so an intensive search was launched before a large tract of desert in southern New Mexico was selected in mid-1944. It was 210 miles (340km) south of Los Alamos and 60 miles (97km) northwest of Alamogordo. The region was named, appropriately, the Jornada del Muerto – Dead Man's Way – where many an unlucky Spanish or Anglo intruder had fallen victim to Apache attackers.

A test date was set: Monday, July 16, 1945, at dawn – the original blast time of 4am was subsequently changed to seconds before 5.30. The few cattle ranchers in the desolate area were bought out as military police guarded against intrusion. On the morning of the test, eggs and French toast were served at 3.45am to the scientific and military personnel inhabiting the base camp, 10 miles (16km) from the detonation point, while others were en route from Los Alamos to observe the momentous explosion.

Shelters were situated north, west and south of Trinity, anywhere from 6 to 20 miles (10–32km) away, and some lighthearted bets were made as to the enormity of what was about to occur – a dread that somehow the whole world might be imperiled was not beyond some idle reckoning. Sirens were sounded, the countdown began, protective glasses were donned, and the observers hunkered down in trenches amid heightened suspense.

The blast far exceeded most expectations. The steel tower that held the bomb was evaporated. Radioactivity was unleashed over a wide area. A 25-ft-deep (8-meter) crater was created. The explosion could be heard 50 miles (80km) away, its flash visible for much more than that – 250 miles (400km) – causing consternation over much of New Mexico and the region.

The observers were stunned by the force. Kistiakowsky, rising after being dazed by the light of the nuclear fireball, was caught off balance by the shock wave and toppled – he and Oppenheimer were 6 miles (10km) away. The blast's impact was equivalent to about 18,000 tons of TNT, making the visiting Columbia University physicist Isidor I. Rabi the winner in the betting pool. Oppenheimer, shaken by the ominousness of the event, made his memorable allusion to the *Bhagavad-Gita*, the classic Hindu devotional poem: "I am become Death/ The shatterer of worlds."

News of the test was relayed to a buoyant Truman at the Potsdam Conference in Germany. He passed the word on to Josef Stalin and wondered at the Soviet dictator's apparent nonchalance. Only much later would Truman learn that a Soviet spy within the British scientific mission at Los Alamos had been keeping Moscow abreast of the Manhattan Project and what was going on in the New Mexico desert.

The spy, Klaus Fuchs, met with his handlers and Soviet couriers just outside Los Alamos. He was unmasked in 1949. One of the consequences of the breach in security and its ensuing political fallout was a fall from grace for the reputedly left-leaning Oppenheimer. Just as the Cold War was heating up, he was favoring a policy of openness on nuclear knowledge. He was eventually stripped of his security clearance.

Something else was happening at the moment of the Trinity bomb blast: the component parts for Little Boy were being placed

aboard the USS *Indianapolis* at a West Coast dock for delivery to the island of Tinian in the Pacific. Then it was loaded onto the *Enola Gay*, the B-29 aircraft which deposited it on Hiroshima on August 6, 1945, at 9.15am. It caused mass destruction and killed 130,000 men, women and children. Fat Boy came next, its devastation at Nagasaki three days later raising the toll by 75,000 additional deaths.

Today the Los Alamos National Laboratory is one of America's leading research institutions, applying science and technology in strategies involving national security. It is operated on behalf of the U.S. Department of Energy by the University of California. ❑

**LEFT:** aerial view of ground zero.
**RIGHT:** three Nobel Prize laureates – Ernest Lawrence, Enrico Fermi and I. I. Rabi – at Los Alamos, 1946.

# MODERN TIMES

*Growing pains afflicted the state throughout the 20th century as a largely rural population learned to deal with industry, tourism and explosive growth*

On March 1, 1994, former city councilor Debbie Jaramillo became the first female Hispanic mayor in Santa Fe history. Promising to rein in runaway development, return city government to the people, and narrow the widening gap between Hispanos and Anglos through a variety of social programs, Jaramillo's low-budget grassroots campaign drew a record 59 percent turnout – a remarkable achievement in a city allergic to any kind of group activity.

"The real politics is not about money or about power. It's about people," said the native New Mexican in her victory speech. "This town is not for sale. It belongs to the community."

Debbie Jaramillo's election was a watershed event for Santa Fe. Although she proved a weak administrator, eventually being ousted amid cries of nepotism, divisiveness and grandiosity, her genuine attempts to improve living conditions in the City Different changed Santa Fe for the better, uniting a community that had become badly divided. While Albuquerque, Roswell, Las Cruces, Farmington, Gallup, Las Vegas and other towns in New Mexico make no pretensions to glamour – what you see is what you get – Santa Fe by 1984 had achieved city status, with over 50,000 residents, but was suffering growing pains. Something had to give.

Santa Fe's perception problem demonstrates just how "different" the City Different had become from the rest of New Mexico. By the end of the 20th century, it had become a victim of decades of self-promotion as a high-end hideout for wealthy visitors. Articles in *National Geographic* and *Esquire* citing Santa Fe as the next "hot" place only widened the gap between fantasy and reality that had been growing since the 1970s. Now, it was official: Santa Fe was "in."

Almost overnight, thousands of wealthy urban refugees cashed out of New York and California and bought cheap fixer-upper adobes

in Santa Fe as retirement or second homes. Santa Feans didn't know what had hit them. Richard Polese, former community liaison for the City of Santa Fe, recalls how apartments that rented for $35 a month – the cheapest in the nation – started renting for ten times that amount.

Even those families who owned their own

homes on Santa Fe's east side were affected. Unable to afford skyrocketing property taxes, many were forced to sell up. A long tradition of subdividing properties among heirs was broken, and many young Hispanics were forced to leave Santa Fe and find affordable housing elsewhere. By the late 1990s, homes within 50 miles (80km) of Santa Fe were fetching more than a million dollars, a real estate boom that continues to the present day.

## City in shock

Long-time residents still talk with sadness about the loss of those qualities that had made Santa Fe home: old-fashioned family-run

**LEFT:** the VLA west of Socorro is one of several high-tech research facilities in New Mexico.
**RIGHT:** Santa Fe architecture is inspired by traditional and contemporary styles.

stores where you could buy a burrito as well as hardware; mixed neighborhoods where everyone helped one another; a real downtown devoid of pricey boutiques and corporate stores; and a community of people interested in each other, who tolerated differences and took the time to talk.

It was just these qualities that had lured earlier generations of Anglos to Santa Fe. Compared with exuberant Albuquerque, which, following the arrival of the railroad in 1880, had grown into a major transportation hub and, later, a high-tech center, Santa Fe in the early 1900s was still a sleepy town of firewood-

had reached the heights of kitsch, spawning images of howling coyotes and flute-playing kokopellis on everything from T-shirts to Christmas ornaments. On a more serious note, the widening gap between haves and have-nots could no longer be ignored. In the remote villages of northern New Mexico, Hispanic and Indian people exhibited signs of what one observer likened to post traumatic stress disorder. Dazed by the rapid transition from a barter economy to a cash society, families struggled to survive. Joblessness, depression, grinding poverty, alcoholism, drug abuse, domestic violence and teen pregnancy rose as once self-

bearing *burros*, wandering Pueblo vendors, and old-time Hispanic and Anglo families who dominated an incestuous political scene. It smiled tolerantly at the eccentric creative types who had left East Coast cities for new homes in the high desert. Indeed, no visit to the City Different was complete without a visit to the 1920 La Fonda Hotel, where a motley assortment of colorful, quipping writers, eccentric artists and roving journalists held court each day, turning the hotel bar into Santa Fe's version of New York's famed Algonquin Round Table.

Press reports extolling the virtues of Santa Fe marked the first time that Santa Fe Style had hit the American mainstream. Before long it

sufficient families resorted to welfare programs.

There were some hopeful signs. More people than ever before were traveling to remote northern New Mexico villages like Abiquiu, Chimayó and Truchas, creating new markets for a growing number of traditional weavers, carvers and farmers.

## Transitions

Until the late 1800s, New Mexico was too far from anywhere to register changes brought about by contact with the outside world. The bloodless coup that put New Mexico in the hands of the United States in 1846 changed the makeup of the state from largely Hispanic to increasingly Anglo (a term used in New Mexico to describe all non-Hispanics). American settlers immigrated west by wagon into New Mexico Territory. Many began trading businesses in Santa Fe and Taos and branches of the Santa Fe Trail. In the torrid Chihuahuan Desert of the southern part of the state, ranchers and farmers from Texas developed Apache land under the protection of U.S. soldiers stationed at forts throughout the region.

In 1880, the railroad bypassed Santa Fe in favor of Albuquerque and Las Vegas in the north and Alamogordo in the south, and those communities quickly grew in importance as

architecture, foods and lifestyle – grew out of Hewett's desire to return the old Casas Reales, or Palace of the Governors, to an authentic regional style. In 1915, architect I. H. Rapp drew on paintings of Acoma and other Pueblo missions by artist Carlos Vierra to create a full-scale Spanish Pueblo Mission Revival building for the Expo in Chicago. The prototype was recreated on the Plaza in 1917 as the Museum of Fine Arts, followed, in 1920, by La Fonda Hotel.

In the subsequent decades, the new Santa Fe Style was popularized by architect John Gaw Meem, who had arrived in Santa Fe tubercular and dying and, like so many other invalids,

tourist and commercial destinations. Santa Fe's economy nosedived to such a degree that Albuquerque made a bid to become the new state capital. The move was narrowly averted by a coalition of local businessmen and land-holding families, such as the Catrons, and powerful newcomers such as the well-connected archaeologist Edgar Lee Hewett, who promoted Santa Fe as headquarters for the newly founded American Institute of Archaeology.

Santa Fe Style – a combination of arts, crafts,

LEFT: power generating station in northern New Mexico.
ABOVE: subdivisions crowd the borders of Petroglyph National Monument on the outskirts of Albuquerque.

made a full recovery in the dry and sunny desert hills. Meem expanded the market for Santa Fe Style to other parts of New Mexico, including Albuquerque, where he designed a number of buildings on the University of New Mexico campus.

## Natural resources

Hewett's renovation of the Palace of the Governors, the oldest capitol in the United States, and promotion of New Mexico's extraordinary archaeological history was a stroke of genius. It seized the imagination of Americans weary with war-torn Europe and inspired them with the glories of their own culture. More important,

New Mexico's increasingly well documented natural and cultural resources meant that granting of statehood was just a matter of time.

When New Mexico became a state, in 1912, it opened the way for important changes. Territorial jobs carried out almost exclusively by Anglos gave way to federal jobs open to Hispanics as well as Anglos. On the downside, the growing interest in New Mexico and demand for national parks, forests and other recreational and resource areas accelerated the loss of Hispanic land grants, as the courts turned over community grazing lands to public and private ownership in rural New Mexico.

Predator reduction programs remained in effect throughout the 20th century. Efforts to reintroduce the wolf were restricted to experimental federal programs supported by zoos and private ranchers like Ted Turner, who also helped reintroduce bison to their native range.

## Indian rights

Preserving the past was also behind a growing interest in New Mexico's native people. Taos society maven Mabel Dodge Luhan's marriage to a full-blooded Taos Pueblo man engendered important gains for Pueblo people. In the 1920s, a coalition of artists, writers, social

These vast public lands attracted a new breed of land manager from back East, who combined scientific training with on-the-ground experience that helped shape land management policy into the 21st century. One of the best known was forester Aldo Leopold, whose work in southwestern New Mexico's Gila National Forest, sparked a lifelong interest in ecosystem management and the setting aside of the country's first wilderness.

Leopold's plea for interspecies harmony, eloquently argued in his classic *A Sand County Almanac*, found stiff resistance among ranchers struggling to protect livestock from predators like coyotes, mountain lions, bears and wolves.

activists like John Collier, and a Pueblo coalition, helped defeat the Bursum Bill, introduced by New Mexico Senator Albert Fall, which would have deprived Pueblos of traditional lands. As a result, American Indians received the vote for the first time and organized into tribal councils in the 1930s, a political first step toward legitimatized government-to-government relations.

The 19 New Mexico pueblos, Navajo Nation, and Jicarilla and Mescalero Apache tribes survived efforts in the mid-1900s to merge them into mainstream society and, today, have never been stronger. In 1970, Taos Pueblo successfully argued for the return of its sacred Blue

Lake on Taos Mountain, and in 2003 Zuni Pueblo won a victory against an Arizona power company to keep out a power plant on its sacred Fence Lake. As the tribes have become wealthy and self-sustaining through arts cooperatives, gaming, hospitality, golf courses, recreational complexes and other businesses, their political clout in the state has grown. State officials work closely with tribes on numerous issues of mutual interest, from tourism and arts festivals to job creation and water rights.

Water remains the most contentious issue for this desert state, pitting the needs of senior users such as Indian pueblos and Hispanic farmers against the demands of developers, industry and other special interests. The situation has been complicated by an extended drought and efforts to restore cottonwood woodlands and protect endangered species such as the silvery minnow and southwestern willow flycatcher.

Fire suppression in national forests and home building in the dangerous urban-wildland interface has led to devastating fires in New Mexico, which destroy hundreds of homes annually. Forest thinning programs on federal lands have made slow progress, stalled by environmental challenges, while public-private partnerships on other lands have managed to prevent disaster in the city-owned watershed above Santa Fe by thinning overgrown forests in the last few years.

## Mutual interests

New Mexico's role in World War II had a lasting impact on this rural state. The Manhattan Project, which built the world's first atomic bomb at a former boarding school in Los Alamos, led to the development of facilities devoted to high-tech defense research at Sandia Labs in Albuquerque, New Mexico Institute of Technology in Socorro, and Holloman Air Force Base near Alamogordo. New Mexico's nuclear legacy has divided the state. Depending on where you live, the defense industry is either an important provider of much-needed work or a worrying environmental accident waiting to happen, such as the contentious Waste Isolation Pilot Project (WIPP), which stores low-level nuclear waste from all over the country in salt caverns in Carlsbad.

A postwar boom contributed to Albuquerque's exponential growth into the North Valley, where the sprawling Rio Rancho development on the west side of the Rio Grande is among the fastest growing in the country. Urbanization is still the exception for most New Mexicans, though. And even as Albuquerque, Santa Fe, Las Cruces and other towns have grown, rural New Mexicans have struggled to survive. Activists like Reies Lopez Tijerina, whose armed Alianza took over the Tierra Amarilla County Courthouse in 1967, focused international attention on the plight of these forgotten people.

As a result, community activism has grown throughout New Mexico, leading to numerous social programs. Low-cost health care clinics, after-school cultural programs and traditional agriculture are sponsored by coalitions of citizens, nonprofit organizations and government which, today, represents a broader cross-section of interests. Among the new challenges are the increasing presence of Mexican nationals throughout the state – not just the borderlands of the south – who are making a permanent home in New Mexico. They, along with thousands of other immigrants from all over the world, are giving new meaning to New Mexico's famed multiculturalism. ❏

**LEFT:** the detritus of the nuclear age is sold at a military surplus shop in Los Alamos.
**RIGHT:** oil rig workers in southern New Mexico.

# THE CULTURAL LANDSCAPE

*Three cultures – Indian, Hispanic and Anglo – imbue New Mexico
with a creative and independent spirit that's far more than the sum of its parts*

One day in the late 1950s, Santa Fe novelist Richard Bradford needed to give directions to his house to an old friend who had just arrived in New Mexico. Street signs were scarce in Santa Fe back then, so Bradford resorted to using landmarks. One of them was a dog.

"Go up Camino del Monte Sol," Bradford told his friend. "It dead-ends where you turn, just go up. At about a hundred yards, on your right you should see a large shaggy black dog sleeping. He's been sleeping there every afternoon since I can remember. When you see the dog, take the first left, and my house is by the biggest cottonwood on the right."

Bradford told this story to John Pen La Farge, who used it as the irresistible title for his Santa Fe oral history, *Turn Left at the Sleeping Dog*. "It never occurred to me that to give directions using living animals as guideposts was a strange thing to do," Bradford said.

## The New Mexico difference

It wasn't, not in New Mexico. Bradford's story illuminates at least four facets of New Mexico's cultural landscape:

● *Improvisation.* New Mexicans always figure out a way to do the job at hand, whether it's giving directions or sustaining life on New Mexico's chronically low-wage work.

● *Tradition.* The shaggy dog could be trusted to park himself in the same shady spot every day. Two-legged New Mexicans, at least those whose families have been around for a few generations, likewise respect tradition.

● *Languor.* Not much happens with alacrity in New Mexico. A dog taking a long afternoon siesta wouldn't be a bad advertisement for the place.

● *Unorthodoxy.* For centuries, New Mexicans have been doing things their own way, with

---

**PRECEDING PAGES:** ceremonial clowns, San Juan Pueblo, 1935.
**LEFT:** rodeo cowboy, Taos.
**RIGHT:** traditional Hispanic dancers.

little if any concern for the conventions of the outside world.

When people hear of the "cultural landscape" of New Mexico, they automatically think: Indian, Hispanic, Anglo. Three distinct cultures elbowing each other in a sometimes uneasy triangle. But there is also an overarching culture

of New Mexico, a place unique in North America, that permeates the land and seeps across ethnic boundaries. It is more a state of mind than a geographic locale.

Robert Leonard Reid, author of *America, New Mexico*, a penetrating survey of the state's people and places, may have explained it best: "Leave behind your foolish romances and preconceptions, and set your spirit to the local time. If your destination is New Mexico, that may mean carrying no bag at all and approaching with all the speed and urgency of a full moon sailing over the Rio Grande."

No bag, the urgency of a sailing moon. Perfect preparation for New Mexico.

## Beyond three cultures

Indian, Hispanic, Anglo: what are they? In New Mexico the answer can be tricky.

Indian cultures of New Mexico comprise Navajo, Apache and more than a dozen Pueblo tribes, with three distinct language families sprinkled among them – Zuni, Keresan and Tanoan. The different languages reflect the varied prehistoric origins of the Pueblo people.

Generally, all tribes accept the term "Indians" today. A recent panel of assorted tribe members agreed that "Indian" is a reasonable catch-all, although the Apache joked, "I'm just glad Columbus wasn't trying to find Turkey."

Many of the Hispanic people of northern New Mexico trace their familial roots directly to Spain, not the mestizo (mixed Indian-Spanish) population of Mexico. Some prefer to be called "Spanish," not Mexican-American, Chicano or Latino. In the younger towns of southern New Mexico, many are first-, second- or third-generation Mexican-Americans. Albuquerque novelist Rodolfo Anaya suggests an all-inclusive term: Hispano.

"Anglo," in the quirky New Mexican vernacular, forms an umbrella for everyone else, regardless of race or ethnicity. Tony Hillerman, writing in his memoir *Seldom Disappointed*,

### PENITENTES

*Los Hermanos Penitentes*, the Penitent Brothers, is a secretive Catholic fraternity that once practiced flagellation and crucifixion to atone for sin. It took root in New Mexico in the late 1600s, filling a vacuum in settlements where there was neither priest nor official government. The church, appalled by the bloody practices, ordered the Penitentes in 1889 to disband, which only drove them underground. The fraternity endures today in northern New Mexico, surfacing for cross-bearing processions during Holy Week.

Controversy has always embroiled the *Penitentes*. In 1888, journalist Charles Lummis was allowed to observe a procession. His account makes readers cringe today. He describes one Santiago Jaramillo, bleeding profusely from a four-inch gash in his torso, being strapped to a cross – all the while begging, "Not with a rope! Nail me! Nail me!"

Lummis was not convinced by the Penitentes' piety. Cynically, he saw the brotherhood as a way for petty criminals to stroke their consciences. "Many of them are of the lowest and most dangerous classes," he wrote, "petty larcenists, horse-thieves, and assassins, who by their devotions during Lent think to expiate their sins of the whole year."

The Penitentes still stage their Lenten processions, sing ancient Spanish hymns, and pray. But instead of torture, they lead peace marches and protest drug-related violence.

recalls an African-American and a Hispanic discussing vote-buying in Santa Fe. The Hispanic asks, "How much they paying for votes?" The African-American replies, "Don't know. They haven't gotten around to us Anglos yet."

New Mexico's 2000 population registered slightly over 1.8 million. Of those, 9.5 percent claimed Indian blood, 42.1 percent were Hispanic, and 44.7 percent called themselves Anglo.

The census numbers, though, don't reflect the feeling of the state, which Robert Leonard Reid calls its "Indianness." He's not speaking of percentage of population, but of a quality that is intangible and indefinable, an enchantment that flows out of the landscape and into every human culture and consciousness. "New Mexico bears witness at every turn to a critical wisdom preserved doggedly by Indians in the face of massive denial by whites," he writes. "The world has a mystical, spiritual nature that is absolutely inaccessible to reason."

## Indian ethos

This mystic or spiritual dimension lies close to the surface in Indian culture. It permeates their history, their art, their ceremonies and their relationships with the natural world. It is difficult for non-Indians to comprehend, but worth the trouble to try.

A wizened Navajo grandmother takes a few moments to tell a visitor her family's story of the Long Walk, the 1864 march from Arizona's Canyon de Chelly to a concentration camp on northeastern New Mexico's bleak prairie. The storyteller's great-grandmother, only 15 at the time, escaped from custody and walked 300 miles (500km) alone to return to her homeland. Traveling only at night to avoid capture, she first followed a benevolent owl's hooting. Then she met a bear, who escorted her through the forest, her hand on his rump for guidance through the dark. Finally, threatened by a pack of wolves, she spoke to them in their own language. "Look at me," she cried. "I am nothing but bones. Go find a fat deer; I just want to go home." Moved by the plea, the wolves spared her.

Bears and wolves don't behave this way in the real world, and modern Navajos are well

**LEFT:** an Albuquerque mural depicting the Bill of Rights, with images of Indian, Anglo and Hispanic voters.
**RIGHT:** Indian vets are honored at the Vietnam Veterans Memorial near Taos.

aware of it: they're keen observers of nature. But the mystical and historical elements of the story twine into one seamless narrative. "In a Navajo story, logical contradictions don't matter," explains a college-educated Navajo. "A wolf and a rabbit may cooperate. It's not important that in the real world the two are natural enemies. To a Navajo, it's all true."

Travelers who drop into New Mexico pueblos on feast days are often welcomed to share meals in Indian homes and watch the ceremonial dances in the plazas (although questions about the proceedings tend to be answered with stony silence). Sometimes an outsider's incli-

nation is to see them as perplexingly quaint, an indulgence of primitive people unwilling to relinquish ancient superstitions. Others may find themselves moved to their spiritual core, as did D. H. Lawrence during the three years he spent roaming New Mexico in the 1920s. Go to Taos Pueblo at some quiet time away from the hubbub of tourists, he wrote, "and you will feel the old, old root of human consciousness still reaching down to depths we know nothing of."

But the Indian reason for the ceremonies, which roll on year after year as reliably as the seasons, is that they sustain community and culture. They ensure that the tribes will not be dissolved into the American mainstream. Navajo and Pueblo people both nurture a quiet belief that modern America will eventually squander the Southwest's natural resources (most obviously its scarce water) and move on. But if the Indians keep their community and traditions alive, they will still know how to live here – as they did for millennia before the Spanish and Anglos arrived.

## Harsh realities and hope

New Mexican Indians today live with a foot in each of two worlds, trying to balance tradition with adaptation, weighing responsibilities to their clans against the realities of making a living in a modern economy. For many, these are over-

dia Pueblo, chairman of the New Mexico Indian Gaming Commission, told the *Albuquerque Journal* that "It's just been phenomenal. Training, location, pride in working for your tribe. When you think what those jobs mean to people and their families, it goes way beyond profits."

Contemporary Indian art likewise goes way beyond profits, and it offers the tribes something gaming and golf cannot: a bridge to the traditions of the past. Pueblo pottery is one of the most treasured Native American art forms, and it is truly "native" – a tradition reaching back more than 2,000 years in the American

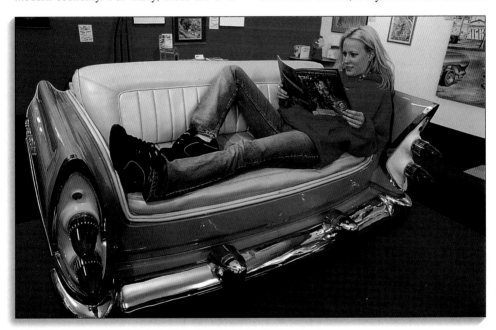

whelming demands. The median income of Indian families in New Mexico is well below the state's average, and New Mexico, overall, leads the nation in percentage of families living below the poverty line – 17.7 percent in the 2000 census. On the reservations, unemployment, alcoholism and drug addiction are persistent plagues.

Still, there are far more employment and entrepreneurial opportunities for New Mexican Indians today than there were just a generation ago. Indian gaming, formally legalized in 1994, quickly caught on: eight years later, 11 of the state's 22 tribes and pueblos operated casinos, and several had begun branching into the resort and golf course business. Frank Chaves of San-

Southwest. Within the last century, Pueblo potters have developed it into a highly refined art, and their ceramics, responding to the market, are today far more intricate, imaginative and beautiful than their ancestors' work.

Navajo weaving dates back at least 400 years to the Spanish introduction of sheep to the Southwest. A Spanish governor observed in 1795 that the Navajo "work their wool with more delicacy and taste than the Spaniards." Navajo rugs today are stunningly beautiful and breathtakingly expensive, but the art, ironically, may be endangered by the very consumer culture that finds it so appealing. "When I was growing up, we didn't have electricity," says one accomplished weaver. "Now all the kids have TV and PlayStations. It's hard for them to develop the patience for weaving with all the modern entertainment and distractions."

## Spanish spirit

Hispanic New Mexico is a remarkably rich stew of tradition and adaptation, a self-contained world that differs in many ways from the Spanish-speaking cultures of other states and nations. It has been that way from the beginning. In the 1620s a Franciscan friar named Jeronimo de Zárate Salmerón reported from New Mexico (with obvious disdain) that the

enjoyed gambling, fighting, unusually liberal sexual mores, and happily borrowed the hallucinogenic drug peyote from nearby Pueblo rituals. Officially the church fussed and fumed (while unofficially some New Mexico priests openly lived with mistresses), but geography inexorably shaped the culture: New Mexico was simply too far from the centers of authority in Mexico to be yanked into line.

Hispanic New Mexicans continued to chart their own course under the Mexican and even the American flags. New Mexico historian Marc Simmons has observed that unlike Texas, Arizona and California – the other states pre-

settlers in the province were "enemies of all kinds of work" who, "as long as they have a good supply of tobacco to smoke, they are very contented, and they do not want any more riches." In fact, the early *paisanos* of New Mexico were not averse to hard work; it was a hard land that demanded it for survival. What Zárate missed was the simple fact that the New Mexicans were determined, in addition, to savor life.

Other chroniclers of Spanish Colonial New Mexico variously observed that the colonists

viously claimed by Spain and then Mexico – New Mexico's Spanish colonial descendants remained the dominant culture at least until the 1940s. Anglo society neither absorbed it nor elbowed it aside. "Simply put, the New Mexicans refused to melt; and at every turn, they repulsed attempts to make them give up their language, their folkways, and their traditional style of life," he wrote.

In the minority today, Hispanic culture persists. Novelist Rudolfo Anaya wrote that his childhood Christmases in New Mexico did not involve toys and malls and football on TV "to distract the spirit and exhaust the mind." Instead, he recalled, families would come to

**LEFT:** hanging out at an Albuquerque tattoo parlor.
**ABOVE:** Margaret and Eremita Campos, owners of an organic farm on the Rio Grande north of Santa Fe.

visit, bringing their histories to share. "The kitchen was warm and filled with good food, and after we ate we listened to the stories." Around Christmas in Santa Fe, the municipal sewer system is still occasionally overwhelmed by the trickle-down effect of grease from the many thousands of tamales being made in Hispanic kitchens around town.

In fact, Hispanic culture does more than persist – it imbues the life of New Mexico. Dozens of craftsmen (many of them Anglo) make a living hand-crafting furniture and architectural ornaments in the Spanish Colonial style. Street names such as Las Cruces' Camino Real and Santa Fe's Paseo de Peralta are authentic reminders of colonial history, not developers' fanciful daydreams. Ancient folk arts such as the sometimes endearing, sometimes grotesque carved wooden *santos* (saints) are alive and well. Española, the lowrider capital of the Southwest, is practically a rolling museum of modern V8-powered folk art. And only in New Mexico is a visitor likely to land a museum tour with a docent who casually lets it slip that his family has been around town "about 300 years, *más o menos*" – more or less.

Arrive for breakfast on a weekday at El Taoseño in Taos or Tia Sophia in Santa Fe, and

SANTA FE FIES
Santa Fe
Ceremonies as

## ACEQUIA CULTURE – MINDING THE DITCHES

In New Mexico they're called *acequias* – communal irrigation ditches that carry water from skinflint rivers to thirsty farms. Snaking between hills and shaded by willows, they can seem picturesque, but the men who struggle to maintain them are seldom impressed. "The ditch is a moody creature," wrote Stanley Crawford in *Mayordomo*, his chronicle of managing an *acequia* in northern New Mexico. "Unpredictable, irritable, irritating, unreliable … You work yourself half to death and think everything's fine. But it isn't. It never is."

New Mexico's *acequias* predate the *entrada*, but the Spaniards overlaid their laws on the system. These abide today, governing some 800 community *acequia* associations.

A *comisión*, or governing board, parcels water out to members and appoints a *mayordomo* to lead the practical battles against collapsing banks, burrowing muskrats and feuding farmers. Keeping the peace requires a dance of diplomacy.

Some ditches are surprisingly beautiful – linear oases in the desert. They nourish riparian mini-forests. But unlike natural creeks, they demand endless attention.

"Next to blood relationships," wrote Crawford, "come water relationships." In New Mexico, ditches are arteries. They sustain life and form a web of community. They generate friendships and bitter rivalries, because in a parched land such as New Mexico nothing is more precious than water.

a visitor can eavesdrop on municipal bureaucrats enjoying coffee and fiery Mexican breakfasts such as *huevos con chorizo*. Civil service jobs in New Mexico still tend to be Hispanic territory, and the bureaucracy carries an indelible tint of Roman Catholic Spain.

Author Richard Mahler wanted to raise the fence of his Santa Fe home a foot for privacy, and in the ancient and honorable New Mexican tradition decided to do it without a building permit. Just before the job was finished, a city official noticed, and red-tagged it.

### HABLA ESPAÑOL?

According to the 2000 census, 29 percent of New Mexicans age 5 and over speak Spanish at home, a higher percentage than in any other state.

In some respects, though, the culture feels threatened. Sometimes from within: Rio Arriba County, mostly rural and Hispanic, sees eight to ten deaths from heroin and cocaine overdoses every year. The district attorney told the *Albuquerque Journal* that Rio Arriba's fatal overdose rate in recent years has been running 300 times the national average.

And sometimes from the outside: New Mexico is one of only two remaining states where cockfighting remains legal (Louisiana is the other), but there are periodic

gas Day
in 1693

Mahler grudgingly filed an application with the city, but it slogged through the bureaucracy for months. Finally, a bureaucrat called to tell him that his request would be on the city council's agenda the next evening.

Mahler, however, was packing for a flight to Singapore on the same day. He pleaded with the bureaucrat. After a moment's contemplation, the city official said, "Well, go ahead and finish your fence. In Santa Fe it's easier to get forgiveness than permission."

**ABOVE:** a re-enactment of Diego de Vargas's entry into Santa Fe during the 1921 Fiesta de Santa Fe, a celebration of Spanish culture that continues to this day.

efforts to kill the sport, rooted in Hispanic rural areas, in the legislature. One cockfighting enthusiast ranted in a public hearing in 2003, "This is a war against our culture. They're trying to turn our traditions into a crime. What about falconry, rodeos and fishing? Why are we singled out?"

The cockfighting ban passed the state House, then died in the Senate.

### Dream chasers

Anglo New Mexico, to use a laughably imprecise and frequently self-contradictory phrase, is impossible to categorize. In Santa Fe, where a substantial fraction of the Anglo community lives in access-controlled faux-adobe compounds (real adobe takes real work to maintain), it's tempting to quote William Ellis's observation in *National Geographic* in 1982: "Often they come as deserters from drudgery, chasing a dream of a new and looser lifestyle." But that's as pat and misleading as reading Navajo, Apache and Pueblos as one monolithic culture. What about Bill Gates and Paul Allen, who started a little company they called "Micro-soft" in an Albuquerque garage? What about the scientists who secretly converged on the Pajarito Plateau in 1943 to invent the atomic bomb? (The town of Los Alamos,

now home of the Los Alamos National Laboratory, still boasts the highest per-capita percentage of Ph.Ds in the country). What about Georgia O'Keeffe?

But at least Ellis's point about people "chasing a dream" is solidly rooted, and not only in the self-consciously chic state capital. The merchants and ranchers who trickled into New Mexico Territory in the first few decades after 1846 were adventurers and optimists – they had to be, taking on a land where nature ran hot and fierce and the prevailing languages and cultures were not anything they could have prepared for. And New Mexico, for at least a century after

## Taos Counterculture

The hippies who converged on Taos in the late 1960s thought they had found nirvana on earth – a landscape of transcendent beauty, a look-the-other-way tradition in local government, and cheap land for their agrarian communes. But they badly misread the culture, and the result was a war, complete with bombings, beatings and shootings.

John Nichols, who later would write *The Milagro Beanfield War*, spotted signs of trouble the day he arrived in Taos in 1969. Someone had tossed a brick through the window of Joe Sage's Macrobiotic Restaurant. A sign in another cafe read HELP KEEP AMERICA BEAUTIFUL, TAKE A HIPPIE TO A CARWASH.

The freak culture was no more welcome in Taos than it would have been in, say, Lubbock, though for different reasons. Native Taoseños saw the hippies as Anglo invaders who were buying up their land and driving up their taxes. Moreover, the free-loving, herb-smoking commune lifestyle deeply offended many Hispanos' conservative family values.

Eventually the communes broke up, the class war relaxed to a simmer, and the hippies drifted into mundane middle-class existence. Quite a few stayed around Taos, selling real estate. And the archetype commune, the New Buffalo in nearby Arroyo Hondo, is now a B&B.

that, proved very good at separating the "desert-ers from drudgery" from those who invested their dreams with energy and adaptability. His-torian Marc Simmons said it perfectly:

"Each generation of Americans, it seemed, had to learn anew what the Spaniards had dis-covered long before: in New Mexico, men could not recreate a life and society they had known elsewhere. Here, the wide and strange land shaped and reshaped human institutions to its own purposes, and one either learned to live with the blazing sun, the scarcity of water, the dust and interminable distances, and the whispering quiet of empty canyons and mesas, or he admitted failure and moved elsewhere."

Anglos have had as many reasons for coming to New Mexico, or if they were born here, for staying (economic rationality would almost always dictate moving elsewhere) as there are definitions of "Anglo." Novelist John Nichols wrote in his memoir *If Mountains Die* that he simply likes a place "where nature can still kick me and all my gadgets in the teeth." Architect Antoine Predock, who acquired an international reputation in the 1980s and '90s, said that New Mexico had erased the rationalist and formalist influences from his buildings. "Living here, something else takes over – not the rational side, but the spiritual side. I see a sky etched full of vapor trails, and think about where they may be going, and at the same time I see a mountain range and the Rio Grande Valley at my feet. It's all over you and into you here." And then there was the artist who fled her native Seattle for a tiny studio and gallery in Truchas: "I could afford to live here."

If there is any common denominator for the "Anglo" culture of New Mexico, it is the remarkable degree to which all the other cul-tures of the region have permeated it. It isn't just an Anglo household's embrace of Spanish Colonial-style furniture, a supply of green chile beer in the fridge and a collection of Pueblo pottery in a display case – any smitten tourist can acquire these things and cart them home. Instead, it's an absorption of the whole historic swirl of attitudes that comprise New Mexico, from a profound and spiritual love of the land to a make-do, desultory attitude toward material

riches. It all circles back to what Robert Leonard Reid called the "Indianness" of New Mexico. Many New Mexicans cannot explain why they live here. They simply know they belong.

## A place within

Throughout its long recorded history, New Mexico has attracted a grand mix of adventur-ers, rednecks, entrepreneurs, visionaries, lunatics, health-seekers, scientists, ski bums, artists, writers, spiritual voyagers, drug-addled longhairs, well-heeled retirees and misfits just wanting to be left the hell alone. The miracle of New Mexico is that it has accommodated all of

these, not without tensions, but with tolerance enough that all the ingredients in this stew could retain their distinctive flavors. New Mexico doesn't assimilate people; instead its residents absorb New Mexico. And somehow, it liberates them to become stronger, more vividly alive.

D. H. Lawrence described the transformation in mystic, raptured language: "The moment I saw the brilliant, proud morning shine high up over the deserts of Santa Fe, something stood still in my soul, and I started to attend ... In the magnificent fierce morning of New Mexico one sprang awake, a new part of the soul woke up suddenly, and the old world gave way to a new."

This is the essence of New Mexican culture,

**LEFT:** chile princess at the Hatch Chile Festival.
**RIGHT:** friendly clerk in gift shop at the Wheelwright Museum of the American Indian, Santa Fe.

and it has little to do with ethnic traditions, or else it reaches across all of them. There is no precise word in English to describe it, but the Spanish *duende* comes close. *Duende*, a not-quite-translatable word, carries connotations of magic and enchantment and some mysterious power. (A great flamenco guitarist would have *duende*, but a competent studio musician likely would not.) New Mexico's undeniable *duende* encompasses love of life and the embrace of absurdity, undergirded by the spirit of ever-cheerful improvisation.

In New Mexico, cultures overlay one another like geologic strata exposed in a

canyon wall. A small-town gas station may have a shelf of hand-carved *santos* for sale, alongside a crock pot of red chile and pork stewing into *carne adovada* – and, of course, a supply of fan belts and motor oil. A couple named Ernesto and Deborah cobble together a living on their northern New Mexico farmstead as if simultaneously occupying two different centuries: Ernesto tends sheep, cattle and horses, cultivates hay and apples, and builds beautiful furniture in the Spanish Colonial style. In the high-tech digital studio on the second floor of their home, Deborah produces radio programs, audio books and CDs. The house, of course, is adobe.

## Proud to be different

The old Spanish sigh of contented resignation, *lo que puede* – that which can be – explains much of contemporary New Mexican life. But what explains the New Mexico legislature, which has declared that the second Tuesday of every February will be "Extraterrestrial Culture Day," in honor of the putative UFO crash near Roswell in 1947? Or the curious inversion of property values in Santa Fe, where as author Susan Hazen-Hammond observed, the richer you are, the more likely you are to live on a dirt road? Or St. John's College, where every student's curriculum consists of the study of 200 "great books," from Plato's *Republic* to Werner Heisenberg's *The Physical Principles of the Quantum Theory*, but there is no workaday major in anything such as accounting or computer science?

In the end, New Mexicans are simply different – and proud of it. They feel endowed by a rich and powerful history, culture and landscape (all shot full of *duende*) that is unlike any other state's, and they will go to any lengths to preserve that difference.

One Territorial governor, Lew Wallace (best remembered for writing the novel *Ben Hur* while residing in the Palace of the Governors), accurately reported: "Every calculation based on experience elsewhere fails in New Mexico." A century later, a couple built a house in Santa Fe with a pointy roof over the kitchen, provoking a municipal feud, waving guns, criminal charges, and ultimately a 4,000-word story about the altercation in the *New Yorker*. (In Santa Fe, roofs are expected to be quiet and lie flat.) New Mexicans love to squabble and file lawsuits, especially over cultural issues, and although it may often seem laughable to the outside world, they do it because they truly care about preserving their uniqueness.

New Mexico is different – it always has been and probably always will be. "Sometimes we're startled by it, sometimes we're pleased by it, and sometimes we're alarmed by it," observed Hazen-Hammond. "But we accept all of it because we have a great desire to preserve who we are." ❑

**LEFT:** young dancers bring decidedly modern sensibilities to traditional *ballet folklorico.*
**RIGHT:** Floyd Montoya with his customized Thunderbird.

# A TASTE OF ENCHANTMENT

*Built upon a foundation of beans, corn and chile, New Mexican cooking runs*

*the gamut from hearty Hispanic dishes to innovative fusions of international styles*

On an unseasonably warm Sunday afternoon in early April, Don Bustos, former president of the Santa Fe Farmers Market, is showing a visitor around his organic farm. Huge, furrowed cottonwood trees shade the community ditch, or *acequia*, that flows through the property, separating the houses on the family compound from the 3½ acres (1.4 hectares) of pale pink earth under cultivation. A greenhouse and temporary hoop houses sport rows of basil, mint and other herbs as well as tender spinach, radishes, baby lettuce and kale destined for the winter market. Water droplets from microsprinklers douse baby carrots, asparagus, tomatoes and garlic, and dance in the strong spring winds, forming tiny rainbows.

As the growing season gets into full swing in May, Bustos will plant sugar-sweet white corn, cucumbers, zucchini squash, eggplant, okra, pumpkins and broccoli. Like other New Mexico farmers, his most eagerly anticipated crop is green chile, which he roasts in small batches for customers at the farmers market, starting in August. Like other growers in the Española Valley, he grows an improved local variety, an 8-inch-long (20-cm) spicy cross between a classic New Mexican Big Jim and the widely available Anaheim pepper. When strung into *ristras* and hung to dry from the eaves of northern New Mexico's pitched tin roofs, it turns bright red and can be ground into a rich, sweet, complex powder and reconstituted for salsas.

## Modern and traditional

Bustos, a powerfully built Hispano with laughing crinkled eyes and a shock of black beard, enjoys the challenge of integrating modern farming techniques with traditional methods. He has just finished flood-irrigating a field of three-week-old peas via a headgate, or *presa*, in

**LEFT:** restaurateurs bring a personal touch to New Mexico's numerous small eateries.
**RIGHT:** locally grown fruit and vegetables are available at the Santa Fe Farmers Market.

the ditch. His share of community water trickles along well-worn pathways that thread through rows of young crops swaddled in high-tech, color-coded plastic weedproof sheeting: red to shut out UV light from his tomatoes, silver to discourage pests on squash, blue to reflect light onto young melons, and black to

warm up his beans. Throughout the year, he alternates his cash crops with plantings of vetch and triticale, which fix nitrogen in the soil and encourage helpful insects like pollinating bees and ladybugs that eat pests. This year, he has planted his first crop of strawberries, a sweet honey-eye variety that explodes with flavor in the mouth. He will be the first grower in the state to offer certified organic strawberries, which presently flood in from California throughout the year.

The Bustos family has been farming the historic Santa Cruz land grant for 300 years. Don Bustos likes to tell how his Spanish ancestors understood how to manage water in arid desert landscapes and how to site a farm to produce the best yield. His earliest memory of farming is accompanying his grandfather and father to Colorado every year to sell wagon-loads of produce. Small-scale family farms like these, in the Española Valley, were established soon after the 1695 Reconquista, when Don Diego de Vargas himself founded Santa Cruz. But it is a way of life fast disappearing as families that have run farms for hundreds of years are squeezed out by newcomers who buy precious water rights for development.

Like José Mondragón, the reluctant protagonist of John Nichols' novel *The Milagro Bean-field War*, farmers who work long hours to keep their land in production are a feisty lot, but "we're more than a bunch of grubby farmers selling produce at the market," Bustos laughs. As he sees it, farmers like him are preserving a time-honored way of life that benefits all of New Mexico's communities. Land is kept in traditional use and children who wish to farm can choose to stay in their communities. State programs provide healthy food for school children. For locals and visitors, it's a rare opportunity to connect on a deeper level with the community, mingle with many different cultures, and feel directly involved with where

their food is coming from. Farms like Bustos's also participate in Community Supported Agriculture (CSA) programs, allowing customers to purchase annual shares in the farm, receive steady produce throughout the year, and help with harvesting, if they wish.

## Farm to table

In a state renowned for nurturing artists, cooking of every style is also considered an art form, from traditional country foods prepared from hundred-year-old recipes in adobe country kitchens to elegant cuisine in one of Santa Fe's upscale restaurants. The demand for fresh organic produce and range-fed meat has grown in recent years, as knowledgeable chefs like Mark Miller of Coyote Café, an ethnobotanist by training, and Café Pasqual's well-traveled Katherine Kagel have encouraged growers to produce heirloom crops and specialty items. Today, handmade goat cheeses, Indian-reared bison, lavender honey, apple cider and other local foods can be found throughout New Mexico, along with the ubiquitous green chile, which infuses everything from beer to cheese, even fast-food burgers.

Chefs like Miller and Kagel have been inspired by the lively mix of Indian, Hispanic and Anglo culinary traditions. New Mexican

soupy mush. Over the centuries, Pueblo people developed special varieties of colored corn, which was not only eaten but used symbolically in sacred ceremonies. Blue corn has become popular in the past 10 years and is grown at pueblos like San Juan for sale worldwide. It is a little more expensive than regular corn but more nutritious and sweet-tasting in tortillas, pancakes and muffins.

## Spanish spice

Adding spice to food was a Spanish contribution to the native foods of New Mexico. When the Spaniards arrived in the 1500s, they were

food has its roots in the Three Sisters – corn, squash, beans – which were introduced from Mexico 2,000 years ago. These important staples were quickly embraced by native people used to harvesting wild sage, lambsquarters, pinyon nuts and a variety of wild game, from rabbits to turkey and bison.

Of the Three Sisters, corn, or maize, is the "staff of life." It can be dried and stored for later reconstitution in meat stews, ground into cornmeal for paper-thin breads, and made into

**LEFT:** artfully prepared dishes are pleasing to the eye as well as the tongue.
**ABOVE:** the dining room at La Fonda Hotel in Santa Fe.

already cooking with many New World foods: potatoes, tomatoes and hot chile peppers from Central and South America; avocados, grapes and melons; spices like cinnamon and nutmeg from the Caribbean Islands that, when mixed with Mexican chocolate, formed a drink revered by Aztec rulers; and foods they had introduced from Europe, such as orchard fruits and wheat. Wild bison, deer, elk and antelope were native to North America and hunted seasonally by Indian people. But it was the Spanish who introduced the concept of ranching. Missionary priests and settlers brought with them thousands of domesticated cows, goats, pigs and sheep that changed the American diet forever. Livestock was raised for meat and eaten fresh or made into dried jerky, a tough, portable food favored by Indians.

Alone on the far north frontier of New Spain, Hispanic cooks learned from their neighbors about local foods and began incorporating them into their dishes. In many Hispanic homes, one still finds a pot of *frijoles*, or beans, simmering on the stove and meats marinating in chile, garlic and other spices for use in *carne adovada* (pork cooked in red chile), *fajitas* (flash-grilled meats served in warm tortillas) and hearty stews. At every meal, there will be stacks of corn tortillas, made fresh daily at the local *tor-*

jalapeños and cilantro). For main dishes, tortillas can be fried into flat tostadas or folded tacos, then piled high with spiced meat, beans, cheese and vegetables. An American Indian variant, Navajo tacos, can be found at pueblos and on the Navajo Reservation at dances and powwows, where they are made with a hot, fresh Indian frybread in outdoor horno ovens.

A sit-down meal in a New Mexico household may feature enchiladas, which, in the local style, are usually stacked (not rolled) and covered with red or green chile sauce and topped with a fried egg. A resurgence in authentic Mexican cuisine has reintroduced

*tilleria*, and kept warm in a basket. Rustic wheat breads, made from organically grown wheat, are also making a comeback. At one time, places like Mora were considered the "bread basket" of New Mexico. Now, thanks to inventive specialty bakeries like Santa Fe's Cloud Cliff, local wheat cooperatives are again in business in northern New Mexico villages.

## Tortilla flats

But corn or wheat tortillas remain the foundation for numerous dishes. They often start the meal as fried tortilla chips accompanied by guacamole (avocado dip) or *pico de gallo* (a fresh Mexican-style salsa of tomatoes, onions,

many New Mexicans to contemporary foods from Mexico City. Bert's Taqueria, Marisco's La Playa and the Old Mexico Grill – all in Santa Fe – offer fresh seafood and meats and unusual salsas that are expanding the local repertoire of Hispanic cuisine.

New Mexico breakfasts are delectable feasts, worth saving up a few calories to enjoy. At old-fashioned haunts like Santa Fe's Tia Sofia's, you'll find local politicos hunkering down around classic egg dishes such as *huevos rancheros*, a substantial meal featuring tortillas, fried eggs, melted cheese, beans (usually served whole in New Mexico, not refried, as in Mexico) and covered in red or green chile. For those with little time, the rolled wheat tortillas known as burritos (little donkeys) are daily fare. Burritos can be filled with a variety of fillings and eaten on the run (the popular new wraps, made on flavored tortillas, are a cold version of burritos). At breakfast, head to Santa Fe Baking Company for one of the best breakfast burritos in town. Three dollars buys an enormous burrito loaded with scrambled eggs, fried potatoes, bacon, cheese and green chile.

## Red or green?

For newcomers, the most perplexing question asked in New Mexico may be "Red or green?" What you're being asked is whether you want red or green chile sauce stuffed into or ladled onto your food. If you're vegetarian, be sure to ask whether meat has been added. Many restaurants now leave it out, but don't assume that they have. More important, ask which is the hottest chile that day. Chile heat varies widely, depending on growing conditions. Fresh or frozen green chile is often fierier, with ripened red chile a pleasing combination of rich flavor and spice. For a taste of both, ask for a "Christmas." It is traditional in New Mexico to serve *sopaipillas*, a hot, puffed, fried yeast bread eaten with honey, to cut the heat of spicy dishes. Dairy foods like yogurt or milk perform the same function.

To learn more about chile, try to visit in August and September, during the chile harvest, when the air is fragrant with the unmistakable smokey smell of fire-roasted chile sold by the bushel on every street corner. The bulk of New Mexico chile is grown along the Rio Grande, at Hatch, near Las Cruces, where new varieties are always being developed as part of the agricultural program at New Mexico State University. The Hatch Chile Festival usually takes place around Labor Day each year. It's an opportunity to mingle with growers and enjoy the strongly Mexican ambiance of the southern part of the state.

At harvest time, traditional restaurants like Café Estevan in Santa Fe serve fresh green chile with everything. A corn, squash and green chile dish known as *calabacitas* (little squashes) is found on many menus, either as

an accompaniment or served alone with melted cheese and boiled potatoes.

Meals usually end with *natillas*, a soft custard, or flan, a Spanish version of crème caramel. You may also be offered *empanaditas*, or fruit-filled turnovers, and small anise-flavored sugar cookies known as *bizcochitos*, which can be dipped into hot cider or spiced Mexican-style hot chocolate.

At Thanksgiving and Christmas, local chefs pull out all the stops, adding a New Mexican twist to traditional American holiday dishes such as turkey (*pavo*) with accompaniments like mole sauce (made with chile and bitter

chocolate). Women in Hispanic families often get together to make tamales, a dish invented by the Aztecs that consists of small cylinders of ground corn placed in corn husks and steamed with different fillings. Even with store-bought varieties widely available, tamales are still traditionally eaten on Chrismas Eve before midnight Mass, after days of preparation.

Another Christmas staple is *posole*, a simmered pork stew flavored with fresh green chile and hominy corn. At any time of year, New Mexicans enjoy eating – and have the waistlines to show for it. But as they say here: *"Panza llena, corazon contento."* Full stomach, contented heart! ❏

**LEFT:** New Mexican farmers produce as much as 95,000 tons of chile annually.
**RIGHT:** cooking *chile rellenos* at the Hatch Chile Festival.

# ARTISTIC SPIRIT

*Inspiring landscapes, desert light and a deep-seated regard*
*for the creative life have nurtured New Mexican artists for centuries*

It's a typical Friday midsummer's eve in Santa Fe. Friends are meeting on the Plaza for Frito pies and ice cream and dancing to a local band from Pecos on a makeshift stage. In the background, a free late opening is attracting a steady stream of visitors to the Palace of the Governors for an exhibit on New Mexican Jews. Across the street, an author is giving a lecture and slide show about Santa Fe poet Alice Corbin Henderson in the 1917 Museum of Fine Arts, the oldest art museum in the state.

All over Santa Fe, a street party seems to be in progress. Women in sundresses and sandals and men in jeans and cowboy boots stroll by, drinks in hand, laughing and golden in the evening light. They wander in and out of art galleries whose diverse offerings underscore the city's reputation as the third largest art market in the United States, generating some $200 million in sales annually.

Opposite St. Francis Cathedral, the Institute of American Indian Arts is holding a lavish reception for a show featuring Navajo artist Shonto Begay and other rising stars of the renowned Indian arts program. On West Palace, "home boys," proud *primos* and enthusiastic fans squeeze into the Cline Gallery to admire the overscaled *santos* and humorous, lowrider-inspired sculptures by hot New Mexico *santero* Nicholas Herrera. And over at Canfield Gallery, the opening of an exhibit of Taos Modern painters is just one of several receptions on Canyon Road, where 150 of Santa Fe's 265 art galleries show everything from pastel southwestern landscapes and prehistoric Indian pottery to folk art from around the world.

## Art lovers

It would be an understatement to say that New Mexico is art friendly. It is positively in love with the creative life. Some 28,000 artists live in the Land of Enchantment – the majority in

and around Santa Fe, where one in six people describe themselves as artists. All are inspired by a setting renowned for its spectacular scenery, picturesque cultures and incomparable desert light. "New Mexico," said the early 20th-century artist Marsden Hartley, "is the only place in America where true color exists."

As long as there have been people in New Mexico, there have been artists. Ten thousand years ago, wandering Folsom and Clovis hunters sat around campfires and chipped beautifully fluted and deadly arrowheads from volcanic chert and chalcedony. In Archaic times, 7,000 years later, hunter-gatherers sculpted tiny human figures from clay, wood and sandstone, and decorated them with feathers and beads, perhaps to ensure fertility or a successful hunt.

As a nomadic hunting and gathering lifestyle gave way to a more sedentary agricultural way of life in villages along the rivers, greater leisure time sparked creativity. People carved images in the black volcanic rocks along the

**LEFT:** artist Karen Pritchett outside her Capitan studio. **RIGHT:** a work in progress on Canyon Road in the heart of Santa Fe's gallery district.

middle Rio Grande, where more than 15,000 petroglyphs are preserved in Albuquerque's Petroglyph National Monument. Many more inscriptions decorate the large sandstone cliff next to a water hole at El Morro National Monument, creating a record of human comings and goings that spans more than 3,000 years.

Pueblo pottery, renowned worldwide for its simple utilitarian beauty and organic forms, began among the Mogollon people of southwestern New Mexico about 2,000 years ago. Mogollon farmers living in the earliest pueblos in the state quickly embraced pottery, a vast improvement over woven baskets for carrying

Grandes, just south of the border in Chihuahua. Western New Mexico University Museum in Silver City and the University of New Mexico's Maxwell Museum in Albuquerque have superb examples of Mimbres pottery, which remains highly prized among collectors.

## Pueblo pottery

The pottery made at New Mexico's contemporary pueblos grew out of an early 20th-century renaissance in ceramics, which had declined following the arrival of Spanish settlers. In the 1920s, excavations at the major trading pueblo of Pecos by archaeologist Alfred V. Kidder

and storing grain and valuables and trading with neighbors. As pottery spread north in the ensuing centuries, individual regions experimented with their own styles using local clays, tempers, slips and designs that evolved over the centuries as individual pueblos rose and fell, moved and took in newcomers.

Early Mogollon pots had a ruddy burnished hue but, as cultural contact increased with Chaco and other ancestral pueblos in the Four Corners, the Mimbres Valley Mogollon developed a beautiful black-on-white style in the 12th century. Using a yucca brush, artisans painted animals and scenes from daily life on a major trading route between Chaco and Casas

uncovered so many different types of pottery, Kidder realized they could be used to distinguish the different cultures living in the Southwest. The Pecos Classification remains an archaeologist's most important dating tool.

Pueblo artists were fascinated by the ancient pots being unearthed in New Mexico. Encouraged by archaeologists like Kenneth Chapman, founder of the Southwest Indian Arts Fund, and School of American Research founder Edgar Lee Hewett, Pueblo people improved the quality of their pottery and began selling it to collectors. San Ildefonso potter Maria Martinez and her husband Julian revived black-on-black ceramics, using techniques from ancient pots excavated by Hewett on the Pajarito Plateau. Their son Popovi Da and grandson Tony Da further developed the style, adding distinctive touches, such as an *avanyu*, or serpent, motif to their ceramics.

Today, Indian arts are New Mexico's greatest draw. Artisans sell direct through home studios, galleries and gift shops at the Museum of New Mexico, Pueblo Cultural Center, and at arts cooperatives such as those at Pojoaque Pueblo and San Juan, which also hosts an annual Eight Northern Pueblos Arts

### SIGN OF THE DIVINE

"Any man who is really an artist," wrote journalist Charles Lummis in 1892, "will find the Southwest… a region where the ingenuity, the imagination, and the love of God are… visible at every turn."

Clara Pueblo also makes blackware, as well as shiny redware. Acoma and Laguna Pueblos specialize in curved pots with geometric designs on a white background. The far northern pueblos of Taos and Picuris make distinctive glittery beige micaceous pottery.

Some Indian potters experiment with traditional ceramic figurines. Cochiti's storyteller dolls, showing a seated woman covered in children, were revived in the 1960s by Helen Cordero. More recently, potters from the Pueblo of Tesuque

and Crafts Show. Many others artists sell a variety of arts and crafts under the portal of the Palace of the Governors and during August's Indian Market on the Plaza.

Each Indian tribe has developed a specialty. Look for intricate silver inlay jewelry and tiny fetish bears from Zuni. The conservative pueblo of Santo Domingo specializes in *heshi*, necklaces made from turquoise disks traditionally mined at nearby Cerrillos. San Ildefonso specializes in black-on-black vases and pots. Santa

**LEFT:** a Taos gallery shows a variety of contemporary arts and crafts.
**ABOVE:** Harry Benjamin at work in his Silver City studio.

have begun making rain god figurines again. Figurines fell out of favor in the 1920s, when potters began mass producing kitschy, inferior quality items for sale to tourists. Today, artists are improving their offerings and reviving the tradition. You can see historic and recent examples at the Wheelwright Museum on Museum Hill in Santa Fe.

### Navajo arts

Pottery is a sedentary occupation but late-arriving nomadic tribes, such as the Navajo, Apache and Ute, better known for Plains style beadwork and leather crafts, also learned to make pottery when they began mingling with Pueblos.

Navajo ceramics are sturdy and pitch-glazed for a shiny look. Contemporary Navajo potters like Bertha Claw decorate their pots with toads, lizards and other rain-making symbols.

Pottery and an increasingly collectable carved wooden folk art sculpture by artisans like Degbert Buck, Johnson Antonio and Mamie Deschillie are relatively recent innovations among the Navajo. They are best known for their fine weaving, learned from Pueblo neighbors in the 1600s, and heavy squash-blossom necklaces, concha belts, rings, bracelets, earrings and other silver-and-turquoise jewelry, taught them by Spanish settlers.

and C. N. Cotton created a major market back East for Navajo weaving in the late 1800s, when they steered Navajo women away from blankets to heavier, more saleable floor rugs. Hubbell introduced new designs as well as bright Germantown anilyne dyes that replaced the subtle ochers, lavenders and pinks created by natural plant dyes. If you're serious about investing in a rug (a good rug will run several thousand dollars), talk to the knowledgeable traders at trading posts like Hubbell in Ganado, Arizona, where you can tour a traditional post and buy local Ganado Red and other rug styles. The monthly Crown Point Rug Auction, just

Navajo arts and crafts are best experienced on the Navajo Nation, where people living in different areas of the reservation continue to weave rugs on upright pole looms outside traditional hogans. A half-dozen unique styles are sold through nearby trading posts, such as Teec Nos Pos, west of Shiprock, and Two Grey Hills, on the east side of the Chuska Mountains. Classic-era blankets, woven in the years following the Long Walk, are rare and generally only found in high-end galleries. The Millicent Rogers Museum in Taos and the Navajo Cultural Museum in Window Rock, Arizona, have particularly lovely collections.

Trading post owners like Lorenzo Hubbell

east of Gallup, has rugs from all over the reservation and is a fascinating place to mingle with the Navajo and find a good deal.

## Hispanic arts and crafts

The mantas, or blankets, woven by Pueblos from locally grown cotton heavily influenced Navajo artisans, as well as Hispanic weavers who began settling in the Rio Grande Valley in the 1600s. Hardy churro sheep, introduced by Oñate in 1598, produced a long-fibered wool prized by weavers in the Chimayo area, where the Trujillo, Ortega and Cordova families became known for distinctive designs: the striped Rio Grande, diamond Saltillo, star-and-diamond Vallero, and more recent Chimayo style rug, a highly recognizable hybrid of the Rio Grande and Saltillo styles. You can visit traditional weaving operations in Chimayo, Los Ojos and Las Vegas and watch wool being sorted, washed, spun, colored with plant dyes and woven on looms into rugs, jackets, waistcoats and *jergas*, or ponchos.

The isolated Hispanic villages on the northern frontier of New Spain, far from the protective presidio garrison in Santa Fe, had to be self-sufficent from the start. Families built scattered ranchos and fortified adobe compounds around a *placita*, or courtyard, surrounded by rooms used for sleeping, eating, storage, cooking and entertaining. Large churches with ornate religious art were built at places like Santa Cruz, Las Trampas and Ranchos de Taos, but they were the exceptions. Most villages set aside a *capilla*, or village chapel, for worship.

Deserted by their priests during the Mexican period, the *vecinos* were forced to make their own *santos*, or sacred objects. Every home had carved *bultos* and painted *retablos* of patron saints, such as Our Lady of Guadalupe and Santo Niño de Etocha, on a homemade altar in one corner. A carved cross decorated with straw appliqué might hang on a wall. Los Hermanos de la Luz, or the Penitente Brotherhood, a secret order of village men committed to upholding the religious calendar and providing aid to neighbors, encouraged this self-sufficiency. The grandeur of the church was replaced by the simple faith of the *morada* meeting house. The Penitente remain active in remote villages like Abiquiu, where large crosses on the hillside indicate the presence of a *morada*.

After a decline in the 1800s, the tradition of the *santero* rebounded when innovative carvers like Patricio Barela in Taos revived the art and the Spanish Colonial Arts Society, founded by architect John Gaw Meem and other influential Anglos in the 1920s, created Spanish Market in Santa Fe. The juried show on Santa Fe Plaza is held every July, concurrent with a Contemporary Spanish Market, sponsored by Santa Fe's El Museo Cultural, dedicated to promoting contemporary Hispanic culture. Traditional *santeros* Marie Romero Cash and Charlie Carrillo win

prizes annually for imaginative, colorful *santos* representing everything from Adam and Eve in the Garden of Eden to Archbishop Lamy and Noah's Ark. Descendants of Patricio Barela show at both the traditional and contemporary markets. A Winter Market is held in December.

Painted *retablos* of wood and tin (introduced during the Santa Fe Trail era) are among the most affordable art pieces, along with award-winning *santos* by children. Traditional needlework, or *colcha*, is also on display, along with worked leather and rawhide, and beautifully carved furniture. Expect to pay as much as $6,000 for a *bulto* by a well-known artist.

## Art colony

In earlier times, wood carving was a time-consuming business for people who were up from dawn to dusk working the fields. Religious items took precedence over furniture in the traditional Hispanic home. The Santa Fe Trail and the arrival of the railroad in 1880 flooded New Mexico with manufactured goods. By the beginning of the 20th century, traditional arts and crafts were on the wane, and Santa Fe was beginning to look like Anytown USA, with Victorian brick houses, pitched-tin roofs, long porches made from milled lumber, and pedimented windows taking the place of traditional flat-roofed adobes with dirt floors.

**LEFT:** a display of Pueblo pottery in Santa Fe.
**RIGHT:** an image of the Virgin of Guadalupe adorns a building in Old Town Albuquerque.

The arrival of East Coast archaeologists, architects, and artists in Taos and Santa Fe changed all that. Fleeing grimy urban environments like New York and Chicago, the new breed of Anglo was quite different from the frontier salesman of the Santa Fe Trail who had successfully Americanized the West. Influenced by the Arts and Crafts movement in England, these well-educated creative types rebelled against mass production, over-regulated city lives and mainstream values. It was more than intellectual boredom. Most were sick with terminal tuberculosis and forced to the western deserts to find a cure at places like Santa Fe's Sunmount Sanitorium, off Camino del Monte Sol. Inadvertently, they found paradise.

The birth of New Mexico as an art colony began with the arrival in Taos, in 1898, of New York artists Ernest Blumenschein and Bert Phillips. In 1915, the two men, along with Joseph Sharp, Oscar Berninghaus and W. Herbert "Buck" Dunton, founded the Taos Society of Artists, which until 1927 promoted the work of the artists through exhibitions throughout the country. Eventually other artists joined, including John Marin, Burt Harwood, Marsden Hartley, Dorothy Brett, Nicholai Fechin and Victor Higgins. Some arrived in northern New Mexico

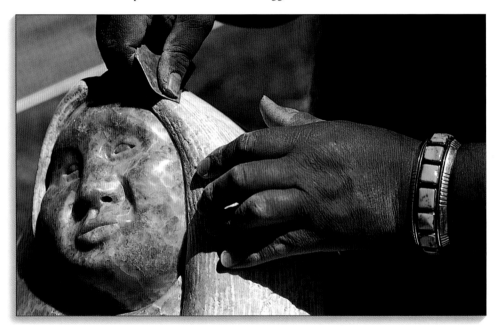

## O'KEEFFE'S MAD COUNTRY

No artist is more closely associated with New Mexico than Georgia O'Keeffe, though she moved permanently to the state rather late in her career. Trained at the Art Institute of Chicago before moving to New York City in 1907, O'Keeffe was "discovered" in 1916 by photographer and promoter of modern art Alfred Stieglitz. She was soon engaged in an affair with Stieglitz, whom she later married, and fell in with the members of the Stieglitz circle, most of whom were inspired by the modernist revolution in Europe.

Unlike so many of her compatriots, however, O'Keeffe didn't travel to Europe during this period. Instead, she went West, teaching in Texas for several years, then, in the summer of 1929, making her first serious visit to New Mexico. It was to be the first of many such stays in the Land of Enchantment, which she described in a letter to Stieglitz as "a perfectly mad looking country – hills and cliffs and washes too crazy to imagine all thrown up into the air by God and let tumble where they would."

In 1948, three years after Stieglitz's death, O'Keeffe moved permanently to her home at Ghost Ranch and, later, Abiquiu, where eroded hills, bleached bones and desert light informed her work for three more decades. She died in 1986 at the age of 98, having won recognition as not only a regional artist but a major figure of 20th-century American art.

at the invitation of Mabel Dodge Luhan, the New York impresario who moved to Taos in 1916. The strong-willed Luhan acted as muse and artistic midwife to several luminaries over the following four decades, including Andrew Dasburg, Georgia O'Keeffe, Ansel Adams and Robinson Jeffers.

Her most famous guest, D. H. Lawrence, and his wife Frieda arrived in 1922. They spent the night in Santa Fe at the adobe home of writer Witter "Hal" Bynner whose lover, Spud Johnson, later moved to Taos and established Laughing Horse Press, a literary journal. Johnson subsequently became Luhan's personal sec-

Corbin were also active in Santa Fe. Corbin had arrived in New Mexico from Chicago with terminal tuberculosis and checked into the Sunmount Sanitorium with her husband William Penhallow Henderson.

Until her tuberculosis went into remission, the influential Corbin, a former editor of *Poetry* magazine, held court in the Sunmount. The seeds of Santa Fe Style, sown by archaeologists at the Museum of New Mexico, took hold in Corbin's salons, where the movement's principal exponents, architect John Gaw Meem and Corbin's husband, popularized the hybrid Pueblo-Spanish Mission style.

retary, a betrayal that Bynner never forgave.

Bynner's home was next to Canyon Road, then the "affordable" quarter of Santa Fe. Other artists had houses nearby, which are still visible today. Painter Gerald Cassidy's home was set on Acequia Madre, while the so-called Cinco Pintores – Will Shuster, Josef Bakos, Fremont Ellis, Walter Mruk and Willard Nash – fixed up rundown adobes on Camino del Monte Sol.

Writers like Mary Austin and Willa Cather and poets Edna St. Vincent Millay and Emily

**LEFT:** Mescalero Apache artist Albert Summa puts the finishing touches on a sculpture.
**ABOVE:** Madrid metal sculptor Michael Wright.

## The WPA in New Mexico

By the 1930s, New Mexico was home to numerous artists, all of whom had come to rely on tourism and art collectors on the East and West Coasts for their income. Most were hard hit by the Great Depression and were left without a livelihood. New Mexico benefited more than most states from the introduction of Franklin D. Roosevelt's Works Progress Administration, designed to put millions of Americans to work. The Albuquerque Little Theater, State Fairgrounds, and several notable buildings on the University of New Mexico campus were constructed with WPA funds. Artists like Gerald Cassidy painted murals in federal buildings, such as the Santa Fe post office.

Spanish-speaking New Mexicans often used the phrase *El Diablo a Pie* (The Devil on Foot), a Spanish transliteration for the acronym WPA, as a tongue-in-cheek commentary about the help offered by the federal government, but traditional artists benefited from the program. Paintings, sculpture and furniture were created for Civilian Conservation Corps programs and parks like Bandelier National Monument, and art exhibits and classes were held in New Mexico Federal Art Centers in Gallup, Las Vegas and Roswell.

– an example of a reemerging Mexican influence in New Mexican art – can be found at the Roswell Museum of Art, Albuquerque Museum of Art and other collections around the state. Humorous welded-metal sculpture is also the medium of choice for Bob Haozous, son of famed Chiricahua Apache sculptor Allan Houser, whose elegant works can be seen outside the Capitol and at the IAIA Museum.

Haozous and fellow Apache artist Darren Vigil Gray offer some of the most exciting examples of modern New Mexican artwork whose power is derived from growing political awareness and freedom of expression

## Regional arts

Roswell, in the ranchlands of southern New Mexico, became an unlikely arts center with the creation of the Roswell Art Museum in the 1930s. Its reputation grew after well-known artist and Roswell native Peter Hurd married Henriette Wyeth, daughter of famed painter Andrew Wyeth, and built a ranch in San Patricio in the Hondo Valley. Today, the valley remains popular with artists attracted to the area by the Roswell Museum's artists-in-residence program. Mexican-American sculptor Luis Jimenez, also a resident of the Hondo Valley, is one of the best-known graduates of the program. His tongue-in-cheek fiberglass sculptures

among American Indians as well as a cross-fertilization of Indian, Hispano and Anglo styles. A graduate of the Santa Fe Indian School art program, Vigil Gray's influences are eclectic, ranging from rock 'n' roll (he's a member of a rock band), traditional Apache ceremonials like the Gaan Mountain Spirit Dance, contemporary Indian portraitists like T. C. Cannon, and Anglo landscape artists like Georgia O'Keeffe. In that respect he's squarely in the tradition of New Mexican art – an original vision inspired by a wide range of cultural influences. ❑

**ABOVE:** *Exodus, Influencias Positivas y Compadrazgo,* 1998, by Frederico Vigil at the Museum of Fine Arts.

# Literary New Mexico

There is no one literature of New Mexico. Modern science fiction, Los Alamos memoirs, genre mysteries, and historical romances rub shoulders with Native American fiction, Hispanic folktales and novels inspired by Latin American magical realism. Local cookbooks, pioneer journals, Spanish romantic epic poems and the diaries of missionaries and explorers sit side by side with cowboy poetry, poetry slam barrio verse and environmental nonfiction.

In a state where anything goes, this is as it should be. Territorial governor Lew Wallace, who braved bullets in Cimarron's St. James Hotel and a sagging roof in Santa Fe's aging Palace of the Governors while writing his epic *Ben Hur*, famously declared: "Every calculation based on experience elsewhere fails in New Mexico." Hispanic New Mexicans, who measure their lives by *dichos* (sayings) and *cuentos* (fables) of all kinds, nodded approvingly.

Literary New Mexico, as an idea, was birthed in the early 1900s in Taos and Santa Fe, under the watchful eye of Taos society queen Mabel Dodge Luhan and Santa Fe poets Witter Bynner and Alice Corbin. Luhan wrote extensively about the spiritual qualities of Taos and prodded her guests to write of their own experiences. Her most famous visitor, English novelist D. H. Lawrence, was fascinated with the pagan landscape of New Mexico during his stay near Taos. "There is something savage, unbreakable in the spirit of the place out here," he wrote. "It is good to be alone and responsible. But it is also very hard living up against these savage Rockies."

As they learned more about their adopted land, it was inevitable that New Mexican authors would be drawn to a variety of causes. In the 1920s, Santa Fe writers Mary Austin, Alice Corbin and Oliver La Farge became outspoken political advocates for Indian rights, both in the courts and on the page. Taos writer Frank Waters's classic *The Man Who Killed the Deer* detailed the consequences of walking in two worlds for one young Pueblo man. More recently, two local writers hit the bestseller lists with New Mexico-themed novels. Retired Albuquerque journalist Tony Hillerman parlayed his interest in Navajo culture into a series

of best-selling mysteries set on the Navajo Nation, introducing readers to the little understood culture. In Taos, writer John Nichols highlighted the struggles of poor Hispanic villagers in northern New Mexico in the satirical novel *The Milagro Beanfield War*, which was filmed in and around Truchas by actor Robert Redford in the 1980s.

By the end of the 20th century, ethnic New Mexican writers were stepping forward to write about their own experiences. The poetry of Acoma poet Simon Ortiz mourns the loss of his homeland to uranium mining and exploitation. The novels of Laguna native Leslie Marmon Silko and N. Scott Momaday, a Pulitzer Prize-winning writer of Kiowa-

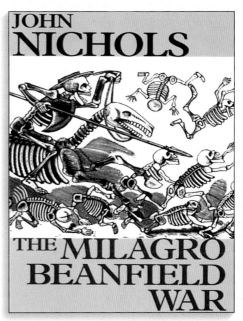

Jemez Pueblo ancestry, offer an unsentimental look at what it feels like to try to retain one's cultural roots in an increasingly Anglo world.

This is ripe territory for Hispanic writers, too. Rudolfo Anaya captured the blurred line between Old and New World America in *Bless Me, Ultima*, where past meets present in the form of a *curandera,* or healer. The exuberance and primary colors of contemporary Mexican-American culture weaves through the passionate novels of writer Denise Chavez, a Mexican-American who grew up in Las Cruces. Chavez's commitment goes beyond the page. Several years ago, she founded the Border Book Festival in Las Cruces. It is now an annual event promoting the literature of the borderlands. ❑

---

**RIGHT:** John Nichols addresses land-use issues in the first volume of his New Mexico trilogy.

# THE NAKED EARTH

*Geologically speaking, the place is a treasure-house of terra firma – mesas and canyons, deserts and mountains, caves and calderas*

Tourism officials pitch New Mexico as the "Land of Enchantment," but the "Volcano State" might be more accurate. New Mexico rivals even Hawaii for the number and diversity of its volcanoes. Moreover, volcanoes in New Mexico are not extinct; they are merely dormant. Eruptions have occurred as recently as 3,000 years ago, and geologists have good reason to believe that the Rio Grande Rift, a dramatic tear in the Earth's crust that pulls apart the center of the state, will remain active and perhaps, one day, widen into an inland sea.

Few travelers come to New Mexico solely for its geological landmarks, but they have been an important part of life here for centuries. Mount Taylor and the towering dark volcanic neck of Ship Rock in the northwestern part of the state feature strongly in the creation stories of the Navajo and other Indian groups. Priests of the prehistoric Chaco culture of the San Juan Basin relied on mountains, mesas and eroded sandstone landmarks as solstice markers to plan ceremonies. Western travelers on the Santa Fe Trail used the distinctive Rabbit Ears to gauge their distance from Santa Fe. For millennia, water percolating through a sandstone bluff at what is now El Morro National Monument in western New Mexico provided thirsty travelers with life-giving water. While they rested, people carved inscriptions on the rock. Today, it preserves thousands of years of New Mexico history.

## Lay of the land

New Mexico contains 20 percent of all U.S. national parks devoted to geological features – more than Arizona, Idaho, Oregon and Washington combined. Northwest of Santa Fe, in the Jemez Mountains, are Bandelier National Monument and Valles Caldera National Preserve, both connected to the world's largest volcanic caldera. West of Albuquerque are Pet-

roglyph and El Malpais National Monuments, with their youthful volcanoes and forbidding lava flows. Carlsbad Caverns National Park, beneath the Guadalupe Mountains on the New Mexico–Texas border, preserves a stunning cave complex carved within one of only two accessible underground Permian Reefs in the

world. Just south of Raton, in northeastern New Mexico, Capulin Volcano National Monument offers a unique opportunity to hike a 1,400-ft-high (420-meter) volcano, in the 8,000-sq-mile (21,000-sq-km) Raton-Clayton Volcanic Field, America's easternmost young volcanic field.

The state can be roughly divided into five geological regions, rising from the low-lying Chihuahuan Desert in the south to high, glaciated mountains on the Colorado–New Mexico border. Southern New Mexico is in the Basin and Range province, which stretches from California to Texas in a series of north-south-trending ranges rising above basins filled with deep

**PRECEDING PAGES:** Ventana Arch rises over the lava flows of El Malpais National Monument.
**LEFT:** Chimney Rock, near Ghost Ranch.
**RIGHT:** erosion forms, north of Chaco Canyon.

sediments. In northern New Mexico, the Rocky Mountains and their southern extension, the Sangre de Cristo Mountains, lie east of the mile-high Colorado Plateau, a 130,000-sq-mile (340,000-sq-km) uplift encompassing parts of New Mexico, Arizona, Colorado and Utah.

In the eastern third of New Mexico are the high-desert grassy plains that sweep to Kansas, Oklahoma and Texas. And dramatically splitting New Mexico north to south is the Rio Grande Rift Zone, home to the Rio Grande, the river that provides most of the precious water that has allowed people to call this arid state home.

But all that was to come. Throughout the Precambrian and Paleozoic Eras, the great laboratory of life was still in the early experimentation stages, out of sight, beneath an ebbing and flowing ocean. North America was part of a vast global supercontinent dubbed Pangaea that tilted down at its western edge, allowing the sea to encroach. Lime deposits from early calcareous algae and other marine lifeforms mingled with coastal sands. As these deposits settled, they were compressed and hardened into horizontal strata cemented by calcium, manganese and iron. The Southwest's first sedimentary rocks – limestone, sandstone and shale – formed during this time.

## Basement rocks

New Mexico's aura – timeless and ancient yet filled with creativity, change and light – may have as much to do with its landscape as its people. For 4 billion years, the state seemed to be biding its time, luxuriating under seawater and building itself up. Then suddenly, beginning 65 million years ago, all that changed. The seismic energy beneath the earth surged to the surface, lifting, dropping, rumbling, twisting and tearing apart everything that had gone before and adding new material to the old. The Rocky Mountains and Colorado Plateau rose, the Rio Grande Rift began to open up, and volcanoes towered over the land.

Brief episodes of mountain building and volcanic activity alternated with long periods of erosion and sedimentation. Movements in areas of weakness, known as faults, provided conduits for heat to escape from the Earth's mantle. Molten rock, or magma, was injected into the sedimentary rocks, uplifting and folding them into tall mountain chains with a core of hard metamorphic gneiss, schist and granite. Attacked by water and wind, they eventually wore down into sediments again, which redeposited, hardened, uplifted and folded several more times.

These ancient rocks can be seen as Vishnu Schist at the bottom of Arizona's Grand Canyon, a formation that is banded and contorted in some places, platey and shiny in others, and filled with large mats of algae known as stromatolites, Earth's first fossils. In southern New Mexico uplift has made Precambrian rocks harder to see. They are found more readily in northern New Mexico in places such as the Sangre de Cristos and Tres Piedras, north of Abiquiu, which have rocks that are 1.3 billion years old.

## Santa Fe-by-the-Sea

The sea continued to cover New Mexico for hundreds of millions of years, building up limestone several miles thick that was uplifted along faults. Southern New Mexico's famous karst topogra-

trapped in a series of large embayments that often dried out before flooding again. One large embayment, the Permian Basin, was filled with sponges, trilobites, ammonites, nautiloids, brachiopods and a type of tiny foraminifera called fusilinids. These marine creatures formed a massive barrier reef, 400 miles (640km) long, dubbed the Capitan Reef. Warm, dry conditions at the end of the Permian Period, 250 million years ago, caused the Permian Sea to withdraw to the west. Eventually, most of this marine life perished in what is still considered the world's greatest mass extinction. Evaporites such as salt, potash and gypsum entombed the

phy was formed now, as groundwater dissolved the limestone into caves and sinks. Some rocks were eroded away altogether, creating a puzzling gap in the geological record. Mountain building began again in the Pennsylvanian Period, 300 million years ago, when the Ancestral Rocky Mountains rose to the north. But they, too, were eventually leveled by erosion, leaving behind coarse sediments atop marine layers.

In southern New Mexico, the sea was now

**LEFT:** Big Skylight Cave, a lava tube, at El Malpais; tourists in Carlsbad Caverns, 1926.
**ABOVE:** limestone caves, like those at Carlsbad, are known for dramatic formations.

Capitan Reef. It would remain buried for more than 150 million years, until the Rocky Mountain Uplift pushed up the Guadalupe and other mountain ranges.

Now above the water table, acidic groundwater began percolating through the rocks hollowing out caves between 12 million and 200,000 years ago. Corrosion was accelerated by the presence of sulfuric acid from hydrogen sulfide gas seeping up from pockets in the shales of the oil-rich Permian Basin. The stalactites, stalagmites, soda straws, helactites, "lily pads" and "cave pearls" of Carlsbad Caverns began forming around 500,000 years ago. Today, most have stopped growing, dried out by exposure to what is now a hot, desert climate that infiltrates the caverns. Only in unvisited wild caves, such as Lechuguilla, is cave formation still a work in progress.

## Where dinosaurs walked

At the beginning of the Mesozoic Era, 250 to 200 million years ago, New Mexico's climate was warm, moist and tropical. Huge conifers and fernlike cycads grew to great heights on the edge of junglelike wetlands. The state was positioned roughly where West Africa is today, as the supercontinent of Pangaea rafted westward on convection currents generated by the

hot magma below the Earth's crust. Sediments left behind by the sea, coastal sands and river deltas mingled with those drifting south from the Ancestral Rockies and volcanic ash. The uranium-rich Chinle Formation, widespread on the Navajo Reservation, was laid down during this time, a rainbow-hued formation of soft, crumbly sediments that have worn away into colorful badlands.

During this Triassic Period, 250 to 200 million years ago, the first dinosaurs appeared, occupying ecological niches left open by the Permian die-off. In the Jurassic Period, 200 to 145 million years ago, the climate changed yet

## HOT SPRINGS

In 1535, Spanish explorer Cabeza de Vaca, one of only four survivors of a shipwreck in the Gulf of Mexico, was led to the hot springs adjoining Poshouinge Pueblo, near Española, where he soaked in the mineral-rich waters before returning to Mexico City. Ojo Caliente, as he called the springs, are "the greatest treasure that I found these strange people to possess... so powerful that the inhabitants have a belief they were given to them by their gods."

Communal bathing in hot springs is an ancient tradition in New Mexico, where centuries ago, Pueblos, Apaches and other Indian tribes laid aside their differences, even in battle, to "take the waters" together. With the arrival of

Anglos in the 1800s, many of these hot springs were developed into rustic resorts, such as today's Truth or Consequences, Jemez Springs, Ojo Caliente and Faywood Springs, still going strong a century later.

Some of New Mexico's best hot springs can still be enjoyed for free, if you know where to go. Montezuma Hot Springs, just north of Las Vegas, is open 24 hours a day, thanks to United World College, which occupies Montezuma Castle next door. Spence Hot Springs is located in the national forest near Jemez Springs. And hot springs along the Gila River beckon in southwestern New Mexico – the perfect reward after a long day's hike in the Gila Wilderness.

again. Hot winds blew sand from coastal areas to the west, piling into tall dunes. Dinosaurs survived by roaming interdunal wetlands, river floodplains and near-shore marshes.

Evidence of dinosaurs is widespread. Their footprints have been found in the red Kayenta Formation laid down as sandy shale, and large fossils have been found everywhere except the Permian Basin. One of the Earth's first dinosaurs, a meat-eater called Coelophysis, was discovered in large numbers in the brightly colored Triassic-era rocks surrounding Ghost Ranch in northern New Mexico. Paleontologists have also found the bones of Jurassic-era

harden into the Dakota Sandstone, Mancos Shale and Mesaverde Group. Below them, sand dunes thousands of feet deep remained virtually unchanged, petrified so perfectly you can see which direction the wind was blowing when they were formed. Calcium cemented the large quartz grains into sandstone. Hematite, derived from iron, tinted it in a range of reds, pinks and oranges.

Today, this sandstone is the most recognizable formation in the West. Throughout New Mexico it is found in exposures of Wingate, Navajo, Entrada, Gallup and Zuni Sandstone. Many of the famous landmarks in Canyon Country are

Stegosaurus, Allosaurus and Camarasaurus. A late Cretaceous-era dinosaur fossil, *Alamoaurus sanjuanensis*, is America's last sauropod. It was uncovered in the Bisti Badlands and De-na-zin Wilderness south of Farmington, where erosion has shaped eerie badlands.

The Sahara-like desert that formed in the Jurassic Period lasted a long time, but eventually the climate changed again and became moister. The sea returned, laying down marine and seashore sediments that would eventually

**LEFT:** visitors view 100-million-year-old dinosaur tracks at Clayton Lake State Park.
**ABOVE:** a free-standing sandstone arch.

made of sandstone: the vertical vermilion cliffs of Red Rock State Park outside Gallup; the haunting Echo Canyon Amphitheater north of Ghost Ranch; Ventana Arch in El Malpais; and the ancient pueblos of Chaco Canyon.

## Continents collide

For the dinosaurs and other living things, the end came when meteors collided with the Earth at the end of the Cretaceous Period, 65 million years ago. This mass extinction is vividly depicted in the new Sea Coast exhibit at the New Mexico Museum of Natural History in Albuquerque. But just as the Permian wipeout made way for the dinosaurs, so too did the late

Cretaceous extinction pave the way for new lifeforms – flowers and mammals. Eventually humans also appeared, many of whom would later find uses for the oil, gas, coal, turquoise, silver, gold and other precious minerals secreted among New Mexico's rocks.

This was the beginning of modern New Mexico. Pangaea broke apart into separate continents. Hot lava from the Earth's interior escaped through a trough in the middle of the Atlantic Ocean, widening the rift between the plates and forcing the North American continental plate west. Inevitably, the North American Plate collided with the Farallon Plate, the

the major rift valleys in the world. West of the San Juan Basin, high plateaus began to form, incorporating the eastern edge of the Colorado Plateau and the volcanic Datil-Mogollon Highlands in western New Mexico. A prominent monocline can be seen near Gallup and to the northeast in the San Juan Basin. Monoclines are some of the most dramatic landforms in the Four Corners, created when strata on one side override those on the other, leaving behind prominent hogbacks and ridges.

In the Tertiary Period, what was not rising in New Mexico was sinking, including the oil- and gas-rich San Juan Basin southwest of the

eastern edge of the Pacific Oceanic Crust off present-day California, forcing the Farallon Plate under the North American Plate along the San Andreas Fault. The reverberations sent seismic shock waves eastward through deep-seated Precambrian faults in the bedrock. The Rocky Mountains, the Sangre de Cristos and the Colorado Plateau began to rise.

## Pulled apart at the seams

Movement along local faults on the Colorado Plateau during the Oligocene Epoch, 30 million years ago, caused other significant landforms to appear. The Rio Grande Rift began to pull apart the land in between, forming one of

Rocky Mountains, which filled with debris eroded from the Rockies.

In southern New Mexico, around 15 million years ago, increasing crustal tension caused uplift along numerous north-south faults. Fault blocks moved up sharply in relation to each other, creating small, craggy ranges and accompanying basins, such as the Organ Mountains near Las Cruces. Nearby, what is now the Tularosa Basin formed when an anticline collapsed, leaving behind the San Andres and Sacramento Mountains on either side. The basin eventually filled with gypsum, blown in from the Permian Basin to the southeast, ending up as the large sculpted dunes of White Sands.

## Recent developments

Within the past 3 million years, rivers entering the Rio Grande Rift, and the Rio Grande itself, cut down into a series of linked basins in the central part of the state, shaping canyons and leaving behind more than a mile of sediments. These hardened into the loose, colorful conglomerate of the Santa Fe Group, which has eroded into mesas, buttes and hills, often preserved by caprocks of lava less than a few thousand years old.

This geological history is easily read today. Roadcuts and stream-carved canyons in the Sangre de Cristo Mountains offer fascinating cross-sections of ancient seas, rivers, coasts and volcanism. Visitors enjoying the tram ride to the top of the Sandia Mountains, east of Albuquerque, can examine fossilized marine rocks that are now 10,000 ft (3,000 meters) above sea level. A drive along NM 14 passes through the Cerrillos Hills, where Ancestral Pueblo people mined turquoise, and into revived ghost towns like Madrid in the Ortiz Mountains, which were once filled with early 20th-century gold miners. From the top of Capulin Volcano, you can see 8,818-ft (2,688-meter) Laughlin Peak, the highest in northeastern New Mexico, 8,720-ft (2,658-meter) Sierra Grande, a Hawaiian-style shield volcano, formed by successive eruptions beginning 4 million years ago, and textbook examples of maars, volcanoes that steam-erupted in water within the past 1.7 million years.

Mount Taylor (11,301ft/3,445 meters), one of the four sacred peaks that make up the Navajo world, was built up from successive eruptions 4 million years ago. Eruptions on side vents have created young lava flows visible in El Malpais National Monument. The state's highest mountain is 13,161-ft (4,012-meter) Wheeler Peak, part of the Taos Mountains that join the Truchas Peaks in the Sangre de Cristo Range north of Santa Fe.

The Jemez Mountains, west of the Rio Grande, began forming 15 million years ago. Valles Caldera appeared 1.2 million years ago. It is the collapsed center of the central Jemez volcanic field, part of which is now Valles Caldera National Preserve. The drive to Valle Grande, the valley overlook inside the caldera, crosses the Pajarito Plateau. This plateau is made of soft volcanic tuff, which was excavated for homes by Pueblo people in what is now Bandelier National Monument. Tuff from another volcano also created the strangely eroded pinnacles of Tent Rocks on the Cochiti Indian Reservation.

Most dramatic of all may be the numerous volcanic necks and dykes and lava flows left behind by erosion, which form a striking contrast with pale sedimentary rocks. The 650-ft-deep (200-meter) chasm cut by the Rio Grande through lava flows west of Taos is part of a huge plateau visible from miles around. Valley of Fires Recreation Area, near Carrizozo, just

east of the Rio Grande, rivals El Malpais for the youngest lava flows in the state. The Puerco Valley of northwestern New Mexico, home to the Navajo Reservation, has more volcanic necks than anywhere else in the world.

To almost all of these rocks are attached stories, a human way of making friends with the lithic world. Places like Three Rivers Petroglyphs in southern New Mexico, the Galisteo Basin and Petroglyph National Monument near Albuquerque have numerous Story Rocks, covered in the inscriptions of generations of Indian, Spanish and Anglo people. Both on and within rocks, we can read stories that tell us where we came from – and where we will return.    ❑

---

**LEFT:** a volcanic dike radiates from Ship Rock; the gypsum dunes of White Sands.
**RIGHT:** petroglyph at Bandelier National Monument.

# LIFE IN A DRY LAND

*From searing lava fields to windswept peaks, New Mexico contains an impressive diversity of plant and animal life*

The Mescalero Apache believe that all life began on Sierra Blanca, the 12,003-ft (3,659-meter) volcanic peak in southwestern New Mexico where their god Essen lives. For anyone who has ever stood on the 10,000-ft (3,000-meter) Windy Point observation platform in the Sacramento Mountains, this is easy to understand. The panoramic views from the overlook are some of the most awe-inspiring in all of New Mexico, taking in arid desert, woodlands on sky-scraping mountain ranges, youthful lava flows, gypsum dunes, grasslands, dry plains and wetlands. This is the only place in New Mexico where you can see so much in one great sweep. God's country, indeed.

New Mexico ranks fourth in the nation for biodiversity in part because of this varied geography. The 122,666-sq-mile (317,704-sq-km) state is centrally located on the southwestern U.S.-Mexico border and overlaps several major ecological regions, including the Chihuahuan and Sonoran Deserts, the Great Plains, the southern Rocky Mountains and the Colorado Plateau. Altogether, the state is home to 4,583 kinds of animals, including 154 species of mammal, 98 reptile and 26 amphibian species, 120 fish species, 447 species of bird, and a whopping 3,305 plant species. A total of 90 species are endemic, meaning that they occur nowhere else on Earth.

## Varied terrain

Elevations in New Mexico range from 2,840 ft (860 meters) in the south to 13,160 ft (4,010 meters) in the north, the result of a pronounced north-south tilt. Most of the year, New Mexico's location between the Sierra Nevada and the Rocky Mountain ranges blocks moist winds blowing onshore from the Pacific, accounting for desert conditions. But in winter, the jetstream changes course and cold, moist

**PRECEDING PAGES:** daisy blossoms throng a meadow on the Continental Divide Trail near Pie Town.
**RIGHT:** a Great Plains toad takes advantage of a summer thunderstorm.

air arrives from the Pacific Northwest, with major accumulations of snow in the Sangre de Cristo and Sacramento ranges that attract skiers from throughout the country. Spring arrives early in southern New Mexico, with strong winds and blooming desert annuals and perennials that provide splashes of eye-popping

color in years of good winter rains. Blossoms don't generally appear until May and June in the north, when the whole state swelters under its hottest, driest period.

Most rainfall arrives between July and September, when warm, tropical air heads north from Mexico via the Gulf of California. Huge cumulo-nimbus thunderclouds build up daily and unleash dramatic thunderstorms and heavy rains, known regionally (but incorrectly) as "monsoons." Late September, October and early November are the best months for travel. In all but the higher elevations, the weather is warm and dry in the daytime and pleasantly cool at night.

## The Chihuahuan Desert

With a mean 15 inches (38cm) of annual rainfall, all of New Mexico is considered desert, but for the real desert, you'll have to head south. The Chihuahuan Desert, stretching from northern Mexico to Albuquerque, stands at an elevation of 3,000 to 5,000 ft (1,000–1,500 meters) and is in the Lower Sonoran life zone. For a desert, it is quite high and has relatively long, chilly winters, with occasional snowfalls that melt fast. Summer temperatures often exceed 100°F (38°C) but are cooled by short, violent thunderstorms that drop most of the 8–12 inches (20–30cm) of annual rainfall.

Conserving moisture is key to survival. Delicate leaves are of little use to a desert plant. Some trees and shrubs shed their leaves and shut down to survive; others close up or tilt fleshy, waxy leaves to keep cool. Cacti have done away with leaves altogether and evolved protective spines. Photosynthesis takes place along the trunk or paddles. Thick, waxy skin keeps moisture in and expands like an accordion to store water during sporadic rains.

In spring, cacti grow showy flowers with large yellow pollen centers. Those trying to attract night pollinators, such as bats and moths, sport creamy phosphorescent blossoms. Birds,

### A FIERCE GREEN FIRE

Hunting in southern New Mexico in 1909, a young forest ranger named Aldo Leopold came across a mother wolf and her cubs and, almost reflexively, shot at them. What followed was a transformative experience for Leopold and a seminal moment in the emerging science of ecology. "We reached the old wolf in time to watch a fierce green fire dying in her eyes... there was something new to me in those eyes – something known only to her and to the mountain. I was young then, and full of trigger-itch; I thought that because fewer wolves meant more deer that no wolves would mean hunters' paradise. But after seeing the green fire die, I sensed that neither the wolf nor the mountain agreed..."

Leopold wrote about the experience in his classic *A Sand County Almanac*, a collection of essays in which he outlines a new "land ethic" that regards the natural world, including humans, as an integrated community. Advancing quickly up the ranks of the Forest Service, he became a passionate advocate of conservation principles. It was largely due to his efforts that the Gila Wilderness – the country's first designated wilderness area– was created in New Mexico. "There are some who can live without wild things and some who cannot," Leopold wrote in *A Sand County Almanac*. "These essays are the delights and dilemmas of one who cannot."

butterflies and other animals active in the day go for loud reds, pinks and yellows. By early fall, the juicy red fruits of prickly pear attract collared peccaries, or javelinas, and other fruit-loving creatures, including humans.

What you won't find in the Chihuahuan Desert are saguaro cacti, those tall gesticulating sentinels that have become icons of the desert Southwest (they grow in the Sonoran Desert to the west in Arizona). Instead, the signature plants of the Chihuahuan Desert are mesquite trees, ocotillo and agaves such as yucca and lechuguilla, which have tall, thick spikes rising from a rosette of fleshy, swordlike "leaves."

Native people traditionally harvested mesquite pods and ground them into protein-rich meal. The roots of the yucca, the state plant, were used for shampoo, the fibers for clothing, and the fruit as a starchy food. The ceremonial life of the Mescalero Apache revolves around agave roasts, and ancient roasting pits can still be seen at Carlsbad Caverns National Park. Seasonal roasting demonstrations take place at Living Desert Zoo and Gardens State Park, just north of Carlsbad, the state's premier institution for interpreting the Chihuahuan Desert and an important breeding site for the Mexican wolf reintroduction program.

Desert animals survive the hot, dry conditions by being active at night and staying cool in burrows or under rocks during the day. Crepuscular hunters like coyotes become active at dusk and dawn and travel between sheltered canyons and desert hunting grounds in search of small rodents such as cottontails, jackrabbits and kangaroo rats, desert specialists who get their water from seeds. McKittrick Canyon in the Guadalupe Mountains shelters thick stands of Texas madrone trees that turn fiery red in fall. It is home to populations of mule deer, the main diet of secretive mountain lions and bobcats that prowl nightly through the scenic area.

## On the border

Wildlife respects no international borders, and in this part of the state you'll find a good many Central American species at the northernmost limit of their range. On the southwestern border, Arizona cypress and alligator juniper min-

gle with Mexican natives like Mexican Chihuahua and Apache pine, while at higher elevations, lush forests of Douglas fir, aspen and ponderosa pine provide browse for white-tailed deer and cover for sulphur-bellied flycatchers, Mexican chicadees and, at the top of just about every birder's wish list, the elegant trogon. Hummingbirds come north to breed in April and can be seen in dazzling numbers outside Silver City in the Gila National Forest.

The lowest parts of New Mexico's Chihuahuan Desert are in the extreme southwestern "bootheel," prime habitat for reptiles. Look for basking collared lizards and huge Gila mon-

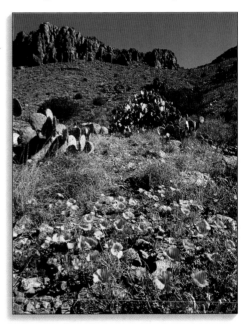

sters early in the morning at places like City of Rocks State Park in the rugged Florida Mountains, near Deming. You may even be lucky enough to glimpse a roadrunner, New Mexico's state bird, a member of the cuckoo family. Desert bighorn sheep, which thrive in the most rugged areas, can be viewed in the Red Rock Wildlife Area, near Lordsburg, where they clamber among rocky hills and come to drink at the lower Gila River.

## Harsh environments

In the Tularosa Basin, gypsum, washed out of the surrounding highlands, has been blown into the unearthly dunes preserved at White Sands

---

**LEFT:** mountain lions are rarely seen. They are stealthy hunters that prey on deer and small animals.
**RIGHT:** Spring poppies bloom in the Chihuahuan Desert.

National Monument. Although they look bare, the dunes support highly specialized life forms like soaptree yucca, which grows fast enough to avoid being buried and whose long roots help stabilize the sand. Fringe-toed lizards and two types of rattlesnakes – western diamondbacks and desert massassaugas – live here, too, as do cottontail rabbits and their chief predator, the ubiquitous coyote. Birds travel easily between mountains and dunes, with finches, doves, thrashers and shrikes giving up

### WHERE THE BLOOMS ARE

Many desert wildflowers remain dormant during periods of extreme heat and aridity, bursting to life in intense displays of color after soaking rains. Check the website www.desertusa.com for information on time and location.

angry-looking lava flows, such as those at Valley of Fires Recreation Area, north of White Sands, in an area known forbiddingly as La Jornada del Muerto, the Dead Man's Way. It may take a century for a few hardy plants to colonize these flows – perhaps a thousand years for anything substantial to grow. Animals have evolved dark coloration to blend into the flows while those living underground have become blind in the darkness. This is also a feature of cave creatures such as eye-

the night sky to nighthawks and owls whose unmistakable hoots carry eerily across the dunes.

Desert basins like the Tularosa are so hot that runoff evaporates, leaving behind dry salt flats, or playas, that sustain only saltbush, iodine bush, pickleweed and other salt-tolerant species. These lowlands come into their own in winter, when they are flooded by rains and attract migratory fowl such as thousands of snow geese and lesser sandhill cranes. Bitter Lake National Wildlife Refuge, east of Roswell, in the Llano Estacado, or Staked Plains, is also noteworthy for its huge number of dragonflies in summer.

Equally unpromising are the sprawling,

less beetles and crickets found in the limestone caves at Carlsbad Caverns. Carlsbad is most famous for its enormous nesting colony of swallows and the 300,000 breeding Mexican free-tailed bats that summer just inside the Natural Cave Entrance. Every evening in summer the bats whirl counter-clockwise into the night sky, one of nature's great spectacles.

## Woodlands and grasslands

The Upper Sonoran zone, found between 4,500 and 7,000 ft (1,400–2,100 meters), is the largest life zone in New Mexico. Predominant species here are dwarf pinyon and juniper trees, scrub oak and native grasses. Pinyon-juniper forest forms a thick green mantle in the foothills of mountains like the Sangre de Cristo range in northern New Mexico, where it surrounds Santa Fe. For millennia, people have relied on the nutritious nuts of the slow-growing pinyon tree. In the 20th century, though, shaggy-barked junipers began to compete with the gracefully arching pinyon as extensive cattle grazing eroded grasslands, allowing invasive shrubs, such as juniper, sagebrush and rabbitbrush to take over.

Grasslands are found throughout the state but really come into their own in northeastern New Mexico, where the Rocky Mountains yield to the Great Plains. This has been ranch country since the state was under Spanish rule, and remains so today, with isolated ranches and cattle and bison herds scattered throughout lonesome short-grass prairies.

Kiowa National Grassland, part of a grasslands-restoration project administered by Cibola National Forest, occupies the land between Clayton and the New Mexico border with Texas and Oklahoma. Any visit here offers glimpses of hundreds of bird species, including wild turkey, pheasant, ducks and geese. Most notable is the flamboyant lesser prairie chicken, whose mating dance attracts avid birdwatchers every spring. The eastern prairies are also home to endangered black-tailed prairie dogs, highly social animals whose "towns" are rapidly disappearing throughout the West. Prairie dogs are the principal diet of black-footed ferrets, one of the most endangered animals in the world.

This quiet area is dubbed New Mexico's Wild West, as much for its wildlands as its gun-toting past. It was once part of the massive Maxwell Land Grant, the largest private land grant in the country. Near Cimarron, the world-famous Philmont Scout Ranch is located on 214 sq miles (554 sq km) of the former Maxwell spread and offers a chance to see herds of pronghorn and bison. South of Raton, volcanoes tower above the grasslands. The centerpiece, 1,400-ft-high (425-meter) Capulin Volcano, has views all the way to Oklahoma's Black Mesa and at least one unusual wildlife event: swarms of ladybugs rest on the forested rim each summer.

---

**LEFT:** coyotes are solitary hunters, though they may join others to take down large game like deer.
**RIGHT:** aspens in fall, Sangre de Cristo Mountains.

## Sky islands

New Mexico's mountains are cool refuges for wildlife and, depending on elevation, sustain very different ecosystems. Above 7,000 ft (2,100 meters), foothill woodlands give way to trees of the Transition zone. The signature trees at this elevation are Gambel oak and ponderosa pine, a tall elegant tree that grows in stands amid clearings called "parks." In summer, the fragrance of pine mingles with vanilla from the tree's plate-like bark in the Sangre de Cristo, Jemez, Sacramento and Mogollon mountains. Nestled beneath the trees are splashy wildflowers, including scarlet penstemon, Indian paintbrush,

lupine and verbena, which bloom in summer.

Wildlife in this habitat include Steller's jays, Abert's squirrels, mule deer and black bears. New Mexico is, of course, famous for its bears. The small cub that was rescued from the Capitan Mountains near Lincoln went on to fame, if not fortune, as Smokey Bear, the U.S. Forest Service's most recognizable mascot.

Above 8,500 ft (2,600 meters), Douglas fir, spruce and thick stands of aspen dominate the Mixed Conifer zone. Hikers in Santa Fe National Forest, for example, enjoy one of the largest aspen forests in the West. The adjoining Pecos Wilderness is one of the most spectacular in the state, with 15 lakes, 30 perennial streams and elevations from 8,400 to 13,100 ft (2,560–3,990 meters). Mule deer, Rocky Mountain elk, yellow-bellied marmots, pika, blue grouse and Abert's squirrels are plentiful, as are tuneful hermit's thrush and Clark's nutcrackers. In winter, snowshoeing and cross-country skiing through the forests atop the Pajarito Plateau in the Jemez Mountains are popular, with views of Valle Grande, part of the Valles Caldera, home to a large herd of Roosevelt elk. In fall, hawks and eagles migrate over New Mexico's central mountains – the Sandias and the Manzanos – important migratory corridors for raptors and other birds.

## Alpine ecology

At 9,500 ft (2,900 meters), Englemann spruce, subalpine fir, corkbark fir, bristlecone pine and other species that can withstand cooler temperatures occupy the Subalpine zone. Over 11,500 ft (3,500 meters), vegetation all but ceases in the windswept tundra above treeline. This Alpine zone exists only on the highest summits in New Mexico – Pecos and Wheeler Peak Wildernesses and the top of Sierra Blanca. The extreme conditions challenge living things as severely as the low desert. To survive, plants must grow in protected areas low to the ground and conserve moisture with woody stems. Flowers are generally very small. A signature

bird of this elevation is the white-tailed ptarmigan, whose snowy plumage allows it to blend with snowfields. The snowshoe hare also employs white camouflage.

## Wetlands

Fully 80 percent of living things in New Mexico rely on rivers, streams, bosque bottomlands, lakes and *cienega* marshes. And with drought an ongoing reality, New Mexicans are working hard to conserve water sources. Adequate water is important not only for irrigating the state's important chile, corn, alfalfa and other crops but to protect endangered fish species like the Rio Grande silvery minnow and Gila trout from loss of riparian habitat.

The Rio Grande, once one of the West's major rivers, has been dammed extensively and has lost many of its important native cottonwood and willow bosque bottomlands. One place where they still exist is next to the Rio Grande Nature Center in Albuquerque. The 270-acre (110-hectare) state park offers glimpses of numerous animals, including Cooper's hawks, Canada geese, black-capped chickadees, and a variety of turtles and toads. Beaver, an important member of the riverine community, whose dams create shady resting areas for fish, insects and other animals, are also present.

Outside Silver City, in southwestern New Mexico, two Nature Conservancy preserves and several federally managed sites along the Gila River support hundreds of species, including endangered southwestern willow flycatchers and common black hawks and wintering sandhill cranes. The Gila has become an important sanctuary for wildlife, thanks in large part to the efforts of environmentalists, land management agencies and local ranchers to reduce the impact of cattle.

New Mexico boasts five spectacular national wildlife refuges. Perhaps the most famous is Bosque del Apache, just south of Socorro, the winter home of thousands of snow geese, sandhill cranes, a few rare whooping cranes and other birds. Birdwatchers come from around the world to view and photograph the spine-chilling sunrise and sunset takeoffs of these migratory waterfowl from bosques along the Rio Grande. Few events in nature are more spectacular. ❑

**LEFT:** Amanita muscaria mushrooms grow in the coniferous forests of the Tusas Mountains.

# For the Birds

**B**irdwatchers are richly rewarded in New Mexico. More than 450 bird species have been sighted in the state, many of them visitors from Mexico and other points south that are rarely found elsewhere in the United States. The Rio Grande Valley serves as a major flyway and is the site of some of North America's most dramatic congregations of migratory birds.

For birding in the Santa Fe area, stop first at the Randall Davey Audubon Center (1800 Upper Canyon, 505-983-4609), set on 135 acres (54 hectares) at the mouth of Santa Fe Canyon. Staff members offer free guided bird walks the first and third Saturday of each month and can fill you in on birding hot spots elsewhere in the area and throughout the state. A trail on the property passes through pinyon-juniper woodland, prime habitat for bushtits, spotted towhees and bluebirds. Stellar's jays, pygmy nuthatches and mountain chickadees are common in stands of ponderosa pine that grow at a slightly higher elevation farther along the trail.

In Albuquerque, the best place to start a birding excursion is Rio Grande Nature Center State Park (2901 Candelaria Rd NW, 505-344-7240), a few miles north of Old Town. The park encompasses 270 acres (110 hectares) of meadows and cottonwood forest along the Rio Grande and is occupied, at one time or another, by more than 200 species, including Cooper's hawks, great-horned owls, ring-necked pheasants, black-capped chickadees and hairy woodpeckers. The glass-walled library overlooks a 3-acre (1.2-hectare) pond, where such waterbirds as great blue herons, Canada geese, mallards and wood ducks congregate. Sandhill cranes and bald eagles are common winter visitors. Free naturalist-led bird walks are offered Saturday and Sunday mornings May through August.

Hawk Watch International, a nonprofit organization dedicated to the protection of hawks, eagles and other raptors, maintains two observation sites in the Albuquerque area – one perched on a ridge in the Sandia Mountains, the other in the remote Manzano Mountains southeast of the city. The group conducts migration counts in spring at the Sandia site and in autumn in the Manzanos.

On a bend in the Rio Grande about 90 miles (145km) south of Albuquerque is Bosque del Apache National Wildlife Refuge (NM 1, 505-835-1828), an expansive area of marshes, ponds, farmland and riparian forest that attracts some 300 bird species. Even more impressive than the variety of birds is the number. Tens of thousands of snow geese, ducks and sandhill cranes arrive in winter, as do bald and golden eagles, kestrels, northern harriers and a few rare whooping cranes. A schedule of nature walks and workshops is offered year-round. The annual Festival of Cranes is held on the weekend before Thanksgiving and is attended by avid birdwatchers from around the world.

In southern New Mexico birders flock to Gila National Forest, particularly along the mountain streams outside Silver City, where such rare birds

as the gila woodpecker and willow flycatcher are found, in addition to some 300 other species, including a dazzling variety of hummingbirds. Among the best places to base yourself is the Bear Mountain Lodge (Cottage San Road, Silver City, 505-538-2538), a bed-and-breakfast owned by The Nature Conservancy. Lodge naturalists lead birding hikes through the Conservancy's Gila Riparian Preserve, demonstrate banding techniques and, in some cases, recruit guests to assist with bird counts and research projects.

For birders it doesn't get much better than this – good meals, comfortable accommodations, an expert staff and some of the best birding anywhere in the Southwest. ❑

**RIGHT:** Gila woodpecker.

# OUTDOOR ADVENTURE

*There's plenty of elbow room in New*

*Mexico's backcountry and lots of exciting ways to explore it*

Opportunities for adventure in New Mexico are more abundant than ever, and it's never been easier to get started. Schools and clubs are available to teach you the basics of wilderness travel as well as adventure sports such as rock climbing and kayaking. There are also a growing number of tour companies that specialize in "light adventure" for people who want to experience the thrill and beauty of the outdoors without committing themselves to months of training or the hassles of planning a trip.

If you're a few years (or several pounds) past your prime, don't panic. Though the ads in outdoor magazines may lead you to believe otherwise, you don't need to be a latte-swilling 20-something with washboard abs. A minimal level of fitness may be required, but in most pursuits good judgment and a willing spirit count for more than brawn and bravado. Which is not to say you'll be dangling by your fingertips or wheeling down a mountainside on your first day out. Making an honest assessment of your limitations – including your tolerance for danger – is an essential first step in any adventure, as is learning to say no when more experienced companions try to pressure you into situations that exceed your abilities.

## Walk on the wild side

For some, hiking is adventure enough. They owe no apologies. A walk in the wilderness is not to be taken lightly, and even a short jaunt can turn ugly if you're not properly prepared.

What gets most people into trouble isn't snakebite, flash floods or falling off cliffs but the far more mundane risk of dehydration – a critical loss of moisture due to extreme heat and aridity. The condition is particularly insidious because in the arid Southwest even mild exertion, like hiking, can cause the body to lose

moisture faster than the brain can generate an urge to drink. In other words, you become dehydrated before you feel thirsty.

Prevention is simple enough. Carry plenty of water and drink it at regular intervals, whether or not you feel thirsty. The rule of thumb is one gallon (4 liters) per person per day, but it's best

to take more than you think you'll need just in case you want to extend your trip or you lose your way. Getting lost is notoriously easy, especially in desert regions where the absence of trees and other landmarks leaves you with few reference points and the abundance of bare ground makes it easy to stray from even a well-marked trail. Coupled with the symptoms of mild dehydration – fatigue, light-headedness, disorientation – losing your way can quickly spiral into a life-threatening situation. Carry a map and compass (or GPS unit) and know how to use them, and leave a travel plan with someone at home, so they know when and where to start looking if you don't turn up.

**PRECEDING PAGES:** mountain bikers enjoy a view of Rio Grande Gorge.
**LEFT:** paddlers take on Rio Grande whitewater.
**RIGHT:** a climber on Wheeler Peak.

Other basics you'll need to take with you are a hat, sunglasses and sunscreen with a high SPF. The New Mexico sun is relentless, and shade is scarce. Left unprotected, your skin and eyes will be fried in no time.

## Feet first

As a hiker, you will rely almost entirely on your feet, so keep them in good shape with the best hiking boots you can afford. Gone are the days of heavy leather clunkers that take forever to break in. Modern boots are lightweight but sturdy enough to protect your feet from cactus and thorny underbrush and need little

choices (and prices) can quickly become overwhelming. Unless you have an experienced friend to show you the ropes, the best advice is to start by doing a little research in books and magazines and on the Web, then go to a reputable camping-supply retailer and work with a salesperson who's willing to take the time you need to make the right decisions. Remember: comfort is key. Roughing it in the outdoors shouldn't be rough at all. The idea is to simplify your life, unload stress, and enjoy the place, people and moment, not aggravate yourself with ill-fitting or poor-quality equipment that leaves you cold, hungry, achy and miserable.

or no breaking in, which helps avoid painful blisters. Wearing polypropylene liner socks under a thick pair of poly-wool outer socks will wick moisture away from your feet and prevent blisters. Avoid cotton socks, which soak up moisture and tend to be rough. If a hot spot develops, cover the area with moleskin (available at camping supply shops) or white athletic tape and allow yourself extra time to rest.

Overnight trips are naturally more complicated to plan and require a rather daunting list of additional equipment, including a backpack, sleeping bag, tent, water-purifying kit and camping stove. The design and quality of camping gear has never been better, though

## Where the wild things are

Now that you're properly equipped, you can begin making the tough decisions about where to go. Trail conditions, topography and weather vary widely in New Mexico, so gathering accurate information about a destination – the length and difficulty of your route, the availability of water, the location of facilities – is essential for planning a successful trip.

The best approach is to let your interests be your guide. Enjoy hiking in forests? Consider a trip through the conifer and aspen groves of the Pecos Wilderness northeast of Santa Fe or among stands of juniper and ponderosa pine in the Sacramento Mountains above the sun-blasted desert of the Tularosa Basin. Have an interest in birding? Thousands of sandhill cranes, geese and other waterbirds flock to the marshes of Bosque del Apache in early winter; hawks and other raptors follow migration routes over the Sandia and Manzano Mountains in spring and autumn. Fancy geology? Explore the lava flows of El Malpais south of Grants or the brilliant dunes of White Sands National Monument near Alamogordo. Fly-fishing? Pull on your waders and cast a line into the San Juan River below Navajo Dam in the state's northwest corner or perhaps the East Fork of the Jemez River in the alpine meadows of the Jemez Mountains.

> **DON'T DRINK THE WATER**
>
> Even clear streams can harbor parasites that cause severe gastro-intestinal illness. All water from wild sources should be boiled for at least a minute, treated with iodine, or passed through a portable filter.

business travelers confined to offices in downtown Albuquerque will find good biking in classic southwestern landscapes only a short drive from the city center. The eastern slope of the Sandia Mountains, for instance, is laced with trails off the Crest Highway about a 30-minute drive from Old Town.

Farther afield, bikers can explore the alpine forests of the Sacramento Mountains on the Rim Trail near Cloudcroft, the volcanic highlands of the Jemez Mountains, the west rim of

## Pedal power

The possibilities become even more enticing when you consider alternate modes of transportation such as mountain biking or rafting, which usually free you from the burden of lugging a backpack and open up territory that may be unreachable on foot. Advances in the technology and design of mountain bikes, for example, make it easier and safer than ever to get started. The clunky, inflexible contraptions of 20 years ago have evolved into sleek and rugged riding machines designed to handle terrain that would reduce an ordinary bike to scrap metal. The advantages are obvious in a place like New Mexico, where much of the backcountry is crosshatched with logging and mining roads. You'll cover more ground on wheels than on foot, and, unlike motorized travel, biking is great exercise, is easy on the environment (so long as you stay on prescribed trails), and lets the landscape unfold at a speed that's more akin to hiking than driving.

While it can take months to master the subtleties of the sport, the basics aren't all that different from riding a road bike. As long as you steer clear of extremely steep, tortuous or rocky routes and technically demanding single tracks (trails just wide enough for one bike), beginners shouldn't encounter too many difficulties.

Best of all, opportunities for mountain biking in New Mexico are virtually endless. Even

the Rio Grande Gorge outside Taos, the steep slopes of Mount Taylor north of Grants, and the rugged mountain trails off the road to the Santa Fe Ski Basin.

Many of the same safety issues pertain to biking as to other wilderness travel. Bring plenty of water and nutritious food, keep abreast of weather conditions, and don't over-tax your skills or endurance. Carry a repair and first-aid kit, and be courteous to Jeeps, horseback riders and hikers who may be sharing the trail. Be particularly wary of logging trucks, which often barrel down backroads at breakneck speed, kicking up a giant plume of dust in their wake. Truckers may not be able to see

**LEFT:** sturdy, lightweight boots protect the feet from cactus, thorny underbrush and rugged terrain.
**RIGHT:** bikers on West Rim Trail of Rio Grande Gorge.

you and probably can't stop in time if they do. Don't let your last thought be: "Funny, I didn't see that truck a moment ago."

## The wetter the better

If, as naturalist Loren Eiseley wrote, there's magic in water, then the rivers of the Southwest are truly a miracle. They bring life to scorching deserts, sculpt rock into canyons, and serve as natural corridors for travelers and wildlife seeking entrée to otherwise impenetrable wilderness.

> **NATURE CALLING**
>
> When nature calls, answer with a trowel. Dig a hole at least 6 inches (15cm) deep for human waste and bury or carry out toilet paper. Pick a site at least 200 ft (60 meters) from water sources.

sponsored by the Adobe Whitewater Club of New Mexico (www.adobeww.org).

The Rio Chama is even more laid back, a one-to three-day wilderness run through sandstone canyons, cottonwood bosques and wildflower meadows. This is a good choice for families with young children and travelers interested in wildlife. Elk, beaver, turkey, bald eagles and black bear are often sighted near the river.

The real beauty of these river trips is that just about anyone can do them. Outfitters authorized

The best paddling in New Mexico is on the upper Rio Grande. Two stretches are particularly popular. A 17-mile (27-km) run through the Rio Grande Gorge known as the Box is a heart-stopping course of Class III-IV rapids strewn with giant boulders, steep chutes and meaty waves. The scenery is breathtaking: a narrow crack in the Earth hemmed in by dark basalt walls. Equally scenic but considerably more mellow is the State Park and Racecourse runs just to the south, which pass through the gentle waters of Orilla Verde National Recreation Area before hitting a series of moderately challenging rapids along NM 68. This last section is the site of the annual Mother's Day races

by the Bureau of Land Management handle all provisioning and navigation. There are even gourmet and wine-tasting trips. About all you have to do – aside from pay the bill – is show up.

Paddling elsewhere in New Mexico can be quite good depending on the season. The level of difficulty ranges from boat-bashing whitewater suitable only for seasoned kayakers to long stretches of calm water that can be floated in a canoe or inner tube. The Pecos, San Juan and Gila Rivers promise solitude, scenery and glimpses of desert wildlife, though water levels are often too low to boat.

Flatwater enthusiasts can explore numerous lakes, ranging in size from 40,000-acre (16,000-

hectare) Elephant Butte Reservoir, which has three marinas and is popular with sailboaters, houseboaters and jetskiers, to diminutive Snow Lake nestled in the Mogollon Mountains at the headwaters of the Gila River.

## Climbing the walls

The learning curve is far more precipitous for rock climbing, although even in this sport, in which technical skill and strength are paramount, the opportunities for beginners are expanding. Not too many years ago, the only practical way to learn rock climbing was to tag along with experienced climbers. Today, it's

## Down and dirty

For those who prefer adventure of a subterranean variety, there's Carlsbad Caverns National Park, one of the most spectacular cave systems in the world and an excellent place to get acquainted with spelunking or, as its practitioners prefer to call it, caving. The Park Service offers a choice of guided tours ranging from an easy underground hike to a four-hour "cave crawl" requiring participants to wiggle through narrow passages, negotiate slippery surfaces and do moderate free climbing. Expect to get dirty.

For experienced cavers, the possibilities are infinitely more interesting. Not only are there

much more common for newcomers to hone their skills at climbing gyms before they actually put flesh to rock. Beginners can learn a few basic maneuvers in just four or five hours, but there's only so much you can do without being out in the field. For that, it's best to contact organizations like the New Mexico Mountain Club (www.swcp.com/~nmmc), which runs a four-week course for novices that covers the fundamentals of climbing techniques, equipment and, above all, safety.

---

**LEFT:** rafters muscle through the rapids of Taos Box on the Rio Grande.
**ABOVE:** cavers explore Carlsbad Caverns.

limestone caves to explore in the Carlsbad area and nearby Guadalupe Mountains but gypsum caves in eastern New Mexico and extensive lava tubes (some with permanent ice ponds inside) around El Malpais National Monument south of Grants. To learn more about New Mexico caving and perhaps join an upcoming trip, contact the Sandia Grotto of the National Speleological Society (www.boim.com/~sandia).

Much less technical but still challenging are the hundreds of peaks that rise from mountain ranges throughout the state. The degree of difficulty varies considerably from one mountain to another, but most require no special skills or equipment and can be climbed in a single day.

Those with little or no experience may want to set their sights on a modest goal – say, a portion of the Sandia Crest Trail outside Albuquerque. Hikers looking for a shortcut can take the tram to 10,678-ft (3,256-meter) Sandia Crest, then walk along the ridge through Sandia Wilderness. On the opposite side of the scale is the lung-searing trek to the top of 13,161-ft (4,012-meter) Wheeler Peak northeast of Taos, the highest point in New Mexico.

## Powder to the people

Considering New Mexico's reputation as a desert state, some people are surprised to learn

that the Land of Enchantment has some of the West's best skiing. There are 10 downhill ski areas, most clustered in the Sangre de Cristo Mountains north of Santa Fe, but the premier site is Taos Ski Valley, at the base of 12,481-ft (3,804-meter) Kachina Peak within the Enchanted Circle northeast of Taos. Family-owned, with few of the high-tech bells and whistles one finds at better-known ski resorts, Taos Ski Valley boasts 2,612 ft (796 meters) of vertical drop, legendary chutes and glades, piles of fluffy white powder, a highly regarded ski school, and a European-style resort village.

Elsewhere in the Taos area, skiers will find excellent conditions at Red River, Angel Fire,

Rio and Sipapu Ski Areas, all of which permit snowboarders (unlike Taos Ski Valley). Three other ski areas are convenienty located for quick getaways. Sandia Peak is minutes from Albuquerque, Pajarito Mountain is just outside Los Alamos, and Ski Santa Fe is within 20 miles (32km) of the Plaza in Santa Fe. Southern New Mexico has two ski areas – Ski Apache and modest Snow Canyon – both in the Sacramento Mountains.

The possibilities for cross-country skiing are even more extensive, with miles of trails at such facilities as the Enchanted Forest Cross-Country Ski Area north of Taos and the Manzano Nordic Ski Center south of Albuquerque.

For those who want to break their own trails, there are countless acres of snow-covered back-country in the national forests, where snow-covered trails and unpaved roads are ideal for cross-country skiers and snowshoers. There's prime nordic terrain in the Mount Taylor and Zuni Mountains areas of Cibola National Forest around Grants, in the Sacramento Mountains around Cloudcroft, in the Jemez Mountains outside Los Alamos, and the Sandia Mountains east of Albuquerque.

## Room to roam

In the end, the deepest rewards of adventuring come not from mastering a particular sport but from simply being outdoors in places where, in the words of the 1964 Wilderness Act, "the earth and its community of life are untrammeled by man, where man himself is a visitor who does not remain."

The Wilderness Act was inspired by the work of Aldo Leopold, a forest ranger, ecologist and gifted writer who in 1924 succeeded in persuading the U.S. Forest Service to designate the Gila Wilderness as the world's first officially protected wilderness area. Today, New Mexico has 1.6 million acres (650,000 hectares) of designated wilderness, 2 percent of the state's total land area, and more than 20 million acres (8 million hectares) of public land administered by state and federal agencies.

What this means in practical terms is that no matter how far or fast you hike, there will always be another canyon to explore, another hill to climb, another trail to follow.  ❑

**LEFT:** a skier rockets over expert terrain on Kachina Peak at Taos Ski Valley.

# Can You Dig It?

Ever wanted to don an archaeologist's battered hat and help dig up an important piece of the past? The romance of archaeology seems to infect everyone. Unfortunately, far more people want to take part in a professionally supervised archaeological dig than there are opportunities for them to do so. But several programs are available, with a limited number of slots open to volunteers.

The U.S. Forest Service operates two programs aimed at archaeology enthusiasts. Heritage Expeditions are tours of archaeological sites in national forests. The popular Passport in Time (PIT) gives you the chance to participate in an actual archaeological excavation in one of the national forests. In recent years, PIT programs have included digs at a 19th-century Spanish hacienda on the Pecos River and Gallinas Pueblo sites in Carson National Forest.

The Museum of New Mexico's Office of Archaeology Studies offers everything from excavation to ongoing lab work for volunteers at sites around New Mexico. In 2002–2003, a high-profile excavation behind Santa Fe's Palace of the Governors, to make way for a new history museum, made headlines. Archaeologists uncovered 195,000 artifacts in four separate layers dating to 1603 (almost certainly pushing back the date of the founding of Santa Fe by seven years).

Also in 2003, Coronado State Monument in Albuquerque, a 1540 site reconstructed in the 1960s, was eagerly recruiting volunteers to help rebuild crumbling adobe walls.

In mid-July each year, the Museum of New Mexico sponsors the Sun Mountain Gathering at the Museum of Indian Arts and Culture/Laboratory of Anthropology on Museum Hill, where you can learn flint knapping and mud plastering as well as how to use an ancient atlatl, or spearthrower. Also in July, the Friends of Tijeras Pueblo holds an archaeology day for kids at the pueblo site east of Albuquerque, with tours, mock digs and other activities.

Salmon Ruin County Park in Bloomfield, preserving one of the largest Chacoan outliers in the Four Corners, is community archaeology at its best. Programs include simulated digs for youngsters, a computerized "virtual tour" of Chaco outliers in the

museum, and occasional public excursions to nearby Navajo pueblitos on state lands, which are monitored by trained volunteers based at the park.

Salmon Ruin's most ambitious project to date is a reconstructed pueblo at Crow Canyon Archaeological Center in nearby Cortez, Colorado. Crow Canyon is the premier place in the Southwest for public archaeology, with ongoing excavations at one of the largest Mesa Verde-era ruins outside the national park. A few miles from Crow Canyon, the Anasazi Heritage Center also offers a variety of archaeology programs, including mock digs and interactive computers.

Still, New Mexico's best offerings are in the arm-

chair archaeology category. Regular ranger tours take place all summer at Bandelier and Gila National Monuments and Chaco Culture and Pecos National Historical Parks.

Special tours of lesser known sites, such as those in the Galisteo Basin, are conducted occasionally by the Albuquerque-based Archaeological Conservancy, Museum of New Mexico, School of American Research and Southwest Seminars. The latter two organizations sponsor a year-round roster of public talks in Santa Fe by famous Southwest archaeologists such as Stephen Lekson and R. Gwinn Vivian, whose amusing tales of digging at Chaco Canyon are the next best thing to getting your own hands dirty. ❑

---

**RIGHT:** a visitor explores the ruins of a Mogollon village at Gila Cliff Dwellings National Monument.

# PLACES

*A detailed guide to the entire state, with principal sites clearly cross-referenced by number to the maps*

**S**un, silence and adobe – that is New Mexico in three words." More than a century has passed since journalist Charles Lummis wrote these words. Little has changed. The chief attractions of this desert state remain the same: diverse habitats; more than 300 days of sunshine annually; and an intriguing mix of Indian and Hispanic cultures, which have not only endured but thrived, even as the rest of America becomes increasingly homogenized.

Water in the desert has shaped the state. The Rio Grande carves a distinctive path through central New Mexico. It occupies one of only a handful of volcanic rift zones in the world, a split that has helped create the southern Rockies and western Colorado Plateau. The Middle Rio Grande supports 90 percent of the state's flora and fauna and numerous human settlements. Most of New Mexico's 19 Indian pueblos and many of its oldest Hispanic land grants are here, using irrigation ditches, known as *acequias*, to water fields laid out centuries ago.

In New Mexico, what lies below the surface is as important as what lies in plain view. The Cerrillos mines, south of Santa Fe, have been mined for their turquoise since Aztec times. Their huge yields of silver, zinc, lead and coal drove Spanish settlement of Santa Fe in the 1600s and fueled the appetites of 19th-century Anglo arrivals.

Oil, gas and coal have helped enrich the Navajo Nation. Uranium found in the region brought the 20th century to rural New Mexico in the 1940s, when scientists used it to create the world's first atom bomb at Los Alamos. Since then, government-funded scientific institutions have been part of the New Mexico landscape in Los Alamos, Albuquerque, Socorro and the Tularosa Basin.

New Mexico has more geological parks than any other state. Carlsbad Caverns, the top attraction, contains one of the most extensive cave systems in the world. Capulin Volcano is in the easternmost volcanic field in the nation. El Malpais contains some of the country's youngest lava flows. But it is for its cultural parks that the state is best known. In the early 20th century, Chaco Canyon, Bandelier National Monument and Pecos National Historical Park attracted the attention of archaeologists. Their work created a model for American archaeology, a legacy that continues in New Mexico's top visitor destination: Santa Fe.

It's not hard to see what attracts more than a million visitors to Santa Fe each year. The country's oldest capital is one of the most beautiful and authentically preserved cities in the United States. Famously laid back, it rivals much larger cities for cultural activities, all in one of the most beautiful mountain settings anywhere. Love it, hate it, it's hard not to be fascinated by it, and to return again and again. ❑

**PRECEDING PAGES:** El Malpais National Monument; White Sands National Monument; Lechuguilla Cave, Carlsbad Caverns National Park.
**LEFT:** West Pueblo, Aztec Ruins National Monument.

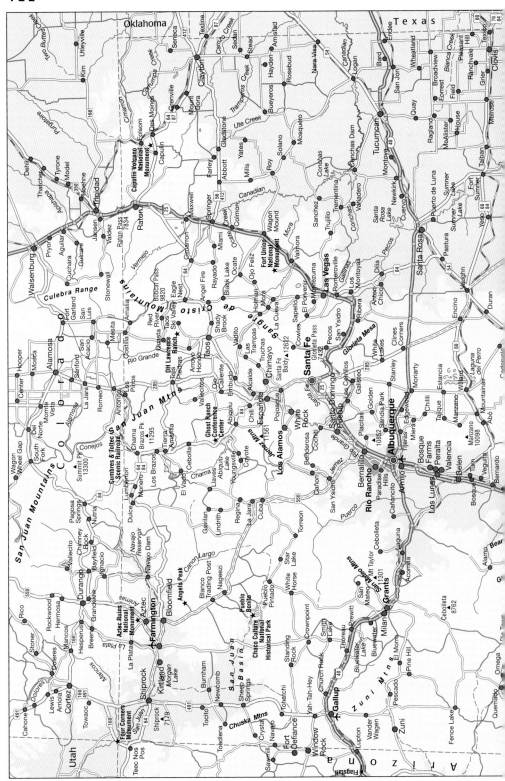

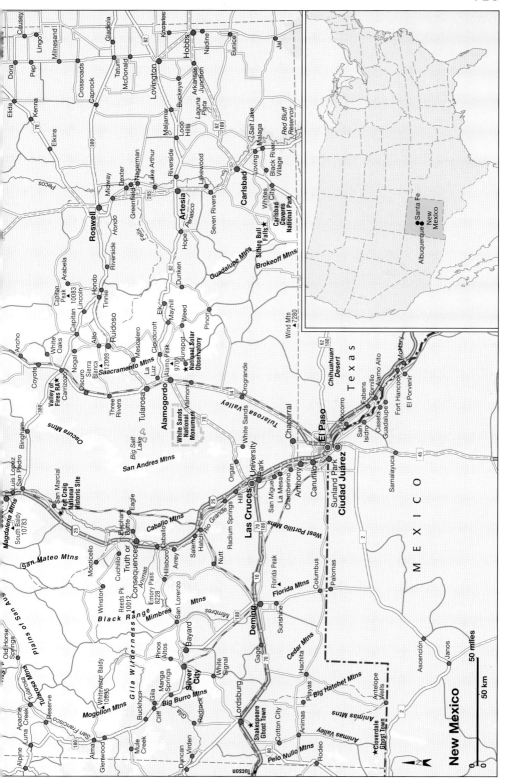

New Mexico

# NORTHERN NEW MEXICO

*Cultures mingle where the Rockies meet the desert, home of classic Southwestern towns like Santa Fe and Taos*

There's a restaurant on the Rio Grande about 35 miles (56km) north of Santa Fe where you can sit in the shade of a cottonwood tree, splash your toes in the river and sip an ice cold draft of green chile beer. The spot is just off NM 68 between Santa Fe and Taos, smack in the middle of New Mexico's Spanish Colonial heart. To the east, strung along the High Road to Taos, modest adobe villages are nestled in the Sangre de Cristo Mountains. They were settled in the early 18th century on what was then the wild fringe of the Spanish empire, and though much has changed in the intervening centuries, life there still revolves around the values of *familia y fé*, or family and faith. It's embodied by the thick mud walls and stout *vigas* (beams) of the village churches, each a treasure of Spanish Colonial architecture.

At the end of the High Road is Taos itself, a town that started, in 1631, as a frontier mission and has remained just beyond reach of the mainstream throughout various incarnations as a trading outpost, an art colony and a hippe hangout. Even today, when summer tourists seem to outnumber residents, Taos retains a scruffy, contrarian spirit.

To the west of the Rio Grande are the Jemez Mountains, created more than a million years ago by a volcanic explosion more powerful than the one that shook up Krakatoa. In its wake was left 1,000 ft (300 meters) of ash, and a bowl-shaped caldera, Valle Grande, more than 15 miles (24km) across. Another explosion of unimaginable force was conceived in these mountains, this time by the hand of man. It was the blast of the world's first atomic bomb, developed during World War II by the top-secret Manhattan Project in a former boarding school at Los Alamos.

Also in this region, in dusty villages on both sides of the Rio Grande, are the descendants of New Mexico's original inhabitants – the Pueblo people, whose ancestors built the ancient villages of Frijoles Canyon, the San Juan Basin and Chaco Canyon, and whose ceremonial dances keep the rain clouds coming, the corn growing, and their communities in harmony with spirit and nature. Farther west, where the mountains yield to the red rock of the Colorado Plateau, is the Big Rez of the Navajo Nation, a place where, in the Navajo view, the land is littered with the petrified bodies of monsters slain by the mythic Hero Twins.

In the midst of all this, both geographically and culturally, is a place known to the Spanish as La Villa Real de la Santa Fée. We call it simply Santa Fe – residents like to tout it as "the City Different." It's a town celebrated for love of art and food, for walkable streets and a vibrant Plaza, for Pueblo architecture and hospitable people. And there's that mellow, accepting spirit. Spanish speakers call it *duende*, a feeling which, as writer Larry Cheek says, "can be felt more easily than it can be translated. Call it 'magic' for starters." ❑

**PRECEDING PAGES:** sheriff's office, J. W. Eaves Movie Ranch near Santa Fe, where flicks such as *Silverado*, *Lonesome Dove* and *Wyatt Earp* were filmed.
**LEFT:** an ultralight "powerchute" floats past Ship Rock.

# SANTA FE

*Deeply rooted in its Spanish past, the City Different
is a vibrant center of art and commerce, home to Indians,
dudes and independent spirits of every stripe*

Map on page 132

It's a chilly December morning in Santa Fe. A light snow is falling on the 400-year-old New Mexico capital, dusting the glowing Christmas *farolitos* outlining the tiered, adobe buildings. Soft collars of white ring the dark *viga* beams supporting the flat roofs. Huge stalactite icicles hang from drainage *canales*. Amid the swirling snowflakes, the low-slung, earthen buildings blend so well with the rolling pinyon-and-juniper-clad foothills at the base of the Sangre de Cristo Mountains, they seem part of the land itself.

On the north side of Santa Fe's historic downtown Plaza, Pueblo Indian vendors arrive and set up beneath the long covered entrance portal of the Palace of the Governors. Huddled in blankets, they arrange their silver jewelry and pottery in front of folding chairs and wait for buyers to arrive. Pueblo people have been selling here so long, they are officially considered "exhibits" of the Museum of New Mexico, headquartered behind them. It's fitting in a way. These living links to the ancient civilizations of the Southwest seem as timeless as the buildings around them.

## City Different

On the face of it, Santa Fe is timeless. Founded as the northern capital of New Spain by colonizing Spaniards in 1610, the "City Different" is the nation's oldest capital. Four flags – Spanish, Mexican, Confederate and American – have flown from the Palace of the Governors, the oldest public building in the country. Beginning in the early 1900s, historic structures have been carefully preserved, reconstructed when necessary, and reinterpreted by historians, archaeologists, artists, architects and others drawn here from throughout the United States and abroad.

By the 1980s, this was being called Santa Fe Style: an aesthetically pleasing fusion of Indian, Spanish and Territorial art, architecture, dress, food and a laid-back lifestyle in one of the country's most beautiful small-town settings. Santa Fe today contains four historic districts and some 3,500 listed buildings, protected by one of the most powerful historical review boards in the country. In a city famous for nonconformity, this is a remarkable achievement.

Some dismiss Santa Fe as an "Adobe Disneyland," a stereotypical theme park city of "lands" filled with sage Indians, colorful Hispanics, aging Anglo hippies, trust-funders consulting alternative healers, and Georgia O'Keeffe wannabe artists. But that misses the point. Santa Fe is both real and imagined – "Fanta Se," as some locals joke – and, in the end, no one would want it any other way. Its stock in trade is to seduce you with beautiful surfaces, romantic images

**PRECEDING PAGES:** Inn at Loretto. **LEFT:** Museum of Indian Arts and Culture. **BELOW:** the Sombrero Man, owner of the world's largest sombrero collection.

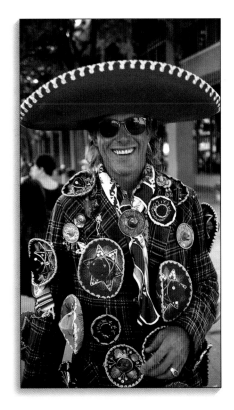

*Gift shops and galleries are filled with American Indian art.*

and teasing glimpses of the endless layers beneath them. Once you're hooked, and have sold all your worldly goods to move here, you get a brief honeymoon before reality sets in with a vengeance, puncturing whatever illusions brought you here – politics, money, ambition, creativity, personal relationships, perhaps spiritual inclinations. This is the beginning of the true, centuries-old Santa Fe Experience. If you survive that, you're a Santa Fean. It's not called the City of the Holy Faith for nothing.

While it's true that the downtown Plaza is no longer the hub of Santa Fe's social and economic life that it was for centuries, it remains the spiritual center of this city of 63,000 – a natural gathering place in times of celebration as well as sorrow, and still a pretty place to while away a warm spring day. Park your car– an inconvenience on Santa Fe's narrow, crooked streets – and begin your walking tour here.

## The Plaza

When the Spaniards first arrived in New Mexico, in 1540, they found some 70 Indian villages, or pueblos. Numerous smaller, earlier pueblos had been abandoned, including Arroyo Hondo and Pindi Pueblos, 5 miles (8km) south and southwest of the Plaza. Pedro de Peralta laid out La Villa Real de Santa Fée, as it was originally spelled, atop the pueblo of Ogapoge, which had been abandoned in A.D. 1425. He used the traditional *ordenanza* plan of a large central defensible plaza, twice as long as it was wide, surrounded by churches, administrative buildings and homes, with communal fields beyond – a layout still found in many of New Mexico's traditional villages. As planned, the colonial plaza stretched all the way to present-day St. Francis Cathedral, one block east

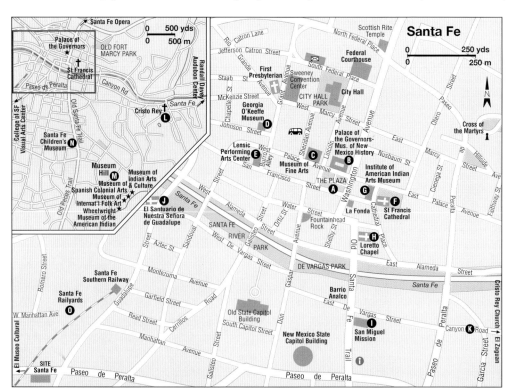

Map on page 132

of the Plaza, and had eight streets running from it: two on each corner and one from the center of each long side.

Whether the original plan was carried out is not known – all government records of colonial Spain in Santa Fe were destroyed in the 1680 Pueblo Revolt – but today's Plaza is quite small, bordered on the north by Palace Avenue, on the south by San Francisco Street, on the west by Lincoln Avenue, and on the east by Washington Avenue. Early photos show shady cottonwood trees and a picket fence around the perimeter, with a bandstand in the center. These have now been replaced by a landscaped square with a commemorative obelisk at the center, benches, and a lawn used for the hugely popular Indian and Spanish Markets and community concerts in summer.

From the **Plaza Ⓐ**, you can see five different building styles: 17th-century Spanish Pueblo, 19th-century American Territorial and Railroad Commercial (Italianate), and early 20th-century Spanish Pueblo Mission Revival and Territorial Revival. By far the oldest is the Spanish Pueblo-style **Palace of the Governors Ⓑ**, or *Casas Reales* (Royal Houses), as it was known. The Palace has been home to 60 Spanish, Mexican and American governors, occupying Pueblo Indians between 1680 and 1692, soldiers, a post office and headquarters of the School of American Archaeology (now the School of American Research on Camino del Monte Sol) as well as the New Mexico Historical Society. The building has grown smaller over the years. It once stretched north to Paseo de Peralta, occupying the locations of the present-day U.S. Post Office and Territorial-era brick Courthouse.

Two of the last governors to live in the Palace are remembered today for their accomplishments. During his 1877–81 tenure, Governor Lew Wallace

**BELOW:**
a Santa Fe art dealer shows her collection of Latin American folk art.

*A wooden Indian stands guard on the Plaza.*

succeeded in both cleaning up crime in the state by capturing Billy the Kid and writing the classic novel *Ben Hur: A Tale of the Christ* in a room whose sagging roof he described as having "the threatening downward curvature of a shipmate's cutlass." The final territorial governor, Bradford Prince, was instrumental in saving the dilapidated Palace from demolition by enlisting the help of the School of American Archaeology's Jesse Nusbaum in restoring the building to its original Spanish Colonial style. When New Mexico became a state in 1912, Prince remained in the building as director of the New Mexico Historical Society while Edgar Lee Hewett headed up both the School of American Archaeology and the Museum of New Mexico.

## Art and asses

There are now four museums under the aegis of the Museum of New Mexico. All four can be visited Tuesday to Sunday, 10am–5pm; admission is free Friday evenings, 5pm–8pm. Otherwise, be sure to purchase the $15 Museum of New Mexico pass, valid for four days – one of the city's best deals – or accompany a New Mexico resident on Sundays, when locals get in free.

The **Museum of New Mexico History** (105 E. Palace Ave, 505-827-6463, www.palaceofthegovernors.org) in the Palace has permanent exhibits of maps, documents, old photographs and artifacts such as guns, spurs, pottery, period furniture, clothing and a ceremonial death cart as well as temporary exhibits. Of particular interest are "archaeological windows" left by recent renovations that reveal the building's history.

One block west of the Palace is the **Museum of Fine Arts ☉** (107 W. Palace Ave, 505-476-5059, www.museumofnewmexico.org), interesting not only for its collection of art by New Mexico painters but its definitive 1917 Pueblo Mission Revival architecture. The building was designed by architect I. H. Rapp, who, in 1910, was responsible for the Scottish Rite Temple, modeled on the Alhambra in Spain, the outlandish pink building at the corner of Paseo de Peralta and Washington Avenue.

**BELOW:**
the Museum of Fine Arts is partly modeled on the mission church at Acoma Pueblo.

MFA concentrates on both traditional and contemporary 20th-century art by New Mexico artists such as Georgia O'Keeffe, the so-called Cinco Pintores (Will Shuster, Willard Nash, Fremont Ellis, Walter Mruk and Josef Bakos), expatriate Taos artists Dorothy Brett and Nicholai Fechin, and others attracted to New Mexico by its combination of cultures, landscape and light. Of special interest are the murals representing New Mexico history painted by Donald Beauregard, Carlos Vierra and Kenneth Chapman in St. Francis Auditorium, a popular venue for concerts.

Georgia O'Keeffe, renowned for her overscaled depictions of flowers, bones and the high-desert mesas and volcanic landmarks around her home in Abiquiu, had a love-hate relationship with Santa Fe and would not allow MFA to display her art during her lifetime. In 1997, her enduring popularity was sealed with the opening of the privately operated, 1,300-square-foot (120-sq-meter) **Georgia O'Keeffe Museum ☉** (217 Johnson St, 505-995-0785, www.okeeffemuseum.org, Tues–Sun 10am–5pm, Fri to 8pm; free Fri eves), the only museum in the United States dedicated to a woman artist. Ten simple galleries feature revolving exhibits of O'Keeffe's work between 1916 and 1980, tracing the artist's development from her Wisconsin roots and early Texas teaching career through her creative partnership with her husband, the influential New York photographer Alfred Stieglitz, and eventual move to New Mexico. The museum hosts special exhibitions of works by contemporaries of O'Keeffe, such as the fascinating exhibition in 2002 exploring the influences of O'Keeffe, Mexican artist Frida Kahlo and eccentric Canadian painter Emily Carr.

A block from the O'Keeffe Museum, quaint Burro Alley links Palace Avenue and San Francisco Street. It was named for its distinctive donkeys, which stood tied to the rails outside trading posts and could often be seen on city streets laden with firewood for sale. On the corner of Burro Alley and San Francisco is the **Lensic Performing Arts Center** ❺ (225 W. San Francisco, 505-988-1234, www.lensic.com). The Lensic (named using the initials of the previous owner's children) was built in 1931 as a movie palace and is Santa Fe's only example of Mexican Baroque Revival architecture. It was built on the site of a casino run by Doña Tules, the most infamous of Santa Fe's liberated women, who shocked newly arrived Americans by living in sin, owning businesses and dancing the Fandango. The Lensic reopened in April 2001, following a stunning $8.2 million restoration, and is now the premier venue for performing arts in the city. It is used by eight Santa Fe organizations, including Lannan Foundation Arts and Lectures, Santa Fe Pro Musica, Santa Fe Opera and Santa Fe Symphony, and also hosts numerous community events.

The southeastern corner of the Plaza, where San Francisco meets Old Santa Fe Trail, is the terminus of the historic **Santa Fe Trail**, the 800-mile (1,300-km)

Map on page 132

**BELOW:** Indian artists sell their work under the portal of the Palace of the Governors, the country's oldest public building.

*A traditional dancer shows her colors at a public performance in the Plaza .*

**BELOW:** the figure of Archbishop Jean-Baptiste Lamy looms large at St. Francis Cathedral.

trade route between Missouri and Santa Fe that flourished between 1821 and 1880. Several inns have stood at the corner of East San Francisco Street and Old Santa Fe Trail, the most recent of which is **La Fonda**, a multileveled Pueblo Mission Revival-style building modeled on Taos Pueblo. The last project of architect I. H. Rapp, it was built in 1920, during the heyday of Southwest tourism that spawned a productive partnership between hotelier Fred Harvey and the railroad. Today, the inn is virtually unchanged and is a must-see for any visitor.

## Lamy's legacy

Another quite different – but no less imposing – landmark can be seen at the other end of this block: the architecturally dissonant but elegant **St. Francis Cathedral** ✪ (213 Cathedral Place, 505-982-5619, open daily). In contrast with the thick-walled adobes around it, this French Romanesque limestone building was built between 1869 and 1886 by the French-born Catholic bishop Jean-Baptiste Lamy, portrayed in Willa Cather's novel *Death Comes for the Archbishop*. It was constructed on the site of the 1717 Parroquia, the adobe church that replaced the first colonial church after it was destroyed during the Pueblo Revolt. A portion of the old Parroquia can be seen inside the soaring building, along with La Conquistadora, the oldest Christian religious statue in the United States. La Conquistadora (the Virgin of the Conquest) was carried back to Santa Fe by a triumphant Diego de Vargas in 1692. It is a key element in the Mass celebrating Santa Fe's annual September fiesta, a Labor Day Weekend extravaganza commemorating the Reconquest. Begun in 1712, this is the oldest community festival in the United States. It culminates in the burning of the huge puppet Zozobra, or Old Man Gloom, a pagan ritual created by artist Will Shuster in the 1920s.

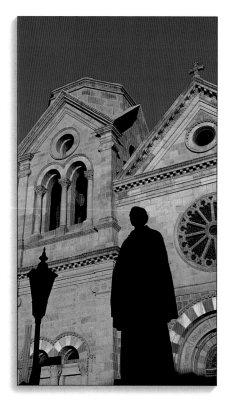

## MARÍA BENÍTEZ TEATRO FLAMENCO

Named the best flamenco dancer of her generation by *Dance* magazine, New Mexico's own María Benítez has been wowing international audiences and winning awards for her inspiring interpretations of traditional Spanish dance since the 1970s. Like swallows flying back to San Juan Capistrano, Benítez and husband Cecilio return to Santa Fe for 12 weeks each summer to perform in the intimate María Benítez Theater in the Hotel Radisson.

Teatro Flamenco, a repertory company comprised of Benítez and flamenco dancers and musicians from the United States and Spain, is showered with *oles* nightly, as its handsome, tightly costumed dancers kick up their elegant heels. The addition of a locally produced tango presentation on certain nights ratchets up the energy still further, as couples locked in tight embraces perform the sensual dance of Argentina's barrios. Call 505-982-1237 or 888-435-2636 for tickets.

Benítez's personal passion is sharing her love of Spain with young people through her performing arts school, the Institute for Spanish Arts. Her Estampa Española, a company of young New Mexican dancers, performs throughout the state. Its free performances on the Plaza during Fiesta week epitomize the legacy of Spain in New Mexico.

St. Francis Cathedral, dedicated to the patron saint of Santa Fe, reasserted the power of the mainstream Catholic Church over the folk religion that had held sway in New Mexico. In the late 20th century, however, it was American Indian power that was reasserting itself. Nothing symbolizes that better than the siting of the **Institute of American Indian Arts Museum** Ⓖ (108 Cathedral Place, 505-983-8900, www.iaiancad.org/museum; May–Oct Mon–Sat 9am–5pm, Sun noon–5pm; admission), the first of its kind, in the old Pueblo Revival post office across from the cathedral. With more than 6,500 pieces representing 3,000 Indian artists, the museum is the largest repository of contemporary Indian art in the world. Entrance is through a symbolic Pueblo kiva, or ceremonial chamber. Five galleries offer revolving exhibits. A large sculpture garden is dedicated to Allan Houser, the renowned Chiricahua Apache sculptor whose works adorn the front of the New Mexico Capitol, the Hotel Santa Fe, the Wheelwright Museum and other locations in Santa Fe.

Walking south on the Old Santa Fe Trail, you pass another of Bishop Lamy's buildings, the **Loretto Chapel** Ⓗ (211 Old Santa Fe Trail, 505-982-0092, www.lorettochapel.com; Mon–Sat 9am–6pm, Sun 10.30am–5pm; admission). The first stone masonry building in Santa Fe, the chapel was built between 1873 and 1878 for the Sisters of Loretto, who taught young women next door at Loretto Academy, now the Inn at Loretto. The decommissioned chapel is one of the most beautiful spaces in Santa Fe, frequently used for weddings and concerts. Its focal point is the **Miraculous Staircase**, an apparently unsupported spiral staircase that rises to the choir loft like a stairway to heaven. According to legend, a mysterious stranger built the staircase, then disappeared without taking payment. The faithful believe it was St. Joseph, patron saint of carpenters.

Map on page 132

**BELOW:** San Miguel Mission is one of the oldest churches still in use in the United States.

*Sculpture is displayed in public places throughout Santa Fe.*

**BELOW:** the Miraculous Stairway at Loretto Chapel.
**RIGHT:** Canyon Road gallery.

Historian Mary Jean Cook uncovered a more-down-to-earth answer, concluding that the staircase was built by a master French craftsman, Francois-Jean Rochas, who moved to a remote New Mexico canyon to become a rancher.

South of the Santa Fe River (a wonderfully shady place to sit and picnic in summer) is **San Miguel Mission ❶** (401 Old Santa Fe Trail, 505-983-3974; daily 9am–5pm, Sun to 4pm; admission). Santa Fe's oldest church is located in Barrio Analco and served the Tlaxcalan Indians who came as servants to the first Spanish colonists. Almost destroyed during the Pueblo Revolt, the church was rebuilt in 1710 and a new wooden *reredos*, or altar screen, installed in 1798. On display are rare images of Christ on buffalo and deer hides. The church's much-photographed exterior has thick buttresses holding up tapered dark brown adobe walls that contrast dramatically with the cerulean New Mexico sky.

Also near **Santa Fe River Park** is **El Santuario de Nuestra Señora de Guadalupe ❶** (100 S. Guadalupe St, 505-988-2027, open Mon–Sat,closed weekends Nov–Apr), thought to be the oldest shrine in the United States dedicated to the Virgin of Guadalupe, the patron saint of Mexico. Built in the late 1700s by Franciscan missionaries, its adobe walls are 3 feet (1 meter) thick. A 1783 oil painting, *Our Lady of Guadalupe* by Mexican artist José de Alzibar, is displayed in the chapel, as are a variety of *santos* (religious woodcarvings) and a photographic history of the building's many incarnations over the years.

## Canyon Road

Barrio Analco, just north of the New Mexico Capitol, has some of the oldest houses in the city. This is also true of **Canyon Road ❻**, an ancient thoroughfare used by Pueblo Indians crossing the Sangre de Cristo Mountains to trade at

Pecos Pueblo, a major pre-conquest village on the cultural frontier between the pueblos and plains. Hispanic settlers used it to haul firewood from the mountains, grazed sheep and goats on the hillsides, and grew chiles, beans and peaches. The main irrigation ditch, the **Acequia Madre**, still runs along the street.

Map on page 132

Starting in the early 1900s, the area became popular with tuberculosis patients from cities back east, seeking a cure in Santa Fe's warm, dry climate. Sunmount Sanitorium, now the Immaculate Heart of Mary Seminary on Mount Carmel Road, designed by I. H. Rapp, was built in 1903. It didn't attract many clients until 1914, when poet Alice Corbin, writer Mary Austin, photographer Carlos Vierra, painter Sheldon Parsons, the Cinco Pintores, and architect John Gaw Meem, among others, began moving to Santa Fe. These Bohemians built inexpensive adobe houses along Camino del Monte Sol, Canyon Road, Acequia Madre and other side roads that can still be seen today. Many are now worth a fortune, sprinkled among high-end restaurants and art galleries offering everything from traditional New Mexican arts and crafts to contemporary Indian and cowboy art.

Don't miss **El Zaguan** (545 Canyon Rd, 505-983-2567, open Mon–Fri 9am–noon, 1–5pm; garden open Mon–Sat 9am–5pm), named for its long, enclosed *portal*, typical of northern New Mexico homes. It was built in 1849 and later bought and expanded by James Johnson, a pioneering Santa Fe Trail trader. It is most famous as the 1880s home of Adolph Bandelier, the self-taught Swiss archaeologist who created the beautiful gardens west of the building. The present owner, Historic Santa Fe Foundation, rents interior apartments to artists but, unknown to many, keeps the gardens open to the public.

Canyon Road is the place to be seen on warm Friday evenings in summer, when a cross-section of Santa Fe comes out for well-attended art openings.

**BELOW:** Canyon Road, known for its numerous shops, galleries and restaurants, is one of the most desirable neighborhoods in Santa Fe.

*Painter's Alley, off Canyon Road, is one of many byways and hidden courtyards worth exploring.*

**BELOW:**
an adobe house
on Canyon Road.

Another local tradition is the annual **Christmas Eve Farolito Walk**, a traditional celebration featuring hundreds of *farolitos*, or brown bag lanterns symbolically lighting the way for the Christ Child. Many Santa Feans bring guests here to walk the 2-mile (3.2km) loop, drink hot cider, and warm themselves around bonfires called *luminarias* to the backdrop of impromptu carol singing and cries of "*Feliz Navidad!*"

Canyon Road winds for 2½ miles (4km) to its terminus in the Santa Fe watershed. One good option is to park and do the gallery walk, then drive up Canyon Road and park at **Cristo Rey Church** ❶ (1120 Canyon Rd, 505-983-8528; daily 7am–7pm; free). Designed by John Gaw Meem in 1940, it is worth seeing for its 1760 carved stone *reredos* altar screen saved from historic La Parroquia.

From here, it's a short walk uphill to the 135-acre (54-hectare) **Randall Davey Audubon Center** (1800 Upper Canyon Rd, 505-983-4609; www.nm.audubon.org; daily 9am–5pm, house tours on Mon in summer; admission), the former home of painter Randall Davey. One of only a handful of Audubon centers in the country, this delightful spot has a bird-viewing garden, nature exhibits and an easy half-mile (800-meter) trail that ascends to a cool ponderosa pine forest. More than 100 bird species use these foothills, some of which can be seen on bird walks offered every Saturday at 8am (9am Nov–Feb).

Trails adjoin those in 190-acre (77-hectare) **Santa Fe Canyon Preserve** (505-988-3867, www.tnc.org/newmexico; open daily; free), donated by the Public Service Company of New Mexico to The Nature Conservancy. Opened in April 2002, you can now hike trails around a Victorian-era dam, native willow and cottonwood bosque, and follow the original route of the Santa Fe River. One of the best things about the preserve is that it links the 25-mile (40-km)

**Dale Ball Trail System**, beginning at **Hyde Memorial State Park** (505-983-7175, 7½ miles/12km north of Santa Fe, off Hyde Park Rd), with **Atalaya Trail** on the south, which leaves from behind **St. John's College** (1160 Camino de la Cruz Blanca, 505-984-6000).

Map on page 132

## Museum Hill

The **Museum of Spanish Colonial Arts** (750 Camino Lejo, 505-982-2226, www.spanishcolonial.org; Tues–Sun 10am–5pm; admission) on nearby **Museum Hill ⓜ** is another of John Gaw Meem's graceful structures. Santa Fe's newest museum is the dream of the Spanish Colonial Arts Society, founded in 1925 to preserve and promote the Spanish influence on New Mexico's art. The society began the well-attended annual Spanish Market on the Plaza and, since 2002, has found a home to display its 3,000 artifacts in the 1930 former residence of the director of the nearby Laboratory of Anthropology, yet another Meem building.

Museum Hill has some of Santa Fe's best-loved museums, so plan on devoting a whole day here. Enjoy the views, walking the permanent labyrinth, and eating in the restaurant on the newly landscaped plaza. There is ample parking, and public transportation runs regularly between the museum complex and the downtown area.

At the top of everyone's list is the **Museum of International Folk Art** (706 Camino Lejo, 505-827-6350, www.state.nm.us/moifa; Tues–Sun 10am–5pm; admission). The museum is the repository of the world's largest collection of international folk art – some 105,000 objects donated by founder Florence Dibell Bartlett in 1953 and the Girard Foundation in 1978. Ten thousand objects

**BELOW:**
the influence of Spanish Colonial style is evident in the work of contemporary artists.

## SANTA FE OPERA

Even if you don't know your arias from your elbow, a visit to the Santa Fe Opera is an experience everyone should have once in a lifetime. Perched on a hillside next to Tesuque Pueblo, the 2,128-seat open-air theater commands panoramic views of the Jemez and Sangre de Cristo Mountains. Founded by John Crosby in 1957, the 600-member company has mounted more than 140 operas to date, including 12 world premieres. Five operas are presented each summer and typically include such favorites as Strauss, Verdi and Mozart as well as a selection of new works. Kiri Te Kanawa, Susan Graham and Dawn Upshaw are just three of the famous singers who perform here, but the Opera also nurtures new talent through its apprentice singer programs. Tickets go fast, so buy early (800-280-4654, www.santafeopera.org). Standing-room tickets are often available. Backstage tours are offered daily.

Do it right. Dress to the nines and enjoy a tailgate picnic. It's traditional to purchase gourmet fixings at nearby Tesuque Village Market. The narrow lanes of Tesuque make a great afternoon drive. Allow enough time to stop at Shidoni Foundry and Gallery and wander the 8-acre (3-hectare) sculpture garden. If you're here on a Saturday afternoon, you can watch bronzes being poured in the foundry.

*The Museum of Indian Arts and Culture sponsors lectures, workshops and field trips.*

**BELOW:** contemporary sculpture greets visitors to the Museum of Indian Arts and Culture.

from 100 countries are displayed in fascinating dioramas in the permanent exhibit *Multiple Visions: A Common Bond*. The new Neutrogena Wing exhibits textiles, costumes and masks donated by Lloyd Cotsen and the Neutrogena Corporation. The Hispanic Heritage Wing features Spanish Colonial folk art in its *Familia y Fe* exhibit.

Across the plaza is the **Museum of Indian Arts and Culture** (710 Camino Lejo, 505-827-6344, www.miaclab.org; Tues–Sun 10am–5pm; admission). MIAC opened in 1987 and displays some of the 70,000 prehistoric baskets, pots, textiles and jewelry collected by archaeologist Edgar Lee Hewett and others held in the collections of the Laboratory of Anthropology. The new exhibit, *Here, Now, and Always*, tells the story of the Indians of the Southwest in an accessible and highly enjoyable way.

Indian culture is also the focus of the small **Wheelwright Museum of the American Indian** (704 Camino Lejo, 505-982-4636, www.wheelwright.org; Mon–Sat 10am–5pm, Sun 1pm–5pm; free). The product of a unique partnership between New Englander Mary Cabot Wheelwright and Navajo medicine man Hastiin Klah, the museum was founded in 1937 to record the rich Navajo culture, which then appeared in danger of being lost forever. Happily that did not happen, and today the Wheelwright has expanded its mission and exhibits of contemporary and traditional southwestern art in a small and atmospheric building designed by artist William Penhallow Henderson. Gifts are available in a replica trading post. Special activities include storytelling on summer weekends and a children's powwow in September. This is one of the few Santa Fe museums open on Monday.

About 2 miles (3km) away, on Old Pecos Trail, is the **Santa Fe Children's**

Museum  (1050 Old Pecos Trail, 505-989-8359; Wed–Sat 10am–5pm, Sun noon–5pm), where kids can explore various aspects of art and science with dozens of hands-on exhibits, including all sorts of building materials, a green-house, a giant bubble-maker, experiments that illustrate the physical principles of motion, color and sound, and a kid-friendly climbing wall and a one-acre (½-hectare) botanical garden. Special events featuring guest artists, live music and nature walks are scheduled throughout the year.

Map on page 132

## A breath of fresh air

In recent years, several brash young newcomers have proved that the Santa Fe arts scene is beginning to shed, once and for all, the folksy frontier image that came out of the town's long romance with the past. The opening of the College of Santa Fe's new **Visual Arts Center** (1600 St. Michael's Dr, 505-473-6011, www.csf.edu) signaled a new era in City Different architecture.

*Navajo rugs are sold at the Wheelwright Museum's gift shop.*

Designed by internationally renowned architect Ricardo Legoretta, the angu-lar, postmodern building dispenses with earth-colored adobe and instead sizzles against the New Mexico sky in a palette of Mexican hot pinks and desert terra-cottas that dance with the light in unexpected ways. A tip of the hat to New Mexico's oft-ignored three decades of Mexican rule, it can also be seen as a wel-come gesture to Santa Fe's more recent wave of Mexican immigrants. These hard-working new arrivals – along with a sizeable population of Tibetan refugees – are becoming a fixture on Santa Fe's rapidly expanding **South Side**. This area now has the city's most affordable housing; restaurants serving cheap, authentic Mexican specialties; and even a Tibetan Buddhist stupa, which lends an air of the exotic to ho-hum housing developments.

**BELOW:** a mural adorns the wall of a school in the Guadalupe District.

Map on page 132

*SITE Santa Fe exhibits contemporary art in a former beer warehouse.*

**BELOW:** Santa Fe Farmers Market.

## Railyard revival

Santa Fe in recent years has expanded its self-image in many ways. Most significant is the need for new community gathering places that offer relaxed settings where all of Santa Fe's diverse residents can mingle. Coffeehouse culture is thriving, and unique partnerships are springing up among the City and County of Santa Fe, government agencies, open space advocates and nonprofit arts, environmental and conservation groups interested in maintaining Santa Fe's famous quality of life even as the city grows by leaps and bounds.

The most important community effort is the redevelopment of the **Santa Fe Railyards ⊙** in the historic **Guadalupe District**, which will occupy about a quarter of the 50-acre (20-hectare) commercial property, just southwest of downtown, for a much-anticipated new city park. This site is already the focal point of a vibrant urban renewal that includes some of Santa Fe's best restaurants, bookstores, movie theaters and shops, as well as the revived historic **Santa Fe Southern Railway** (410 S. Guadalupe, 505-989-8600, www.sfsr.com), which offers daily scenic rides to the main rail station at Lamy.

On the south side of the property, contemporary arts organizations are breathing new life into old warehouses. Since 1995, **SITE Santa Fe** (1606 Paseo de Peralta, 505-989-1199, www.sitesantafe.org; Wed–Sun 10am–5pm, Fri to 7pm; admission) has used a former beer warehouse to host the work of internationally known artists, such as environmental artist Andy Goldsworthy, whose earthwork installations wowed critics and casual visitors. **Warehouse 21** (1614 Paseo de Peralta, 505-989-4423) offers opportunities for Santa Fe's underserved teens to learn photography, music recording, radio announcing and theater. Across the street is Eric and Elise Gent's dynamic **Railyard Performance Center** (1611 Paseo de Peralta, 505-982-8309), which pulsates regularly with African dance and drumming classes and all-ages concerts.

## Santa Fe spirit

Next door is **El Museo Cultural** (1615-B Paseo de Peralta, 505-992-0591; Tues–Sun 1pm–5pm; free), an exciting work-in-progress whose mission is to highlight nothing less than the contemporary Hispanic culture of the Americas. To that end, El Museo hosts conferences, Spanish-language plays, poetry workshops, dance and marimba classes, photo exhibits and community events such as 2002's *Moving Waters, Growing Traditions*, featuring exhibits, field trips, readings and weekend lectures exploring the role of water in New Mexico's land-based cultures.

There is no better example of Santa Fe's support of its rich multicultural agricultural traditions than the well-attended **Santa Fe Farmers Market** (505-983-4098; year round; Tues and Sat 8am–noon in summer; Nov–April winter market is held Sat 9am–1pm inside El Museo Cultural). The lively market brings together a cross-section of northern New Mexico – young and old, newcomer and native, Hispanic, Anglo and Indian – to enjoy traditional foods, organic produce grown on farms throughout the region, flowers, folk crafts, music and light-hearted, easygoing camaraderie. This is what Santa Fe is all about. ❏

# Festivals and Fiestas

"**B**urn him! Burn him!" shouts the mob packed into Fort Marcy Park. The object of their scorn is a 44-ft-high (13-meter) puppet with glowing eyes called Zozobra. As night falls, Old Man Gloom, as he's known, moans and growls in a gravelly voice, his complaints the personification of all the mistakes and disappointments of the year. Fire Dancers and children dressed as Little Glooms dance around him in a pagan frenzy. Then, suddenly, Zozobra goes up in flames. The crowd roars. *Que Viva La Fiesta*!

The burning of Zozobra has marked the beginning of Fiesta in Santa Fe since 1926, when artist Will Shuster reinvented the traditional ceremony commemorating the 1692 Reconquest of New Mexico as a four-day street party celebrating Spanish Colonial culture. Held the week after Labor Day, festivities include a reenactment of Diego de Vargas's entry into Santa Fe, the crowning of a Fiesta Queen, plays, mariachi concerts, entertainment on the Plaza, the popular Desfile de los Ninos (Pet Parade), and the Historical/Hysterical parade, with floats, marching bands and waving politicians. The finale is a Fiesta Mass at St. Francis Cathedral and a candlelight parade to Cross of the Martyrs.

Fiesta is just one example of the rich multicultural blending that makes Santa Fe such a wonderful place to let your hair down. Much of the action is on the Plaza, which hosts festivities year-round, from free concerts, Fourth of July pancake breakfasts and lowrider car rallies to October's annual Aids walk.

By far the most popular events are the juried Spanish and Indian Markets in July and August, respectively, where buyers from all over the world converge on Santa Fe to meet the top traditional and contemporary artisans in the Southwest. Indian Market (known affectionately as "Indian Markup" by participants) is the largest contemporary American Indian art event in the world. Some $130 million is generated for the roughly 1,200 exhibiting artists, galleries, and the tourism industry.

Summer brings the crowds, but it's Christmas that steals a visitor's heart forever. Fairy lights and *farolito* lanterns twinkle in the snow, and an elaborate Santa Claus ice sculpture carved by chefs from La Fonda Hotel lasts for weeks on the Plaza, preserved by the frigid temperatures. In early December, Todos Vamos a Belen (Let's All Go to Bethlehem), a series of sketches and songs celebrating Christmas in New Mexico, kicks off festivities in the Museum of Fine Arts. Just before Christmas, Las Posadas (The Inns), a traditional reenactment of Mary and Joseph's search for lodging, takes place on the rooftops around the Plaza.

On Christmas Eve, thousands congregate on Canyon Road to drink hot cider and sing carols by *luminarias* (bonfires), lit by residents to guide the faithful to the Christ Child. On Christmas Day, it is traditional to visit nearby Indian pueblos to view winter dances celebrating the Buffalo and Deer. Both Hispanic churches and Indian pueblos perform the Matachines, a dance commemorating the meeting of Old Spain and New World in a centuries-old costume drama. ❑

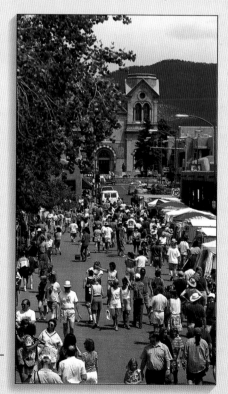

**RIGHT:** shoppers crowd the streets during Spanish Market.

# JEMEZ MOUNTAINS AND PAJARITO PLATEAU

Map on page 150

*Indian pueblos – ancient and contemporary – surround
the birthplace of the atomic bomb in a spectacular
volcanic mountain range*

The 11th and 12th centuries were a period of enormous upheaval in New Mexico. An extended drought, coupled with cooler temperatures, led to the sudden collapse of the agriculturally based Chaco empire. Thousands of desperate farming families from villages all over the San Juan Basin fled to the surrounding mountains, where moisture was greater and wild game and plants were abundant.

Many headed southeast into the volcanic Jemez Mountains, a traditional pilgrimage spot for obtaining obsidian for tools and arrowheads. On the other side of the enormous volcanic caldera, they found the unpopulated Pajarito Plateau, a 300-mile-long (480-km) mesa that had been created by ash fallout from the 1.2-million-year-old volcano. There, on the moist eastern edge of the mountains, overlooking the Rio Grande basin, the refugees found sanctuary.

It must have been with joy and relief that they put down roots amid the mesas and deep canyons carved by tributaries of the Rio Grande. Their homes were an inventive mixture of what they already knew: small masonry pueblos built directly against soft volcanic tuff cliffs that could be carved into simple cave rooms for winter retreats. Food was again abundant, with deer, elk and other game that were hunted in winter and wild foods, such as the nutritious nuts that grew on surrounding pinyon trees, that were harvested every fall. Women even began making their distinctive black-and-white pots again, creating unique mugs, bowls and effigy pots that celebrated their new home.

Frijoles Canyon, the gateway to Bandelier National Monument, was the center of this new Jemez civilization. Here the banks of the year-round Frijoles River could be farmed close to homes with warm southern exposures. A new wave of Four Corners immigrants built Tyuonyi, a large pueblo on the canyon floor, in the late 1200s. But not long after, swelling populations and colder temperatures forced another migration. Clans united by shared languages and customs moved to warmer lowlands and began building self-contained pueblos along the Rio Grande, where their descendants live today.

## Hidden worlds

The 150-mile (240-km) loop drive from **Santa Fe ❶** on the **Jemez Mountains National Scenic Byway** is immensely satisfying. It takes in eight of New Mexico's 19 pueblos and passes several important ancestral pueblo sites. The high country offers cool, pine-scented campgrounds and miles of trails perfect for hiking in summer and cross-country skiing in winter.

**PRECEDING PAGES:**
Santa Clara Pueblo.
**LEFT:** Bandelier
National Monument.
**BELOW:** kiva ladder
at Coronado State
Monument.

Geologists will enjoy numerous volcanic features in the mountains, many now protected in **Valles Caldera National Preserve**, the state's newest natural park.

Most fascinating of all is the sense of entering hidden worlds in the mountains. In the government defense town of Los Alamos, industrial-park-style buildings mysteriously emerge from the ponderosa forest with no identifying features except a series of cryptic numbers. One of the world's largest concentrations of archaeological sites (7,000 at last count) hides in plain sight on the Pajarito Plateau, waiting to be discovered in backcountry canyons still sacred to modern pueblos. And in the rustic little resort town of Jemez Springs, natural and developed hot springs emerge right in the river, offering sanctuary for stressed-out weekend refugees from fast-track Albuquerque.

## Cultural revival

Begin your tour on US 285/84 at **Tesuque Pueblo ❷** (RR 42, Box 360-T, Santa Fe, NM 87506; 505-983-2667), 9 miles (15km) north of Santa Fe. This conservative pueblo encompasses 17,000 acres (7,000 hectares), including irrigated farmland near the Rio Grande and ponderosa high country in Santa Fe National Forest. The current pueblo, with a population of 450 people, is situated around a large plaza dating to 1694. It replaced a pre-1200 pueblo that was abandoned during the Pueblo Revolt. Sadly, the historic church was burned down by arsonists in 2002. It was rebuilt and rededicated in 2005.

Tesuque Pueblo operates a suites hotel in Santa Fe, the **Tesuque Flea Market** next to the Santa Fe Opera, and **Camel Rock Casino** (US 285/84; tel: 800-GO-CAMEL), which features top name acts and is popular with summer visitors to the Santa Fe Opera, just to the south. There are dances at the pueblo on the Feast of

**BELOW:**
a young dancer at
Santa Clara Pueblo
feast day.

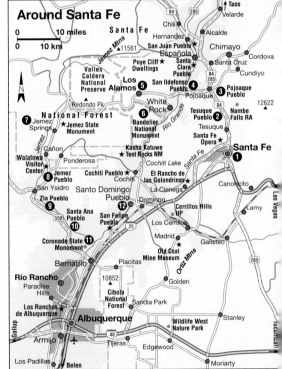

San Diego, Christmas Day, Kings Day in January, and the Corn Dance on the first weekend of June. The pueblo is known for its brightly painted ceramic rain god figurines, which, after many years, are again being produced by Tesuque artists.

Six miles (10km) up the road, **Pojoaque Pueblo** ❸ (505-455-3334), which straddles the highway at the junction of US 285/84 and 501, is making a big comeback after being abandoned in 1915 following a smallpox epidemic. The Tourist Information Center offers travel information, maps and recommendations on many northern New Mexico attractions. Modern tribal enterprises include a shopping center, restaurants, two hotels, a casino, a gas station and the 36-hole Towa Golf Course. Although it appears modern, Pojoaque remains firmly rooted in the past. Like several other pueblos, it is reintroducing buffalo on its lands and encouraging young people to learn traditional arts under the tutelage of established potters, painters, sculptors and weavers. Art classes are offered at the attractive Poeh Cultural Center. Pojoaque's feast day is celebrated on December 12, a day it shares with the Virgin of Guadalupe.

US 502 heads west into the mountains along the southern margin of the Española Valley. To the north are the prominent badlands, or Las Barrancas, a series of pinkish eroded rocks where paleontologists have found skeletons of extinct southwestern camels. Numerous small Hispanic villages with names like Jacona and El Rancho line the fertile valley floor, clustered around shady bosques along the Pojoaque River. Any of the turnoffs here offer an interesting backway through tiny settlements wedged into Indian lands in the shadow of Black Mesa, an isolated volcanic promontory east of the Rio Grande.

Pueblos in the Española Valley consider Black Mesa sacred, none more so than **San Ildefonso Pueblo** ❹ (505-455-3549) a few miles up the road, whose residents barricaded themselves atop the mesa and resisted the Reconquest of New Mexico by Diego de Vargas in 1694. The ancestors of today's residents of San Ildefonso moved from Bandelier National Monument during the 1300s, following a long drought.

The ancestral link to Bandelier bore unexpected fruit in 1919, when archaeologist Edgar Hewett shared examples of the pottery he was uncovering with San Ildefonso elder Julian Martinez and his potter wife Maria. The Martinezes, and later their son Popovi Da, revived the subtle black-on-black pottery that is now a hallmark of the pueblo. It is found in major collections throughout the world. The pueblo museum has examples of Maria's work, and a number of small, family-owned shops sell pottery as well as Pueblo paintings, embroidery, moccasins and silver jewelry. Visitors are welcome at ceremonial dances on the historic plaza throughout the year, including the evocative Christmas Day Buffalo Dance and feast day celebration on January 23.

Black-on-black, as well as polished red pottery, is also found at **Santa Clara Pueblo** (505-753-7330), just north of San Ildefonso on NM 30. With 2,600 residents, Santa Clara is the second largest of the Eight Northern Pueblos, with 50,000 acres (20,000 hectares) of land. Unique among these pueblos, Santa Clara's ancestral home is set nearby at the **Puye Cliff Dwellings**, in the lower reaches of the Pajarito ("little

**Map on page 150**

**BELOW:** dancers take a break during festivities at San Ildefonso Pueblo.

*A Los Alamos "museum" sells laboratory surplus.*

**BELOW:** Robert Oppenheimer figures prominently in an exhibit on the Manhattan Project at the Bradbury Science Museum.

bird") Plateau. Unfortunately, these ruins are presently closed to the public, after 700 acres (280 hectares) of pueblo land were damaged by the 2000 Cerro Grande Fire. You are welcome to explore the modern pueblo along the Rio Grande, which was founded in the 1400s. Santa Clara Pueblo owns Big Rock Casino and Bowling Alley in Española, as well as Black Mesa Golf Course, and celebrates its feast day on August 12.

## Los Alamos and Bandelier National Monument

After crossing the Rio Grande via Otowi Bridge, US 502 winds onto the Pajarito Plateau to **Los Alamos ❺**. You can bypass the town by picking up NM 4, which takes you directly through White Rock to Bandelier, or visit the town and return to NM 4 via US 501.

When Manhattan Project leaders Robert Oppenheimer and General Leslie Groves visited this mesa in the fall of 1942, it had been used for more than 20 years as Los Alamos Ranch School, an academy where well-to-do boys studied the classics and received an outdoor education. Beginning in April 1943, the government took over the facility, installing scientists who raced to beat Germany in developing the atomic bomb. You can learn more about the Manhattan Project at the **Bradbury Science Museum** (15th and Central, 505-667-4444; Tues–Fri 9am–5pm, Sat–Sun 1pm–5pm; free). Also of interest is the **Los Alamos Historical Museum** (1921 Juniper St, 505-662-4493; Mon–Sat 9.30am–4.30pm, Sun 11am–5pm; free), which has exhibits on the area's geology, anthropology and recent history. The **Fuller Lodge Arts Center** next door is also worth a stop to view fine arts. Both are housed in historic Ranch School buildings.

Just south of Los Alamos is **Bandelier National Monument ❻** (off NM 4,

505-672-3861, www.nps.gov/band; open daily; admission). Highlights along the 1.4-mile-long (2.3-km) Main Loop Trail through Frijoles Canyon include Long House, Alcove House and other cave-like homes carved into south-facing cliffs; two-story Tyuonyi Pueblo; and Ceremonial Cave, located at the top of three very steep ladders 150 ft (46 meters) above the canyon floor. More than 2,600 archaeological sites have been found here, most in the 75 percent of the park protected as wilderness. Seventy miles (110km) of trails make this a hiker's paradise. One of the best day hikes is the Falls Trail, which descends to the Rio Grande to two waterfalls, passing a rare maar volcano.

Bandelier is named in honor of the famous Swiss-born archaeologist Adolph Bandelier, who explored most of New Mexico's pueblos on foot in the 1880s. Bandelier was led to the park that eventually bore his name in 1880, following a guide from Cochiti Pueblo, whose members make regular pilgrimages here. Excavation of the site did not take place until 1919, when Edgar Hewett, founder of the School of American Research in Santa Fe, began working on the Pajarito Plateau. Hewett lobbied tirelessly for the whole Pajarito Plateau to be made a national park and wrote the landmark 1906 Antiquities Act that allows the U.S. president to protect threatened cultural resources by naming them national monuments. Bandelier was granted such protection in 1916.

Bandelier erupted in controversy in May 2000, when a prescribed burn at the park went out of control in hot, windy conditions. The Cerro Grande Fire destroyed thousands of acres of national forest and some 400 homes in Los Alamos, forced the evacuation of 18,000 people, and led to the resignation of the park's longtime superintendent. The heartbreaking sight of blackened tree trunks is still visible along NM 4.

*An exhibit at the Bradbury Science Museum chronicles the development of nuclear weapons.*

**BELOW:** Long House Ruins, Bandelier National Monument.

## ADOLPH BANDELIER

Swiss-born Adolph Bandelier developed a passion for anthropology during the American Civil War while working in an office in Illinois. After reading extensively about North American archaeology, he apprenticed himself to anthropologist Lewis Henry Morgan, whose theories on social evolution later influenced Friedrich Engels and Karl Marx. Under Morgan's tutelage, Bandelier wrote an important series of monographs on the political organization of the Aztec culture. He had never even been to Mexico.

Wanderlust caught up with Bandelier in 1880, when, with the help of Morgan and the newly formed Archaeological Institute of America, he received funding to collect data on the native cultures of the Southwest. For the next five years, he devoted himself to his subject, traveling constantly throughout New Mexico, mostly on foot. "I have known many scholars and some heroes," said journalist Charles Lummis. "But they seldom come in the same package."

Bandelier's 1890 report on the Indian ruins of the Southwest led directly to the founding of the School of American Archaeology in Santa Fe. Its director, archaeologist Edgar Lee Hewett, undertook extensive excavations of the Pajarito Plateau in 1907 and lobbied hard for the national monument that would eventually bear Bandelier's name.

*The Santa Ana Star is one of more than 10 Indian casinos in New Mexico.*

**BELOW:** Jemez State Monument.

## Valles Caldera and the Jemez Mountains

A few miles west of Bandelier, a pleasant forest trail leads to a scenic overlook above Frijoles Canyon. In winter, cross-country skiers enjoy this loop. Continuing east, the highway skirts majestic Valle Grande, part of the 16-mile (26-km) caldera protected as **Valles Caldera National Preserve** (877-851-8946; www.vallescaldera.gov). Roadside interpretive signs tell the story of the volcanic activity that led to the explosion, more than a million years ago, that created the Jemez Mountains. The preserve is open for hiking, fishing, hunting and wagon rides, by reservation only. Call for information.

**Redondo Peak** in Valles Caldera remains sacred to the people of Jemez Pueblo who migrated into the nearby Jemez Springs area from the vicinity of Mesa Verde in the 1100s. They built numerous multistory pueblos on the steep mesa tops of San Diego Canyon, but by the early 1600s, European diseases and warfare had decimated the population. The survivors coalesced into two pueblos: Guisewa in Jemez Springs and Walatowa, a few miles to the south. By 1630, even Guisewa had been abandoned, leaving only a handful of people at Walatowa.

Guisewa is now protected as **Jemez State Monument** (NM 4, 505-829-3530; daily 8am–5pm; admission), at the north end of **Jemez Springs ❼**. If you spend the night here, you'll have plenty of time for a leisurely soak in the 1870s **Jemez Bath House** (Jemez Springs Plaza, 505-829-3303; daily 10am–7.30pm, extended summer hours), enjoy a hearty meal at a nearby inn, and explore the monument.

At Jemez State Monument, the ruined 1622 Spanish mission church dominates the scene, with its adjoining *convento* and cloisters. The unexcavated remains of the large farming pueblo are now buried beneath hummocks, and only a restored great kiva hints at its former importance. The small museum has

excellent interpretive exhibits, incorporating both anthropological and tribal viewpoints. Kids will enjoy touching the reproduction turkey-feather blankets in the rear and grinding corn on a mano and metate.

Map on page 150

A highlight of the museum is rare Jemez black-on-white pottery whose utilitarian beauty is still evident centuries later. In 1706, when the remaining Jemez moved to Walatowa, they ceased making black-on-white pottery and destroyed most of what remained to protest the Spanish Reconquest. When Jemez pottery was later revived, it resembled the distinctive black-on-red and black-on-tan ware made at neighboring Zia Pueblo. **Jemez Pueblo ❽** has more than its share of well-known artists and writers, including Pulitzer Prize-winning author N. Scott Momaday and sculptor Cliff Fragua, whose rendering of Popé, a leader of the Pueblo Rebellion, is one of two statues representing New Mexico in the U.S. Capitol.

Jemez is a closed pueblo, only open on the Feast Day of San Diego on November 12 and for holiday dances. Its main contact with the public is at its attractive new **Walatowa Visitor Center** (7413 Hwy 4, 505-834-7235, www.jemezpueblo.com; open daily), amid the glorious red rocks north of Walatowa. The facility has exhibits on the area's geology, natural and cultural history, a small museum, tourist information and pottery displays. Cultural tours and fishing trips on the pueblo can also be arranged here.

## Pueblo resort

Just west of the junction of NM 4 and US 550 is **Zia Pueblo ❾** (505-867-3304), whose sun sign now appears on the state flag. On arid lands, Zia has struggled throughout its history and was shunned by other pueblos after its members allied with the Spanish during the Reconquest. About 700 people live here and are known mainly for pottery. Fishing is available on Zia Lake.

In contrast, there's plenty for visitors to see and do at **Santa Ana Pueblo ❿** (2 Dove Rd, Bernalillo; 505-867-3301). The tribe has several well-run enterprises, including a new casino showcasing popular entertainers, a championship golf course with a clubhouse featuring gourmet dining, and a wholesale agriculture business specializing in organic produce. Elements of all these endeavors are incorporated into the pueblo's star attraction, the 500-acre (200-hectare) Hyatt Regency Tamaya Resort and Spa, the first luxury resort on Indian land in northern New Mexico. Guests can golf, take a walk with a naturalist along a restored bosque on the Rio Grande, tour sacred lands on horseback, dine in gourmet restaurants, and relax in a full-service spa using native-inspired products.

Santa Ana artisans are renowned for their crosses of inlaid straw and polished polychrome pottery, which were revived several decades ago to great acclaim. These and other artworks adorn every room of the hotel whose circular, multistory layout evokes the pueblo architecture of Chaco Canyon. The ancestral pueblo of Tamaya, 9 miles (15km) away, is closed to visitors except on feast days, but the hotel runs a small attractive cultural center, where you can learn about history and customs from a tribal member.

By the time Coronado wintered in the Albuquerque area in 1540, the Keresan-speaking people of Tamaya

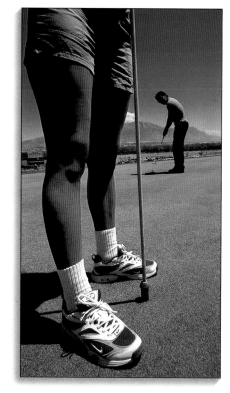

**BELOW:** Santa Ana Pueblo's Tamaya Resort features a championship golf course.

Map on page 150

*Drinking buddies at Silva's Bar, Bernalillo.*

**BELOW:** Tent Rocks.
**RIGHT:** Upper Frijoles Falls, Bandelier National Monument.

had moved closer to the Rio Grande. Their nearest neighbor was the Tiwa-speaking pueblo of Kuaua, one of a dozen towns in the province of Tiguex, a 30-mile (50-km) corridor flanking the Rio Grande. Founded in AD 1300, Kuaua grew into a 1,200-room fortress at the crossroads between the Ancestral Pueblo and Mogollon cultures. Although no hard evidence has been found, historians believe that its leaders may have offered the entire pueblo of Kuaua to Coronado and his men as winter quarters, after news of their conquest of Zuni spread north.

## Historic homesteads

**Coronado State Monument ⓫** (NM 44, Bernalillo, 505-867-5351; Wed–Mon 9am–5pm; admission) is one of those places where so little remains of the past, you'll have to imagine the rest. An excellent self-guided trail circles the park, with stops at capped adobe walls and reconstructed kivas that show both Mogollon and Ancestral Pueblo influences. A small museum offers an overview of the Indian and Hispanic history of the area, where kids can try on Spanish armor and beat a drum. A separate building showcases the park's main draw, its mysterious ceremonial kachina murals, which were removed for safekeeping from the great kiva following excavations by the Civilian Conservation Corps during the 400th anniversary of Coronado's arrival.

There are several historic homesteads in the Hispanic town of **Bernalillo** and nearby **Placitas**, a charming village in the Sandia foothills with terrific views of Mount Taylor, the Jemez Mountains and Cabezon Peak. A short way north on Interstate 25 is **San Felipe Pueblo**, (PO Box 4339, San Felipe Pueblo, NM 87001, 505-876-3381), founded in 1706, which sits nestled against the west bank of the Rio Grande beneath Black Mesa. The tribe runs the popular Hollywood Casino east of the interstate. The Pueblo itself is usually closed to visitors except on feast days.

The tribe's lands adjoin those of **Santo Domingo** ⓬ (PO Box 99, Santo Domingo Pueblo, NM 87052, 505-465-2214), one of New Mexico's largest Indian villages, with about 3,200 residents. Highly traditional Santo Domingo is known for its turquoise jewelry and huge Corn Dance, held on its feast day in August. The tribe runs a small arts and crafts center at the pueblo and a discount gas station with the best prices in northern New Mexico.

**Cochiti Pueblo** (PO Box 70, Cochiti Pueblo, NM 87041, 505-465-2244) is situated in the volcanic country to the west of the La Bajada incline not far from its ancestral home at Bandelier. The focal point of this Keresan-speaking community of 1,200 residents is the 1598 **San Buenaventura de Cochiti Church**, which hosts the tribe's feast day ceremonies on July 14.

Cochiti is well known for its ceremonial drums and storyteller pottery figures, which were first popularized by Helen Cordero. **Cochiti Reservoir** has boating and a large campground. Outdoors enthusiasts will also enjoy the pleasant 2-mile (3-km) loop hike at **Kasha Katuwe Tent Rocks National Monument** (435 Montano Rd NE, 505-761-8700; daily 7am–6pm; day-use fee), which protects 4,100 acres (1,700 hectares) of eerie minaret-shaped cones of pale volcanic tuff on lands sacred to the Cochiti. ❑

# GEORGIA O'KEEFFE COUNTRY

*Traditional Hispanic and Indian villages are set
in a desert landscape whose stark beauty captured the
imagination of a visionary American artist*

Map on page 162

"It fit me exactly," artist Georgia O'Keeffe said of northern New Mexico. And touring her Abiquiu home, one sees just how close the fit was. Particularly revealing is her studio – a high-ceilinged room almost completely devoid of color. Whitewash covers adobe walls. Ceilings, doors and cupboards are unadorned wood. A huge worktable is thriftily constructed of plywood atop sawhorses. Even O'Keeffe's artwork in this room is white: a sinuous sculpture as smooth as gleaming bone on a sideboard, one of her cloud paintings on the wall, and a simple pot she made in the last years of her life on a windowsill.

The meditative calm of the room is a telling counterpoint to the magnificent view of the Chama River Valley framed by huge picture windows which, as O'Keeffe might say, "fills the space in a beautiful way." On the lush banks of the Rio Chama are the three cottonwoods whose skeletal forms she painted in winter. Farther east are the pastel-hued mesas and crumbling badlands of the White Place. O'Keeffe spent countless hours walking here, picking up the rocks and bones that for her symbolized the "wideness and wonder of the world as I live in it."

**PRECEDING PAGES:**
Gallina Canyon,
Abiquiu.
**LEFT:** Ghost Ranch.
**BELOW:** Georgia
O'Keeffe, ca. 1940.

## Historic hot spots

A tour of the country O'Keeffe called home begins in **Española ❶**, a busy agricultural center 20 minutes north of Santa Fe at the junction of US 84 and 285. Founded in the mid-1800s, Española today is an odd mix of traditional and contemporary. Here, the Saints and Sinners Liquor Store sits across from the Oasis Cyber Café. Roadside stands sell strings of bright red chiles, sweet peas and corn in the shadow of Wal-Mart. And the traditional Saturday night *paseo* of young men courting pretty girls involves not fine clothes but Española's famous "lowrider" cars, bucking up and down like prancing ponies with bright paint, flashing lights and ear-splitting stereos.

Española has always been at the crossroads of history. Two miles (3km) north of town, adjoining the Tewa village of San Juan Pueblo, are the remains of New Mexico's first capital, founded by Don Juan de Oñate in 1598. Another former Spanish colonial settlement, **Santa Cruz**, is 3 miles (5km) east of Española. Founded by Don Diego de Vargas in 1693, it was for some years second in size only to Santa Fe.

The people of **San Juan Pueblo ❷** (505-852-4400), who in the 1500s were living in two Rio Grande villages – Ok'he and Yunge – were the first to bear the brunt of Spanish colonization. When Oñate and his 400 settlers arrived in New Mexico, they first moved into Ok'he, which Oñate renamed San Juan de los Caballeros. When this site proved inhospitable, he took over Yunge and renamed it San Gabriel. In 1675, a San Juan religious leader named Popé was

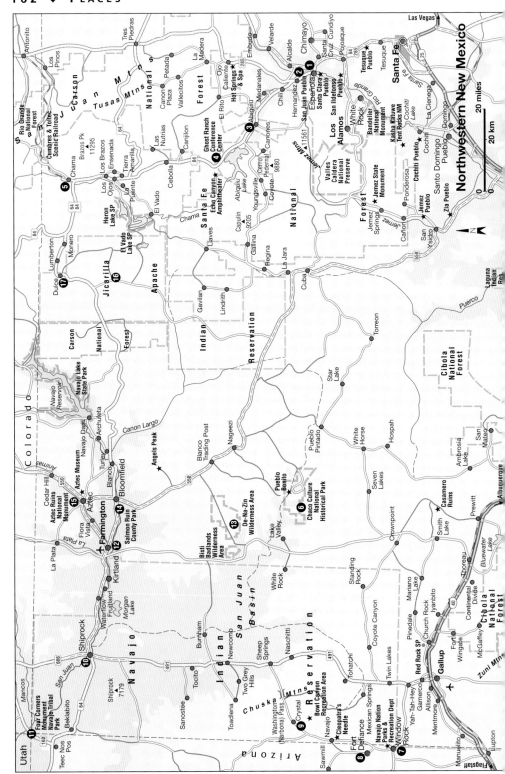

Northwestern New Mexico

flogged for practicing what the padres regarded as sorcery. Soon after, Popé began plotting an uprising that resulted in the Pueblo Revolt of 1680.

Today, San Juan serves as the administrative headquarters of the Eight Northern Pueblos, which in 2003 opened the attractive **Eight Northern Indian Pueblos Visitors Center** (505-747-1593; www.8northern.org) at the pueblo. As well as offering an information center, museum and gift shop, the new building is the permanent home of the annual **Eight Northern Indian Pueblos Artists and Craftsmen Show**, an event that rivals Santa Fe's Indian Market in popularity. The other highlight of the year is the pueblo's feast day on June 24, when hundreds of traditional dancers throng the plaza. The O'Ke Oweegne Arts and Crafts Cooperative is a good place to buy the pueblo's famous incised red pottery.

The modern residents of San Juan Pueblo are descendants of immigrants from the Mesa Verde area of Colorado, who moved south to the Rio Grande following a long drought in the 1200s. They built farming villages on river terraces throughout the Chama valley, spacing them roughly a day's walk, or 5 miles (8km), apart. The remains of the 700-room pueblo of Poshouinge can be seen from a half-mile trail just off US 84, 2½ miles (4km) south of Abiquiu.

## Open-door policy

Poshouingue was inhabited for about a century before its residents moved on, this time to the larger San Juan and Santa Clara Pueblos on the Rio Grande. Their departure may have been hastened by the arrival of Navajos and Apaches. Their presence, and the subsequent arrival of Utes and Comanches from the northern Plains, delayed settlement of the lower Chama River Valley until the 1700s and even later in the upper Chama. A few Spanish families founded the village of Santa Rosa de Lima, 3 miles (5km) south of modern-day Abiquiu, in 1734, but were forced to abandon it after several colonists were killed by Comanches.

In 1750, settlers reoccupied the village but this time brought with them a group of *genizaros*, former Indian captives who had become Hispanicized. Considered the lowest rung on New Mexico's complex social ladder, they were given land in exchange for establishing villages on the frontier, which served as buffers between hostile natives and Hispanic settlements. In 1754, a group of *genizaros* moved 3 miles (5km) upriver to settle a former Indian pueblo, which they renamed Santo Tomas de Abiquiu.

Santa Rosa is long gone but **Abiquiu ❸** was an instant success. Its open-door policy was a magnet for settlers unable to get ahead in socially conscious Santa Fe. By 1793, Abiquiu had a population of 1,363 and was New Mexico's third largest town. Abiquiu's location on a cultural frontier was a distinct advantage. Plains Indians arrived every fall to trade deerskins for Spanish horses, corn and slaves. Then, in 1829, Antonio Armijo blazed the 1,200-mile (1,900-km) Spanish Trail from Abiquiu to the Pacific Coast, and traders began arriving to outfit themselves in Abiquiu before setting off in their wagons.

By the mid-1800s, trade at Abiquiu equaled that of Taos. One store was owned by Taos entrepreneur and former mountain man Ceran St. Vrain. The army also

Map on page 162

**BELOW:** deer dancer, San Juan Pueblo, 1935.

*A roadside grave-stone marks the final resting place of an unfortunate traveler.*

**BELOW:** a strip of reddish-brown earth leads drivers into the backcountry near Abiquiu.

used the village as a base from which to patrol the surrounding area for Navajos, Utes and Jicarilla Apaches. From 1852 to 1873, Abiquiu was headquarters for a Ute Indian agency and trading post.

It helps to know something about Abiquiu's remarkable history because very little of it is visible in the sleepy village today. Crumbling adobes slumber in the sun around a large plaza, anchored on its east side by the lovely church designed in the 1940s by architect John Gaw Meem. Two Penitente *moradas* and a series of crosses around the village hint at the struggle between Archbishop Lamy's church and the Penitente order that took hold in remote northern New Mexico after the area was abandoned by Spanish priests.

## Ghost Ranch and the O'Keeffe house

It took 10 years for Georgia O'Keeffe to talk the Catholic Church into selling her the ruined adobe in Abiquiu, parts of which date to 1760. She moved into the place in 1949, four years after an extensive remodeling of the 3-acre (1.2-hectare) property by close friend Maria Chabot. From then on, she spent winters in Abiquiu and summers at her Ghost Ranch property until ill health forced her to move to Santa Fe in 1984. She died there in 1986 at the age of 98.

Today, the home is a walled oasis, with shade trees, flower beds and a vegetable garden watered by the community *acequia*. Inside, thrifty Midwestern touches, such as cupboards built into the two-foot-thick adobe walls and well-maintained mangles, refrigerators and other 1950s appliances, blend seamlessly with design elements inspired by the lofts of New York City – floor-to-ceiling windows and elegant Eames chairs topped by bright cushions designed by Andre Girard. The Georgia O'Keeffe Foundation runs one-hour tours of the house by appointment

only on Tuesday, Thursday and Friday, April to November. Group size is limited to 12. Call well in advance for reservations (505-685-4539).

Tours of the O'Keeffe property begin at the Foundation's offices, across the street in the **Abiquiu Inn** (505-685-4378 or 800-447-5621; www/abiquiuinn.com). The attractive adobe complex is a pleasant place to spend the night or enjoy a Middle Eastern meal. It is part of the 1,600 acres (650 hectares) owned by **Dar Al Islam** (505-685-4515; www.daralislam.org), which began building a Muslim community here in the 1980s that has since been reorganized into an educational and retreat center. Its large mosque, designed by renowned Egyptian architect Hassan Fathi, is behind the inn, off FR 155. Visitors are welcome.

This area has a long history of religious tolerance, and Dar Al Islam isn't the only religious community that has made its home here. **Christ in the Desert Monastery** (www.christdesert.org) was built by Benedictine monks in 1962 and is located 13 miles (21km) down FR 151 in Chama River Canyon, 27 miles (44km) north of Abiquiu. Drive out here to walk, meditate, and enjoy the silence. There is a gift shop, where you can make arrangements for a longer retreat.

Twelve miles (19km) northwest of Abiquiu is **Ghost Ranch Conference Center ❹** (877-804-4678; www.newmexico-ghostranch.org). Started as a dude ranch by publisher Arthur Pack, who later donated the property to the Presbyterian Church, Ghost Ranch is a destination unto itself. Visitors can take a workshop, hike into the canyons, and enjoy inexpensive lodging and meals in a peaceful atmosphere. Two excellent museums are on the property. The **Florence Hawley Ellis Anthropology Museum** traces the human history of the area, while the **Ruth Hall Paleontology Museum** has information about the colorful rock formations behind Ghost Ranch and the dinosaurs that were unearthed there.

**BELOW:** crosses stand sentinel outside a *morada*, a meeting house of the secretive Penitente fraternity.

*Small chapels remind travelers of the Church's deep roots throughout the region.*

**BELOW:** eroded bluffs similar to those that inspired Georgia O'Keeffe rise above a Ghost Ranch pond.

From Ghost Ranch, you have a good view of **Pedernal**, the flat-topped volcanic plug that Georgia O'Keeffe painted so often. Explore Pedernal up close by driving a few miles north of Abiquiu and heading west on NM 96 between **Abiquiu Lake** (a popular boating and fishing spot) and **Cuba**, where US 550 heads north through the Jicarilla Apache Reservation. NM 96 crosses the dam, then passes below Pedernal and the tiny villages of **Coyote** and **Gallina**, founded by people from Abiquiu. This is spectacular high country, with brightly colored sandstone "amphitheaters" similar to those found in southern Utah. One of them, **Echo Canyon Amphitheater**, is off US 84 about 3 miles (5km) north of Ghost Ranch.

## Ride the rails

The craggy profile of the San Juan Mountains walls the northern skyline as you head north on US 84 into the Tierra Amarilla Valley, where snowmelt from the mountains trickles through pastures laced with spring wildflowers. To the west are **El Vado** and **Heron Lakes**, both state parks on dammed sections of the Chama River. The distinctive grey granite cliffs rising vertically on the east are the 11,403-ft-high (3,476-meter) Los Brazos, the western edge of the Tusas Mountains.

The people who founded the communities of **Tierra Amarilla**, **Los Brazos** and **Los Ojos** in 1860 were sheepherders and farmers from Abiquiu. Emboldened by the presence of U.S. soldiers, they built communities on the common lands, or *ejidos*, of the 1832 Mexican land grant they had been grazing for decades. A hundred years later, the loss of those lands, following a U.S. court decision revoking their communal status, ignited a firestorm over the inequities of land distribution in northern New Mexico. At the peak of the controversy, in 1967, a group of armed Hispanic men led by the charismatic Reies López Tije-

Map on page 162

rina stormed the Rio Arriba County Courthouse in Tierra Amarilla, aiming to make a citizen's arrest of the district attorney. Angered by the D.A.'s absence, the men shot up the courthouse, wounded two lawmen, and fled with two hostages before being captured by the National Guard.

In the 1990s, the nonprofit Ganados de Valle was formed to encourage local businesses to draw on traditional resources and skills. The group's first venture was a women's weaving cooperative using the long-fibered wool of locally reared churro sheep, the hardy breed brought to New Mexico by Spanish settlers 400 years earlier. A visit to **Tierra Wools** (91 Main St, Los Ojos, 505-588-7231, www.handweavers.com) offers an inspiring glimpse into the soul of Hispanic culture in northern New Mexico. Here you can watch freshly sheared wool being graded, hand spun and colored with natural dyes, and purchase beautiful blankets and jackets woven on looms in the back. Other Ganados de Valle businesses are showcased in **Los Pastores** (505-588-0020), an 1890 general store next door.

For most visitors, the highlight of a drive through the Chama River Valley is a ride on the narrow-gauge **Cumbres and Toltec Scenic Railroad** (888-286-2737, www.cumbrestoltec.com), built in 1880 to serve mining camps in the San Juan Mountains and revived in the 1960s. The 64-mile (103-km), one-way train trip to Antonito, Colorado, leaves **Chama ❺** at 10am on Tuesday and Saturday; bus transportation is available for the return. Plan on doing the ride in late September or early October, when aspen leaves light up the mountains with autumn color.

## Ojo Caliente Hot Springs

From Chama you can hike and camp in more than a million acres (400,000 hectares) of **Carson National Forest** or head to one of the nearby lakes for boating and fishing. There are numerous pullouts, campgrounds and picnic spots on scenic NM 64, which takes you east into the Tusas Mountains to **Tres Piedras**, where you can either continue to Taos via the Rio Grande Gorge or loop back to Española via US 285. If you have time, consider exploring the backcountry on one of the forest roads just south of Tres Piedras that wander through pretty mountain villages such as Vallecitos, La Madera and El Rito.

After a long day on the road, don't pass up the opportunity to have a long soak at **Ojo Caliente Hot Springs and Spa** (50 Los Baños Drive, Ojo Caliente, 505-583-2233, ojocalientespa.com), which has been in use for more than a thousand years. Some 100,000 gallons (400,000 liters) of hot mineral water, at temperatures between 103° and 109°F (39°–43°C), emerge from the volcanic rocks along the river. You can choose from several different pools containing a unique combination of mineral waters said to have curative properties: arsenic for arthritis, stomach ulcers and skin conditions; lithia for depression; soda for digestion; and iron for the blood. Following a fire in the 1990s, the spa and hot springs are being upgraded by new owners into a full-service resort, with expanded massage and bodywork services, a wide selection of healthy foods at its Artesian Restaurant, private cliffside pools, and several new lodging options in addition to rooms in the historic 1916 hotel. ❏

**BELOW:** the Cumbres and Toltec Scenic Railroad runs from Chama, New Mexico, to Antonito, Colorado.

# CHACO CANYON

*Ruins are all that remain of ancient Indian pueblos
where artists crafted beautiful pottery, pilgrims came with
precious goods, and priests watched the stars*

Map
on page
162

ugust 1849. U.S. Army Lt. James Hervey Simpson is leading an army
survey team through the vast sagebrush country of northwestern New
Mexico, part of the new American territory. The landscape has a deep,
spare, monochromatic loneliness unfamiliar to Easterners. Fascinated, Simpson
records various geological features while his colleague, Richard Kern, makes
sketches of the landmarks.

A prehistoric village appears, silhouetted on the horizon. The guides refer to
the three-story structure as Pueblo Pintado. Simpson marvels at the fine
stonework: "...so beautifully diminutive and true are all the details of the structure as to cause it, at a little distance, to have all the appearance of a magnificent piece of mosaic work." As they push west, they find themselves in **Chaco
Canyon ❻**, a 15-mile-long (24-km) valley cut by a shallow ephemeral wash and
enclosed by 300-ft-high (90-meter) sandstone cliff walls. Eleven miles (18km)
in, just past the small easternmost ruin of Wijiji, the canyon opens out and spectacular Fajada Butte dominates the southeastern horizon.

As they proceed westward along the base of the cliffs, Simpson and his col-
leagues find many more large village sites, which their Mexican and Indian
guides call pueblos. These stone villages dominate the canyon's north side and
extend to the south and onto the mesa tops. Each has
high walls, an enclosed plaza, large and small ceremonial chambers, and numerous small rooms with
narrow doorways, openings and recesses. The state
of preservation is remarkable. Simpson and his men
leave the canyon and report on their findings. Chaco
has been officially "discovered."

Nearly 150 years later, Chaco Canyon still has the
power to stop you in your tracks with its remote
grandeur. At least 3,600 archaeological sites have been
located in the canyon and surrounding area, along with
a 400-mile (640-km) road system connecting Chaco to
satellite villages, or "outliers," in the 25,000-sq-mile
(65,000-sq-km) San Juan Basin. The Chacoan ancestors
of today's Pueblo people dominated the Southwest
between AD 950 and 1150, then fragmented and merged
with other Ancestral Puebloans. Archaeologists, skilled
detectives all, can only guess why. What has been
dubbed the Chaco Phenomenon is exactly that – an
exceptional occurrence that may never be explained.

## First things first

Everything about a journey to Chaco Culture National
Historical Park (505-786-7014; www.nps.gov/chcu;
open daily; admission) supports the impression that
this was – and remains – a place of pilgrimage. From
Albuquerque, it's a 144-mile (232-km) drive via US
550 (formerly NM 44) to the park turnoff, just south

**PRECEDING PAGES:**
Pueblo Pintado,
Chaco Culture
National Historical
Park.
**LEFT:** New Alto ruins.
**BELOW:** ancient
potsherds.

of Nageezi, then another 21 miles (34km) across the Navajo Reservation. Plan to bring food, camping gear and a full tank of gas, as none of these is available in this minimally developed park. Try to arrive by early morning in order to avoid intense summer heat and secure a spot in the small campground.

On the first day, explore the main ruins, which sit on either side of Chaco Wash, the ephemeral stream that cut this wide, 300-ft-deep (90-meter) canyon. A paved 9-mile (15-km) loop road leads to the major pueblos on the north side of the canyon – Chetro Ketl, Pueblo Bonito, Pueblo Del Arroyo – and to a trail that accesses two 12th-century pueblos – Casa Chiquita and Kin Kletso. The main loop then returns to the visitor center via the south side of the canyon, with stops at the great kiva of Casa Rinconada, the largest in the canyon, and its associated small village sites across from Pueblo Bonito.

A good plan on the second day is to pick up a free permit and hike to back-country sites such as Pueblo Alto, Tsin Kletsin, Wijiji, and Peñasco Blanco. These buildings around the perimeter of the canyon relate directly to the main canyon and probably served as communication stations for weary travelers arriving at Chaco from across the San Juan Basin.

**BELOW:** Pueblo Bonito, the largest structure at Chaco Canyon, rose to five stories on one side and encompassed hundreds of rooms and more than 30 kivas.

## The flower of Pueblo culture

Although there are many beautiful buildings in Chaco Canyon, few people forget their first view of Pueblo Bonito, the highlight of any trip. The 3-acre (1.2-hectare), D-shaped great house was built by successive generations of Chaco masons. It eventually rose four to five stories in the back, dipped to one story in front, and contained 650 large rooms around a plaza dotted with three great kivas and more than 30 small kivas. The high, tapering walls employ core-and-

veneer construction, a technique in which two walls several feet apart are filled with rubble and mortar for strength.

Chacoan walls are, as Simpson observed, like mosaics. They are made of dressed sandstone tablets laid in courses and alternated with perfectly fitted smaller stones. This beautiful stonework was once plastered with mud and painted, which speaks volumes to us today about the worldview of these inspired artists. Equally amazing is the amount of timber used for lintels and roof beams – wood that was hand-carried from mountain forests 30 to 60 miles (50–100km) away.

Pueblo Bonito was first excavated by cowboy archaeologist Richard Wetherill and the Hyde Expedition between 1896 and 1899. Further excavations were performed by Smithsonian curator Neil Judd and a National Geographic Society Expedition in the 1920s. Pueblo Bonito has yielded impressive amounts of unusual black-on-white pottery, raw and worked turquoise (including a stunning multi-strand necklace), carved effigies inlaid with precious stones, Pacific shells, Mexican copper bells and colorful macaw feathers and bones. Also unearthed were bone awls, scrapers and ceremonial items such as 375 carved wooden staffs that may have been prayer sticks. It was "the very symbol of Pueblo civilization in full flower," marveled Judd, who never got over his seasons at Chaco.

Wetherill approached Pueblo Bonito through a southeast entryway that passes through what he thought was a large midden (trash mound) but which some archaeologists now believe is landscape architecture related to a network of roads that converge on the canyon. This landscaping at Pueblo Bonito consists of a 10-ft-high (3-meter), leveled mound filled with rubble, enclosed with masonry, and covered in plaster. Subsurface imaging has revealed an extensive network of rooms, kivas and foundations extending toward Chetro Ketl. This

Map on page 162

500-room great house was begun in AD 1010 and has a particularly beautiful back wall, the second largest great kiva in the canyon and two unique features: a raised plaza and a 12th-century Mesoamerican-style colonnade indicating that trade with Mexico also left a mark on the culture.

## Humble beginnings

What led to this remarkable Chaco Phenomenon? Construction of the great houses at Chaco began in the 10th century, but Chaco's human story goes back much farther. After the Ice Age, the San Juan Basin was used by Paleo-Indian hunters. But when the climate warmed, killing off big game, they were succeeded by Archaic hunter-gatherers who hunted small game such as deer and rabbits but relied on wild seeds, berries, roots and tubers for the bulk of their diet.

By 2,000–3,000 years ago, family groups of Archaic people had learned from southerners how to cultivate corn and were occupying pithouses atop Chacra Mesa in Chaco Canyon and other sites with adequate moisture. They used plant fibers to make baskets, sandals and traps, leading archaeologists to call them Basketmakers.

In the 8th century AD, Basketmaker clans began banding together and building the first above-ground masonry-and-timber hamlets. They were now skilled dryland farmers, raising hardy corn, nutritious beans and various squashes, and they followed the seasonal progress of the sun, moon and the constellations in the night sky to gauge when to plant and harvest. Ceremonies were held in underground kivas, a link to the womblike pithouses of old. Crops were stored in stone mealing bins in rooms adjoining small family quarters. With more hands making lighter work, steadier food supplies, communal living, widening trade networks and an accompanying exchange of ideas, these Chacoans flourished.

**BELOW:** Richard Wetherill's gravestone. Though not formally trained, Wetherill was one of the most influential archaeologists of the American West.

## ALL ROADS LEAD TO CHACO

The need to move around the San Juan Basin's rough topography may partially account for the far-reaching prehistoric road network in and around Chaco. Arrow-straight roads, some as wide as 30 ft (9 meters), lead to great houses in Chaco and outlying communities. Several, however, seem to mysteriously lead nowhere.

A series of line-of-sight signaling stations roughly a day's walk from each other facilitated communication. While the roads eased transportation of timber and resources, they also may have had a symbolic role. Modern Puebloan people continue to use direction as a means of tying their physical and spiritual worlds together; it is quite possible that Chacoans did the same.

Chacoans may have planned for their future by building this road system and the many outliers along it. Aztec Ruins, a settlement to the north, seems to have become the new Chacoan center after the canyon was gradually abandoned in the 12th century. For the next hundred years, Pueblo people in the Mesa Verde area dominated the Four Corners, but eventually a combination of drought, resource depletion and overpopulation apparently took its toll. Ancestral Puebloans scattered and joined the Rio Grande and Hopi pueblos, where their descendants live today.

## Golden age

In the 10th century, Chaco entered a golden age. Pottery replaced baskets for storage of seeds, dried produce, mineral paints, precious stones and other important supplies. Chacoans refined a black-on-white pottery that goes far beyond simple practicality and is, even today, unmatched in form and beauty. The dark, airless rooms of the pueblos were too cramped for daytime living, so the work of the community generally took place on the plaza. Women ground corn using handstones (manos) on rectangular slabs (metates), made cooking and storage pots, cooked mush and stew over fires, looked after the children, and patted new mud plaster onto pueblo walls. Men hunted and attended to ceremonies, planting, harvesting, tool carving, weaving, and even found time for games.

Map on page 162

Chaco's planned great houses began construction at this time. They may have functioned primarily as trading and spiritual centers, with suites of rooms for pilgrims and traders, great kivas for staging community events and ceremonies, and smaller kivas used by clansmen for discussion, working turquoise and weaving. Chacoans seem to have engaged in turquoise trading with Mesoamerica and the Pacific, as well as neighboring southwestern tribes, such as the Mimbres to the south and the Sinagua to the southwest. Turquoise, mined in Cerrillos, near Santa Fe, and brought west to Chaco for processing and distribution, may have been as important to southwestern cultures as gold is to us today.

## Ancient astronomers

Religion, the arts, trade and agriculture became more deeply intertwined as Chacoan society grew more complex. Its most powerful citizens may have been priests, skilled in the arts of agriculture, astronomy and ritual. Members of this elite class may have resided year-round in Chaco's great houses, which were designed to catch the sun during frigid winters.

There is evidence that these ancestral Puebloans were monitoring the skies and the seasons. What appear to be astronomical features have been found throughout the canyon: a possible solstice marker in the great kiva of Casa Rinconada, a corner doorway alignment in Pueblo Bonito, and manipulated stones atop Fajada Butte that could have marked the seasons in the way that Stonehenge did in England. At certain times of year, one can imagine people from outlying communities traveling from far away to attend ceremonies to guarantee successful harvests.

Just how many people lived at Chaco is still being debated. There is a general absence of living quarters, hearths and mealing bins in the canyon, and a dearth of burials. Those burials that have been found are mainly of high-status individuals, accompanied by fine jewelry, ceremonial items such as staffs, prayer sticks and quantities of fine turquoise. Curious, too, is the huge amount of broken pottery – perhaps a sign of ceremonial breakage. A large number of ancient irrigated fields have been mapped on the north side of Chaco, but archaeologists estimate that they could only have supported a few thousand year-round residents.

By the early 12th century, Chaco culture was on the wane. The reasons are unclear. Recent work by

**BELOW:** a pictograph at Peñasco Blanco may be a record of a supernova

Map on page 162

archaeologists offers some new theories. A long-running tree-ring dating project found that Pueblo Bonito was initially constructed 50 years earlier than originally thought. And its construction, along with that of Peñasco Blanco atop a mesa in the western canyon, coincided with a particularly wet period in the Southwest. Chaco Canyon, an unlikely place for a ceremonial center, may have become important mainly for its central location.

A short drought in the 11th century seems to have triggered a flurry of construction activity at Chaco, perhaps to build extra storage space for redistribution of food. When a long drought cycle occurred in the 1100s, the system seems to have broken down. Chaco leaders may have had no way of satisfying an increasingly hungry and desperate people who depended on their predictions and who perhaps felt their gods had deserted them.

In the 1100s, people throughout the region seem to have focused attention on getting by instead of constructing masterpieces. Architecture of this late McElmo Phase, as seen at Kin Kletso, Wijiji and Casa Chiquita, is functional but lacks the finesse and careful planning of earlier times. Existing buildings were often clumsily remodeled. This is most obvious in the rear of Pueblo del Arroyo, which also sports an unusual triwalled kiva, a style more commonly associated with the northern San Juan area, suggesting that newcomers may have moved in for a while.

**BELOW:**
doorways at Pueblo Bonito provide ample evidence of the Chacoans' skill as builders.

Eventually, everyone left, seeking better-watered farmlands along the Rio Grande, Puerco Wash and the Little Colorado River, where their descendants, the modern Pueblo people, live today. These descendants offer many clues to what may have happened at Chaco. Pueblo migration stories tell of a White House to the north, and Navajo oral histories include stories about The Great Gambler, a powerful man who controlled the Chacoan world from his house at Pueblo Alto. Researchers are also taking another look at the role of Sun Chief in modern-day Pueblos. Like Chacoan priests, these ritual specialists are responsible for watching the movements of the sun, moon and stars and making accurate predictions for the seasonal planting calendar and associated ceremonies.

## Becoming a park

Fears about looting led to Chaco being declared a national monument in 1907. In 1980, to protect the newly discovered Chacoan outliers and road network from burgeoning oil and gas development, the park was expanded to 53 sq miles (137 sq km) and officially designated a national historical park. Although Chaco Canyon is remote, visitation and impacts have increased over the years. Park managers have closed the original north entry road to protect nearby fragile structures from vibration damage. Revegetation and stabilization are constant projects, carried out by crews made up of permanent and seasonal park staff, volunteers and student interns.

Along with the Galapagos Islands off Ecuador and Machu Picchu in Peru, Chaco Canyon is now a World Heritage Site – significant for what it tells us about life on earth. The secrets of Chaco Canyon may never fully be known, but such places remind us of who we are and what dreams can build. It is a legacy each of us must protect.                    ❑

# Pueblo Architecture

The dramatically situated pueblos of New Mexico have had a powerful grip on the non-native imagination ever since Spaniards laid eyes on them in the 16th century. Even as they sought to breach the walls of the huge ancestral pueblos, Coronado's conquistadors marveled at their size and strength.

The layout of the towns was even more impressive. Mud-plastered stone buildings, oriented toward cardinal directions and lined up with landforms for solsticial readings, rose three to four stories high, as if funneling the power of the landscape into the large plazas in their midst. The central plaza was a unifying feature. Then as now, it brought together clansmen in a daily round of social interactions, including, most important of all, seasonal kachina dances in which the whole community participated in order to ensure successful harvests.

Pueblo architecture evolved over centuries, as people in the Southwest shifted from a hunter-gatherer lifestyle to one invested in agriculture and towns. In early Pueblo times, changing environmental conditions and the needs of a dynamic society stalled permanent development. Until the early 1300s, the standard pueblo home was a pithouse – a small oval shelter dug into the ground with an earthen roof supported by huge timbers. The pithouse never really disappeared. It remains today as an archetype in all pueblo villages in the secret ceremonial chamber known by the Hopi word *kiva*. Kivas are an important link to the spirit world, signified by the *sipapu*, a hole in the floor through which Pueblo people symbolically emerged into the world.

The celebrated cliff dwellings of Mesa Verde and great houses of Chaco Canyon are, in fact, anomalies: a brilliant but short-lived attempt by a powerful elite to use architectural solutions to control communities polarized by severe drought, crop failures and social breakdown. At Chaco Canyon, between AD 900 and 1125, this resulted in a formula of great house and great kiva communities surrounded by small farming pueblos linked by an elaborate road network. At Mesa Verde, Chaco's successor in the 13th century, a less rigid arrangement was employed, incorporating pithouses and small pueblos on top of mesas with large towns built under canyon overhangs.

Executed over generations, these planned communities seem forlorn today, the ambitions of their founders overblown in the fickle high desert they occupied. Chaco's high, tapered, core-and-veneer walls, mosaic-like masonry, odd T-shaped doorways, and numerous kivas offer glimpses of an agricultural society preoccupied with power and symbolism, yet destined to fail. A similar air of desperation hangs over the hundreds of 13th-century cliff dwellings, from the Gila River in southern New Mexico to the San Juan drainage in the Four Corners. Didn't their inhabitants know such desperate measures were unsustainable? Apparently not. Like so much great architecture, the pueblos of New Mexico – both ancient and modern – are a testament not only to the builders' skill but the strength of their convictions. ❑

**RIGHT:** a modern structure echoes the style of ancient Pueblo architecture.

# NAVAJO COUNTRY

*At home among remote canyons and mesas, the Navajo
and their Jicarilla Apache neighbors tread a path between
centuries-old rituals and modern lifestyles*

Map
on page
162

Dine Bikeyah. The homeland of the Dineh, the People, commonly called the Navajo. Nowhere else in America is there such a remarkable place. Red rock mesas and black lava promontories reach to an endless horizon. Rainstorms and rivers carve serpentine pathways through bare rock. Green mountains rise from a high-desert ocean of dry sagebrush. And every nook and cranny echoes with the stories of those who have called these 25,000 sq miles (65,000 sq km) of New Mexico, Arizona and Utah home for more than 500 years.

This tour begins at Gallup and explores the original 1868 reservation on the Arizona–New Mexico border. It then heads northeast across the Chuska Mountains and into the San Juan Basin, where the Navajo Reservation covers 7,500 sq miles (19,500 sq km) of northwestern New Mexico. Allow a long weekend. This is a place that rewards travelers willing to slow down and enter the rhythm of a different way of life.

## Indian capital

Exit Interstate 40 at Lupton just west of Gallup and follow Navajo Highway 12 to **Window Rock ❼**. This busy little town is the capital of the Navajo Nation. Its name refers to the large eroded sandstone window in the town center. A good time to visit is during the **Navajo Nation Fair** in September, the "World's Largest American Indian Fair." Thousands of people pour into town during this four-day event, which includes a popular Pro-Indian rodeo, a powwow, the Miss Navajo Nation pageant, and traditional music, dance and food. For more information, call the Navajo Nation Fair Office at 928-871-6478.

Just off NM 264, stop at the **Navajo Nation Parks and Recreation Department** (928-871-6647/6636) for information on the 15 national monuments and historic sites and eight Navajo tribal parks on the reservation. Founded in 1957, the Parks and Recreation Department has a million acres under its jurisdiction. The best-known tribal park is Arizona's Monument Valley, which gets 400,000 visitors a year. The other tribal parks include cool high-country forests and lakes in the Chuska Mountains and cultural monuments that are all but unknown to non-Navajos. Staff members here are happy to help you plan your trip and sell you the required visitor use permits for backcountry hiking and camping, fishing, hunting and other recreational activities.

One tribal park is next door. The **Navajo Nation Zoo and Botanical Park** (off AZ 264, Window Rock, 928-871-6573; daily 8am–5pm) is the only tribal zoo in the country. This wonderful facility uses natural sandstone walls to exhibit animals native to the reservation. Despite fiscal challenges, the zoo has suc-

**PRECEDING PAGES:**
kiva reconstruction,
Aztec Ruins
National Monument.
**LEFT:** a young
Navajo cowboy.
**BELOW:** doorways
and kiva ladder,
Aztec Ruins.

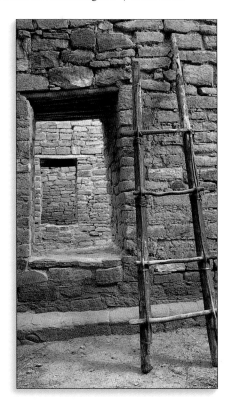

cessfully bred Mexican wolves for reintroduction into the Southwest ecosystem, as well as Spanish churro sheep, prized by Navajo weavers for their hardiness and fine wool. It's a thrill to encounter mountain lions, skunks, elk, golden eagles, wild turkeys, owls, coyotes, jackrabbits, snakes and even a rarely seen old-style "male" forked-stick hogan. Interpretation is in English and Navajo and explains the Navajo worldview in an informative and accessible way. Don't miss it.

Across from Parks and Recreation is the **Navajo Nation Museum** (off AZ 264, 520-871-6673; Mon–Fri 8am–5pm). Built in the style of a contemporary hogan, this attractive cultural center opened in July 1997 with a splash, featuring a traveling historic rug exhibit from the Smithsonian's Museum of the American Indian and a traditional blessing ceremony in the atrium lobby. Its state-of-the-art exhibits offer an excellent introduction to Navajo culture from the tribe's perspective. You can hire Navajo guides to show you around.

### Their finest hour

As with all Indian reservations in the United States, the Navajo tribe is a sovereign nation with its own government, police force, schools and health centers. For insight into tribal politics, visit the **Navajo Nation Council Chambers** (928-871-7160) during one of its four annual sessions. The government building is in the shape of an eight-sided hogan with a door facing east to allow the Holy People to enter. A large mural by Navajo artist Gerald Nailor depicts Navajo history.

A proud part of that history is the role Navajo soldiers played in the U.S. military. Navajos fought bravely during World War II, Korea, Vietnam and the Persian Gulf War. Perhaps their finest hour came during World War II, when Navajo Code Talkers foiled Japanese codebreakers by communicating in Navajo, one of the most complex (and hard to learn) languages in the world. To commemorate the tribe's distinguished military service, the **Navajo Nation Veterans Memorial Park** (928-871-6413) was dedicated in 1995 in Window Rock Tribal Park. It has many symbolic structures: a circular path outlining the four cardinal directions, 16 angled steel pillars with the names of war veterans, and a healing sanctuary featuring a sandstone fountain used for reflection and solitude.

Northwest of Window Rock is **Fort Defiance ❽**, the site of an 1851 fort built by the U.S. government to quell clashes between the Navajo and Anglo settlers. By 1863 the situation had deteriorated into all-out war. Christopher "Kit" Carson, under the orders of U.S. Army General James H. Carleton, instigated a scorched-earth campaign to drive out the Navajo. Homes and possessions were burned, fruit orchards cut down, and livestock slaughtered. As many as 8,000 Navajo were exiled on what they dubbed the "Long Walk" – a forced march of 300 miles (480km) to Bosque Redondo in eastern New Mexico. Some 400 died along the way. There the Navajo suffered more hardships: scarce supplies, undrinkable water, poor soil, disease, hunger. Finally, in 1868, after conditions at the Bosque were publicly condemned, the Navajo were allowed to return to their homeland and rejoin thousands of refugees who had sought sanctuary in the remote fastness of Canyon de Chelly, the Grand Canyon and Monument Valley.

Map on page 162

## Trading places

Drive north on Navajo Highway 12 into the foothills of the Chuska Mountains, past Navajo family homesteads, or outfits, generally consisting of a trailer, a government-built house, one or two ceremonial hogans, livestock corrals and cornfields. Turn right on NM 134 toward **Crystal ❾**. Soon after the turnoff, you will see the site of a historic trading post run by J. B. Moore between 1890 and 1920. Like Lorenzo Hubbell, whose trading post is now a national historic site in Ganado, Moore encouraged Navajo women, long known for their superior weaving, to make rugs for sale. The traditional Crystal pattern is one of several designs associated with specific locations. To see others, stop in at **Toadlena** and **Two Grey Hills Trading Posts**, just north of the NM134/491 junction.

The 7-mile (11-km) dirt road on the right leads to **Assayi Lake and Bowl Canyon Recreation Area**, a tribal park favored by boaters, fishers, campers, picnickers and hikers. Glistening Assayi Lake and several other lakes in the Chuska Mountains are stocked with trout and other sport fish. When you stop at Parks and Recreation in Window Rock, ask what's biting. The road climbs out

**LEFT:** Navajo rug and concho belt.
**BELOW:** the face of a Navajo elder reflects years of hard work.

## CODE OF HONOR

Navajos have fought bravely in every major American military engagement in the last century, but their most important contribution came during World War II, when 400 Navajo Code Talkers served with the U.S. Marine Corps throughout the Pacific, sending and receiving messages in a disguised version of their native language. The code, which was never broken by the Japanese, is now recognized as having been one of the keys to victories at Iwo Jima and other major battles.

It was the brainchild of Philip Johnston, a white missionary's son who grew up on the reservation. In 1942, Navajo recruits at Camp Pendleton, California, devised their own code, using three Navajo words for each letter – e.g., ant, ax and apple for A, or badger, bear and barrel for B.

So secret was their work, Code Talkers didn't receive national recognition until 1982, when President Ronald Reagan proclaimed August 14 National Navajo Code Talkers Day. In 1999, President Bill Clinton visited the reservation and gave a speech that included a few words in Navajo code. For Navajos, the symbolism of that speech lay not so much in a recognition of their people's patriotism but in the use of a language that, for years, the U.S. government actively worked to stamp out as un-American.

*Manuelito led Navajo resistance against the U.S. Army throughout the Long Walk period.*

of the pinyon-juniper zone (elevation 4,500-6,500ft/1,400–2,000 meters) through ponderosa-oak forest, finally arriving among spruce, aspen and ponderosa at an elevation of 8,000 feet (2,400m). Watch for bluebirds, red-tailed hawks and eagles.

## Mythic landscape

Return to NM 134 and head east over **Washington Pass**. The Navajo have renamed the route **Narbona Pass** in honor of Navajo headman Narbona, who was murdered by Americans in 1849. In Narbona's place rose his son-in-law Manuelito, a hero of the Long Walk who helped bring his people home. Narbona Campground lies close to the road and makes a convenient stop, or look for picnic tables at Owl Springs on the downward slope.

From the top of the pass, the view over the San Juan Basin is spectacular. Dark volcanic landmarks rise out of a pale sagebrush steppe scored by numerous washes and ringed by distant mesas and the Sangre de Cristo Mountains. The homeland of the Navajo, Dinetah, lies to the northeast. The Dineh believe they evolved through four lower worlds, helped by the Holy People who created First Man and First Woman and, later, Changing Woman. Changing Woman holds great significance because she is the mother of the Hero Twins, Monster Slayer and Born for Water, whose exploits are celebrated in Navajo origin stories.

The mythic Hero Twins undertook a long and difficult journey to their father, the Sun, and gained all of the sacred teachings necessary to rid Dinetah of its monsters. The Dineh were then free to follow the peaceful Beauty Path. Modern Navajo still strive for *hozho*, a state of harmony with all things, and consider most problems to be the result of falling out of balance with the teachings of the Holy People.

Geographic landmarks offer visual reminders of the rich mythology of the Navajo. Marking the boundaries of the Navajo homeland are four sacred peaks: Mount Hesperus to the north, Mount Blanco to the east, the San Francisco Peaks to the west and Mount Taylor to the south, while the creation mesas of Gobernador Knob and Huerfano Mesa sit to the northeast. On their mythic journey, the Hero Twins passed safely through the crushing rocks of Narbona Pass by invoking sacred powers. The Chuskas themselves represent the head of Yootzill, a prone male god whose torso is the Lukachukai Mountains and feet the Carrizos. **Ship Rock**, to the north, a 1,700-ft (520-meter) volcanic plug with radiating dikes, is the petrified form of Tse Bitai, the man-eating eagle monster killed by Monster Slayer.

## Four Corners

Beyond Ship Rock, on Highway 491, lies the town of **Shiprock ⑩**. This town is the commercial center of the northern reservation, with plenty of chain motels, fast-food joints and other businesses. The **Northern Navajo Nation Fair** is held here every October, and the town is known statewide for its award-winning high school athletic teams. Many Shiprock residents work at the nearby Four Corners Power Plant, which has the dubious honor of having the largest open pit mine in the western U.S. It burns 7 million tons of coal a year and generates 2,085 megawatts of electricity. Farther east, the Navajo Irrigation Project pumps groundwater to irrigate crops in a landscape that is otherwise dry and dusty.

At Shiprock, turn west on NM 64, skirting the **Carrizo Mountains**. The road passes through glorious red rock country toward Kayenta, Arizona, where you turn north for Monument Valley. Be sure to stop at **Teec Nos Pos Trading Post**, about 22 miles (35km) west of Shiprock (just over the Arizona border), one of several historic posts in the area. Check out the rug room. Teec Nos Pos is the most elaborate Navajo rug style, reminiscent of Persian rugs, and with a price to match, but you may find sale items in the pile.

Map on page 162

Five miles (8km) north of Teec Nos Pos is **Four Corners Monument Navajo Tribal Park ⓫**, the conjunction of four states – Colorado, New Mexico, Arizona and Utah. To the north is the San Juan River, one of Navajo Country's major rivers, and enigmatic Sleeping Ute Mountain in Colorado. Local people sell jewelry, rugs and other crafts as well as the ubiquitous fry bread.

## Rugs, rivers, ruins

Return now through Shiprock and head east on NM 64. The route travels above the San Juan River, past orchards and farms, to Mormon-founded **Kirtland** and **Farmington ⓬**, a former ranching and agricultural center near the confluence of the Animas, La Plata and San Juan Rivers, which together provide 60 percent of the surface water in New Mexico. Homely Farmington is better known as a burgeoning oil-and-gas boomtown, with activities as diverse as the Connie Mack World Series Baseball Tournament in August and a balloon festival in May. The excellent **Farmington Museum and Visitors Center at Gateway Park** (505-599-1174, www.farmingtonmuseum.org), headquartered at Gateway Park, also includes the **Riverside Nature Center** (505-599-1422), **E³ Children's Museum**

**BELOW:** a Navajo woman tends sheep on the eastern edge of the reservation.

*Visitors explore the backcountry on horseback.*

**BELOW:** Ship Rock, the eroded remains of a volcanic plug, is known to the Navajo as Tse Bitai, the Rock with Wings.

**& Science Center** (505-599-1425), and **Harvest Grove Farm and Orchards**, all close to the lovely Animas River.

Thirty-eight miles (61km) south of Farmington, on NM 371, is the surreal landscape of the **Bisti Badlands and De-Na-Zin Wilderness** ⓭ (505-599-8900), where erosion has created toadstool-like hoodoos in the rocks. Bring plenty of water and provisions; there are no services. NM 371 continues south to Thoreau and Interstate 40 via **Crownpoint**, known for its monthly rug auction. Weavers from all over the reservation sell here, and visitors with a good eye will find bargains.

Just before you reach Crownpoint, NM 57 turns east and continues for 30 bone-shaking miles (48km) to the south entrance of world-famous **Chaco Culture National Historical Park** (see page 171). Allow a full day to view the empty monumental pueblos and kivas in this remote canyon, which, between AD 950 and 1150, was the cultural center for the powerful Chaco culture, ancestors of today's Pueblo people.

Throughout the San Juan Basin, the Navajo live near the remains of hundreds of Chacoan villages ("outliers"). **Casamero Ruins**, a 22-room outlier built in AD 1000, is just southeast of Crownpoint in the Rio Puerco drainage. Turn east on MC 48, then pick up MC 19 to view the pueblo. It is thought that Navajo farming, weaving, certain beliefs and even the name Navajo (a Tewa word, Navaju, meaning "great fields") grew out of close relations with these former neighbors.

## Ancient gardeners

From Farmington, stay on NM 64 to visit two important Chacoan outliers near Bloomfield, which were linked to Chaco Canyon by the Great North Road, a major roadway on the 400-mile (640-km) Chaco road system. **Salmon Ruin County**

**Park ⑭** (505-632-2013; open daily 9 am–5pm), 2 miles (3km) west of Bloomfield, preserves a 217-room pueblo built in AD 1088. Salmon is a classic Chacoan outlier. It has a great house with tapered core-and-veneer walls, several kivas (ceremonial chambers), including a great kiva, numerous hearths, pottery, tools, mealing bins and evidence that macaws from Mexico were used in ceremonies.

Map on page 162

Residents at Salmon had "waffle gardens" – fields laid out in a grid of square, water-conserving depressions – where they specialized in growing a new strain of corn that was probably traded into Chaco Canyon along the extensive road system. Goods probably passed through Kurtz Canyon and the San Juan River, via Aztec Pueblo to the north and Twin Angels Pueblo to the east. Salmon was abandoned in 1138, then reoccupied briefly in 1185 by people from Mesa Verde whose distinctive black-on-white pottery was plentiful among the 1½ million artifacts pulled from the ruins in the 1970s.

The ruins can be viewed on a self-guided trail. The trail passes through the **Salmon Homestead Complex and Heritage Park**, where you can see a Navajo hogan, a Ute brush wickiup, a Jicarilla Apache tipi and the adobe home of a 19th-century settler. The kiva-shaped visitor center has a museum with exhibits and a computer program that allows visitors to do a virtual tour of 16 Chacoan outliers.

## Cultural confluence

Unlike Salmon, **Aztec Ruins National Monument ⑮** (84 CR 2900, 505-334-6174; www.nps.gov/azru; daily 8am–5pm; admission), just outside the pretty town of Aztec on the Animas River, has been completely excavated and stabilized. Its large great kiva is the only one in the Southwest that has been reconstructed, offering a unique opportunity to imagine ceremonial life in the pueblo in the

**BELOW:** bizarre shale formations are found throughout the Bisti Badlands.

Map on page 162

1100s. Also unusual are the tri-walled kivas. Archaeologist Gordon Vivian excavated the one on display, but others have been found at an unexcavated site nearby.

Even more fascinating is the mingling of Chacoan and Mesa Verde characteristics at this site, prompting some archaeologists to theorize that it was never abandoned but occupied by a transitional people blending the best traits of both cultures. Aztec is wonderfully photogenic at sunset. Try to plan your visit for late in the day.

End your trip to Navajo country by visiting the original Dinetah area, east of Bloomfield. During the Pueblo Revolt of 1680, Pueblo people moved in with Navajo in this area. Then, during Ute raids in the 1700s, Navajo employed Pueblo techniques to build defensive, towerlike pueblitos. Ask at Salmon Ruins about tours to view 18th-century Navajo *pueblitos* such as **Three Corn Ruin** and **Truby's Tower**, recently placed on New Mexico's Most Endangered Places list.

This part of New Mexico is also filled with opportunities for outdoorsmen. **Navajo Lake State Park** (505-632-2278), above Navajo Dam on the San Juan River, is one of the top places in New Mexico for fishing, with abundant native brown trout, kokanee salmon, black bass, bluegill and crappie. Camping is available at several campgrounds. Cottonwood Canyon Campground provides rare, shaded spots among the red rocks. Arrive early. This is a popular place.

## Northern Apache

Outdoor lovers will also enjoy visiting the 722,000-acre (290,000-hectare) **Jicarilla Apache Nation**  (P.O. Box 507, Dulce, NM 87528, 505-759-3242), set in the scenic mountains and mesas near the Colorado border. Fishing is available at seven beautiful mountain lakes, from 30 to 400 acres (12–160 hectares) in size, and birders can view thousands of ducks and a huge variety of waterbirds. Hunting is popular at the **Horse Lake Mesa Game Park**, the largest single elk enclosure in the country. Otherwise, the reservation is a great place for hikers and campers, with nearly 750,000 acres (300,000 hectares) of wilderness. For permits, contact the Jicarilla Apache Department of Game and Fish at P.O. Box 313, Dulce, NM 87528, 505-759-3255.

The capital of the Jicarilla nation is **Dulce**, reached by staying on NM 64 from Bloomfield. This quiet town is among the most open of Indian capitals, with plenty of overnight accommodations and no camera permit required. Be sure to stop by the **Jicarilla Arts and Crafts Shop Museum** (Jicarilla Blvd, 505-759-3242 ext. 274; daily 8am–noon, 1pm–5pm), to see Jicarilla beadwork, baskets, paintings and ribbon shirts. Darren Vigil Gray, one of New Mexico's top contemporary Indian artists, grew up on the reservation and was inspired by the area's wild beauty.

There are a number of special events. The **Little Beaver Roundup** in July includes a rodeo, dances and a crafts fair. The **Go-Jii-Yah Feast**, in September, is an Apache campout at Stone Lake south of Dulce, with feasting, crafts, dances and a relay race between the Llaneros (plains people) and Olleros (mountain people), representing a traditional social division among the Jicarilla. The two teams also represent the sun and moon in a mythical race to escape the underworld. ❏

**BELOW:** ceremonial relay race at the Stone Lake campout.
**RIGHT:** Jicarilla Apache man, 1904.

# SANTA FE TRAIL

Map on page 194

*In an epic undertaking, gold-diggers, mountain men, merchants and a steady stream of opportunists blazed a path and altered history over this famed frontier thruway*

Northeastern New Mexico, where the southern Rocky Mountains meet the high plains, is quiet, remote and lightly populated. Beyond Las Vegas, huge isolated ranches and scattered herds of bison, pronghorn and domestic cattle graze the native shortgrass prairie that covers the eastern third of New Mexico and spills into Texas, Colorado, Oklahoma and Kansas. In winter, lakes and marshes in these dry grasslands are a haven for hundreds of migratory and resident bird species protected in several national wildlife refuges.

For humans, northeastern New Mexico has always been a frontier. Ancient Folsom hunters pursued big game on the plains, leaving behind important archaeological evidence of their presence. During the Spanish era, Jicarilla Apaches and Moache Utes frequented the deep canyons of the Sangre de Cristo Mountains, using them as bases for raiding and trading with settlements on the Rio Grande.

Against this backdrop, the 1821 opening of the Santa Fe Trail, linking Independence, Missouri, and Santa Fe, was an epic undertaking. Almost overnight, Spanish New Mexico, locked for more than two centuries in political and geographical isolation, was exposed to a flood of new ideas and manufactured goods. Over the next 50 years, explorers, mountain men, traders, gold seekers, military expeditions, immigrants, tourists, ranchers and outlaws made their way west. It was the greatest cultural collision since Coronado appeared in the Zuni pueblo of Hawikuh in 1540.

**PRECEDING PAGES:** "mountain man" gathering. **LEFT:** a bronc buster prepares for a wild ride at a Cimarron rodeo. **BELOW:** Fort Union National Monument.

## Uncle Dick's road

Begin your tour of New Mexico's Wild West Corner on Interstate 25, north of Raton, on the Colorado–New Mexico line. A small pull-off, 1½ miles (2.5km) north of **Raton Pass** (7,834-ft/2,387-meter elevation) offers excellent views of the Santa Fe Trail as it passes through Uncle Dick Wootton's Ranch in the adjacent canyon. The highway follows the Mountain Branch of the Santa Fe Trail, which split in Kansas into northern and southern routes. The northern Mountain branch linked Bent's Fort, Colorado, and Fort Union, New Mexico. Although longer and very rugged, it was safer than the alternative route, the Cimarron Cutoff, which crossed exposed waterless plains frequented by Indians.

Wagons struggled to cross the mountainous terrain until 1866, when a mountain man and Indian scout named "Uncle Dick" Wootton blasted a route through the mountains and set up a toll gate, charging everyone who passed. Trail ruts are still visible above the base of the pass, 11 miles (18km) north of Raton. Travelers rested at Willow Springs Station, at what was later the town of Raton. In 1879, the Atchinson, Topeka & Santa Fe Railroad bought the toll road from Uncle Dick, and Raton become a busy railroad, mining and ranching center, and the seat of Colfax County.

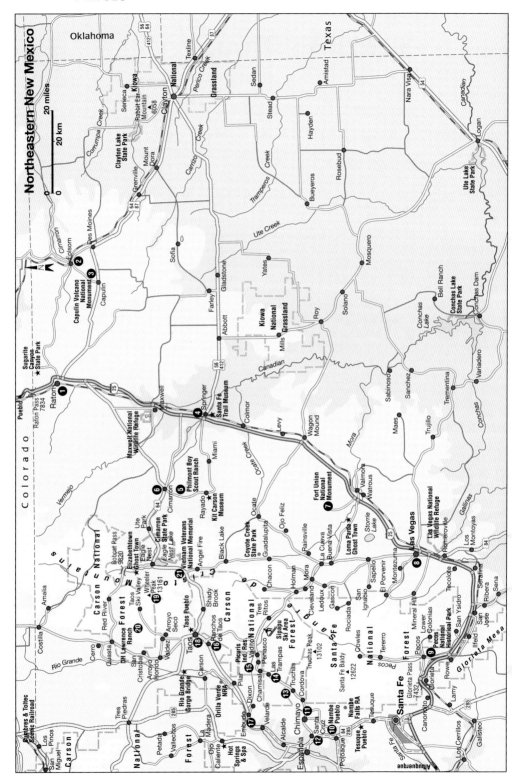

## Ancient hunters and a young volcano

Most of what there is to see in **Raton ❶** can be found in the blocks around the historic railroad depot, which is the first stop in New Mexico for westbound passengers on the Amtrak train between Chicago and Los Angeles. Seventy well-preserved Victorian buildings are on the National Historic Register, including the 1915 **Shuler Theater** (131 N. Second St, 505-445-2052), which has a 1930s mural depicting local history painted by WPA artist Manville Chapman.

*Ranching remains a family business in northeastern New Mexico.*

Ten miles (16km) northeast of Raton, off NM 72, is **Sugarite Canyon State Park** (505-445-5607). You can still see the foundations of the prosperous coal camp that operated here in the early 1900s. There are several lovely hiking trails through ponderosa forests and wildflower meadows, trout fishing in three stocked lakes, and two large campgrounds. The best time to visit is fall, when turning oak leaves offer a dramatic counterpoint to dark basaltic rocks. Sugarite Canyon is on the west end of Johnson Mesa, formed from columnar lava flows (palisades).

In a few miles, the road enters tiny **Folsom ❷**. At one time, Folsom was the most important stockyard west of Fort Worth, but the town declined in 1880, after the railroad reached Santa Fe, and was virtually destroyed in a major flood of the Dry Cimarron River in 1908. Not long after, the foreman of the Crowfoot Ranch, an ex-slave named George McJunkin, stumbled upon huge bison-like bones washed out of the riverbank. Excavations uncovered a beautiful fluted arrow point in the ribs of a long-extinct bison and the recognition of a prehistoric culture, the Folsom, which hunted extinct short-faced bear, bison and other game at the end of the Ice Age. The dusty **Folsom Museum** (summer: 505-276-2122, winter: 278-3616; www.folsommuseum.netfirms.com; open 7 days Memorial Day to Labor Day, 10am–5pm, weekends in May, Sept., rest of the year by appointment), situated in the 1896 mercantile store, has all kinds of odd artifacts celebrating Folsom Man.

**BELOW:** Capulin Volcano rises above grasslands scattered with chunks of volcanic rock. The volcano's crater is about 415 ft (127 meters) deep and a mile in circumference.

Tours of McJunkin's old "Bone Pit" are offered annually by staff members at nearby **Capulin Volcano National Monument ❸** (off NM 325 just north of Capulin, 505-278-2201, www.nps.gov/cavo; daily in summer 7.30am–6.30pm, in winter 8am–4pm). Capulin, a pleasingly symmetrical cinder cone rising 1,400 ft (425 meters) above the surrounding grasslands, was born about 60,000 years ago, a comparative youngster in the 8,000-sq-mile (21,000-sq-km) Raton-Clayton Volcanic Field. Don't bypass this little national monument; it's one of New Mexico's lesser-known gems. A historic 2-mile (3km) paved road winds up to the 8,182-ft (2,494-meter) summit. From there, you can hike the short **Crater Vent Trail** or circumvent the rim on a mile-long (1.5km) trail that offers unparalleled views of nearby volcanoes and four surrounding states.

Several historic trails are visible from the rim. To the southeast are ruts associated with the Fort Union-Granada Road, which was used by soldiers as a supply route once the railroad reached Granada, Colorado, between 1873 and 1875. The Goodnight Trail, used by cattle king Charles Goodnight, also ran nearby. In the late 1800s, it was used by cattlemen to drive cattle from Texas to Folsom for shipping. On the far southeastern horizon is 6,058-ft (1,847-meter) **Rabbit Ear Mountain**. Named for its two eroded peaks, it is the burial

*The Santa Fe Trail Museum in Springer is housed in a 19th-century courthouse.*

**BELOW:** Cimarron was a favorite haunt of outlaws such as Clay Allison and "Black Jack" Ketchum.

ground of an Indian chief, Rabbit Ear, and a landmark on the Cimarron Cutoff of the Santa Fe Trail. Several trail crossings and exceptionally good exposures of wagon ruts can be seen east of Clayton, via US 64/87. The Clayton Complex, beginning at McNees Crossing, near the Oklahoma line, and extending southwest for 35 miles (56km) to Round Mound, became an historic landmark in 1964.

## Sea of grass

It's easy to see why long trains of loaded Conestoga wagons were known as "prairie schooners" when you visit **Kiowa National Grassland** (714 Main St, Clayton, 505-374-9652, www.fs.fed.su/r3/cibola), surrounding Clayton. A sea of swaying grasses hides all but the tallest landmarks and provides sanctuary for threatened prairie chickens, scaled quail and many other birds. This is a wonderful place for camping, hiking, mountain biking and bird watching in summer.

Another unit of the Kiowa Grassland can be found south of US 56, near **Springer ❹**, where you'll find the **Santa Fe Trail Interpretive Center and Museum** (614 Maxwell Ave; 505-483-5554, summer 9am–4pm; admission) in the 1882 county courthouse. Just to the north is **Maxwell National Wildlife Refuge** (off I-25 outside Maxwell, 505-375-2331). Some 200 species of birds have been seen, including burrowing owls and overwintering geese and ducks.

From Springer, you can pick up NM 21, which takes you into the last intact section of the historic **Maxwell Land Grant**. In 1847, larger-than-life mountain man Lucien Maxwell inherited a Spanish land grant from his father-in-law and began ranching in the Rayado area with fellow guide Kit Carson. The land baron built up his holdings to 1.7 million acres (700,000 hectares), the largest private property in the Western Hemisphere. After he sold it to a syndicate of

Map on page 194

English investors in 1870, the property was broken up. The largest ranches in the area can be found on remaining segments of the old land grant. **Valle Vidal**, famous for its elk hunting and wilderness activities, lies north of town. So, too, does **Vermejo Park Ranch**, a luxury hunting resort owned by media mogul Ted Turner, whose holdings rival Maxwell's for acreage.

A large section of the land grant, south of Cimarron, was bought in 1922 by Waite Phillips, founder of Phillips Oil. Phillips dreamed of raising cattle but, in 1938, donated the 127,395-acre (51,555-hectare) property to the Boy Scouts of America. **Philmont Boy Scout Ranch** ❺ (505-376-2281) is now used by thousands of scouts to test their backcountry skills. Much of the ranch is open to the public. In summer, you can tour Waite's Mediterranean-style **Villa Philmonte** and enjoy living-history demonstrations at the **Kit Carson Home and Museum** in Rayado. The **Philmont Museum** and **Seton Library** are open year-round. Bison and other wildlife are visible from the highway in winter.

Maxwell planned to capitalize on traffic on the Santa Fe Trail. In 1864, he built the **Old Mill Museum** (220 W. 17th St, Cimarron; 505-376-2417; open weekends) and supplied flour to the U.S. Army and Indian agency. The four-story Aztec Mill is now a museum run by the CS Cattle Company.

The mill is just one of 14 historic locations on a fascinating downtown walking tour of **Cimarron** ❻, named by early Spaniards whose run-ins with local Apaches and Utes led them to call the area *cimarron*, or wild and unruly. The undisputed highlight is the 1880 **St. James Hotel** (505-376-2664 or toll-free 866-472-5019). The St. James was built by Henri Lambert, former cook for Abraham Lincoln, and was the first hotel west of the Mississippi to offer running water, gourmet food and luxurious furnishings. Buffalo Bill planned his Wild West shows in the bar with Annie Oakley, and notorious figures such as Bat Masterson, Blackjack Ketchum and Jesse James were frequent guests. The hotel's 1872 saloon (now a dining room serving highly rated gourmet food) was famously violent, as bullet holes in the pressed-tin ceiling attest. Recent owners have ensured that guests have an authentic Wild West experience. But be warned: The hotel is reputed to be haunted. The ghosts are mostly benign, except for one malevolent spirit, a man named TJ, who allegedly won the hotel in a poker game but was gunned down before collecting his prize. Hotel owner Roger Smith, mayor of neighboring Colfax (pop. 1), keeps TJ's room locked but will open it on request.

**BELOW:** a costumed interpreter stands guard at Fort Union National Monument.

## Fort Union

Return to Interstate 25 and head south to **Watrous**. En route, you'll pass the **Wagon Mound**, a small butte that resembles a wagon and served as a major landmark on the Santa Fe Trail. Exit the interstate at NM 161 and follow the signs to nearby Watrous, named for Samuel Watrous, a Santa Fe Trail trader who built a store here in 1849. Six miles (10km) north of Watrous is the ghost town of **Loma Parda**. Founded as a quiet Hispanic farming settlement, it was later nicknamed "Sodom on the Mora," when it became a rowdy brothel and drinking haven for soldiers from Fort Union.

**Fort Union National Monument** ❼ (NM 161, 8 miles/13km northwest of Interstate 25, 505-425-8025,

*The Plaza Hotel was built in Las Vegas in 1881 to meet the needs of burgeoning commercial traffic.*

**BELOW:** melting adobe walls are all that remain of the Fort Union hospital.

www.nps.gov/found; daily 8am–6pm; admission) was once one of the largest and most important forts in the West. Built in 1851, close to where the two branches of the Santa Fe Trail converged (trail ruts here are very easy to see), the fort served as a supply depot for other military outposts in the Southwest, and it protected travelers. Two replacements were later built, but by 1891 the fort was abandoned. You'll also find exhibits on the Santa Fe Trail in the museum. Living-history weekends with costumed interpreters are popular in summer.

## On "the meadows"

Fort Union is 19 miles (31km) north of **Las Vegas ❽**, which became the capital of New Mexico for two months during the Civil War when Confederates held Santa Fe. Much of the older part of Las Vegas (named for its *vegas*, or meadows) has been designated a historic district. More than 900 listed structures can be seen, from elegant Victorian brick buildings like the **Plaza Hotel** to Spanish colonial adobe homes on winding side streets. During the Spanish-American War, Teddy Roosevelt blew into town and recruited scores of eager Spanish-speaking volunteers for his team of "Rough Riders." Find out more about New Mexico's prominent role in the Spanish-American War at the **City of Las Vegas Museum/Rough Riders Memorial Collection** (727 Grand Ave, 505-454-1401, ext. 283; open weekends May–Oct; free), a quirky little institution.

Like Raton, Las Vegas was a rest stop on the Santa Fe Trail. **Haye Springs Well**, situated at 2213 Hot Springs Boulevard, is the oldest surviving well on the trail. Las Vegas boomed when the railroad reached town, and by 1900 it had a greater population than Santa Fe. Every summer, adventurous wealthy folk rode the rails west to enjoy luxury resorts built by entrepreneurs like Fred Harvey in

partnership with the railroad. One of the most exclusive lies just north of town, at the mouth of Gallinas Canyon. **Montezuma Castl**e (5 miles/8km northwest of Las Vegas via NM 65, 505-454-4200) was an elegant Grande Dame hotel built around mountain hot springs. A multimillion-dollar restoration by **United World College** (tour info: 505-454-4221; www.uwc-usa.org), a small private institution attracting students from around the world, has returned the building to its former glory. The hot springs are open to the public.

Map on page 194

## Pecos

West of Las Vegas, the Santa Fe Trail continues through the scenic Pecos River valley, with the 13,000-ft-high (4,000-meter) Sangre de Cristo Mountains walling the northern horizon and the Tecolote Mountains and their western extension, Glorieta Mesa, rising on the south. After 1858, one of the last rest stops before reaching Santa Fe was Kozlowski's Stage Stop, 3 miles (5km) east of Pecos, where travelers enjoyed Mrs. Kozlowski's famous fried trout, pulled from the icy waters of the Pecos River, and visited the nearby ruins of Pecos Pueblo.

By the time Kozlowski built his stage stop, using timbers from the ruined Spanish mission church at Pecos, the powerful trading pueblo of Cicuye, a 650-room, 15th-century fortified city-state dominating the frontier between the Rio Grande pueblos and the Plains, had been empty for about 20 years. Its former residents had migrated to live with Towa-speaking relatives at Jemez Pueblo, on the other side of the Rio Grande. In its heyday, though, the multistory pueblo atop the ridge in Pecos Valley inspired awe in all who saw it. Even the Spaniards, whose zealous missionary efforts and introduced diseases would doom the population, were impressed. In 1540, chronicler Pedro de Castaneda wrote, "It is feared throughout the land … [T]he people of this pueblo pride themselves that no one has been able to subdue them, while they subdue what pueblos they will."

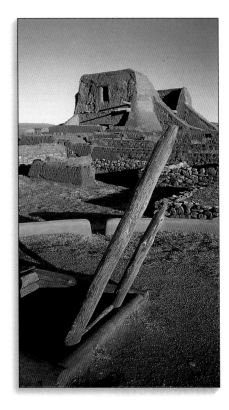

**BELOW:** mission church ruins and a reconstructed kiva at Pecos National Historical Park.

Among the pueblo's many visitors was General Stephen Kearny and his Army of the West, who camped here in 1846 on the way to complete the handover of New Mexico from Mexican authorities in Santa Fe. In March 1862, a less peaceful military encounter took place at nearby **Glorieta Pass**, where, after a three-day battle, Union troops routed Confederate interlopers, saving western gold fields for the Union.

Today, after several expansions of the national monument, surrounding sites like these are part of **Pecos National Historical Park** ❾ (NM 63, 505-757-6417, www.nps.gov/peco; daily 8 am–6pm; admission), a fitting place to end your tour. Be sure to stop at the E. E. Fogelson Visitor Center, an attractive building with a small museum and bookstore. The remains of the old pueblo and mission church can be visited by walking a paved, 1½-mile (2.5-km) trail.

The park offers tours of Civil War sites, Santa Fe Trail ruts, and the Forked Lightning Ranch House, designed for rodeo entrepreneur Tex Austin in 1926 by Santa Fe architect John Gaw Meem. Other programs focus on wetlands preservation on the Pecos River, skywatching, and wildlife. There are also daily demonstrations of bread making, basketry, blacksmithing and silversmithing at Kozlowski's Trading Post in summer. ❑

# HIGH ROAD TO TAOS

*Family, faith and art are the foundations of life in the traditional Hispanic villages of the Sangre de Cristo Mountains*

Map on page 194

The heartbeat of traditional Hispanic culture resonates as strongly as ever in the tiny mountain villages of the Upper Rio Grande Valley. Here, far from the mainstream, poor but fiercely independent Hispano families have worked the western foothills of the Sangre de Cristo Mountains for centuries, their lives tied to *familia y fé* (family and faith) and high-elevation agriculture, where the growing season is short and winters long and fierce.

Much of the younger generation has left for reliable jobs in nearby Los Alamos, Albuquerque and Santa Fe. But the old ones, *los viejitos*, hold on in their ancient haciendas of thick-walled adobe. They graze livestock in family *potreros*, or pastures, and irrigate corn, squash, chile, apples and other crops with water from the community ditch, or *acequia*. When nights are long, the people gather to sing songs, play scratchy fiddle music, dance, and tell folk stories known as *cuentos* in the ancient Spanish dialects peculiar to each village.

Massive buttressed churches, tiny *capillas* (family chapels), and less obvious religious meeting houses are important gathering places in every village. They provide a refuge for families struggling with unemployment, illness, crime and drug problems that have taken the lives of too many young people. Every village has artisans whose skills have elevated everyday objects and religious paraphernalia to fine art. The studios of weavers, needleworkers, tinsmiths, potters and wood carvers along the winding road between Nambe and Taos are the highlight of any tour of this region. An annual 100-studio **High Road to Taos Studio Tour** (505-732-8267 or toll-free 800-732-8267, www.highroadnewmexico.com) takes place two weekends in September and is well worth planning a trip around.

**PRECEDING PAGES:** Rio Grande raft trip. **LEFT:** a Chimayo lowrider. The cars often bear religious images. **BELOW:** Leona's take-out restaurant, Chimayo.

## The tour begins

For convenience, this tour begins in Santa Fe, follows the High Road to Ranchos de Taos, then returns via the Low Road, along the Rio Grande. Head north on US 84/285 through Pojoaque and turn right on NM 503, a two-lane route that winds through bottomlands crowded with cottonwood, alder and willow. In about 2 miles (3km), you reach **Nambe Pueblo ⑩** (505-455-2036).

Founded in 1300, Nambe, which in the Tewa language means "Mound of Earth in the Corner," was once a major religious center, but today only about 600 tribal members live on the 19,076-acre (7,720-hectare) pueblo. The tribe has a small buffalo herd, and residents sell pottery and jewelry from their homes. Its main attraction is **Nambe Falls Recreation Area** (505-455-2034), a scenic area with three waterfalls and a lake, where you can fish, swim and camp. It is the focal point of a July 4 celebration that includes Indian dances, food vendors and arts and crafts. Dances are also held on October 3, the day before the pueblo's feast day.

*Traditional Hispanic
art forms, like the
painting of religious
icons, are a specialty
of local artists.*

**BELOW:** El Santuario
de Chimayo.

## Chimayo

Follow NM 503 through badlands composed of eroded rocks washed down from the Sangre de Cristo Mountains. Turn left on NM 520 and descend into **Chimayo** ⓫, a village of several connected neighborhoods, or *placitas*, built in the early 1700s. Set at the confluence of three rivers, Chimayo was settled by Tewa Indians who named their community Tsi Mayoh, "Hill of the East," in honor of the large hill that was recognized as one of the four corners of the world. A corruption of that Tewa word was used for the first Hispanic settlements here in the 17th century.

Hispanic farmers returning to the area following the 1680 Pueblo Revolt were offered a land grant on the condition that they build their homes close together, around defensible, pueblo-style plazas that protected the inhabitants from Comanche and Apache raiders. Chimayo's 1740 Plaza of San Buenaventura, now known as **Plaza del Cerro**, is one of the best-preserved plazas in New Mexico. Sway-backed adobe buildings in various stages of repair surround the overgrown plaza. A *torreon*, or watchtower, is still visible on the southwest corner.

On the west side of the plaza is a crumbling *capilla*, a family chapel owned by the Ortegas, which served parishioners unable to travel to the main church in Santa Cruz. On the south side of the plaza is the old Ortega mercantile store and residence, which now houses **Rancho Manzana** (505-351-2227, www.ranchomanzana.com), a bed-and-breakfast renowned for its authentic architecture, cooking classes and organically grown fruits, vegetables and lavender.

Chimayo is known for its weaving. Eight generations of Ortegas have perfected the craft, developing a variant of the Rio Grande style, using wool from Spanish churro sheep and designs that emphasize bright stripes and diamond patterns. **Ortega's Weaving Shop** (505-351-4215), at the junction of Highway 520 and 76,

has been in business since 1900. You can watch family members weaving rugs on large looms and buy a variety of weavings, from place mats to floor rugs.

Another old Ortega home on the Plaza del Cerro houses the **Chimayo Museum** (505-351-0945, www.chimayomuseum.org). This delightful community museum features revolving exhibits on village history and offers information on walking tours. Its main mission is to preserve local culture with programs such as Los Maestros, which teaches youngsters traditional Hispanic arts, and a conservation partnership with the nonprofit Trust for Public Lands that keeps historic family-owned pastures and farmland in traditional use.

Map on page 194

## Sacred ground

One such pasture is behind **El Santuario de Nuestro Señor de Esquipulas**, the religious shrine dubbed the "Lourdes of America." Some 300,000 people a year visit this former family chapel on the south end of the village. Most come during Easter Week, when Catholics from all over northern New Mexico make the pilgrimage on foot, some carrying crosses. They have been coming here since 1814, when a priest from the Santa Cruz church, Bernard Abeyta, reputedly discovered a cross in these pastures. Three times the cross was taken to Santa Cruz, and three times it miraculously reappeared in the same field. Eventually, Abeyta received permission to build a shrine around the well of soil in which the cross was found.

A tiny room now houses El Pozo, the holy well. Visitors purchase candles and small baggies for sacred dirt at nearby stores. Many return to the shrine with testaments of healing and leave shoes, photos, crutches and other items in front of a statue of Santo Niño de Atocha, the child saint reputed to wear out his shoes nightly helping poor villagers. The original cross, displaying the Black Christ of Guatemala, now sits on the altar of the adjoining adobe chapel. Mass is said daily in this chapel. The combination of traditional folk art, centuries of prayer and peaceful cooing doves in the eaves imbues the sanctuary with a moving spirituality that remains in the heart long after you leave. No matter what your faith, this is a place worth seeing.

Chimayo's other claim to fame is its superb chile, which ripens slightly later than Hatch chile in southern New Mexico. You can buy it green, but it is best ripened on strings, known as *ristras*, then ground, which brings out its sweet, complex wine-like flavor. You can buy reasonably priced bags from vendors in Chimayo or enjoy some hearty *carne adovada* or other chile-infused entrée at **Rancho de Chimayo Restaurante** (505-351-4444), run by the Jaramillo family in their old hacienda, between the Santuario and the Plaza del Cerro.

**BELOW:**
the Santuario's altarpiece was created by a celebrated 19th-century *santero* known as Mollero.

## Santa Cruz, Cordova, Truchas

Before heading north on the Taos High Road, plan on making a side trip west on NM 76 to visit **Santa Cruz** ⓬. Several artisans have studios on this main road between Chimayo and Española, including the **Trujillo Weaving Shop** (505-351-4457), where you can visit with Chimayo's other famous weaving family and purchase rugs and other items. On the south side of the highway, in **Cuarteles**, you'll find a restored Penitente *morada*, one of the best examples of the meeting houses

*Hanging around
the back yard.*

**BELOW:**
family farms rely
on direct sales to
the public for much
of their income.

used by the religious brotherhood that rose to prominence in the early 1800s.

Santa Cruz was founded in 1695 by conquistador Don Diego de Vargas. **Holy Cross Catholic Church** (505-753-3345) was built in 1733 and houses a number of important 18th-century religious paintings from Mexico City. Its 1795 wooden altar screen is the oldest in New Mexico. Santa Cruz is also home to **Siri Singh Sahib Sikh Dharma**, North America's biggest Sikh community. Their large gated compound is just off US 285, opposite the **Wildlife Center** (505-753-9505, www.thewildlifecenter.org), a rehabilitation facility that cares for raptors, cougars, coyotes and other injured animals.

Double-back to Chimayo and continue east on NM 76 to the village of **Cordova**, which is renowned for its woodcarving. San Antonio de Padua Church here has a large altar screen painted by famed *santero* Rafael Aragon, and several studios are open to visitors. A few miles farther on, the High Road ascends a broad 8,000-ft-high (2,400-meter) plateau at **Truchas ⓭**, named for the trout that are often pulled from nearby streams. Magnificent 360-degree views take in 13,102-ft (3,994-meter) Truchas Peak, the state's second highest summit, as well as the Rio Grande Valley, Jemez Mountains and Sandia Mountains.

Founded in 1754 by 12 families from Chimayo, Truchas's exposed setting made it extremely vulnerable to Comanche attack. With no help from an over-stretched colonial government, the people were forced to fend for themselves. As in Chimayo, they built their homes around a defensible plaza close to the edge of the plateau. Over time, people began to occupy ranchos closer to community pastures along the *acequia*, east of town.

About 1,000 people now live in Truchas, which has several quaint *tienditas*, including an old-fashioned mercantile, on the main street. Pedro Antonio Fresquis, a famous *santero* known as the Truchas Master, lived here in the 1700s. The village church has a number of *bultos* on display. Contemporary arts are the focus of **Hand Artes Gallery** (800-689-2441), which has an interesting selection of sculptures, paintings and other works. Movie buffs will recognize Truchas from the 1987 film adaptation of John Nichols's *The Milagro Beanfield War*, centered on the clash between traditional New Mexicans and contemporary developers in the 1970s.

## Las Trampas and Picuris

North of Truchas, the highway enters aspen and mixed conifer forest in 1½-million-acre (600,00-hectare) Carson National Forest. The tiny hamlet of Ojo Sarco, named for its well, has a *Sound of Music* setting surrounded by high country that has attracted several artists whose studios are open to visitors. It lies a few miles south of **Las Trampas ⓮**, another land-grant settlement founded by families from Santa Fe in 1751. Las Trampas (the Traps) is a quiet little town with one very popular attraction: **San José de Gracia Church**, one of the best examples of monumental adobe mission architecture still standing in New Mexico. A favorite of photographers, the church was built in 1760 and has enormous buttressed walls, twin bell towers and a flat roof drained by gutters known as *canales*. Its huge, carved wooden doors offer a hint of the treasures inside: carpentry by masters like Nicolas de Apodaca and Juan Manuel Romero. To see the interior, inquire at La Tiendita, a mercantile opposite the church.

A few miles beyond Las Trampas is **Chamisal**, on the **Picuris Indian Reservation** ⓖ (505-587-1099, www.picurispueblo.com). With 100 tribal members, Picuris is the smallest and most remote of the Rio Grande pueblos, although once it was one of the largest. It's worth a visit today to view the restored 18th-century **San Lorenzo de Picuris Church**, which replaced the original 1621 church destroyed in the Pueblo Revolt. To reach the pueblo, head west on NM 75, just before Peñasco, and follow the signs. Stop at **Picuris Pueblo Museum** (505-587-2957) to pick up permits to tour the village and take photographs. On sale are pottery, weaving and beadwork. A restaurant serves tasty New Mexican food.

Map on page 194

### Toward Taos

Back on NM 76, continue through Peñasco to NM 518. To see more of the Sangre de Cristo Mountains and Carson National Forest, turn right on NM 518 and drive east to Mora and Las Vegas. En route, you'll pass **Sipapu Ski Area** (505-587-2240), popular with skiers in the Taos and Las Vegas area. In summer, this high-country area is a cool getaway for hiking and camping. For more information, stop in at the **Camino Real Ranger District Office of the Carson National Forest** (15160 NM 75, Peñasco; 505-587-2255).

If, on the other hand, you're headed in the direction of Taos, turn left at NM 518, drive past **Fort Burgwin**, a reconstructed 19th-century fort and museum, and rejoin US 68 at **Ranchos de Taos** ⓗ. Taos Indian farmers founded this small community, south of Taos proper. Today, it is a quiet, rather artsy roadside village, with several good galleries and restaurants. It is best known for the

**BELOW:** San Lorenzo de Picuris Church has been fully restored by the residents of Picuris Pueblo.

## LOW AND SLOW

Dave Jaramillo of Chimayo dreamed of transforming his 1969 Ford LTD into a "lowrider" – a car with a lowered suspension and custom paint and interior. It was more than just a hobby; it was a personal calling. "A true lowrider is when you start from scratch and build it all," says El Rito *santero* Nicholas Herrera. "It is a changing art exhibit."

The first lowriders appeared in Los Angeles in the 1940s, a blatant appropriation of an Anglo icon. But the "waxed to the max" lowriders cruising Española's Riverside Drive on Saturday night do more than catch the eye. They are an expression of Hispanic values – faith, family and art – that have united the villages around Española for centuries.

The village of Chimayo demonstrated that kind of unity when Dave Jaramillo died, leaving his car unfinished. Family members worked together and, two years later, had turned an ugly duckling into a beautiful swan, with velvet upholstery, a color TV, fuzzy dice and a portrait of the Jaramillo family painted on the side.

The story of Jaramillo's lowrider attracted the attention of the Smithsonian Institution, which bought the car in 1992. It received a uniquely New Mexican send-off. More than 500 people attended Mass at the Santuario to bless the car. By then, everyone knew its name: "Dave's Dream."

Map on page 194

1730 **San Francisco de Asís Church** on its old plaza. The enormous buttresses and adobe walls in the back of the church have inspired numerous artists, including photographer Ansel Adams and painter Georgia O'Keeffe, both of whom rendered the church many times during their careers.

## Down by the river

*Rafting the Orilla Verde section of the Rio Grande.*

**BELOW:**
San Francisco de Asís Church.
**RIGHT:** a view of the Rio Grande from Embudo.

From Ranchos de Taos, NM 68 (also known as the Low Road) drops south into the **Rio Grande Gorge**, where the river flows within a narrow volcanic canyon. This part of the river was set aside as a state park in 1959 and became popular with river runners attracted by the state's best whitewater. The most popular run, a section dubbed "the Box," was transferred to federal ownership when the Rio Grande was designated a Wild and Scenic River in 1970. The state park has now been transferred to the Bureau of Land Management and renamed **Orilla Verde National Recreation Area**. The **Rio Grande Gorge Visitor Center** (505-751-4899) is at the intersection of NM 570 and NM 68 in Pilar.

**Pilar** was settled by Jicarilla Apache farmers. In 1795, 20 Hispanic families were granted land here by Governor Fernando Chacón. They moved in with the Apache, who had returned to the area after being chased out by de Vargas in 1694. The Apache staged frequent raids on the settlers, but a peace treaty signed in the mid-1800s resettled the Jicarilla on a new reservation between Cuba and Farmington. Pilar today is home to a lively community of artists.

After a day of river running, there are few things more pleasurable than a meal accompanied by a home-brewed cold beer at historic **Embudo Station** ⓱ (505-852-4707). Housed in the remains of the area's last narrow-gauge railroad station, this popular spot has everything a visitor could want: a restaurant serving quick lunches and elegant dinners, a microbrewery producing 24 ales (including a spicy green chile beer), a winery and organic garden. You can also spend the night in a small cabin.

In addition to growing their own produce and flowers, the owners buy them from their neighbors the Campos family, whose 20-acre (8-hectare) organic farm is about a mile down a rutted dirt road that runs along the river. Margaret Campos and her mother are not only gracious hosts, they give you an insider's look at farming in rural New Mexico. You can rent small *casitas* on the property and help the family harvest onions, broccoli, carrots, chiles, beets, peppers, artichokes, garlic and other crops (the farm produces about 1,500 pounds/700kg of tomatoes a week in summer). The Campos also offer **Comida de Campos** (505-852-0017, www.comidadecampos.com), cooking classes in which guests learn about traditional New Mexican cuisine using an outdoor clay oven, or *horno*.

There's no shortage of good things to eat in this area. Apples are the main crop in Embudo and nearby Velarde, known for its quaint fruit stands. In Dixon, a few miles east of Embudo on NM 75, you'll find numerous art studios (a tour is offered every November), apple orchards and the **Chiripada Winery** (Hwy 75, Dixon, 505-579-4437), the highest vineyard in New Mexico, where you can sample a selection of some of the state's best homegrown wines. ❑

# TAOS

*Art and nature meet head-on in Taos Valley,
an "edge place" of international renown where energy
flows like the waters of the Rio Grande*

t is late afternoon on Christmas Eve in **Taos** . Last-minute shoppers dart into galleries and stores on the historic plaza. A fiery winter sun shoots its dying rays low over the sagebrush plateau, skimming the black gash of the Rio Grande Gorge to the west. The snow-capped Sangre de Cristo Mountains are bathed in alpenglow, their angular forms massed on the eastern horizon more than a mile above the broad sweep of Taos Valley.

Three miles (5km) to the north, in Taos Pueblo, people are arriving in the North Plaza for Christmas ceremonies. They stand around huge *luminarias*, stretching their hands toward the bonfires to stay warm as the temperature plummets below freezing. From inside the whitewashed walls of the 1850 church of San Geronimo, on the South Plaza, comes the faint sound of vespers being sung. This is the second church here. The first was built in 1619, in the North Plaza, 21 years after Spanish missionaries had moved into the pueblo. It was burned down during the 1680 Pueblo Revolt, which was planned at Taos Pueblo.

As evensong ends, the church bells ring, and voices raised in song can be heard from inside the church. Several village men begin pouring gasoline over dozens of unlit *luminarias* on the plaza and rooftops, setting them alight with the touch of a match. They stand back as orange flames and swirling black smoke engulf the stacks of pitchy ocote wood, illuminating the expectant faces of the crowd.

Suddenly, the old wooden doors of the church open, and a procession emerges. In the front are Pueblo men who shoot live ammunition in the air. They are followed by the priest and his acolytes and six men bearing a statue of the Virgin Mary on a litter. At the rear are village elders chanting in Tiwa and beating drums. As the procession ends, people break away to socialize around *luminarias*, lit at this time every year since Spanish Catholicism first reached Taos Pueblo in 1598.

## Art and energy

New Mexico is famously multicultural, but nowhere is the collision of landscape and culture more intense than at Taos. Geography has a lot to do with it. Taos – actually three small communities: Taos Pueblo, historic Taos and Ranchos de Taos – is concentrated between New Mexico's tallest mountains and its deepest gorge. There's no doubt that this is an "edge place." You feel the energy as soon as you climb out of the Rio Grande Gorge into Taos Valley (elevation 7,200 ft/2,200 meters). Your pulse quickens. You feel a little uncomfortable. Something ancient and primitive stirs.

From its official founding in 1725, Taos has attracted people with a spirit of adventure attracted to this wild energy like moths to a flame. Local history is a veritable who's who of renegade priests, celebrated

**PRECEDING PAGES:**
Taos Pueblo.
**LEFT:** hikers at the Rio Grande Gorge.
**BELOW:** proprietor of a Taos "cowboy boutique."

*Taos shops are filled with Indian arts and crafts.*

mountain men, writers, artists, spiritual seekers and healers of many cultures. The town first garnered international attention in 1918, when wealthy heiress Mabel Dodge Luhan and her new husband, Taos Pueblo native Tony Luhan, built a home here and attracted some of the most creative people of their day, not the least of whom were Carl Jung and D. H. Lawrence. In the 1970s, actor Dennis Hopper moved into the former Luhan home, lured by that same sense of danger. Hopper filmed much of the seminal 1969 movie *Easy Rider* in Taos and attracted a host of hippie followers. Many found a niche and stayed, working as community activists, writers and artists. Taos is a hard place to leave.

These newcomers have not always been welcome in this largely Hispanic area – as Taos writer John Nichols so brilliantly captured in his novel *The Milagro Beanfield War* – but by now an uneasy truce has been established. Whereas class-conscious Santa Fe often seems more interested in image than substance, Taos remains a scrappy little town of 6,000 where art is not so much viewed as experienced through authentic living. This goes some way to explaining Taos's love of diversity. You can buy souvenirs at the shops around historic **Taos Plaza Ⓐ**, then attend a lecture on the evils of consumer culture. Have organic veggie salad and align your chakras over lunch, then enjoy steak, beer and bluegrass music at a local bar at night. Hike to a mountain lake to fish for trout in the morning, then don clean jeans and cowboy boots for an art opening in the evening. Anything goes.

The spirit of Taos is best summed up in its popular solar-powered local radio station, playing everything from jazz to screaming punk. KTAO sponsors the laid-back Taos Solar Music Festival in Kit Carson Park every June. If you want to know what makes Taos tick, check out its roster of musicians. Even Harry Belafonte gets a little bit alternative in Taos. It has that effect on people.

**BELOW:**
historic Taos Plaza.

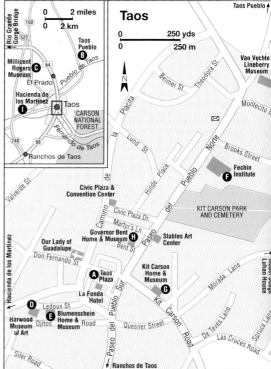

## Taos Pueblo

Whenever the temptation to sell out rears its ugly head, Taoseños have only to look to nearby **Taos Pueblo** ❽ (505-758-1028; www.taospueblo.com) for inspiration. As recognizable as Delicate Arch in Utah or the Empire State Building in New York, the thousand-year-old pueblo rises beneath sacred Taos Mountain like a force of nature, stirring the hearts of all who see it.

For sheer artistry alone, this pueblo is unequaled in the native world. Its stacked architecture, massed high like a Cubist painting, echoes the blocky granite façades of mountains born two billion years ago. It's easy to see why Spanish conquistadors thought they had found their longed-for golden cities of Cíbola in the 1500s. Pale straw in the adobe walls and flecks of mica in the tribe's pottery glitter in the sunlight, beckoning travelers with the hint of treasures within.

Long before Europeans arrived, Taos Pueblo was known as a great trading place. Every fall, Comanches and Utes and other Plains people arrived to trade deer skins, buffalo hides and beadwork for pottery, corn and other foods grown at the southern Rio Grande pueblos. The men of the mountain pueblo were also great hunters, who became known for their finely crafted deerskin moccasins and drums. The sound of drumming and the smell of smoke and sagebrush after a heavy summer rain are quintessentially Taos experiences that linger in the memory long after you leave.

The people of Taos have lived in Taos Valley for centuries. The main pueblo is thought to have been built between A.D. 1000 and 1450, making it one of the oldest continuously occupied communities in America. The pueblo incorporates 99,000 acres (40,000 hectares), including land along the Rio Grande Gorge and 48,000-acre (19,500-hectare) Blue Lake on Taos Mountain, which

Map on page 214

**BELOW:** galleries, shops and restaurants are clustered around the Plaza.

## MABEL DODGE LUHAN

**D**earest Girl, Do you want an object in life? Save the Indians, their art – culture – reveal it to the world!" When artist Maurice Sterne wrote this note to his soon-to-be ex-wife Mabel Dodge Sterne in 1917, he changed the course of history. Within a year, New York's most famous salon hostess had abandoned her avant-garde uptown apartment, moved to Taos and married Taos Pueblo Indian Tony Luhan, and with his help built a 22-room hacienda near Taos Pueblo.

Over the next 40 years, Mabel's "Big House" became a hothouse of creativity, attracting renowned artists, writers and social reformers, among them D. H. Lawrence and Carl Jung. "This Taos Myth – It is just unbelievable," wrote Georgia O'Keeffe after her visit in 1929. "One perfect day after another – everyone going like mad after something."

Born in Buffalo in 1879, Mabel had been "going like mad" all her life, marrying four times, living in New York and Italy, and surrounding herself with people whose work she valued over her own. In Taos, she found enough peace to pull forth the creativity within herself, writing an autobiography, *Edge of Taos Desert*, in which she chronicles her search for healing. Mabel Dodge Luhan House is now an inn and retreat center, imbued with the former owner's creative energy and expansive vision.

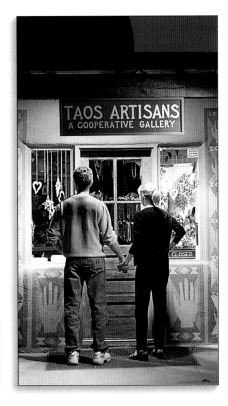

*Indian art at the Millicent Rogers Museum.*

**BELOW:** a fancy dancer at Taos Pueblo powwow.

was taken from the tribe in 1906 to become part of the national forest and returned in 1970, following a long fight with the U.S. government.

Today, Taos Pueblo is recognized as both a UNESCO World Heritage Site and a National Historic Landmark. But you'll find no "museum Indians" here. Taos is a vital, modern pueblo, whose members wear contemporary western attire except on ceremonial days. Most work in nearby Taos or run tribal enterprises, such as art galleries, horseback riding tours and the tribe's small Mountain Casino. About 150 tribal members live in the old pueblo, where, by tribal decree, no electricity or plumbing is allowed and all drinking water comes from the Rio del Pueblo.

Because of the restrictions, most of the 1,800 other tribal members live nearby in modern homes but maintain buildings in Old Taos for ceremonial purposes and as art galleries, where you can buy pottery, beadwork, moccasins, drums and other handicrafts. The pueblo is open seven days a week, from 8am to 4.30pm, except for 10 weeks in spring, when it closes for ceremonial purposes. Traditional dances take place year-round; Christmas and the tribe's San Geronimo feast day on September 30 are the most popular. Separate fees are charged for admission, photography, videotaping and sketching. Pay the money. This is one experience you will want to remember.

## Small town, big culture

Mabel Dodge Luhan wasn't the only strong-willed woman to come to Taos. In 1947, oil heiress Millicent Rogers gave Taos's most formidable hostess a run for her money when she moved to town and, in the five short years before her tragic death at age 50, accumulated one of the premier collections of Southwestern art in the region. After she died, her art collection was put on public display in a

private home a few miles northwest of downtown. **The Millicent Rogers Museum ©** (Millicent Rogers Rd, 505-758-2462, www.millicentrogers.org; daily 10am–5pm, closed Mon Nov–Mar; admission) is an excellent place to get an overview of the historic and contemporary art of the Southwest.

Map on page 214

Room after room holds dazzling collections of Navajo rugs, Hopi kachinas, painted and carved Hispanic *santos* and furniture, old and modern Pueblo pottery, and Apache baskets. A courtyard has a lovely sculpture by famed Navajo artist R. C. Gorman, who died in 2005 and for many years maintained a gallery on Ledoux Street in downtown Taos. The collection of pottery by San Ildefonso potter Maria Martinez and her family alone warrants a visit. It is the only such collection donated by the potter's family and provides details about the creative interplay between generations, including letters, drawings and family snapshots.

Rogers' own interest in Indian cultures is evident. When she moved to Taos, she adapted the traditional velvet dress of Navajo women into a unique personal statement and amassed an extraordinary collection of silver, turquoise, coral and inlaid shell Indian jewelry. Many of her own designs are displayed here, along with her mother's important collection of paintings by Indian women artists like Pop Chalee, taught by Dorothy Dunn in The Studio in Santa Fe in 1932.

## Taos Society of Artists

By the time Rogers moved here, Taos had been an art colony for nearly 50 years. As the story goes, it began in the autumn of 1898, when New York artists Bert Phillips and Ernest Blumenschein decided to make a sketching trip to New Mexico on the recommendation of fellow painter Joseph Sharp. The pair took the train to Denver and hired a wagon to travel south. When their wagon wheel

**BELOW:** an exhibit of Spanish pottery at the Millicent Rogers Museum.

*Boots, chaps and other cowboy gear are available at a variety of specialty shops.*

**BELOW:** Ernest L. Blumenschein, founder of the Taos Society of Artists.

broke in Taos Canyon, they were forced to stay in town to get it repaired. This unexpected delay sealed their fate. They fell in love with Taos and decided to stay.

Phillips moved in right away. Blumenschein visited every summer until 1919, when he, his wife Mary Greene Blumenschein, and daughter Helen bought an old adobe and moved in permanently. In 1912, Blumenschein and Phillips organized the Taos Society of Artists in the living room of Bert's sister Helen and her husband, Doc Martin, whose home sat where Historic Taos Inn is located today. The group eventually also included Sharp, Victor Higgins, John Marin, Marsden Hartley and Dorothy Brett, among others.

Paintings by Taos Society artists of churches, villages, mountains, Taos Pueblo elders, cowboys and other frontier characters can be found in several worthwhile museums in downtown Taos. One of the best is the **Harwood Museum of Art ⑩** (238 Ledoux St, 505-758-9826, harwoodmuseum.org; Tues–Sat 10am–5pm; admission), named in honor of artist Burt Harwood, who came to Taos for his health in the early 1900s. The museum was founded in the family adobe in 1923 by Harwood's widow and is the second oldest museum in the state. In 1936, the University of New Mexico took over administering the museum and hired well-known architect John Gaw Meem, the principal exponent of Santa Fe style, to create an elegant expansion.

Today, you'll find some of the best paintings by the Taos Society in an elegant downstairs room. A nearby gallery dedicated to works by contemporary artist Agnes Martin, a Taos resident, makes an interesting counterpoint. Martin's ultramodern, white-on-white gridded canvases couldn't be more different from the organic black-on-black pottery by pueblo potter María Martínez on display at Millicent Rogers Museum. But like Martínez, Martin is a New Mexico resident, with work that has put this art museum on the national map. This interesting juxtaposition continues upstairs. Traditional northern New Mexico carved furniture sits next to the neo-primitive carved *bultos*, or saint statues, created by Patricio Barela, considered a master *santero* in the 1940s. Nearby are some unusual articulated *bultos* donated by Mabel Dodge Luhan.

A few doors east of the Harwood is the **E. L. Blumenschein Home and Museum ⑤** (222 Ledoux St, 505-758-0505; daily 9am–5pm; admission). A typical organically grown adobe, with rooms dating to 1797, the home of the founder of the Taos Society of Artists is cool and dark with low ceilings made of huge *viga* beams and interwoven aspen *latillas*. The house has a strong 1920s feel. Furniture is minimal: simple beds, tables and chairs, and day beds that do double duty as couches and guest beds. Artwork, however, abounds, with numerous paintings by "Blumy" and his contemporaries on every wall. This museum is one of three former residences administered as Taos Historic Museums – the Blumenschein Home, the Kit Carson Home, and the Martínez Hacienda – which may be visited with a combined pass.

A very different artist's home can be found just north of Kit Carson Park. The building preserved as **Taos Art Museum at the Fechin House ⑥** (227 Paseo del Pueblo Norte, 505-758-2690; www.taosartmuseum.org; Wed–Sun 10am–2pm; admission) is a true Taos original, created by renowned immigrant Russian painter Nicholai Fechin from an historic adobe between 1927 and 1933. The son of a woodcarver, Fechin carved all the furniture, doors, windows and corbels in the house, which seamlessly blends a Russian monastic interior with a traditional northern New Mexico exterior. Even today, the creative force that went into imagining such a dwelling is staggering. Fechin and his daughter Eya left the home in 1933, following his divorce. In 2003, the Fechin home was renovated by the City of Taos to house the Van Vechten-Lineberry art collection. Fechin's exuberant portraits and detailed drawings share space with fine originals by Taos Moderns like Larry Bell.

Map on page 214

## Pioneers and mountain men

The former residence of another Taos original, mountain man Kit Carson, lies just to the south, preserved as the **Kit Carson Home and Museum** ❻ (Kit Carson Rd, 505-758-0505; daily 9am–5pm Apr–Oct; admission), half a block along Kit Carson Road. Carson first came west from Missouri on the Santa Fe Trail in 1826 in search of his fortune. For the next 42 years, he made his permanent home in Taos, while pursuing a rugged life in the mountains as a trapper, mountain man, translator, scout for explorer John C. Frémont and eventually an army officer, dealing with "the Indian problem" following the Civil War. The four modest rooms that date to 1825 were bought by Carson as a wedding gift for his young bride María Josefa Jaramillo in 1843. They spent the next 25 years here, raising seven children.

When Carson and his wife died suddenly in 1868, their belongings were sold to care for their orphaned children. Much of what you see today are furnishings of the period donated by Taos residents. Exhibits interpret Carson's unexpected rise to fame (Frémont recalled that Carson was "quiet and unassuming") and his

**BELOW:** exterior and interior of the Harwood Museum of Art.

*A bell hangs over a bed-and-breakfast inn near the Plaza.*

life in Taos. One room has guns from the period. Another showcases a Trappers Hall of Fame. Kids will enjoy the walk-through mountain man's camp.

Carson and fellow mountain men Ceran St. Vrain and Charles Bent founded Taos's first freemason brotherhood in the mid-1800s. By then, Ceran St. Vrain had moved to Taos and opened a store on the south side of the Plaza. **La Fonda Hotel** now stands on the site of the former mercantile. Bent was installed as the first governor of New Mexico in 1846, after the United States seized New Mexico. The following year, he and other Americans were murdered by a group of Hispanic settlers and Taos Indians in a three-week uprising. The **Governor Bent House and Museum ⊕** (117A Bent St, 505-758-2376; daily 10am–5pm) is open to visitors.

## Beyond Taos

Kit Carson arrived in Taos just after the opening of the Santa Fe Trail, which broke Spain's economic stranglehold on New Mexico by making inexpensive finished trade goods available to New Mexicans living under Mexican rule. New Mexico immediately benefited from the reversal in fortunes. Goods made in the East arrived in Santa Fe and Taos and were sent down the Camino Real to Mexico City along with New Mexico exports, such as woven goods, to markets eager to receive them.

**BELOW:** Hacienda de los Martínez has been restored to its appearance in the early 19th century.

The first trader in Taos to capitalize on this new trade was Hispanic settler Severino Martínez and his wife María del Carmel Santiestevan, who, in 1804, moved near Ranchos de Taos and built a fortified ranch and trading post at the northern end of the Camino Real. The eldest of their six children became a priest and championed the rights of the Hispanic people under U.S. rule. Padre Antonio Martínez battled French Archbishop Lamy to preserve the Hispanic

character of the Catholic Church in the territory, opened Taos's first coeducational school, and founded Taos's first newspaper.

Today, the restored **Hacienda de los Martínez ❶** (Ranchitos Rd, 505-758-0505; daily 9am–5pm Apr–Oct; admission) offers a rare chance to examine frontier life in the early 1800s. Twenty-one rooms with cedar shake ceilings, known as *rajas*, surround two pleasant courtyards, or *placitas*. The main *placita* was used by the family and includes bedrooms, trade rooms, a chapel, a dispensary and a *sala*, or family room, with a wooden floor. A large kitchen with an unusual shepherd's bed over the fireplace, weaving rooms and storerooms surround the adjoining servants' *placita*. Demonstrations of traditional handicrafts take place in summer.

US 64 heads north from Taos through pastoral country grazed by Indian paint ponies, cows and sheep. Just beyond Millicent Rogers Road, a right turn on US 64 takes you past several popular restaurants near the arts village of Arroyo Seco to Taos Ski Valley, known worldwide for its superb ski conditions. A few miles west of the junction is the **Rio Grande Gorge Bridge**, dubbed the "Bridge to Nowhere" when it was built in 1965, because the road dead-ended on the other side of the gorge. At 650 ft (200 meters) above the river, this is the second highest suspension bridge in the country. Be careful walking across or leaning over the railings. Winds are very strong here.

Maps
Area 194
City 214

*A sign beckons to shoppers from the window of a Taos boutique.*

## The Enchanted Circle

The 86-mile (138km) scenic byway known as the Enchanted Circle begins north of the Ski Valley turnoff and loops east at artsy Questa, around 13,161-ft-high (4,012-meter) **Wheeler Peak ⓳**, New Mexico's tallest mountain, via NM 38. The loop passes through several former mining towns, including 1892 Red

Map on page 194

*D. H. Lawrence Ranch and Memorial.*

**BELOW:** a typically diminutive adobe house.
**RIGHT:** a rafter takes on the Taos Box of the Rio Grande.

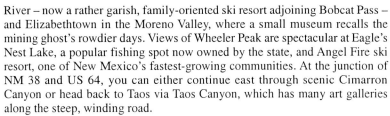

River – now a rather garish, family-oriented ski resort adjoining Bobcat Pass – and Elizabethtown in the Moreno Valley, where a small museum recalls the mining ghost's rowdier days. Views of Wheeler Peak are spectacular at Eagle's Nest Lake, a popular fishing spot now owned by the state, and Angel Fire ski resort, one of New Mexico's fastest-growing communities. At the junction of NM 38 and US 64, you can either continue east through scenic Cimarron Canyon or head back to Taos via Taos Canyon, which has many art galleries along the steep, winding road.

Two stops on this tour stand out. Just beyond Arroyo Hondo, a right turn at San Cristobal takes you on a dirt road to Lobo Mountain, where the University of New Mexico preserves the **D. H. Lawrence Ranch ㉔**. The 160-acre (65-hectare) Kiowa Ranch was given to the writer and his wife Frieda by Mabel Dodge Luhan in 1924, when Lawrence returned to New Mexico aiming to create a Utopian community he called Rananim. During the summers of 1924 and 1925, the Lawrences and their only convert, Lady Dorothy Brett, together with Taos Pueblo artist Trinidad Archuleta and his wife, experimented with group living, painting, writing, fixing up cabins, milking cows, plowing fields and baking bread. The 14-month experiment ended when Lawrence was diagnosed with tuberculosis and he returned to Europe.

Lawrence died in Vence, France, in 1930. In 1935, Frieda's Italian lover Angelo Ravagli brought the writer's ashes back to Taos, where his former wife interred them in a small whitewashed concrete shrine at the ranch. At her request, she was buried outside the Lawrence Memorial, where a break in the forest offers spectacular views of Taos Plateau. Frieda Lawrence willed the ranch to the University of New Mexico in memory of her husband, and the public is welcome to visit. For fans of D. H. Lawrence's work, a pilgrimage to this shrine is a must. Be sure to read the visitor's book inside the shrine, which contains many poignant comments about the writer's impact on individual lives.

### War and remembrance

Equally poignant, but for very different reasons, is the **Vietnam Veterans National Memorial ㉑** (877-613-6900; www.angelfirememorial.com), high on a hillside near the turnoff for Angel Fire. Funded and built by Dr. Victor Westphall in 1971 to honor the memory of his son David, who was killed with 12 comrades in Vietnam in 1968, this is a place where, like the phoenix above Lawrence's shrine, you feel the spirit reborn and flying free. A slender whitewashed building designed in the shape of a pair of folded dove's wings encloses an intimate chapel containing a small altar, photographs of the deceased, and meditation cushions.

The site is now recognized as a national memorial and has a well-conceived visitor center, with exhibits and an extensive research library. An attractive museum uses artifacts, photographs of soldiers and Vietnamese people, and quotations to get its message of the futility of war across. A moving PBS documentary, drawing on home-movie footage, soldiers' letters home and contemporary music, captures the reality of the Vietnam experience beautifully. ❏

# CENTRAL NEW MEXICO

*Albuquerque, the state's largest city,*
*anchors a region of varied attractions*

**D**espite all the people – about 450,000, the largest number of any place in the state – Albuquerque makes no big claims about itself. It's a city laid out in typically sprawling Sun Belt fashion, but somehow it manages to cling to a small-town attitude.

There are no major-league sports for would-be boosters to brag about. Nor any gold-domed capitol glinting in the sun (Santa Fe is the capital city). There's no architectural icon on the scale of anything like the Empire State Building in New York or, on the other coast, the Golden Gate Bridge. Even the slogan dreamed up by the Convention and Visitors Bureau – "Albuquerque: it's a trip" – evinces a good-natured recognition that the city isn't quite in the same league as, say, Los Angeles or Phoenix.

And what about the name of Albuquerque's new triple-A baseball franchise, the Isotopes? Was it inspired by the city's connection with cutting-edge nuclear research? Up to a point, say the team's owners. The chief inspiration, they confess, was an episode of television's hit series *The Simpsons* in which Homer thwarts a plan to move his favorite baseball team, the Springfield Isotopes, to Albuquerque.

Funny thing is, Albuquerque needn't be humble. There may be bigger, flashier, higher-profile towns, but few offer the same quality of life at so reasonable a cost. Encompassed within the metropolitan area is a major university, a bustling business district, historic Old Town, scores of excellent restaurants, a dozen fine museums and a vibrant arts scene.

For those who can't bear to be separated from wild places, Albuquerque is within easy reach of what one writer calls the "faraway nearby." A 30-minute drive from downtown can put you on the crest of the Sandia Mountains or in a lovely shaded bosque along the Rio Grande (a blessing on a sweltering summer day). To the northeast of the city, along a backcountry road dubbed the Turquoise Trail, are the tumble-down remains of mining camps and the funky shops of Madrid, a ghost town resurrected by a quirky coalition of artists and entrepreneurs.

Ghost towns of a very different sort are found along the Salt Trail – ruins of Indian Pueblos and 17th-century Spanish missions at Salinas Pueblo Missions National Monument. To the west, straight down speedy I-70, is the mesatop home of the Acoma people, perhaps the oldest continuously inhabited village in the United States, as well as Zuni and Laguna pueblos. Here, too, is Mount Taylor, the Navajo's sacred Turquoise Mountain, and the Zuni Mountains, both laced with excellent hiking and Jeep trails, as well as the unearthly El Malpais, a forbidding lava sea (monster's blood, the Navajo say) rimmed with sandstone bluffs.

Back in town, folks nod with a knowing smile when outsiders say that Albuquerque isn't quite up to big-city standards. They're right. Albuquerque is different. It's the home of the Isotopes. And it's a trip. ❑

---

**PRECEDING PAGES:** New Mexican rancher, with a winter supply of firewood.
**LEFT:** *farolitos* – traditional Christmas lights – illuminate Old Town Albuquerque.

# ALBUQUERQUE

*It's the Big Enchilada of New Mexico, a brash urban
entity that keeps straining its borders even as
it embraces its historic roots*

I n a state that seems caught in a centuries-old time warp, **Albuquerque ❶** is brazenly modern in its outlook. Perhaps it's because, in common with other Sun Belt cities like Phoenix, the "Duke City" came of age during the postwar boom. Certainly its location in the center of the state has made it a popular crossroads for centuries. The Camino Real and Santa Fe Trail both passed through here, and the city grew overnight when the railroad depot was built just east of Old Town in 1880.

But since Route 66 was first blasted through here, in the 1920s, Albuquerque has been a city dedicated to auto travel. The clearest evidence of this is the recent completion of what has become known locally as the "Big I," where Interstates 40 and 25 intersect in a surprisingly harmonious series of soaring flyover bridges painted in pleasing pinks and tans that echo the pastel tones of the desert. In laissez-faire New Mexico, there's room for just about anything to take root.

The Duke City seems comfortable with its status as the only major city in a sleepy rural state. This urban-rural conjunction has made for a number of strange bedfellows. Traditional Indian pueblos sit next to sprawling Anglo subdivisions in the 'burbs. Spanish Pueblo Revival buildings add much-needed gravitas to a confusing mixture of more recent styles, from postmodern glass boxes to neon-lit roadside attractions born in the age of motor tourism. And even its critics acknowledge there's genius in siting the new state-run National Hispanic Cultural Center – an eclectic assortment of buildings whose architecture echoes Spanish styles around the world – in the Barelas neighborhood, a place where old New Mexico meets new. Almost overnight, the historic barrio has become the hot new place to discover authentic homestyle restaurants and receive a much-needed infusion of urban renewal.

**PRECEDING PAGES:**
Sandia Peak
Tramway.
**LEFT:** San Felipe
de Neri Church.
**BELOW:** a trail guide
shows his charges
a horny toad.

## Squeeze play

With pueblo lands north and south of the city limiting expansion, Albuquerque has developed sideways instead, following the Interstate 40 corridor. The burgeoning suburb of Rio Rancho is swallowing up West Mesa, the black lava bench where thousands of historic rock inscriptions are protected at Petroglyph National Monument. To the east, the city has spread from Old Town right into the foothills of the 10,000-ft (3,000-meter) Sandia Mountains.

In between is the lush Rio Grande, its banks a ribbon of green in spring and appealing russets in winter. Mature bosques of cottonwoods and willows line the river, attracting a huge variety of riparian creatures, such as migratory and resident waterfowl and even beavers at several nature preserves. The North Valley is where much of Albuquerque comes to play. Residents

*Squash blossom necklace at the Turquoise Museum.*

enjoy birdwatching, horseback riding, hiking, biking, golf, ballooning and roller blading on miles of City Open Space along the Rio Grande **acequia madre**, between Interstate 40 and Alameda Boulevard. Nearby, in October, the world's largest mass ascension of balloons takes place at **Balloon Fiesta Park** (505-821-1000; www.balloonfiesta.com), where, in 2005, a new museum tracing the history of ballooning opened its doors.

## Old Town

Any tour of Albuquerque begins in **Old Town** Ⓐ. This is where, following the death of Diego de Vargas, the ambitious acting governor, Francisco Cuervo y Valdez, founded Albuquerque in early 1706. By the time Governor Cuervo wrote to the Viceroy of New Spain, the Duke of Alburquerque, to inform him of the new settlement, 35 families were living at a 1632 *estancia*, or ranch, known locally as El Bosque Grande de Dona Luisa. Soldiers and others attracted by land grants built homes made of *terrones*, or sod bricks, not traditional adobe, and kept live-stock in adjoining corrals. Fields were sown and irrigated, using a network of nar-row ditches running from the Rio Grande. A church had already been completed.

To head off official criticism for having founded a new settlement without the required royal permission, Cuervo told the Viceroy he had named the new com-munity La Villa de San Francisco de Alburquerque in his honor. The only expense to the royal treasury would be bells, missals, chalices and other neces-sities for the church. Backed into a corner, the Viceroy agreed to send the items up El Camino Real to the remote northern frontier settlement. Cuervo was, however, instructed to rename the town. In a political move at least as overt as Cuervo's, the Viceroy decreed that the new administrative center should be

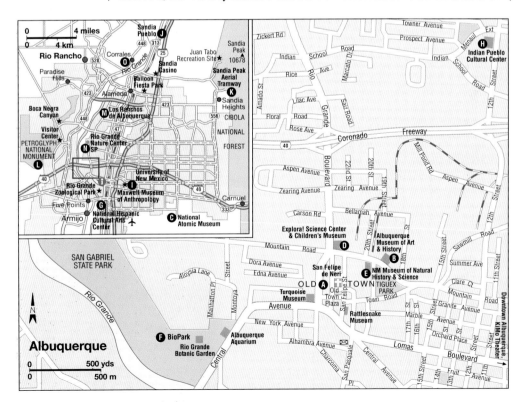

called La Villa de San Felipe de Alburquerque, to honor King Philip of Spain. Only later would Alburquerque lose its first "r" when, as the story goes, the station master at the new railroad depot anglicized the Spanish name.

**San Felipe de Neri Church** was originally west of the Plaza but was moved to the north side in 1793. Although small, the church with the double bell tower aspires to grandness, with a pulpit, a Spanish *reredos* (altar screen), pious European-style statuary, and fussy linens. Mass is held regularly, and in May the church has its annual Blessing of the Animals. In June, a popular **Old Town Fiesta** brings mariachi music, food and celebrations. Then, nine days before Christmas, traditional Las Posadas (the Inns) processions circle the Plaza in candlelit reverence, reminding the faithful how Mary and Joseph sought shelter for the birth of baby Jesus. On Christmas Eve, the plaza glows with thousands of *farolitos*, small brown paper bags with votive candles inside, traditionally put out to light the pilgrim's way to the Christ Child.

Around the Plaza, historic buildings contain restaurants and galleries representing some of the most prestigious artists in the state. As in Santa Fe, you'll find Indian artisans selling under the portals of some buildings. Before buying jewelry, you might want to visit the **Turquoise Museum** (2107 Central Ave NW, 505-247-8650; Mon–Sat 9.30am– 5.30pm; admission) to learn how to distinguish genuine turquoise from clever fakes. This museum is a mine – forgive the pun – of information about the history of turquoise and has many beautiful displays.

## Cultural corridor

A block east of the church is the **Albuquerque Museum of Art and History ⓑ**, (2000 Mountain Rd NW, 505-242-7255, www.cabq.gov/museum; Tues–Sun 9am–5pm; admission). As you might expect, the main exhibition at this child-friendly museum chronicles four centuries of Albuquerque history, with a strong emphasis on the Spanish experience. Highlights include a life-size armored conquistador and horse, a reconstructed 18th-century hacienda, and a 300-year-old *repostero*, or armorial wall hanging, donated to the city in 1956 by the 18th Duke of Alburquerque. The *vaquero* exhibits are particularly interesting, featuring ornate chaps, saddles, bridles and paintings of the original American cowboys.

The other highlight of the museum is its large collection of art by well-known New Mexico artists such as Warren Rollins, John Marin, Roxanne Swentzell and Georgia O'Keeffe. Look for several compelling portraits by Taos painter Ernest Blumenschein of various Indian acquaintances. Works by Apache bronze sculptor Allan Houser and Hispanic *enfant terrible* fiberglass artist Luis Jimenez can be found in a pleasant sculpture garden.

The Albuquerque Museum opens onto the beautifully landscaped **Tiguex** (Tee-gwesh) **Park** on Mountain Road in what is fast becoming Albuquerque's most important cultural corridor. The federally funded **National Atomic Museum ⓒ** (1905 Mountain Rd NW, 505-245-2136, www.atomicmuseum.com; daily 9am–5pm; admission) may not be everyone's cup of tea. It owns the world's largest collection of artifacts

Map on page 232

**BELOW:** *Earth Mother* by Jemez Pueblo artist Estella Loretto is displayed in the sculpture garden of the Albuquerque Museum of Art and History.

*The American International Rattlesnake Museum features exhibits of live rattlers.*

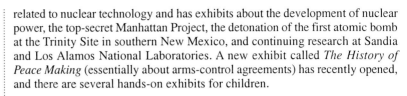

related to nuclear technology and has exhibits about the development of nuclear power, the top-secret Manhattan Project, the detonation of the first atomic bomb at the Trinity Site in southern New Mexico, and continuing research at Sandia and Los Alamos National Laboratories. A new exhibit called *The History of Peace Making* (essentially about arms-control agreements) has recently opened, and there are several hands-on exhibits for children.

## Life science

Lighter in tone is **Explora! Science Center and Children's Museum** (1701 Mountain Rd NW, 505-224-8300, www.explora.mus.nm.us; Mon–Sat 10am–6pm, Sun noon–6pm; admission) just down the road. Explora moved into a spectacular new two-story building in late 2003, where "interactive" is the key word. More than 250 exhibits explore the properties of electricity, light, gravity and water. Highlights include a Kinetic Sculpture and a series of exhibits where kids can experiment with motion, force and energy. A dome in the entryway offers a clever demonstration of acoustics. This is a fun place for the whole family. Exhibits are designed to pique kids' curiosity on their own; volunteers are available to help with questions. Parents can learn alongside youngsters or relax in the water play area or outdoor playground with the tiny tots.

Explora shares a parking lot with the superb **New Mexico Museum of Natural History and Science** (1801 Mountain Rd NW, 505-841-2800, www.nmnaturahistory.org; daily 9am–6pm; admission) next door. Among the highlights are the Sea Coast and Dinosaur exhibits, which feature dinosaur skeletons unearthed in New Mexico's Bisti Badlands and the Clayton area. This is *the* place in New Mexico to learn about the state's volcanoes, with clever displays about geology, including one that mimics a volcanic eruption. The most recent new attractions are the Lodestar Astronomy Center, where the planets come to life in a domed auditorium, and a 266-seat large-screen theater.

**BELOW:** a bronze *Albertosaurus* looms just outside the entrance of the New Mexico Museum of Natural History.

You can get up close with wildlife at **BioPark** (2601 W. Central Ave NW, 505-764-6200, www.cabq.gov/biopark; daily 9am–5pm, to 6pm in summer; admission). This is really three separate facilities: the **Albuquerque Aquarium**, the **Rio Grande Botanic Garden** and the **Rio Grande Zoological Park**. The Aquarium does a fine job of exploring the role of water as it passes through the New Mexico desert, using as its theme the journey of a drop of water traveling from the source of the Rio Grande in Colorado to its terminus in the Gulf of Mexico. Displays of Gulf creatures include a floor-to-ceiling shark tank and a spooky walk-through moray eel and schooling fish exhibit.

Next door, the 16-acre (7-hectare) Botanic Garden includes an airy 10,000-sq-ft (930-sq-meter) conservatory with exhibits of Mediterranean plants and those that grow in the Southwest's Chihuahuan and Sonoran Deserts. Outdoor paths wind through many native plantings and a new Children's Fantasy Garden, a unique interactive experience where kids can learn about plants in a topsy-turvy, magnified Alice in Wonderland setting.

The 60-acre (24-hectare) Rio Grande Zoo (903 10th St SW, 505-764-6200; daily 9am–5pm; admission) is located a few blocks away, close to the Rio Grande. On the beautifully land-scaped grounds are an aviary, petting zoo and a reptile house with 6-ft (2-meter) cobras, 20-ft (6-meter) pythons and Komodo dragons. Polar bears have their own pool, waterfall and air-conditioned cave. There are also elephants, Australian animals, primates, Mexican wolves and a new Tropical America area. The zoo's naturalistic enclosures have received kudos from wildlife advocates.

## Hispanic and Indian cultures

Hispanic culture worldwide is the ambitious undertaking of the spectacular new **National Hispanic Cultural Arts Center ⑥** (1701 4th SW, 505-246-2261, www.nhccnm.org; Tues–Sun 10am–5pm; admission), south of Old Town. The first phase of the $34 million project was completed in 2000 and includes a genealogical research center, a library and an 11,000-sq-ft (1,000-sq-meter) art museum. Three galleries feature work by Hispanic artists from around the world. The museum, administered by the state's Office of Cultural Affairs, isn't afraid to take chances. In 2003, it featured a contemporary exhibit curated by Chicano comedian and art lover Cheech Marin.

For an overview of New Mexico's complex Pueblo Indian cultures, be sure to visit **The Indian Pueblo Cultural Center ⑪** (2401 12th St NW, 505-843-7270; www.indianpueblo.org; daily 9am–5.30pm; admission), a few blocks north of Old Town and just north of Interstate 40. The cultural center is owned by the 19 pueblos of New Mexico, each with an area showing its unique arts and crafts. If you've ever wanted to sample an Indian taco, but can't make it to a pueblo feast, the small restaurant serving native foods is the place. On summer weekends, members of different tribes perform dances on the patio; photography is permitted.

Map on page 232

**BELOW:** fanciful mural on Central Avenue, along old Route 66.

*A young visitor enjoys an Old Town fiesta.*

**BELOW:**
human evolution
exhibit at the
Maxwell Museum
of Anthropology.

## Urban renewal

The City of Albuquerque has recently finished a near miraculous overhaul of what was once a soul-less, 1970s-era, downtown area near the railroad station. Although flanked by two modern high-rises (dubbed The Twin Peaks by wags), historic **La Posada Hotel**, Conrad Hilton's first property, holds its own for sheer charm. The Pueblo Revival lobby has a cool elegance, with dark mission-style wood furniture, an old-fashioned bar, ceiling vigas and a colorful wall mural showing the Indian pueblos. A block south, **The District**, as it's now known, is a walker's paradise. Central Avenue (formerly Route 66) has new landscaping, the city's hippest clubs and restaurants, lofts, art galleries and studios, classic hotels and diners, western wear shops and the well restored **KiMo Theater** (505-768-3522), a top example of ornate Pueblo Deco architecture in the state.

Contemporary architecture along Central cleverly pays homage to the neon-lit diners, gas stations and motor courts that lined Route 66 in its heyday in the 1950s and '60s. Follow Central east, under Interstate 25, to the **University of New Mexico ❶**, where architecture and anthropology are two of the university's highly regarded programs. The two disciplines come together seamlessly in the **Maxwell Museum of Anthropology** (505-277-4404; Tues–Fri 9am–4pm, Sat 10am–4pm; free), one of a number of campus buildings designed by famed New Mexico architect John Gaw Meem in the 1930s. Meem's Pueblo Revival building is a perfect home for the Maxwell, which has exhibits on world cultures as well as an extraordinary collection of Southwest artifacts, including a stunning collection of black-on-white Mimbres pottery from near Silver City.

Don't leave the University District without enjoying a huge breakfast burrito smothered in hot chile at the city's best bargain eatery, the **Frontier Restaurant**, opposite UNM's main entrance. The 24-hour diner is an Edward Hopper classic, with 1950s Googie architecture and servers in white hats. You'll find more upscale dining, as well as unique shops, at the popular **Nob Hill Shopping Center**, a few blocks away.

## Beyond the city

The **Sandia Mountains** – a massive uplift of granitic rock topped with limestone on the east side of Albuquerque – dominate the city aesthetically, recreationally and climatically. The mountainsides facing the city are rugged and steep; the other side is gentler, with forested slopes. Both sides offer miles of hiking trails in **Cibola National Forest**.

**Sandia Pueblo ❷** (Box 6008, Bernalillo 87004, 505-867-3317, www.sandiapueblo.nsn.us), 14 miles (23km) north of Albuquerque, has fertile bottomland for farming and has capitalized on its proximity to Albuquerque by encouraging tourist-related industries such as its attractive Ancestral Pueblo-style **Sandia Hotel and Casino** (800-526-9366), the highly rated Bien Shur Restaurant and concerts at its huge outdoor amphitheater. **Sandia Peak** is sacred to the pueblo. Look for the tribe's herd of buffalo on the south side of the road and a large arts and crafts center on the road to the Sandia Peak Tram.

**Sandia Peak Aerial Tramway ❸** (505-856-7325; daily 9am–10pm; admission), the longest in America, goes up the west side of the mountains. By day, one can see mountains 100 miles (160km) away. At night, eat at a restaurant at the top while the lights of Albuquerque, Santa Fe and Los Alamos twinkle below. In winter, skiers take the tram to **Sandia Peak Ski Area** or drive up the other side. Built in 1966 by a Swiss company, the tramway spans 2.7 miles (4.3km) and climbs 3,819 ft (1,165 meters). The ride takes about 15 minutes; the elevation at the terminal is 10,378 ft (3,163 meters).

Immediately west of the Rio Grande is **Petroglyph National Monument** ❶ (off Unsor Blvd, 505-899-0205; www.nps.gov/petr; daily 8am–5pm; admission). Established in 1990, it is jointly managed by the City of Albuquerque and the National Park Service. It had suffered significant degradation even before it was set aside. Now, with housing subdivisions and a highway just feet away, it's struggling to hold its own. The monument contains land sacred to the Pueblo people, whose ancestors left thousands of petroglyphs along 17-mile-long (27-km) West Mesa, a volcanic formation that erupted 110,000 years ago along the still active Rio Grande Rift Zone. There are several trails in three main areas: Boca Negra Canyon, Rinconada Canyon and Volcanoes, which is reached from the opposite side of the monument. The 15,000-plus petroglyphs here – the earliest is over 2,000 years old – also include a number of historic Spanish and cowboy inscriptions.

## Town and country

Ranching and farming remain popular pursuits in Albuquerque's North Valley. You can buy a latte at a tack shop, sample wines at some surprisingly good vineyards, and dine al fresco in the **Dietz Farm Plaza** while enjoying a *sandia* (watermelon)-hued sunset on the mountains. The ranches and farms in the villages of Los Ranchos and Corrales have been worked since Ancestral Pueblo

Map
on page
232

**LEFT:** mountain lion image in Rinconada Canyon, Petroglyph National Monument. **BELOW:** desert biking on the outskirts of town.

Map on page 232

*Only segments of Old Route 66 remain in New Mexico.*

**BELOW:**
Sandia Mountains.

times, and a number of Indian villages lie beneath the rich loam. In the 1700s, people from Puebla, Mexico, took over abandoned Indian farmlands and created *estancias* and *ranchos*, irrigating from a network of ditches off the Rio Grande.

Farming is woven into the history of **Los Poblanos** (4803 Rio Grande Blvd, 505-344-9297, www.lospoblanos.com) in **Los Ranchos de Albuquerque ❿**, now a historic bed-and-breakfast inn and lavender farm occupying 26 acres (11 hectares) atop an ancient pueblo. The present estate was developed from the 19th-century Armijo homestead by Congresswoman Ruth Hanna McCormick Simms and her husband. The couple, major philanthropists in Albuquerque, remodeled the property in 1934 and started Creamland Dairy on the site.

Among the estate's unique features is its Mexican-style hacienda, considered one of architect John Gaw Meem's most pleasing Spanish Territorial buildings. The formal English garden was laid out by famed landscape artist Rose Greeley. Rock paths by New Mexico's foremost folk artist Pop Shaffer add a touch of humor with the names of the Simms' prize dairy cows spelled out in the rose garden. **La Quinta Cultural Center** next door, designed by Meem as a public entertainment venue, is currently being used for that purpose by owners Armin and Penny Rembe, who took over the property in 2000. The Rembes' extensive collection of *santos*, tinwork and other New Mexico art objects sits alongside a mural by Peter Hurd and unusual carved doorways by printmaker Gustave Baumann in the banquet hall.

## Wild at heart

Hands down the best place in Albuquerque to learn about native wildlife is the nearby **Rio Grande Nature Center State Park ❶** (2901 Candelaria NW, 505-344-7240; daily 10am–5pm; admission). This 270-acre (110-hectare) preserve has three ponds, nature trails, an outdoor classroom, a native herb and wildflower garden, and access to the Rio Grande open space corridor. The concrete visitor center blends into the bosque and has exhibits on Rio Grande water and porthole windows out to the main pond. The library viewing area, with its miked sounds of red-winged blackbirds, geese, ducks and other birds at the pond, is an enchanting place to spend an afternoon. Guided hikes and family activities are offered regularly. The park also runs a rehabilitation center for injured birds that is occasionally open to the public.

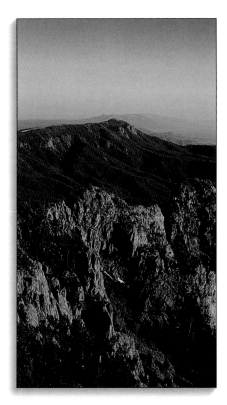

You'll see all manner of unusual animals, including sheep, goats, llamas, emus, even ostrich, on tiny homesteads in the nearby village of **Corrales ❶**, which bills itself as "animal friendly" and offers its own scenic byway. Delightful art galleries, studios, inns, restaurants and lots of massage therapists run businesses amid fragrant apple orchards and leafy lanes (come for the art studio tour at the beginning of May). In the historic center of Corrales, the 1860s **Old San Ysidro Church** (505-897-1513) makes a great photo op. Opposite is **Casa San Ysidro** (505-898-3915 for tours), an 18th-century adobe hacienda that once belonged to the descendants of Don Felipe Gutierrez, recipient of the Bernalillo land grant in 1704. San Ysidro, the patron saint of farmers and rain, works overtime in this delightful spot, which feels like a million miles from Albuquerque. ❏

# The Mother Road

Dispossessed Okies and Arkies in the 1930s. African-American ex-GI's in the 1940s. Wild-eyed Beat poets in the 1950s. Vacationing families in station wagons in the 1960s. What they all had in common was a burning desire to get into the car, turn on the ignition, and head west on Route 66 to see America. Between 1926 and 1985, its final year, the 2,448-mile (3,940-km) highway linking Chicago and Santa Monica, California, became a rite of passage for thousands of travelers, their ticket to a better life just around the corner.

When it was built in 1926, the original 506-mile (814-km) route through New Mexico followed a circuitous path using existing roads. It began in eastern New Mexico at Glenrio, then headed west through Tucumcari to Santa Rosa, where it wandered north to Romeroville, then returned west to Santa Fe, following the Santa Fe Trail. It then dropped south along El Camino Real to Albuquerque and Los Lunas, challenging drivers at La Bajada Mesa, where they were forced to negotiate the steep switchbacks by putting the car in reverse and backing down! The route passed close to a number of pueblos, including Santo Domingo and, to the west, Acoma. After leaving Acoma, it headed west to Arizona via Gallup, taking in a large section of the Navajo Reservation.

Late in 1926, ousted governor A. T. Hannett exacted a final revenge on northern New Mexican voters by ordering the highway department to blade the 67 miles (108km) between Santa Rosa and Moriarty, initiating a realignment of Route 66 that bypassed Santa Fe. By 1938, the route through New Mexico was not only paved but 107 miles (172km) shorter. Travel on the improved highway boomed in the 1940s and '50s, then tapered off as the old road was buried beneath the new interstate system.

Of the six segments of Route 66 still visible in New Mexico, Albuquerque's neon-lit Central Avenue is one of the best preserved, with more than 100 diners, motor courts, theaters and other classic structures built in a variety of architectural styles, from Streamline Moderne to Pueblo Deco. In Tucumcari, the down-home friendly Blue Swallow Motel is still going strong 55 years after it was given to owner Lillian Redman as an engagement present. The grande dame of Gallup, the 1937 El Rancho Hotel, once hosted Ronald Reagan, Robert Taylor and many other Hollywood actors who stayed here while filming westerns between 1940 and 1964. John Wayne stayed so frequently, he got his own room next to the bar.

In the end, though, Route 66 is all about cars and the open road. You'll find classic T'birds and 'Vettes and other tricked-out roadsters in the Route 66 Auto Museum in Santa Rosa, which along with Tucumcari, Grants and Albuquerque is host to an annual Route 66 festival. The eastern part of the state still echoes with the strains of Buddy Holly, who recorded his hits here in the 1950s. Perhaps that's why it seems only natural to grab a burger and fries at Joseph's in Santa Rosa and take in a drive-in movie. The Mother Road still beckons. ❑

**RIGHT:** Central Avenue, also known as Old Route 66.

# TURQUOISE TRAIL AND SALINAS MISSIONS

Map on page 244

*Two winding backroads lead into New Mexico's past –*
*one to a ghost town resurrected by artists, the other*
*to the ruins of 17th-century Spanish missions*

F ew people think of New Mexico as having a colorful mining history. Perhaps that's because lucky strikes in other states yielded such untold riches, they get more play in history books. Prepare to be surprised. A scenic byway between Santa Fe and Albuquerque offers a fascinating exploration of New Mexico's colorful mining past.

Promoted as the Turquoise Trail (www.turquoisetrail.org), NM 14 and its lesser-known southern extension, the Salt Mission Trail, make for an unusual long weekend trip. Along these winding backroads are the oldest mines and salt-collection areas in North America, silent Spanish missions, Mexican haciendas, artsy ghost towns, odd roadside attractions and an abundance of local character.

One of the first sights, as you pick up NM 14 from the north, is a little incongruous: the **New Mexico State Penitentiary**. In 1980, the vacant building on the right was the scene of the bloodiest prison riot in U.S. history. Today, it is used mainly to shoot movies, but the minimum security prison and North and South facilities are still operational, along with the new Santa Fe County Jail, on the left side of the road.

Just ahead, the road winds through an area of hills, arroyos and dramatically upended rocks known as the **Garden of the Gods**, the northwestern margin of the Galisteo Basin. For an interesting detour, turn left when you see signs for Galisteo and follow the gravel road to this quiet Hispanic community.

## Pueblos past

**Galisteo ❷** was founded in 1588 on the ruins of Galisteo Pueblo. In the early 1800s, it was famous for its sheep ranches, which supplied wool for the profitable New Mexico weaving industry. Today, the village is a haven for spiritual seekers, writers, artists and those in search of peace and quiet.

Following the great drought of 1276–99, the Galisteo Basin had one of the biggest concentrations of Indian pueblos in the state. Defensive towns were built by people leaving the overcrowded Rio Grande area for secondary farming districts. For most pueblos, the gamble didn't pay off. Arroyo Hondo, one of the largest, collapsed by the 1400s, its residents dead from starvation. By the time the Spanish arrived, most people had coalesced into a few powerful pueblos that were self-sufficient and highly specialized. Cicuye, in the adjoining Pecos River valley, was an important trading center. San Marcos Pueblo in the Galisteo Basin focused on making a new kind of pottery that used a galena glaze derived from lead mined in the Cerrillos Hills.

**PRECEDING PAGES:**
artist Michael
Wright at his
Madrid studio.
**LEFT:** pueblo ruins
at Gran Quivira.
**BELOW:** all smiles on
the Turquoise Trail.

*"Virtue triumphant" is the theme of the Madrid melodrama, an authentic re-creation of a 19th-century "traveling show."*

**RIGHT:** enigmatic petroglyph in the Galisteo Basin.

## Cerillos mines

The **Cerrillos Historic Mining District** surrounding the village of **Los Cerrillos** ❸ ("Little Hills") is the oldest in the United States. By AD 1000, turquoise mining camps at Mount Chalchihuitl were supplying the precious stones for trade to the Aztec empire in Mexico and Chaco Canyon, where huge quantities of turquoise have been found. In 1541, Coronado and his Spanish conquistadors passed through the Galisteo Basin en route to Pecos, obsessed with gold, and missed the mines.

Not long after Coronado returned to Mexico empty-handed, silver was discovered in the northern provinces of Mexico. The subsequent mining rush revived interest in the Southwest. In 1581, the brazen Rodriguez-Chamuscado expedition sneaked into New Mexico illegally and was led to the mines in the Cerrillos Hills by miners from San Marcos Pueblo. Within three years of Juan de Oñate's arrival in New Mexico, he and his partner Vicente de Zaldivar were mining silver and lead at Cerrillos. Historians suspect they built a camp near the mines. If so, it predates Santa Fe as the first colonial settlement in this area.

An important lead mine, El Mino del Tiro, was opened during the Mexican period. Then, in 1879, American miners from Leadville, Colorado, flooded into the area. The village of Cerrillos was laid out in 1880, the same year the railroad reached the settlement. In its heyday, the village had 3,000 residents, 21 saloons, five brothels, four hotels and eight newspapers. The **Clear Light Opera House** where Sarah Bernhardt and Lily Langtry sang is still on Main Street. Thirteen movies have been shot in the sleepy village, including scenes from *The Hi Lo Country* and two Walt Disney films.

Mining continued sporadically well into the 20th century but has now ceased due to local opposition. In 2000, residents succeeded in getting 1,100 acres

(445 hectares) of the mining district set aside as open space. **Cerrillos Hills Historic Park** (505-424-0807, www.cerrilloshills.org), opened in 2003, has hiking trails, interpretive signs and an informative website.

## A ghost resurrected

Just beyond Cerrillos, in the Ortiz Mountains, another ghost town, **Madrid ❹**, is the oldest coal-mining region in New Mexico, with mines dating to the mid-1850s. A railroad spur in 1892 linked the community, then known as Coal Gulch, to the main line of the Santa Fe Railroad. By the early 1900s, Madrid (pronounced MA-drid) was owned by the Albuquerque and Cerrillos Coal Company and boasted a population of 2,500. The company built schools, a hospital, a company store, a tavern and an employees club. Miners were required to donate to civic causes and participate in town events, such as Madrid's famous Christmas illuminations, which boasted 150,000 Christmas lights powered by 500,000 kilowatts of electricity from the town's coal-fed generators. Madrid's ballpark was the first flood-lit park in the country. It is now used for bluegrass and jazz concerts in summer.

The death knell sounded for Madrid during World War II, and by the 1950s the mines were closed. In the mid-1970s, the town's current owner, the late Joe Huber, son of the former mine superintendent, tried to revive the town. The old clapboard "shotgun shacks" were sold at fire-sale prices to artists and others keen to start a new community. Today, Madrid is an arty little town, fully wired to the Internet (www.mad-rid.com). Its 300 residents run a plethora of art galleries, cafes, restaurants and museums, and a Madrid Holiday Open House (505-471-1054), complete with Christmas lights, is once again a popular tradition. Madrid is unapologetically counter-culture, making for some odd sights as you approach town. One must-see is the Bone Zone, the creation of Tammy Jean Lange, an artist who creates sculptures out of bones, then places them in her gardens.

On weekends, people come from Santa Fe to a popular watering hole known as the **Mine Shaft Tavern** (505-473-0743). Its 50-ft-long (15-meter) lodgepole pine bar is the longest in New Mexico. You'll meet all kinds of folks enjoying strong drinks, good burgers and live music. The mine shaft can be viewed at the **Old Coal Mine Museum** (505-438-3780) next door, which has exhibits on the town's history, as well as a restored 1900 locomotive. Visitors can also enjoy Victorian melodramas in the adjoining Engine House Theatre.

## Sandia Crest and the Manzanos

Compared with Madrid, there's not much left of **Golden ❺** except for a charming whitewashed adobe church. But in 1825, this unassuming ghost town a few miles south of Madrid made history as the site of the first gold rush west of the Mississippi. In 1879, a second gold strike created a boom, but a lack of water made mining difficult and the town quickly emptied.

About 12 miles (19km) south of Golden, Sandia Crest Scenic Byway (NM 536) winds to the top of 10,000-ft (3,000-meter) Sandia Crest. Two miles (3km) up the road, behind a wall made of thousands of glass bottles, you'll find **Tinkertown** (505-281-5233; Apr–Oct 9am–6pm; admission). The life work of wood carver Ross

**BELOW:** Golden's church and cemetery are a favorite of photographers.

Map on page 244

*Splashes of bright paint add color and whimsy to Madrid mailboxes.*

Ward and his potter wife Carla, the homegrown museum displays a three-ring circus and miniature Wild West town. You can hike and picnic and ski in winter on Sandia Crest, but strangely, no camping is allowed. If you want to camp, pitch your tent in Cedar Crest, next to the privately run **Museum of Archaeology and Material Culture** (22 Calvary Rd, Cedar Crest, 505-281-2005; Apr–Oct daily noon–7pm; admission). The brainchild of archaeologist Bradley Bowman, the museum displays numerous artifacts from the past 12,000 years.

NM 14 joins Interstate 40 at **Tijeras ❻**, a few miles east of Albuquerque. Tijeras sits astride the passage between the Sandia and Manzanita Mountains and was the site of an important gateway pueblo occupied between AD 1300 and 1450. Today, you can visit the 80-room pueblo behind the **Tijeras Pueblo/Sandia Ranger Station** (11776 Hwy 337, 505-281-3304; Mon–Fri 8am–5pm, Sat–Sun 8.30am–5pm) of Cibola National Forest, just south of Interstate 40 on NM 337/14. Pick up maps and information on hiking and camping in the national forest.

There is abundant wildlife in these mountains. **Wildlife West Nature Park ❼** (87 N. Frontage Rd, 505-281-7655; daily 10am–6pm; admission) in nearby **Edgewood** is a good place to learn more. The sanctuary cares for non-releasable animals, such as injured cougars and raptors, which become ambassadors in public education. The Manzanita and Manzano Mountains, bordering southbound NM 337/14, attract migratory raptors, and every winter birders converge on a remote lookout in the Manzanos to count them. Volunteers are always needed. For more information, contact Hawkwatch (505-255-7622, www.hawkwatch.org). The count site is reached via **Manzano Mountains State Park** (505-847-2820) near Manzano. This 160-acre (65-hectare) preserve is set at an elevation of 7,600 ft (2,300 meters) and is a delightful spot for wildlife viewing, hiking, camping and fishing.

## The salt missions

East of the mountains are the low-elevation grasslands of the Estancia Basin, the beginning of the Plains. Estancia is named for its many ranches but, in the past, it was better known for another resource – salt.

Humans have lived in the Estancia Basin for more than 12,000 years. During the Ice Age, it encompassed a lake frequented by paleo hunters. More than 10,000 years later, after the lake dried up, people of the Mogollon culture built pithouses in the basin. Later still, Pueblo people from the north, speaking several different languages, moved in. They had been living in villages here for centuries when the Spanish arrived in 1598 and quickly saw the potential of the salt deposits and free Indian labor. In the early 1600s, Franciscan priests oversaw the construction of missions at several pueblos in the area. **Salinas Pueblo Missions National Monument** (Ripley and Broadway, Mountainair, 505-847-2585, www.nps.gov/sapu; daily 9am–5pm), set aside in 1980, protects three of the best preserved missions.

**Quarai ❽**, 8 miles (13km) north of Mountainair on NM 55, and **Abó ❾**, 9 miles (14km) west of Mountainair on US 60, are typical 17th-century missions. Each has a large, attractive church of vermilion-colored sandstone built with wall-and-lintel construction, high tapering walls, a long nave, transepts, a choir loft and clerestory windows that lit up the altar to maximum effect. Next door is a *campo santo* (cemetery), *portería* (waiting room), patios, *ambulatarios* (walkways), cells, kitchens and livestock corrals. Abó also included the *visitas*, or satellite parishes, of neighboring Tenabó and the southern missions of Tabira and Gran Quivira. As a mark of its importance, the small church of San Gregorio de Abó, the first to be built in the area in 1622, was replaced by a much larger church in 1651.

The ruins of the beautiful mission church of Nuestra Señora de la Purísima Concepcíon at Quarai, founded in 1626, still dominate the well-watered valley, a mile west of Punta del Agua. It soars above the former Tewa-speaking pueblo of Cuarac, now buried beneath grassy mounds. Today, this is a peaceful spot to stroll around and have a picnic. But its tranquility belies a turbulent history.

Spanish settlers placed huge demands on Pueblo people. They were required not only to convert to Christianity and work for the Franciscan friars but to support an *encomienda*, or tribute, system, which allowed soldiers and settlers to collect cloth, grain and other goods annually from Pueblo people in return for "protection."

Complicating matters further, the Salinas province was subject to widening political rifts between Spanish civil and clerical authorities in the 1660s. Quarai was the headquarters of the Spanish Inquisition, which terrorized colonists by collecting evidence (usually unfounded) of disrespect for the clergy and other sacrilegious acts. One unfortunate settler, a German named Bernard Gruber, was jailed for a year without trial on charges of heresy. He escaped, only to die along a torrid 90-mile (145-km) stretch of the Llano Estacado now known as La Jornada del Muerto – the Dead Man's Way.

Map on page 244

**BELOW:** "Rusty" the sheriff keeps an eye on Madrid.

Map on page 244

*Outhouse at the Old Coal Mine Museum.*

**BELOW:** Quarai ruins, Salinas Pueblo Missions National Monument.

## Gran Quivira

The largest of the pueblo missions, **Gran Quivira** , is not typical at all. It lies 26 miles (42km) south of Mountainair, off NM 55, in open country. Today, it seems quite forlorn, with its fallen limestone buildings and lonely setting. At the time of Spanish arrival, though, Gran Quivira was a powerful trading hub, known as Pueblo de las Humanas. It sat on the southernmost frontier between the Rio Grande pueblos and the Plains Apaches and was a bustling melting pot of native cultures that bartered animal products, pottery, pinyon nuts, corn, cloth and more. Traces of all these cultures have been found at the pueblo, including both circular and rectangular kivas, the latter offering strong evidence of Mogollon influence.

The pueblo was constructed of local limestone, but water was an ongoing problem. Indian residents used *pozos*, or cisterns, to collect water and managed quite well by dry-farming and hunting. However, the remote setting and lack of water doomed missionary efforts. Father Francisco Letrado began the church of San Isidro in 1629 but left it uncompleted when he transferred to Zuni Pueblo, where he was later martyred. The Humanas mission was served by a priest from Abó for years, until a new priest, Father Santander, was dispatched in 1659.

Santander's church, San Buenaventura, was never finished either. The disruptions brought by the Spanish were exacerbated by a drought and Apache raids. In 1669, Father Juan Bernal wrote of seeing Indians "perished of hunger, lying dead along the roads… There were pueblos, like Las Humanas, where more than 450 people died of hunger." By the time of the 1680 Pueblo Revolt, the Salt Missions were empty, their residents dispersed among the pueblos of the middle Rio Grande.

Each Pueblo has a small visitor center with exhibits. Park headquarters is in tiny **Mountainair**, at the corner of Ripley and Broadway off NM 66. Mountainair is now a quiet ranching community, although it was once dubbed the Pinto Bean Capital of the World. Diversions are few here – a couple of homespun restaurants and a few dusty shops. Mountainair is known for one famous site: the 1923 Pueblo Deco **Schaeffer Hotel**, built by folk artist Pop Schaeffer, whose "environmental sculptures" are on display.

## Back to Albuquerque

From Mountainair, return to Albuquerque on Interstate 25, via US 60 and NM 47. The highway passes through **Belen** ⑪, once an important stop on the Camino Real, the Royal Road to Mexico City. Every three years colonial administrators used this route to send important supplies north to missions in New Mexico, which then sent back local goods such as woven cloth, rugs, salt and captive Apache laborers.

Just beyond Belen, in rich farmland, is **Isleta Pueblo** ⑫ (505-869-3111), one of the pueblos that took in refugees from the Salt Missions. Historic **St. Augustine Church**, built in 1612, is set on the main plaza. The tribe welcomes visitors and operates several businesses, including Isleta Casino & Resort (800-460-5686), a large complex with five restaurants and a sports bar, and a championship 27-hole golf course with beautiful views. **Isleta Lakes Recreational Complex** (505-877-0370) has year-round fishing, picnicking and RV campsites. ❏

# El Rancho de las Golondrinas

El Rancho de las Golondrinas (The Ranch of the Swallows) is a 200-acre (80-hectare) farm with a historic past. It was acquired by Miguel Vega y Coca in about 1710 and inherited by descendants of the Baca family who married Coca's daughters. During Spanish Colonial times, the ranch was often mentioned in diaries as the final *paraje*, or stop, on El Camino Real, the Royal Road between Mexico City and Santa Fe. In 1778, Governor Juan Bautista de Anza and his men camped here while on an expedition to Mexico.

Since 1972, El Rancho de las Golondrinas has been operated as a nonprofit living history museum, dedicated to fostering understanding of the language, culture and history of Spanish Colonial New Mexico. Dozens of 18th- and 19th-century buildings have been brought to the ranch and restored in period style. Costumed volunteers demonstrate blacksmithing, baking in *hornos* (adobe ovens), sheepshearing, traditional weaving and wool dying, folk music and dance, storytelling, and other activities.

This may well be the best place in all of New Mexico to take the whole family. Visit an 18th-century *placita*, a home built around a courtyard with thick adobe walls and a defensive *torreón*, and duck into cool, dark rooms furnished with carved wooden furniture and lit only by candles. Watch flour being ground in a mill powered with water brought by log flume from the *acequia*. Kids can visit a frontier-era schoolhouse, splash in the river, net tadpoles in the old pond, and pet sheep and goats. And just past the old *morada*, or Penitente chapel, you can visit a family hacienda, complete with miniature grandmother's house, corrals and cornfields.

The ranch holds theme weekends throughout the summer. During these lively events, volunteers dress in traditional costumes, chat with visitors, and demonstrate the skills early settlers needed to survive on the frontier. The museum comes alive with dancing, music, food and crafts. Among the most popular offerings are Civil War reenactment weekends and the Spring and Fall Harvest festivals, with a Mass honoring San Ysidro, the patron saint of farmers, and a procession through the fields to bless the crops.

El Rancho de las Golondrinas (505-471-2261; www.golondrinas.org) is in La Cienega, 15 miles (24km) southwest of Santa Fe. To reach it take I-25 to exit 276 and bear right on NM 599. Turn left at the traffic light onto the frontage road and right just before the racetrack on Los Pinos Road. The museum is 3 miles (5km) from this intersection.

The ranch is open for self-guided tours, Wed–Sun, 10am–4pm, Apr–Oct. A modest admission fee is charged. Allow at least two hours for a tour and be prepared for a lot of walking in hot sun. Bring water and a picnic if visiting during the week or on a non-theme weekend. Healthful and delicious food is also available at the Blue Heron Restaurant at Sunrise Springs Resort, a retreat center in La Cienega, just before reaching the ranch. Sunday brunch is particularly recommended. ❑

**RIGHT:** costumed volunteers re-enact the past.

# ALBUQUERQUE TO ZUNI

*Here, where Coronado and his comrades first encountered
Pueblo people centuries ago, visitors can imagine
how it was when two worlds collided*

Map
on page
254

To the west of Albuquerque, I-40 unfurls like an asphalt ribbon through windswept desert speckled with juniper and sage. Square-shouldered mesas rise on the horizon, their slopes furrowed like rhino skin. This is the land of the three western pueblos – Laguna, Acoma and Zuni – and their Navajo neighbors, as well as the city of Gallup, the self-proclaimed Indian Capital of the World.

This is also the setting of Coronado's earliest meeting with the Pueblo people of New Mexico, an encounter that did not bode well for the Indians. One can only imagine the conquistador's fury upon laying eyes on the Zuni pueblo of Hawikuh – not the fabled City of Gold, as he was led to believe, but a poor village of mud and stone. He ordered the Indians to surrender, threatening to "make war against you… take you and your wives and children… make slaves of them… and do to you all the harm and damage that we can." The Zuni responded with stones and arrows but were no match for gunpowder and steel. Coronado's mounted soldiers overran the village in a matter of hours.

**PRECEDING PAGES:**
La Ventana Arch,
El Malpais National
Monument.
**LEFT:**
Comanche dance,
San Juan Pueblo.
**BELOW:**
NM 117 leads
into El Malpais.

## City in the sky

Start this tour by driving west from Albuquerque on I-40. About 15 miles (24km) beyond the city limits, you cross into the **Laguna Indian Reservation ❶**, home to 2,927 tribal members and 888 other community members residing in six small towns. Laguna was established in the late 17th century by Keresan-speaking refugees evicted by the Spanish from villages along the Rio Grande. Best time to visit is during the Feast of St. Joseph in March and September, which features buffalo, corn and eagle dances and dozens of arts and crafts booths at the village of **Old Laguna**. At other times, stop at Old Laguna for a look at **San José de Laguna Mission Church**, a brilliant whitewashed adobe set on a hill surrounded by the squat, stone houses of the pueblo. The 1699 church is a national historic landmark.

To the west is the exit for Laguna's **Dancing Eagle Casino and Travel Center** (I-40 exit 108, Casa Blanca, 505-552-7777, www.dancingeaglecasino.com), with over 500 slots, an attractive restaurant, a travel center, and fast food. The tribe also owns New Mexico's newest casino, **Route 66 Casino and Travel Center** (I-40 exit 140, 505-352-7866), a retro-themed complex with 1,200 slots, bingo, two restaurants, and a 2,800-seat theater attracting big musical acts.

There's a larger and more elaborate casino just a short drive farther down the highway on the neighboring **Acoma Indian Reservation ❷**. The **Sky City Casino** complex (I-40 exit 102, San Fidel, 505-552-6017, www.skycitycasino.com) encompasses 62,000 sq ft (5,800 sq meters), with poker, blackjack, craps and roulette tables, and more than 600 slot machines. An

*Caution is always a good policy when hiking in the backcountry.*

all-you-can-eat buffet in the adjoining restaurant is a good place for a meal before hitting the road. A hotel and conference center are also on the grounds.

Those who want a deeper understanding of Pueblo culture should take the scenic 16-mile (26km) drive to the old pueblo of Acoma, now known as **Sky City**. Perched atop a mesa 365 ft (111 meters) above the valley floor, Sky City, founded before AD1150, is one of the oldest continually inhabited villages in the United States. Although most Acoma people live in outlying towns, the old pueblo is still inhabited year-round by about a dozen families and is kept in excellent repair for a variety of ceremonial events. The two- and three-story buildings, many entered only by ladder, have no electricity or plumbing. Rainwater is still collected in "water pots" carved into the rock 800 years ago.

After visiting Acoma in 1540, one of Coronado's officers reported that the pueblo was "one of the strongest ever seen, because the city is built upon a very high rock." Sadly, the mesa walls did not repel a contingent of Spanish soldiers bent on revenge. After the Acoma killed a party of Spanish tribute collectors in 1598, including one of Juan de Oñate's nephews, an army of 70 Spanish soldiers stormed the pueblo and slaughtered hundreds of Indians in revenge. Oñate himself sentenced 20 Acoma men to the amputation of one foot and 20 years of slavery. Acoma women and children were condemned to 20 years of servitude. In a particularly cruel stroke, he ordered two Hopi men who were captured at Acoma to have their right hands hacked off, then set free in order to "convey the news of this punishment" to other Indians contemplating defiance.

To visit Sky City, park and register at **Sky City Cultural Center** (800-747-0181, www.skycitytourism.com), at the base of the mesa, where you can buy camera permits, sign up for a tour, or hire a guide. The tour includes a stop at **San**

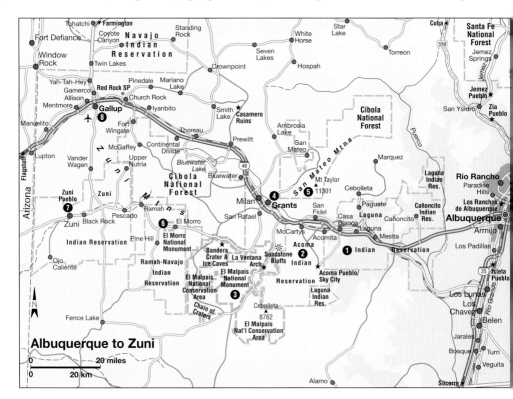

Map on page 254

**Esteban del Rey Mission**, a monumental adobe church built in the early 17th century under the direction of Friar Juan Ramírez. All the construction materials were carried to the mesa top by Acoma laborers, including the soil that fills the graveyard and the church's massive ceiling beams, which came from Mount Taylor, nearly 50 miles (80km) away. Legend has it that the giant logs never touched the ground. There are plenty of opportunities during the tour to buy Acoma pottery. Prices and quality vary, but the most valuable pieces are hand built, thin walled and painted in painstaking detail with natural dyes and yucca brushes.

## The best of a bad land

Return to I-40 via NM 38, continue west to exit 89, and follow the signs to **El Malpais National Monument** ❸ (PO Box 846, Grants, NM 87020, 505-783-4774, www.nps.gov/elma). Dubbed El Malpais – the Badlands – by Spanish sojourners who found the tortured black formations nearly impossible to cross, the lava flows encompassed by the park are the product of more than 30 volcanoes that erupted with some regularity over the past 3 million years. Even more compelling is the juxtaposition of the jagged volcanic rock with the smooth red-and-cream sandstone that rises up around it.

Stop first at the ranger station on NM 117 just beyond the park entrance. Here you'll find exhibits on the Acoma, Laguna and Zuni Indians and their ancient predecessors as well as information on the region's natural history. As always, an excellent selection of books and maps are on hand, and a ranger is available to offer tips on hiking and camping. Though this isn't a terribly large park, the terrain is extremely rugged. Lava has sharp edges and is sweltering in summer, and the landscape can easily disorient even experienced hikers.

You can appreciate the formidable size of El Malpais a few miles away at the **Sandstone Bluffs** overlook, where a rimrock formation juts like a ship's prow into a sea of black lava. The road winds deeper into the park, skirting the base of sandstone cliffs streaked with "desert varnish" and eroded into a riot of knobs, niches and other extraordinary formations, including dramatic **La Ventana Arch**, New Mexico's largest natural arch, about 9 miles (15km) farther on. A short footpath leads to the base.

The road beyond La Ventana passes through the **Narrows**, a passage squeezed between towering sandstone bluffs and sprawling lava. A picnic area along this stretch serves as the trailhead for the Narrows Trail, which leads hikers about a mile along a sandstone ledge with magnificent views of the lava field.

Get a closer look at this unforgiving terrain on the mile-long (1.6km) **Lava Flows Trail** several miles farther along, which leads hikers over the the park's youngest lava flow – a mere 3,000 years old. Take note of the the two types of lava – *aa*, which cools quickly and breaks into sharp chunks, and *pahoehoe*, which is viscous and ropey and forms telltale ripples. Juniper and pinyon pine have colonized the flows. Some are several hundred years old, though poor soil and relentless winds have stunted their growth.

Travelers with an adventurous spirit and a four-wheel-drive vehicle can follow the **Chain of Craters**

*Zuni-Acoma Trail, a strenuous 7½-mile (12-km) trek across four lava flows, follows the path of an ancient Pueblo trade route.*

**BELOW:** El Morro rises 200 ft (60 meters) above the valley floor. More than 2,000 inscriptions and petroglyphs are on its sandstone walls.

*The Candy Kitchen
Rescue Ranch near
Ramah is a sanctuary
for captive-bred
wolves and wolf-dog
hybrids. Visitors are
welcome. Telephone
505-775-3304 for
information.*

**Backcountry Byway** to the **Big Tubes** area, where a system of lava caves, some with ceilings more than 90 ft (27 meters) high, extends for miles. Within some of the caves are permanent ice ponds caused by cold air settling into dark, well-insulated chambers. Exploring the caves is risky, but you can visit a developed 17-mile (27-km) lava tube and ice cave at **Bandera Crater** (off NM 53, 505-783-4303, www.icecaves.com, daily 8am–sunset; admission), northwest of the monument. Also rare are the rescued wolves and wolf-dogs that live at **Wild Spirit Wolf Sanctuary** (378 Candy Kitchen Road, off NM 53, 505-775-3304, tours year round Tues–Sun 11am, 1, & 3pm; donation), 20 miles (32km) southeast of Ramah. The sanctuary survives on donations and sales of wolf-themed gifts and really loves to see visitors. Call for directions.

## Gateway town

Back on I-40, it's a short jump to **Grants** ❹, a ranching town that boomed briefly during the uranium rush of the 1950s and '60s. You can learn more about uranium mining at the **New Mexico Mining Museum** (100 N. Iron Ave, 505-287-4802; Mon–Sat 9am–4pm; admission), a relatively modest affair with exhibits on mining technology, gems and minerals, and a re-created mineshaft.

**BELOW:**
Acoma Pueblo, also
known as Sky City,
is one of the oldest
continuously
inhabited villages in
the United States.

Grants is also a convenient launchpad for a variety of backcountry excursions, including driving and hiking tours of 11,301-ft (3,445-meter) **Mount Taylor** ❺, one of the Navajo's four sacred peaks and site of the annual **Mount Taylor Winter Quadrathalon**, a grueling four-event (running, biking, skiing, snowshoeing) race to the summit. To the south of I-40, a network of unpaved roads and hiking trails leads into the remote and scenic **Zuni Mountains**. For details, stop at the attractive **Northwest New Mexico Visitor Center** (I-40 exit 85,

Map
on page
254

505-876-2783; daily 9am–6pm) on the far east side of town across I-40. It's an invaluable source of information on travel opportunities throughout the region.

## Pasó por aqui

From Grants, follow NM 53 south toward El Malpais, then west over the Continental Divide to **El Morro National Monument ⑥** (NM 53, 505-783-4226, www.nps.gov/elmo; daily 9am–5pm), a small park dedicated to the preservation of natural features, ancient Indian ruins and an unusual historic document. El Morro is a *cuesta*, a ramp-like sandstone formation with a gradual incline on one side and steep ramparts on the other. It isn't merely the majestic upward thrust of the formation that makes it a noteworthy landmark but the pool of precious water in a protected alcove at its base. Fed by runoff from the rock above, the pool has served as a lifegiving – and sometimes life-saving – source of water for travelers making the difficult journey across the western desert.

We know people stopped here because they left their names. Like graffiti on a bus station wall, inscriptions engraved in the sandstone cliffs record the passing of dozens of desert wayfarers. *Pasó por aqui* (he passed here) say several Spanish inscriptions, including one left in 1605 by Juan de Oñate, who camped at El Morro on his return from an expedition to the Gulf of California. It is the oldest non-native inscription on the rock. More than eight decades later, in 1692, Don Diego de Vargas recorded his passage on the rock after reconquering Santa Fe, then heading west to reimpose Spanish dominion over Zuni and Acoma. Americans left messages, too. The first, in 1849, were Lieutenant James Harvey Simpson and artist Richard H. Kern, members of an Army mapping unit surveying territory acquired from Mexico under the Treaty of Guadalupe Hidalgo. Kern returned the following year and inscribed his name a second time before being killed by Indians in Utah.

A cultural record of a different sort is at the top of El Morro – the ruins of **A'ts'ina**, an Indian pueblo built in the late 13th century. At its peak, A'ts'ina encompassed 875 chambers and housed as many as 1,500 people. Only a portion of the village has been excavated, including round and square kivas, storage areas and living quarters. The trail to the top is quite strenuous, first switchbacking up the side of the rock, then following the rim of a box canyon to the pueblo site. The round-trip from the visitor center is about 2 miles (3km).

## The Middle Place

The people of A'ts'ina abandoned El Morro in the mid-14th century. Their descendants, the Zuni, settled in several villages to the west, including Hawikuh, where Coronado made his dreadful entry in 1540. Today most Zuni live in two towns – Black Rock, a modern subdivision of houses and trailers, and **Zuni Pueblo ⑦**, occupied for some 700 years and known to the Zuni people as Halona Idiwan'a, the Middle Place of the World.

To get to **Zuni**, continue west on NM 53 through the **Ramah Navajo Indian Reservation**, the largest Navajo community outside the "Big Rez." The little town of **Ramah** was established in 1874 by Mormon

**BELOW:** the world's largest drill bit is mounted in front of the New Mexico Mining Museum.

Map
on page
254

*Petroglyphs near
Zuni Pueblo.*

**BELOW:** Acoma
man, 1904.
**RIGHT:** Red Rock
State Park.

farmers, who dammed Cebolla Creek and formed Ramah Lake. Irrigated fields, many visible from the highway, are still diligently worked.

Before entering Zuni Pueblo, stop at the **Visitor Information Center** (1222 NM 53) in the Zuni Arts and Crafts Building. Here you can get information about local artists, see exquisite handmade jewelry (the Zuni are renowned for inlay work), and ask about visiting historic **Our Lady of Guadalupe Mission**. You might also inquire discreetly about upcoming dances. Keep in mind that these are ceremonial events and not intended as tourist attractions. Visitors are usually welcome but not really encouraged. If you're lucky enough to catch one, behave as you would at any religious gathering – respectfully, quietly, inconspicuously. And don't even think about bringing a camera. Photography is strictly prohibited. Another good source of information is the **A:shiwi A:wan Museum and Heritage Center** (Ojo Caliente Rd, off NM 53, 505-782-4403; Mon–Fri 9am–6pm), which has programs and exhibits exploring various aspects of Zuni culture and can arrange for a guide to show you around Hawikuh ruins.

## Indian capital

Directly north of Zuni is the city of **Gallup** ❽, the "Indian Capital of the World" and perhaps the best place in the state to find a good deal on Indian jewelry. Make no mistake, this isn't Santa Fe. At heart, Gallup remains the hardscrabble mining town it was in the 1880s. Its charm – if you can call it that – comes from a bygone West: the lonesome wail of a freight train rumbling through town, the honky-tonks and pawn shops on a long stretch of Old Route 66, and the threadbare nostalgia of the 1937 El Rancho Hotel, once a favorite bolt-hole of Hollywood stars. Still, it appeals to serious collector of Indian art and crafts. Scores of pawn shops do business in Gallup, serving Indian craftsmen as suppliers of raw materials, distributors of finished goods and a ready source of cash.

For visitors, most of the action in Gallup is in the downtown area between Route 66, Coal Avenue, 1st and 4th Streets. You'll find a little slice of Bohemia on Coal Avenue, where the ornate 1928 **El Morro Theater** and neighboring **211 Gallery and Coffee House** (211 W. Coal Ave., 505-722-5315) attract local artists. The former Santa Fe Depot, built in 1927 by architect Mary Elizabeth Colter (known for her glorious national park lodges), now serves as the **Gallup Cultural Center** (201 E. Route 66, 505-863-4131; Mon–Fri 8am–5pm), with exhibits on the city's history and galleries dedicated to native arts.

A few blocks away, the **Rex Museum** (300 W. Route 66, 505-863-1363; Mon–Fri 9am–3.30pm, Sat 9am–3pm) is filled with tools, furniture and other household items from the coal-mining days of the late 19th and early 20th centuries. About 7 miles (11km) east of town, the sandstone outcroppings of **Red Rock State Park** (NM 56, off I-40; 505-722-3839) are the backdrop for the **Inter-Tribal Indian Ceremonial**, an August celebration that brings together as many as 30 tribes and 50,000 spectators for five days of dances, rodeo, art shows, parades and educational programs. The **Red Rock Museum** (505-863-1337) has year-round exhibits of Southwest Indian arts. ❏

# SOUTHERN NEW MEXICO

*Geological wonders, historic sites and wild mountains are just a few of the attractions that lure travelers to the southern desert*

**D**ead Man's Way, the Spanish called it – *Jornada del Muerto*. It's a 90-mile (145-km) stretch of the Chihuahuan Desert notorious for scorching heat, a lack of water, and hostile Apache. Hardly an inviting picture, but in the minds of many people – including a good many New Mexicans – this is the essential image of southern New Mexico.

There's more than a little truth in it. Much of the state's southern tier is hot, dry and unforgiving. Few places are less hospitable, for example, than the gypsum dunes of White Sands National Monument, or the jagged, black lava flows of Valley of Fires, or the sere, sun-blasted flats of the Bootheel.

But that's only half the picture. What many people don't realize is that southern New Mexico also boasts snow-capped mountains, refreshing alpine breezes, icy streams, forest-clad canyons, and one of the world's best-known bird sanctuaries. They're part of the region, too, and they shouldn't be lost sight of.

Consider Gila National Forest, a 3.3-million-acre (1.3-million-hectare) expanse encompassing five mountains ranges, three wilderness areas, the ruins of 13-century Mogollon cliff dwellings, numerous ghost towns, and enough hiking, biking and horseback riding trails to keep outdoorsmen busy for a lifetime.

In addition to White Sands, geologic points of interest include the Stonehenge-like monoliths of City of Rocks and the subterranean fantasia of Carlsbad Caverns, one of the largest and most spectacular limestone cave systems in the world.

As for historic sites, there's the town of Lincoln, where a young and notorious gunslinger gained international renown as Billy the Kid. There are ghost towns like Steins, Shakespeare and Mogollon where abandoned buildings and broken dreams still rattle in the wind. And there are the melting adobe ruins of Fort Selden, a 19th-century military outpost manned by a contingent of so-called "buffalo soldiers."

Under the rubric of unexpected pleasures are the delightful shops and lively Spanish-flavored atmosphere of Old Mesilla Plaza; the art studios and galleries on Yankie Street in Silver City; exhilarating downhill skiing at Ski Apache in the Sacramento Mountains; Roswell's fine art museum and out-of-this-world UFO culture; the giant radio telescopes of the VLA (Very Large Array) west of Socorro; and the mysterious *Lightning Field*, a work of conceptual art by Walter de Maria composed of 400 stainless steels rods in a remote prairie on the windswept Plains of San Agustin.

Yes, there's Dead Man's Way. And much more besides. ❑

**PRECEDING PAGES:** sunflowers bloom around the ghost town of Chloride, a mining camp in the Black Range of southwestern New Mexico.
**LEFT:** branding day at the Burnt Well Ranch near Roswell.

# LAS CRUCES, SILVER CITY AND THE SOUTHWEST CORNER

*A region of varied charms, including ghost towns, a lively Spanish plaza, ancient cliff dwellings and a vast mountain wilderness, lures travelers off the beaten path*

Map on page 268

Often overlooked by travelers, New Mexico's southwest corner is a vast and sparsely populated territory encompassing deserts, mountains, ghost towns and, surprisingly, even to some New Mexicans, the second largest city in the state. **Las Cruces ❶**, a city of some 80,000 residents, sprawls in the Chihuahuan Desert 42 miles (68km) north of El Paso, Texas. It's a booming place, one of the fastest-growing cities in the Southwest, with a historic (if somewhat rundown) core surrounded by a halo of newly minted subdivisions.

Efforts to rejuvenate the downtown area have been concentrated around a five-block pedestrian mall, site of the **Branigan Cultural Center** (500 N. Water St, 505-541-2155; Mon–Fri 9am–4.30pm, Sat 9am–3pm, Sun 1pm–5pm) and intriguing new **Museum of Fine Arts and Culture** (490 N. Water St, 505-541-2155; Tues–Fri 10am–2pm, Sat 9am–3pm) as well as a community theater and cavernous used bookstore. Also in the area is the **Bicentennial Log Cabin Museum** (Main and Lucero Sts), featuring a miner's cabin built in 1890, and the **New Mexico Railroad and Transportation Museum** (351 N. Mesilla St, 505-541-2155, open Sat only, 9am–1pm), in the former Santa Fe Railroad depot a few blocks away.

**PRECEDING PAGES:**
City of Rocks
State Park.
**LEFT:** dancer
performs at
Old Mesilla.
**BELOW:**
chiles for sale.

Also attracting a great deal of interest in Las Cruces is the smartly conceived **NM Farm & Ranch Heritage Museum** (4100 Dripping Springs Rd, 505-522-4100; www.frhm.org Mon–Sat 9am–5pm, Sun noon–5pm; admission), an expansive complex on the outskirts of town that chronicles 3,000 years of agricultural development in New Mexico from the earliest Mogollon gardeners to the advent of mechanized farming. Churro sheep, burros, longhorn cattle and other traditional livestock are kept on the grounds, and demonstrations of blacksmithing, candle making, weaving, milking and other farm skills are presented regularly.

## Old Mesilla

Adjacent to Las Cruces on the southwest side is the little community of **La Mesilla ❷**, founded in 1850 by Mexican loyalists who tried to escape American rule by settling on the opposite side of the Rio Grande. The effort proved futile. The United States annexed the Mesilla Valley (and much else) in the Gadsden Purchase of 1853. Then, as if to emphasize the point, the Rio Grande changed course, putting both Mesilla and Las Cruces on the eastern shore.

The big attraction here is **Old Mesilla Plaza**, a traditional Hispanic square with shops and restaurants catering mostly to tourists. Among the historic buildings around the Plaza are La Posta, which served as a way station on the old Butterfield Overland Mail route

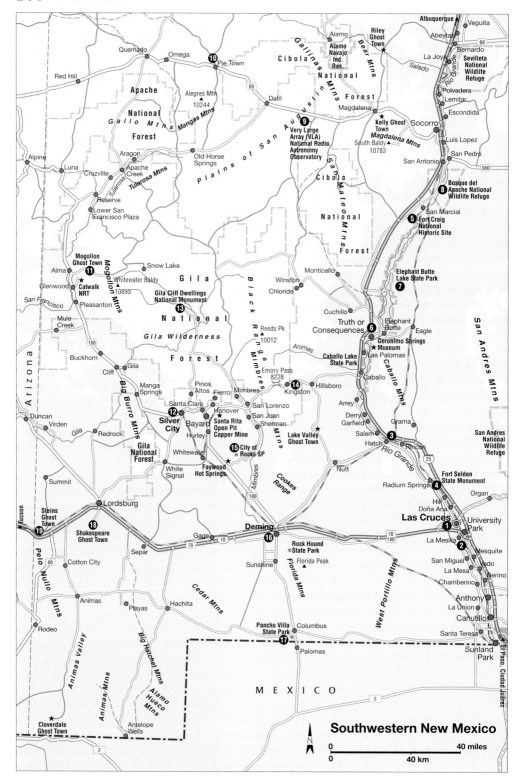

Southwestern New Mexico

0 ——————— 40 miles

0 ——————— 40 km

starting in 1858, and the Billy the Kid Gift Shop, originally a courthouse where the Kid was sentenced to hang in 1881. The Double Eagle Restaurant is housed in a restored 1848 mansion, with gold-leaf ceilings, crystal chandeliers, antique furnishings and 19th-century paintings. Handsome **San Albino Church**, on the north side of the Plaza, was built in 1906 on the foundations of the original 1856 adobe church. If possible, visit Mesilla during the twice weekly **Farmers Market**, held in the Plaza on Thursday 10am–2pm and Sunday noon–4pm.

*A Mesilla shop occupies the courthouse where Billy the Kid was sentenced to die.*

## The royal road

To the north and south of Las Cruces, in the rich bottomlands of the Rio Grande valley, are agricultural zones dedicated almost exclusively to two cash crops – pecans and chiles. **Stahmann Farms**, about 10 minutes south of Las Cruces, is the largest family-owned pecan grower in the world, with more than 180,000 trees on 4,000 acres (1,600 hectares). Visitors can drive through the orchards on Route 28 and stock up on pecan products – pie, cookies, brittle, toffee and more – at the farm store (Route 28, San Miguel, 505-526-8974; Mon–Sat 9am–6pm, Sun 11am–5pm). Guided tours are offered weekly; call the store for details.

For chile, head north to **Hatch ❸**, the self-described Chile Capital of the World, and site of the annual Chile Festival on Labor Day weekend. In autumn, during harvest time, the smell of roasting chiles permeates the air and strings of dried chiles, or *ristras*, are sold from roadside stands.

Travelers interested in military history should make a point of stopping at nearby **Fort Selden State Monument ❹** (1280 Ft. Selden Rd, Radium Springs; 505-526-8911; daily 8.30am–5pm), where they can wander around the adobe ruins of a military garrison built in 1865 to protect settlers and railroad workers. A contingent of black troops, known to the Indians as "buffalo soldiers," was stationed here, and here lived a young Douglas MacArthur, whose father was commander in 1884–86. The visitor center is worth a visit.

Less dramatic are the ruins at **Fort Craig National Historic Site ❺** (off Route 1 near San Marcial, 505-835-0412; open dawn–dusk), about 105 miles (170km) north of Fort Selden in a remote spot off I-25, where a few crumbling foundations and masonry walls bake in the sun. Union soldiers stationed at the fort were repulsed in 1862 by an invading Confederate army at the Battle of Valverde, just to the north. A marker on I-25 identifies the battlefield.

**BELOW:** Old Mesilla Plaza is surrounded by shops and restaurants.

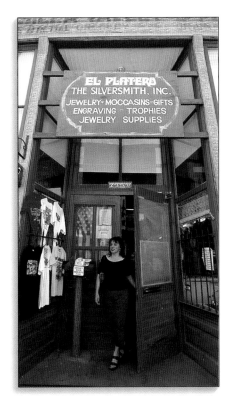

## The lure of water

Hot springs at **Truth or Consequences ❻** attracted Indians for centuries before achey cowboys came to "take the cure" in the 1880s. Warm desert temperatures and inexpensive rustic hot spring resorts lured winter "snowbirds" and retirees, starting in the early 1900s. These days, T or C's laid-back style attracts artists, such as the late H. Joe Waldrum, whose daughter now runs the edgy **Rio Bravo Gallery** in the artist's former studio. Along with an increasing number of funky art galleries, bookstores, cafes, restaurants, and health centers, there's the French-owned **Sierra Grande Lodge**, an elegant, renovated 1920s inn with a gourmet restaurant, spa, and the town's most deca-

*A blacksmith demonstrates iron-working at the New Mexico Farm & Ranch Heritage Museum.*

**BELOW:** thousands of snow geese flock to Bosque del Apache in late fall and winter.

dent hot springs bath house. And what of that strange name? In 1950, to commemorate the 10th anniversary of the popular game show, the town—then known as Hot Spring – renamed itself in return for national publicity. The name stuck.

Fishermen, boaters, windsurfers and swimmers flock to nearby Caballo Lake and Elephant Butte Lake State Parks. **Elephant Butte Lake ❼** (Route 51, Elephant Butte, 505-744-5421; open daily; admission), just north of Truth or Consequences, is the larger and more visited of the two. The lake was created by a dam in 1916 and takes its name from a pachyderm-shaped island – actually the eroded core of an extinct volcano. Bass fishing is excellent here. **Caballo Lake** (off I-25, Caballo, 505-743-3942; open daily; admission), about 15 miles (24km) south of Truth or Consequences, is well-known for attracting bald and golden eagles, which nest in the area beginning in late October.

Birds by the thousands flock to **Bosque del Apache National Wildlife Refuge ❽** (NM 1, 505-835-1828; one hour before sunrise–one hour after sunset), an area of ponds and marshes on a gentle bend in the Rio Grande about an hour farther north. The 57,000-acre (23,000-hectare) sanctuary attracts nearly 15,000 sandhill cranes in late autumn and winter, as well as thousands of Arctic geese, innumerable ducks and shorebirds, bald eagles and a small number of endangered whooping cranes. Information about birding tours, photography workshops, lectures and the annual Festival of the Cranes is available at the visitor center.

## High lonesome

It was liquor rather than water that attracted people to **Socorro** during the silver boom of the 1880s. At its peak, the town had 44 saloons where local miners could blow off steam after weeks in remote mining camps. Today, Socorro is

## LIGHTNING FIELD

**W**alter de Maria's *The Lightning Field* isn't the sort of art you can hang over the living room sofa. It's a work of conceptual art or, more precisely, earth art, a movement conceived in the 1960s involving monumental works that alter or are integrated into the landscape. In this case, the sculpture – if that's the right word for it – is composed of 400 stainless steel poles spaced exactly 220 ft (67 meters) apart in a rectangular grid measuring one mile by one kilometer. Each pole is 2 inches (5cm) in diameter and 20 ft (3 meters) high.

What does it mean? That's for you to decide. And you'll have plenty of time to think about it. The work is set in an isolated prairie about an hour's drive north of Quemado. The only way to see it is to make reservations well in advance, then rendezvous with a driver in Quemado. Visitors are required to spend the night in a nearby log cabin in order to observe how changes in light and weather alter the work over time.

For information or reservations, contact the New Mexico office at The Lightning Field, P.O. Box 2993, Corrales, NM 87048; tel: 505-898-3335; info@lightningfield.org. Fees start at $110 per person, including transportation, lodging and two meals.

notable mostly for the pretty adobe San Miguel Mission and the New Mexico Institute for Mining and Technology, which runs a geology museum with samples of ore and minerals from the Magdalena and San Mateo Mountains.

The college also serves as the administrative center of the **Very Large Array** ❾ (505-835-7000; www.nrao.edu; self-guided tours 8.30am–dusk; free), a cluster of 27 radio telescopes on the Plains of San Agustin 50 miles (80km) west via US 60. The dish antennas, each 82 ft (25 meters) wide, are mounted on rails allowing them to be maneuvered into a number of configurations, depending on the task at hand. A modest, unstaffed visitor center has exhibits on radio astronomy.

Beyond the VLA, US 60 leads into wild and woolly Catron County, a mountainous ranching district with only 3,500 residents spread across an area larger than Connecticut. This is big, lonesome country with few amenities, though you should make a point of stopping at **Pie Town** ❿ for – what else? – a big piece of pie at the **Pie-O-Neer Cafe**. Here weary travelers join cowboys, cattle haulers and the occasional radio astronomer for a selection of "house pies" such as strawberry-rhubarb, coconut macaroon and oatmeal-pecan. The population of Catron County nearly doubles during the annual Pie Festival in September, which includes pie-eating contests, hot-air ballooning, fiddle music and square dancing.

## Into the Gila

Continue west to Quemado, then south on NM 32 for a spectacular drive over the Gallo Mountains into **Gila National Forest**, 3.3 million acres (1.3 million hectares) of soaring peaks, deep canyons and leaping streams ranging in elevation from 4,200 to 10,895 ft (1,280–3,320 meters) and containing three wilderness areas, including the nation's first, the **Gila Wilderness**, designated in 1924.

Map on page 268

**BELOW:** 27 radio telescopes probe the heavens at the Very Large Array.

*Spring poppies bring a splash of color to the Chiricahua Desert.*

**BELOW:** the Catwalk leads hikers into Whitewater Canyon.

Acquaint yourself with the forest's rugged terrain by making a side trip on NM 159, a harrowing 9-mile (15-km) drive up a winding, single-lane mountain pass. The road deposits you in **Mogollon** , a resurrected ghost town wedged into Silver Creek Canyon. During its heyday around 1915, the town produced about $5 million of gold and silver, and boasted 1,500 residents, five saloons, four general stores, a theater, a hospital and two redlight districts. More than 20 buildings remain, including the ruins of the Little Fanny Mine, several abandoned shacks, a saloon, a general store and a scattering of rusty equipment.

Allow plenty of time to wander through the **Mogollon Museum** (505-539-2015), a hodgepodge of cast-off items such as clothing, a bathtub, mining lamps, photos, newspapers, a small collection of Mogollon pottery, and an enormous iron vat probably used as a still. Across the street, the Silver Creek Inn (866-276-4882), an inviting bed-and-breakfast, is housed in a restored 1885 adobe that was once a barbershop and general store. Pies are baked daily by innkeeper Kathy Knapp, the original "pie lady" of the Pie-O-Neer Cafe.

Return to US 180 and continue south about 3 miles (5km) to Glenwood, where you'll find signs directing you to the **Catwalk National Recreation Trail** (505-539-2711). Originally built by the Civilian Conservation Corps in 1935, the Catwalk is a series of suspended footbridges that lead hikers about 2 miles (3km) into narrow Whitewater Canyon over the chutes and waterfalls of Whitewater Creek. The walkway follows the route of a water pipeline built in 1893 to service the 200 residents of Graham, a mining camp that once clung to the canyon walls, now reduced to a few broken-down timbers near the Catwalk entrance. The canyon was also a favorite hideaway of Butch Cassidy and the Wild Bunch, who holed up at the nearby WS Ranch between "jobs."

## Silver City

Back on US 180, it's a pleasant 60-mile (100-km) drive down to **Silver City** , a town of about 12,500 that sprang to life in the 1870s after Captain John Bullard opened the Legal Tender silver mine. Henry McCarty, aka Billy the Kid, was a boy of 14 in 1873 when his mother, "a jolly Irish lady, full of fun and mischief," died here of tuberculosis. "The Kid" worked briefly at a hotel but was jailed in 1875 for stealing clothes from a Chinese laundry. He soon escaped, the first of several jailbreaks that would burnish his legend. In 1895 the town was struck with the worst of a series of calamities. A flood tore through Main Street, gouging out a gully more than 30 ft (9 meters) deep. The Big Ditch, as it came to be known, is now a municipal park.

Get your bearings in Silver City by first stopping at the **Murray Ryan Visitor Center** (201 N. Hudson St, 800-548-9378; Mon–Sat 9am–5pm), in the compact downtown area near the site of the Kid's former home. Gather up a bundle of brochures and maps, then head over to the **A.I.R Coffee Company** (112 W. Yankie St, 866-892-3009) for a stiff cup of java and a chat with managers Jacqueline Shaw and Sharifa Renfro, who preside over a daily gathering of artists, shopkeepers and curious visitors. Browse the excellent galleries on Yankie Street, then stroll around the corner to the **Silver City Museum** (312 W. Broadway,

505-538-5921; Tues–Fri 9am–4.30pm, Sat–Sun 10am–4pm), a modest but interesting collection of Mimbres pottery, household items from the mining era, and dramatic photos of the 1895 flood. Ask at the gift shop for a self-guided tour of the historic districts.

More impressive is the **Western New Mexico University Museum** (10th St, 505-538-6386; Mon–Fri 9am–4.30pm, Sat–Sun 10am–4pm), which has a peerless collection of Mimbres pottery. The refined black-on-white vessels offer clear evidence that the Mimbres people, a branch of the Mogollon culture based around the Mimbres River about AD1000, had an elaborate belief system and a deep appreciation of beauty. Also exhibited are woven yucca sandals, baskets, pottery from Casas Grandes in Mexico, and a mining display detailing the hardships of frontier life.

## Restless ghosts

You can visit the ruins of a Mogollon village at **Gila Cliff Dwellings National Monument** ⓭ (505-536-9461; daily 9am–4pm, extended summer hours), 44 miles (71km) north of Silver City on spectacular but tortuous NM 15. Tucked into natural caves under a canyon ledge, the site encompasses 40 apartment-like rooms, granaries and kivas, occupied for about 60 years starting in AD 1270.

En route to the national monument, you'll pass through **Pinos Altos**, another ghost town brought back to life by a few hearty and creative residents. The **Pinos Altos Historical Museum** (Main St, 505-388-1882; daily 10am–5pm) keeps a collection of vintage tools, furnishings, photographs, maps and other artifacts in a log cabin built in the 1860s shortly after gold was discovered in nearby Bear Creek. Food, drink and entertainment are offered at the authentic

**Map on page 268**

*Sadie Orchard, a native of London, operated a Kingston brothel… on Virtue Street.*

**BELOW:** pooch and pal on Yankie Street in Silver City, a small but intriguing district of galleries and boutiques.

*Rattlesnakes are not generally aggressive. If you see or hear one, move away slowly and warn others in the area.*

**Buckhorn Saloon** (Main St, 505-538-9911; open Mon–Sat 3pm), dating roughly to the same period. The **Pinos Altos Melodramatic Theater** (505-388-3848, late Jan–Thanksgiving) in the old Opera House next door stages hilarious spoofs Friday and Saturday night.

From the cliff dwellings, follow NM 35 over the Continental Divide and along the Mimbres River to NM 152. To the west, back toward Silver City, is the **Santa Rita Open Pit Copper Mine**. At 1,000 ft (300 meters) deep and a mile (1.6km) across, this tiered, multicolored hole is one of the largest open-pit mines in the world and the oldest active mine in the Southwest, having been worked commercially by the Spanish as early as 1800 and by the Apache for centuries before them. The actual town of Santa Rita, once one of the largest in the region, was eventually swallowed up by the mine that gave it birth.

To the east, NM 152 cuts a head-spinning path up and over the Mimbres Mountains to a trio of former mining towns. It's awfully quiet in scruffy little **Kingston ⓮** (pop. 30), though it wasn't always that way. Some 7,000 people resided in the "Gem of the Black Range," as the town was known during the silver boom of the 1880s. Today, it's noteworthy for the Black Range Lodge, a bed-and-breakfast built from the ruins of Pretty Sam's Casino and the Monarch Saloon. A community museum occupies the old Percha Bank.

**Hillsboro**, 9 miles (14km) farther east, is a bit livelier. Stop by for a bite to eat at the Barber Shop Cafe or General Store (in operation since 1879, two years after gold was discovered on the east side of the Mimbres Mountains), check out the antique shops, and poke around the Black Range Museum, originally a hotel and brothel operated by enterprising madame Sadie Orchard, now packed to the gills with an assortment of artifacts and memorabilia.

**Lake Valley**, about 16 miles (26km) south of Hillsboro on NM 27, is a ghost town in the truest sense. During its brief lifetime, the nearby Bridal Chamber mine produced nearly $3 million of silver, more than enough to support the town's 4,000 residents, 12 saloons, three churches and two newspapers. The silver panic of 1893 devastated the town soon after, and a fire in 1895 destroyed what little remained. A few tumble-down buildings are all that is left.

Map on page 268

## The Bootheel

South of Silver City, the elevation drops, temperatures soar and isolated mountains – dark and naked – rise from the desert floor like crooked spines. Perhaps the most curious geological formation in this region is the huddle of monolithic blocks at **City of Rocks State Park** ⓯ (off US 180, 505-536-2800). Composed of volcanic tuff deposited more than 30 million years ago and subsequently exposed by erosion, stone knobs some 40 ft (12 meters) tall stand like thumbs in the torrid flats of the Chihuahuan Desert. A gravel road loops around the park, but it's much more fun to wander through the maze-like passageways between the rocks.

*Lunchtime at the Hillsboro General Store.*

Continue south to **Deming** ⓰, a windblown ranch and railroad town founded in 1881 at the junction of the Santa Fe and Southern Pacific lines. The **Deming Luna Mimbres Museum** (301 S. Silver St, 505-546-2382; Mon–Sat 9am–4pm, Sun 1.30pm–4pm), housed in the 1916 National Guard armory, has an excellent collection of Mimbres pottery, Pueblo baskets, period furnishings and antique dolls. **Rockhound State Park** (NM 497, 505-546-6182), southeast of town on the slopes of the Little Florida Mountains, is of interest mostly to rock collectors due to the abundance of agate and quartz. About 33 miles (53km) south of Deming, in the border town of Columbus, **Pancho Villa State Park** ⓱ (505-531-2711) commemorates the spot where in 1916 the Mexican rebel led an attack on an American military outpost, killing 18 people. President Wilson dispatched General "Black Jack" Pershing and an army of 6,000 men to punish Villa, but they gave up the chase after 11 fruitless months.

**BELOW:** the Gila Cliff Dwellings, built in the late 13th century, were occupied for about one generation.

Two well-tended, privately owned ghost towns are preserved in the desert west of Deming. **Shakespeare** ⓲ (off I-10, 505-542-9034), just outside the town of Lordsburg, sprang to life in the 1870s during an early silver boom. Among the buildings preserved here is the modest Stratford Hotel, where Billy the Kid reputedly worked as a dishwasher after busting out of the Silver City jail. Shakespeare is open only on select weekends or by appointment. Call for information and be sure to ask about the schedule of living-history performances.

**Steins Ghost Town** ⓳ (off I-10, 505-542-9791; daily 9am–7pm), near the Arizona border, was once a thriving railroad town of about 1,300 people. When the Southern Pacific switched from steam to diesel after World War II, eliminating the need to stop for coal and water, the station was closed and the town was abandoned. The surviving structures are being restored; most contain a miscellanea of original artifacts ranging from pots and pans to roller skates, wagons, bottles, parasols, old-fashioned washing machines and other personal items. ❏

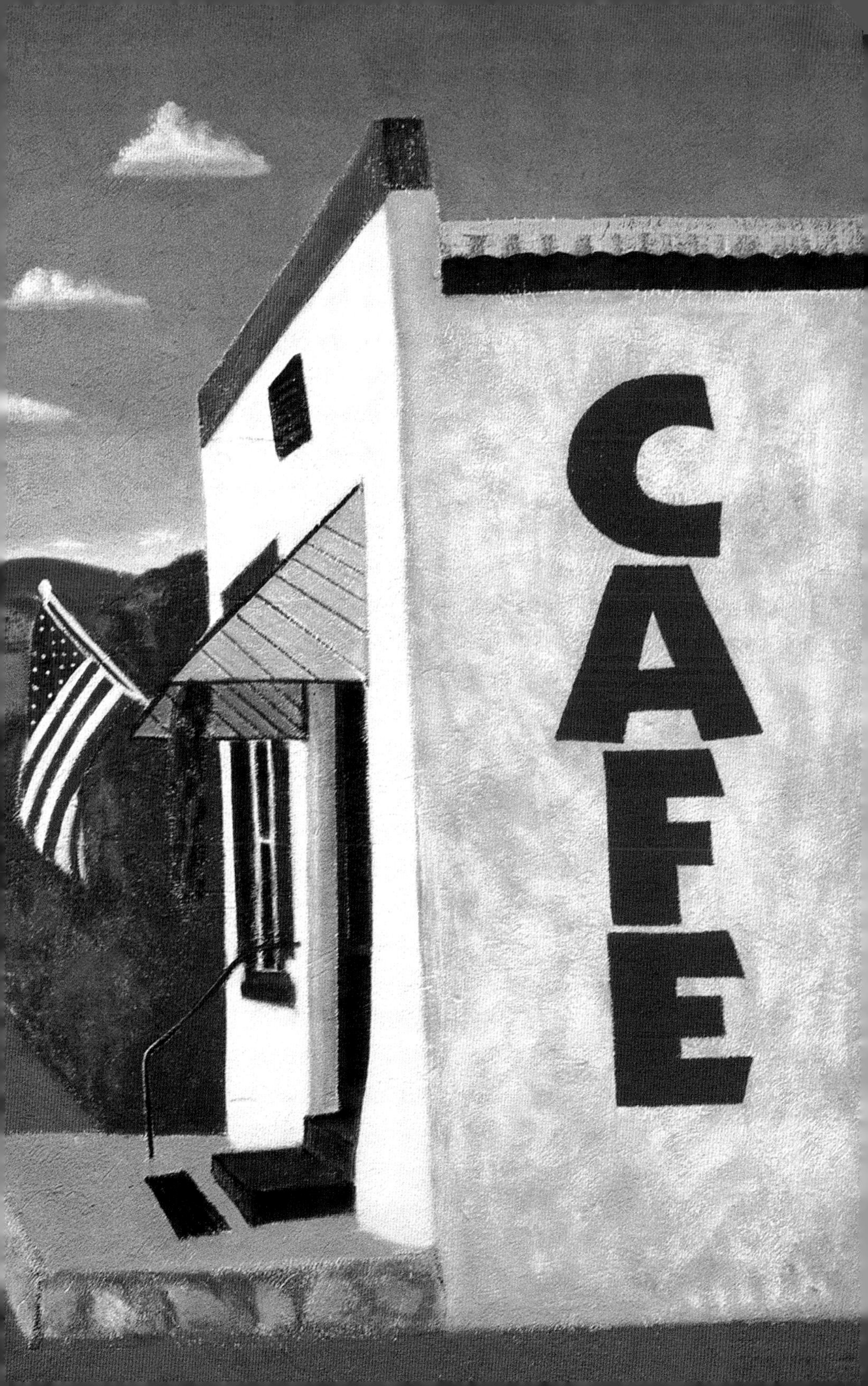
CAFE

# BILLY THE KID COUNTRY

*The young gunman-turned-icon who shot his way into the
history books is the main draw here, where one of
the West's deadliest feuds took place*

Map
on page
280

There are few pastoral settings more lovely than Lincoln County in south-eastern New Mexico. Tiny settlements hug the banks of the streams rushing from the Sacramento Mountains to join the Pecos River, which winds south through eastern New Mexico into Texas. Roadside stands sell fresh-picked fruit from irrigated orchards. Horses and cattle twitch tails in front of picturesque barns. Famous artists sell their work from historic buildings. And looming above it all is 12,003-ft-high (3,658-meter) Sierra Blanca, sacred to the Mescalero Apache whose 40,000-acre (16,000-hectare) reservation is centered in the fragrant evergreen forests of the Sacramento Mountains.

It's all a far cry from the mid-1800s, when Hispanic farmers cultivated the river valleys and the only building in Ruidoso was Dowlin's 1853 Mill. These early settlers arrived with the U.S. Army at nearby Fort Stanton, which had been built to guard the Rio Grande and Pecos communities from Apache attacks. Far from markets on the remote frontier, the government and local people formed close relationships, both politically and economically. Soldiers provided protection to settlers who, in turn, hoped to prosper by supplying beef and grain to the fort and, later, the newly formed Mescalero Indian Agency.

**PRECEDING PAGES:** a
mural in Hillsboro.
**LEFT:** a costumed
guide leads visitors
through Lincoln.
**BELOW:** Lincoln
tombstone.

## A house divided

From the beginning, the fortunes of one community in the Rio Bonito Valley, Lincoln, originally called La Placita, were tied to nearby Fort Stanton. By the 1870s, a business monopoly by two ex-soldiers, L. G. Murphy and his successor James J. Dolan, backed by Santa Fe Ring lawyer Thomas Catrón, had alienated the local Hispanic population, who had become deeply indebted to what was dubbed simply "the House."

When an ambitious young lawyer named McSween, a former employee of the Murphy-Dolan Store, set up a rival ring with an equally ambitious young Englishman, John Henry Tunstall, and Pecos cattle baron John Chisum, many Lincoln residents saw their chance to free themselves from the House's grip, too. But things became ugly, as the financially ailing Murphy-Dolan Store took up the gun to maintain its hold on Lincoln.

The shooting of John Tunstall at his ranch on February 13, 1878, by a sheriff's posse attempting to collect on an old debt of McSween's would trigger one of the most violent episodes in frontier history. The Lincoln County War would eventually pit the new governor of New Mexico, Lew Wallace, a glamorous figure best known for his novel *Ben Hur*, against the young folk hero Billy the Kid, whose mythic status has only grown with each passing year.

No place in New Mexico has stronger links to Billy

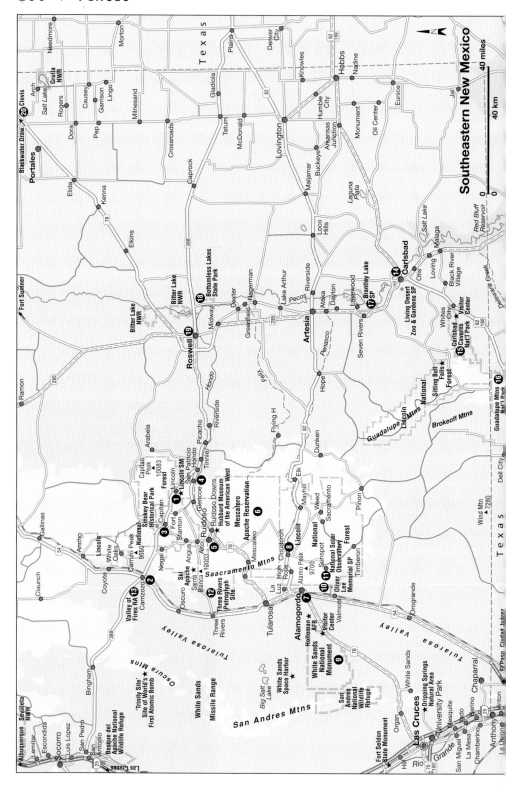

Southeastern New Mexico

than **Lincoln ❶**. This dusty, one-horse town (pop. 68), in the heart of south-eastern New Mexico's vast ranch lands, was the scene of the Kid's greatest escapades. The entire town is preserved as a national historic landmark, with more than a dozen beautifully restored structures operated by a cooperative agreement between the Museum of New Mexico's Lincoln State Monument and Historic Lincoln, a division of the Hubbard Museum of the American West. Both offer historic tours by arrangement.

Map on page 280

## A legend is born

Begin your walking tour in Historic Lincoln's **Anderson-Freeman Visitors Center and Museum** (P.O. Box 98, Lincoln, NM 88338, 505-653-4025, www.hubbardmuseum.com; daily 9am–5pm; admission), on the eastern end of town, which has exhibits on the Mescalero Apache, Fort Stanton and its famous buffalo soldiers, Hispanic settlers, and a whole room dedicated to the life of Billy the Kid and the Lincoln County War.

*Deputy Sheriff Robert Ollinger was killed with his own shotgun during Billy's most daring jailbreak.*

The kid's origins are shrouded in mystery, but it is thought that he was born Henry McCarty in a grim New York City ghetto in 1859 and grew up in Kansas. His first recorded presence in New Mexico was in March 1873, when he witnessed the marriage of his 43-year-old mother to her longtime companion, Bill Antrim, 30, in Santa Fe. The family moved south to Silver City, a booming mining camp near the Santa Rita Mine, where his schoolteacher described the quiet adolescent as a "scrawny little fellow with delicate hands and an artistic nature."

At 15, Billy's life took a turn for the worse, when his mother died of tuberculosis and his stepfather abandoned him. Searching desperately for an identity, the lonely teenager adopted his runaway stepfather's name, then the name William H. Bonney. In 1880, a year before he died, he was being called Billy the Kid and would later be immortalized by his killer, Pat Garrett, in a popular novel.

**BELOW:** William H. Bonney, aka Billy the Kid, about 1879.

Kid Antrim's first recorded crime was the theft of several pounds of butter from a Silver City ranch. Soon after, he killed a bully in Fort Grant, Arizona, reportedly in self-defense, and returned to New Mexico wanted by Arizona authorities. In 1877, he spent a few weeks with Jesse Evans's gang of horse thieves, known as The Boys, then fell in with a band of 30 gunmen who, on November 17, 1877, broke Jesse Evans out of the Lincoln jail. The Kid found a home in Lincoln. Tunstall and McSween's operation was growing, and there was work for a youngster with a loyal disposition who was handy with a gun. The Kid was quickly hired as a cowhand at the Tunstall Ranch on the Rio Felix, south of Lincoln.

Legend has it that the Kid and Tunstall were good friends, leading him to avenge Tunstall's death as part of a group dubbed the Regulators. There is little evidence to support this contention, but the Kid was well liked locally. He spoke fluent Spanish and enjoyed singing and dancing and was often the guest of Juan Patrón, a well-educated Hispanic who ran a store in his home and would become the youngest speaker of the New Mexico legislature. The Kid was particularly friendly with fellow cowhand Fred Waite, a Choctaw Indian, with whom he hoped to start a ranch on the Rio Peñasco.

*Billy the Kid slept at the Ellis Store – and so can you.*

**BELOW:** Virginia Vigil whips up gourmet goodies at Lincoln's Ellis Store.

## Making a killing

That dream died on April 1, 1878, when the Kid and four other gunslingers shot and killed Sheriff Bill Brady from an adobe corral adjoining Tunstall's store. The Kid was seen searching Brady's pocket for McSween's arrest warrant before escaping into the hills. After months of escalating warfare, the final showdown of the vendetta came on the night of July 14, 1878.

The Kid and McSween rode back into town with 45 gunmen. Some took up positions in the Montaño Store, across from the fortified tower known as the Torreón, which had been used by early settlers to defend themselves from Indian attacks. The Kid, McSween and a few companions settled into McSween's house, on the other side of the Tunstall Store. The rest of Lincoln's 400 inhabitants fled or hid in their homes.

During what came to be called the Five Days Battle, the two sides emptied their guns at each other. Then soldiers arrived, aiming a howitzer and a Gatling gun at the Montaño Store. Soon the only Tunstall partisans still fighting were those holed up with the Kid in McSween's house. Deputies torched it. The Kid bolted first. He darted unscathed through a shower of lead, then vanished. McSween wasn't as lucky. With the timbers of his house collapsing around him, he made a run for it, only to be shot in his own back yard.

## Lincoln landmarks

Visitors to Lincoln today see a frontier town that has been so well restored it looks much the same as it did on the day those shots rang out. There are no souvenir shops and only a handful of businesses offering casual fare, lodging and dining. Restoration work continues on several homes, including the **Dr. Woods House**, on the west end of town, and the **Gallegos House**, next door to the visitor center. **Casa de Patrón**, the 1860s home and store of Juan Patrón, has been privately restored. It sits next to the **Montaño Store**, an attractive adobe with exhibits on Lincoln. Following his conviction in Mesilla for killing Sheriff Brady, the Kid found himself under house arrest at the Patrón house, and, as the story goes, was serenaded nightly by locals who looked upon him as an adopted son.

The Kid was also held at the **Ellis Store** (800-653-6460), which had served as a headquarters for the Regulators. In 1905, the Ellis Store was bought by a doctor from Fort Stanton and turned into a tuberculosis sanitorium. Several of the rooms that were added are now part of a bed-and-breakfast operation, including a converted millhouse in the rear that was used as nurses' quarters. Particularly lovely are Dr. Law's unusual white-washed tree-trunk portal along the front of the house and an elegant great room. The latter is presently used to great effect as the setting for Virginia Vigil's award-winning gourmet candlelit dinners.

**Lincoln State Monument** is headquartered in the **Tunstall Store** (P.O. Box 36, Lincoln, NM 88338, 505-653-4372, www.museumofnewmexico.org; daily 9am–5pm; admission), which still displays some 1,000 items from Tunstall's original inventory, including coffee grinders, spittin' tobacco, buttons, shoes and garments. The western half of the store was used

Map on page 280

as Lincoln County's first bank. The site of McSween's house is next door and beyond it the 1881 **Wortley Hotel** (877-967-8539; www.wortleyhotel.com), a living history museum originally built as a mess for the Murphy-Dolan Store. The **Old Schoolhouse Art Center**, the original 1921 adobe that held the school, is across the street. The beautifully renovated building is Lincoln's newest addition. It displays work by local artists, offers classes, and provides space for theater.

When it was built, the two-story Murphy-Dolan Store was lauded for its elegant architecture. By the late 1870s, the assets of the bankrupt "house" had been taken over by Thomas Catrón in Santa Fe, and the store closed. A few years later, the building was turned into the **Old Lincoln County Courthouse**, the highlight of any visit to Lincoln. In April 1881, the Kid was held here under armed guard, still hoping for a long-promised reprieve from Governor Lew Wallace for turning state's evidence after witnessing the killing of the widow McSween's lawyer.

By April 28, 1881, the Kid figured – correctly – the reprieve would never come. He managed to slip his slender hands from the handcuffs and blast his way out of jail, killing two guards (bullet holes can still be seen in the wall). Still wearing ankle manacles, he severed the chain between his legs with a pickax and looped the remnants around his belt. He proceeded to chat with unnerved townspeople outside the Wortley Hotel before commandeering a horse and heading west.

## The last escape

The end of the Kid's life is as mysterious as his beginnings. Most historians believe that on the night of July 14, 1881, while hiding in the home of Pete Maxwell, near Fort Sumner, northeast of Lincoln, the Kid saw a figure crouched in a darkened room and called *"Quien es?"* (Who is it?) The figure, Sheriff Pat Garrett, fired in the direction of the voice, and Billy the Kid fell dead. He was apparently interred in this lonely spot, which now bears his grave and the Billy the Kid Museum.

The Kid died a few years before the macabre habit of photographing dead gunmen was introduced to verify reward claims, and there are those who say he did not expire that night. Reports have surfaced that Billy made it to England (perhaps courtesy of the Tunstall family) and died a natural death in Preston, Lancashire, where he is buried in a churchyard. Another report has him fleeing to Hico, Texas, where he eventually revealed his identity.

In May 2003, the Lincoln County sheriff reopened the case of Billy the Kid. The hope was to use DNA evidence from the Kid's mother's grave in Silver City to settle once and for all Garrett's claim on the reward. In the meantime, most of the hoopla in Lincoln is the town's three-day **Last Escape of Billy the Kid Pageant** in August, which features a re-enactment of bloody moments from the Lincoln County War, a fiddling contest, Apache dancing and handicraft items.

## Hot on the Kid's trail

Undoubtedly the Kid visited many of the historic communities on the 84-mile (135-km) **Billy the Kid National Scenic Byway,** but none has as strong a claim as Lincoln. **Carrizozo ❷**, a small 1900 railroad

**BELOW:** hikers can explore miles of jagged, black lava flows at Valley of Fires Recreation Area.

*Windmills, a fixture on the plains, pump water to the surface.*

town at the junction of US 380 and NM 54, has been the seat of Lincoln County since 1912, when New Mexico achieved statehood. Carrizozo today retains its sleepy charm. It is known for its apple cider and nearby **Valley of Fires Recreation Area** (505-648-2241), a young lava flow in the northern Tularosa Basin.

A few miles north of Carrizozo is the old mining town of **White Oaks**. In 1879, this ghost town was the site of a gold strike, bringing new economic opportunities to Lincoln County. The Brown Store Building, the School House Museum, Hoyle Castle and the Miners Museum are among the remaining buildings in White Oaks, which holds an annual Miners Day celebration the first Saturday in June.

The whole village of **Capitan ❸** is dedicated to just one furry creature: Smokey Bear, a real-life bear cub who, on May 9, 1950, was rescued from a forest fire in the Capitan Mountains. The charming **Smokey Bear Historical Park** (118 Smokey Bear Blvd, 505-354-2748, www.smokeybearpark.com; admission) is not your average small-town museum. It has real historical value and does a fabulous job of telling the story of Smokey Bear, the famous fire prevention mascot, through an informative film and exhibits even small kids will like.

One section of the museum traces the history of the Smokey Bear fire prevention campaign ("Only you can prevent forest fires"), which predated the rescue of the tiny cub who was initially dubbed "Hotfoot Teddy" by his rescuers. Another section offers an excellent explanation of fire ecology in the West, the need for controlled burns, fire ethics, and the lives of "hotshot" firefighters, or "smoke jumpers," who work the frontlines of a wildfire. Smokey Bear, who lived out his life in Washington DC's National Zoo, is buried in the back of the museum along a pleasant little nature trail, which allows you to pass through six different life zones, from desert to mountain top.

**BELOW:** in Billy's day, firearms were essential equipment.

## FORT SUMNER

Billy the Kid is a big deal at tiny Fort Sumner northeast of Lincoln County. The outlaw's rifle and spurs are displayed in the Billy the Kid Museum, along with a jail cell he once occupied. You'll find letters from both Pat Garrett and Kid Antrim, and out back is the Kid's grave. The headstone has been stolen so often, it's now enclosed in an iron cage.

It's ironic that the injustices done to and by one charismatic young thug should be the main draw at Fort Sumner today. Surely, the suffering of 9,000 Navajos and 450 Mescalero Apaches imprisoned at Fort Sumner between 1862 and 1868 is a far more poignant lesson in inhumanity. The story of the Navajos' Long Walk, a forced 300-mile (480-km) march, makes chilling reading. Two thousand Navajo died from illness and starvation before the Army agreed that the concentration camp had failed and allowed the Navajo to return home.

The visitor center at Fort Sumner State Monument has exhibits about the ill-fated Army campaign but as yet no official memorial. The construction of a memorial, designed by a Navajo architect, remains stalled at the fund-raising stage. Pause for a moment at a large pile of stones outside the museum. They were carried from the Navajo Reservation by people who have never forgotten. Nor should we.

## Military outpost

Just before you get to Lincoln, there is a turnoff for **Fort Stanton** (P.O. Box 1, Fort Stanton, NM 88323, 505-354-0341, www.fortstanton.com; Thurs–Mon 10am–4pm; free), the 1855 fort that figured prominently in the events surrounding the Lincoln County War. The fort was also used by Colonel Kit Carson as a headquarters during the incarceration of local Apaches and Navajos at Fort Sumner in 1864-1868. Colonel "Black Jack" Pershing, whose army battled Pancho Villa along the border, also began his career here. In 1866, following the Civil War, a contingent of African-American soldiers known to the Apache as "buffalo soldiers" was headquartered at the fort.

After it closed, in 1896, the fort was used as a U.S. Marine tuberculosis sanitorium, a World War I concentration camp, and more recently as a drug rehab center and halfway house for prisoners. A nonprofit organization is presently trying to restore the fort and open it to the public. It runs a small, rather confusing museum in the old chapel, which it hopes to improve. Presently, Fort Stanton is open one summer weekend a year for reenactments.

*Cowboy collectibles are found in shops throughout the Lincoln area.*

East of Lincoln is the **Hondo Valley**, where US 380 meets US 70. A right turn at the junction takes you into the tiny 1875 community of **San Patricio ❹**, a favorite haunt of Billy the Kid and the Regulators, several of whom had ranches here. One of those operations, the Coe Ranch, was painted by one of Roswell's most famous native sons, Peter Hurd. Hurd, who married Henriette Wyeth, daughter of renowned East Coast artist N. C. Wyeth, in 1929, returned to the area in the 1930s and built Sentinel Ranch in San Patricio. The couple lived here the rest of their lives, entertaining friends like writer Paul Horgan, putting on polo matches, and participating in the life of the little Hispanic community.

**BELOW:** artist Georgia Stacey at her Nogal studio.

Today, visitors may tour the attractive **Hurd-La Rinconada Gallery** (P.O. Box 100, San Patricio, NM 88348, 800-658-6912, www.wyethartists.com) and view examples of Hurd's and Wyeth's portraits, still lifes and scenes of the Hondo Valley. Their son Michael, also an accomplished artist, has fixed up the old ranch hands' quarters for use as guest houses. The Hondo Valley has attracted numerous creative people. **Benson Fine Art Gallery** is next door to the Hurd Gallery, and contemporary Mexican-American sculptor Luis Jimenez, whose colorful oversized fiberglass sculptures can be seen in collections throughout New Mexico, maintains his studio here.

## High country

San Patricio is 20 miles (32km) east of the busy little mountain town of **Ruidoso ❺** (elev. 6,900 ft/2,100 meters, pop. 4,500), named for its "very noisy" river, a waterway that is now obscured by cabins clustered along its banks. Texas license plates far outnumber New Mexico plates, and you'll hear many a Texas twang among the residents here.

Ruidoso adjoins 1.1-million-acre (445,000-hectare) **Lincoln National Forest** (505-257-4095) and the **Ski Apache Resort** (505-336-4356; www.skiapache.com), and most folks come here for outdoor pursuits such as hiking, mountain biking, camping, golf and skiing. Be sure to visit **Monjeau Lookout**, a 1930s fire lookout at

Map on page 280

10,356 ft (3,156 meters), where you can see the dark lava flows of the Tularosa Basin below and take in all of New Mexico's life zones.

If the great outdoors doesn't appeal, you may wish to know that Ruidoso has a smattering of good restaurants and several cultural attractions. North of town, off NM 48, is the extraordinary new **Spencer Theater for the Performing Arts** (888-818-7872), designed by New Mexico architect Antoine Predock. Situated halfway down Airport Road, this spectacular building looks like a spaceship has landed in the middle of a prairie.

The somewhat trapezoidal building has a clear view of 12,003-ft (3,658-meter) **Sierra Blanca** and its roofline angles up to it, paying homage to the Apache's sacred peak. Even stranger is the prism-like glass atrium on the building's north side, which breaks up the view of the surrounding high country in interesting ways. The center has already gained a reputation for its top-of-the-line Broadway shows. Tours are offered Tuesday and Thursday at 10am.

West of Ruidoso proper is **Ruidoso Downs Race Track and Casino** (505-378-4431). This is one of the most popular tracks in the Southwest, with races every weekend from Memorial Day to Labor Day, including the All-American Futurity quarterhorse race – at $2 million, the richest purse in the world. The disappointing **Billy the Kid National Scenic Byway Visitors Center** (505-378-5318) is next door. The exhibits are hokey, but the tourist information is useful.

Ruidoso Downs is owned by entrepreneur R. D. Hubbard, a name you'll see everywhere around town. Hubbard's friendship with wealthy Patagonia, Arizona, horse lover Ann Stradling led to her bequest of 10,000 horse-related items in 1992 and the founding of the **Hubbard Museum of the American West** (505-378-4142, www.hubbardmuseum.com; daily 10am–5pm; admission) next

*Christ as an Apache holy man at St. Joseph church on the Mescalero Apache Reservation.*

**BELOW:** Hubbard Museum of the American West. **RIGHT:** second-hand treasures at a Ruidoso shop.

Map on page 280

door to the race track. An affiliate of the Smithsonian Institution, the hangar-like Hubbard Museum hides most of its treasures until you get inside. One you can see from the road is the specially commissioned, larger-than-life sculpture *Free Spirits at Noisy Water*. This celebration of seven different breeds of horse by local sculptor David McGary makes it clear that this place is all about horses.

The museum's open-plan layout works well for displaying its large collection of bridles, saddles and unusual wagons, including a stagecoach, a child's hearse and a Conestoga wagon used on the Santa Fe Trail. The fascinating *Hollywood Guns* exhibit has firearms, holsters, chaps, Stetsons and other props used in famous Hollywood westerns such as the *Magnificent Seven* and numerous John Wayne films. A 15-minute video of *The Great Train Robbery* runs in its entirety, followed by rare footage of Annie Oakley. You'll also find a kid's dress-up corner, and the Race Track Hall of Fame downstairs. An upstairs gallery features revolving exhibits.

## Apache homeland

The **Mescalero Apache Reservation** ❻ lies just outside Ruidoso and offers a number of attractions for visitors. The tribe's Ski Apache resort gets an average snowfall of more than 15 ft (5 meters) and has New Mexico's largest lift capacity. Golfing is popular at the 18-hole Inn of the Mountain Gods Golf Course, one of the highest in the United States. The lakeside greens are part of the top-rated luxury resort **Inn of the Mountain Gods**, which in 2003 was completely razed to make way for a spanking new Lake Tahoe-style casino resort. The new resort includes expanded facilities and new outdoor opportunities on Apache land, including guided tours of the backcountry. The tribe's casino remains as popular as ever. A new Travel Center on US 70 has restaurants, a gas station and a smoke shop.

The Mescalero Apache have lived in the Sacramento Mountains for centuries and, like the Navajo, trace their origins to northwest Canada, where they were hunter-gatherers. The Mescalero are named for their use of mescal, or agave, which is still collected from the desert and used in ceremonies. Tribal members learned ranching and horsemanship from Spanish and Anglo settlers and have today become accomplished stockmen and cowboys. The highlight of the year is the annual Fourth of July celebration, which includes a powwow, a rodeo, dances featuring the spectacularly costumed *gaan*, or mountain spirit dancers, and the important three-day puberty ritual that is the cornerstone of every young woman's life.

You can find out more if you drop in at the **Mescalero Apache Cultural Center** (open daily 9am–5pm) near the tribe's headquarters in **Mescalero**. Before leaving, consider visiting the lovely **St. Joseph Apache Mission** (626 Mission Trail, Mescalero; 505-464-4473), a soaring 1939 sandstone cathedral dramatically situated on a hill near Mescalero. Among the unique highlights are a beautifully rendered painting of the Apache Christ behind the altar, Mexican tinwork light fixtures, and a painting of the Apache mountain spirits whose presence can be felt throughout these sacred mountains. ❑

**BELOW:** Mescalero Apache leader San Juan, 1882.

# WHITE SANDS AND THE TULAROSA BASIN

*A region of curious geological formations evokes ancient Indian life, old Spanish missions and brave new worlds of space-age technology*

Map on page 280

Santa Fe
Albuquerque

There's more than a touch of the surreal about the Tularosa Basin in southern New Mexico. Soft silvery gypsum dunes and jagged black lava flows sit uneasily side by side at White Sands National Monument and Valley of Fires Recreation Area. Traces of ancient and modern Indian cultures, ill-fated Spanish missions, pioneer American ranches, and a quaint historic mountain railroad linger in the foothills of nearby mountains. And silent Stealth bombers glide across liquid-blue morning skies like stylized bats en route to top-secret military hangars.

With most of this unearthly landscape now under government ownership, it's hardly surprising that, since the 1940s, the Tularosa Basin has become synonymous with air and space research. A space shuttle landing strip lies ready for use at Holloman Air Force Base. The British Royal Air Force used the original base for practice during World War II and, ironically, the German Air Force uses it for similar purposes today. A rare solar observatory is hidden among the cool forests of the Sacramento Mountains. And, inevitably, White Sands Missile Range was chosen to test the world's first atomic bomb in July 1945, ushering in a nuclear industry that casts a long shadow over New Mexico.

**PRECEDING PAGES:**
Organ Mountains.
**LEFT:** White Sands
National Monument.
**BELOW:** anti-war
protestors at the
Trinity site.

## Simple beginning

Begin your tour in **Alamogordo ❼** (pop. 29,000), founded by the Eddy brothers in 1898 on the former ranch of controversial Texas cattle baron Oliver M. Lee. Alamogordo's proximity to rivers emerging from the 12,000-ft (3,660-meter) **Sacramento Mountains** to the east and seasonal lakes on the gypsum flats to the west has always been a powerful magnet for wildlife and humans. Folsom hunters killed mammoth, bison and other big game here when the Ice Age ended 10,000 years ago. Archaic people hunted and gathered in cool mountain forests 3,500 years ago, leaving behind evidence of their presence at sites like Fresnal Shelter, between Alamogordo and Cloudcroft.

By the early Christian era, Pueblo and Mogollon farmers from the Rio Grande region were living in pithouses and pueblos along permanent water sources. Alamogordo is built atop a large 11th-century pueblo that was abandoned in the 1300s, when a long drought and Apache raiding made life too difficult. The arrival of the U.S. Army at Fort Stanton in 1855 was the beginning of the end for Apache warriors fighting to hold onto their adopted homeland. In the 1880s, the Apache were forced to make peace and moved to a reservation near Ruidoso, allowing Anglo settlement of the Tularosa Basin and surrounding river valleys to begin.

The Eddys built their new community as a division

*A Little Joe rocket towers over the "rocket garden" at the New Mexico Museum of Space History.*

of the El Paso & Northeastern Railroad. By 1901, the model town had attracted 4,000 residents, who ranched, farmed, and made railroad ties from lumber brought down from the adjoining Sacramento Mountains. The tiny community of **Cloudcroft** ❽, built by the railroad, then as now was a popular summer getaway for desert dwellers. Nobs and ordinary folk rode the rails, picnicked in the forest, and stayed overnight at a modest pavilion until it was destroyed in a fire.

The new **Lodge at Cloudcroft** (1 Corona Place, Cloudcroft, NM 88317, 505-682-2566), a Bavarian-style castle, complete with tower, pond and croquet lawn, opened in 1909. Over the years, it has hosted Mexican revolutionary Pancho Villa, every governor since New Mexico became a state, and Judy Garland and Clark Gable, who carved their names in the tower. Rebecca's, the four-star restaurant, is renowned for its fine European dining and views of the Tularosa Basin. It is named for the hotel's resident ghost, a redheaded chambermaid who met an untimely end in the 1930s at the hands of her jealous lover.

Like Los Alamos, Alamogordo's prosperity since World War II has come from government defense contracts, high-tech research and aeronautics. Downtown is an odd mix of fast-food outlets, quiet parks, uninspired modern architecture, and a scattering of historic buildings. On the east side, near the foothills, are large homes and the town's most interesting public buildings, housing a medical center and a branch of New Mexico State University.

## The final frontier

Behind the NMSU campus is the **New Mexico Museum of Space History** (Hwy 2001, 505-437-2840, www.spacefame.org; daily 9am–5pm; admission), Alamogordo's main visitor attraction. The four-story "cube," as it is known, is

a temple to everything astronomic. Some of the most fascinating exhibits are about rocketry pioneer Robert Goddard, whose first jet fuel propulsion experiments on the plains east of Roswell in the 1920s helped launch the U.S. space program. (For more on Goddard, visit the Roswell Museum, which has carefully recreated his lab and named its planetarium after him). There are also models of the Apollo Command Module and the ill-fated Skylab, as well as other milestones in the space program.

Former astronauts are inducted annually into the International Space Hall of Fame in a special October ceremony. Outside, the Stapp Air and Space Park displays a rocket sled from the 1950s and actual rocket stages. The Astronaut Memorial Garden commemorates astronauts who lost their lives in space missions. An adjoining building holds the Clyde W. Tombaugh IMAX Dome Theater and Planetarium, which offers large-format films, star tours and laser-light shows. You may even want to leave the kids here. Weeklong space camps are offered in summer.

For most people, the highlight of any trip to Alamogordo is a visit to **White Sands National Monument** ❾ (off US 70, 505-479-6124; www.nps.gov/whsa; daily 8am–4.30pm, to 7pm in summer and midnight on full moon; admission), 15 miles (24km) southwest of town. Stop at the visitor center for an orientation, then take the 16-mile (26-km) loop drive through the dunes. Interpretive signs and trails explain their formation. Running barefoot in the dunes is encouraged! You can also picnic in the Heart of the Dunes for a dining experience in perhaps the world's strangest setting. Primitive camping is occasionally allowed.

These white sands are really a 275-sq-mile (712-sq-km) expanse of fine gypsum washed into the basin from the San Andres Mountains to the west and the Sacramento Mountains to the east. The sediments are trapped in low-lying ephemeral lakes that evaporate in the sizzling heat, leaving behind gypsum crystals that are blasted apart by extreme temperatures and winds. The gypsum was originally deposited at the bottom of an ancient Permian-era sea that became landlocked and evaporated 250 million years ago. The sedimentary layers hardened and domed up, then, about 10 million years ago, the center collapsed, creating the two ranges that flank the basin today.

The dunes move constantly, reshaped by winds that funnel between the mountains. At the eastern edge of the basin are crescent-shaped parabolic dunes anchored by hardy plants such as four-wing saltbush and soaptree yucca. Barchan dunes, also crescent shaped even though their noses point into the wind and their arms trail behind, measure up to 65 ft high (20 meters). They are found in the middle of the basin, along with transverse dunes, which form undulating ridges like a string of waves at sea. The park road exits through a band of dome dunes, the youngest and most active, migrating some 30 ft (9 meters) a year.

Surrounding White Sands are **Holloman Air Force Base** and **White Sands Missile Range**, best known for the **Trinity Site**, where the world's first atom bomb was detonated. You can visit this national historical landmark on the first Saturday of April and October, with military escort. Tours begin at 8am and return at 3pm. Call 505-437-6120 or toll-free 800-826-0294 for more details.

Map on page 280

**BELOW:** the New Mexico Museum of Space History, known affectionately as "the cube," features a planetarium, IMAX theater and exhibits on the development of space science.

*A desert gift shop beckons drivers in Three Rivers.*

**BELOW:** Three Rivers Petroglyph Site.
**RIGHT:** instruments at the National Solar Observatory on Sacramento Peak allow astronomers to study the sun safely.

## Sun watchers

Oliver M. Lee's ranch headquarters has been rebuilt and is now part of **Oliver M. Lee Memorial State Park** ❿ (409 Dog Canyon Rd, 505-437-8284; open 24 hours; admission), 12 miles (19km) south of Alamogordo. This little-known gem has an immaculate, 50-site campground that makes a good base for campers and those who wish to hike in the Sacramento Mountain foothills. A rocky 5½-mile (9-km) trail, once used by Indians, leads into Dog Canyon and ascends 3,100 ft (945 meters) to Joplin Ridge (elev. 7,500 ft/2,290 meters). The visitor center has exhibits on colorful early settlers, plants and animals, and Oliver Lee, who was tried for murdering a rival, found innocent, and went on to serve in the state legislature.

In 1898, Lee moved into the Sacramento Mountains and built Circle Cross Ranch, near tiny Timberon, eventually amassing the largest ranch in New Mexico. The 20-mile (32-km) scenic drive into the mountains, via US 82, is one of the most dramatic in New Mexico, climbing abruptly from 4,350 ft (1,325 meters) at Alamogordo to almost 9,000 ft (2,740 meters) at Cloudcroft. The road passes through the state's only automobile tunnel, and several pullouts have spectacular views of White Sands. At Cloudcroft, winter visitors enjoy the family-oriented ski area and cross-country skiing on old logging roads. Forest trails like the popular 2.6-mile (4-km) Osha Trail, which begins just west of Cloudcroft across the highway from the historic railroad trestle, are popular in summer.

If you're keen on astronomy, don't miss the **National Solar Observatory and Apache Point Observatory** ⓫ (NM 6563, 505-434-7000, www.nso.edu/sosp/pr; daily May–Oct 10am–6pm; admission), atop 9,200-ft-high (2,800-meter) **Sacramento Peak** in the tiny forest community of **Sunspot**, 16 miles (26km) south of

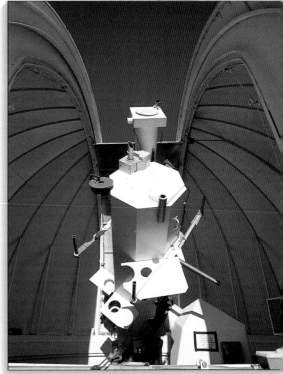

Cloudcroft. You can do a self-guided tour of the grounds and view exhibits on solar and other planetary research in the visitor center from May to October. To find out how astronomers safely view the sun, you'll need to take a guided tour, available on Saturday only. It's worth it. The telescopes here are amazing and include the Dunn Solar Telescope, a rotating instrument that rises 330 ft (100 meters) from a subterranean chamber.

From Cloudcroft, US 82 continues to Ruidoso, via the spectacular Mescalero Apache Reservation, where you may glimpse tipis, ceremonial brush shelters, and cowboys rounding up stock in early fall.

Map on page 280

## Dead man walking

From Alamogordo, US 70 continues past White Sands, over the San Andres Mountains to Las Cruces, while US 54/70 continues north through the Tularosa Basin through irrigated fields. The family-owned **Eagle Ranch Pistachio Groves** (7288 US 54/70, 505-434-0035, www.EagleRanchPistachios.com; Mon–Sat 8am–6pm, Sun 9am–6pm), west of the highway, has 12,000 trees and is the state's oldest and largest pistachio grower. You can tour the groves; sample brittle, biscotti, and pistachios flavored with chile, garlic and other seasonings; and purchase them in an attractive visitor center/gift shop. Ask about picnicking and camping in the groves. Another shady spot to picnic is nearby **La Luz**, founded as a Spanish presidio and mission in 1719. Today, it's a tiny community of shaded streets, art galleries and old adobe walls.

Enjoy the shade while you can. The north end of the Tularosa Basin is searingly hot lava country. About 36 miles (58km) north of Alamogordo, turn east on CR B30 and drive 5 miles (8km) to the **Three Rivers Petroglyph Site ⓬** (CR B30, 505-525-4300; open daily; admission). A short trail leads past 21,000 extraordinary petroglyphs, representing hand prints, sun bursts, masks, birds and other cryptic symbols left behind by the mysterious Jornada Mogollon people a thousand years ago. Sadly, many have been defaced, but managers now hire onsite stewards to watch over the site. Continue along the trail to view a partially excavated pithouse and pueblo village. You can picnic and camp here, if you wish, but there's little shade in summer.

It's hotter than Hades in summer at **Valley of Fires Recreation Area ⓭** (off US 380, 505-648-2241; open daily; admission), west of Carrizozo. Try to time your visit for early in the morning. The 220-sq-mile (570-sq-km) Carrizozo Lava Flow is one of the youngest in the United States. The name Valley of Fires is an Indian term given by people whose ancestors are said to have witnessed the lava erupting from a small peak near the northern end of the *malpais* (badlands) a thousand years ago. Incredibly, a number of plants and animals have made a home in this stark terrain. Ocotillo and yucca have managed to root in moist crevices in the lava, and, if you spend the night here, you may glimpse deer, coyotes and ring-tail cats silhouetted against the jagged black rocks. Little wonder, considering the forbidding, sun-blasted landscape, that this region of New Mexico was dubbed Jornada del Muerto – Dead Man's Way. ❏

**BELOW:** sorting nuts at the Eagle Ranch Pistachio Groves.

# CARLSBAD CAVERNS AND THE SOUTHEAST CORNER

*Temperatures sizzle in New Mexico's southern desert, to which visitors from far and wide flock for a look at a phenomenal world beneath the earth's surface*

Map on page 280

L ittle Texas, they call it – and it's easy to see why. The flat plains of southeastern New Mexico blend seamlessly into a West Texas horizon that won't quit. Howling winds chase tumbleweeds, and whirling dust devils skitter across lonesome highways. Oil pumps, windmills, cattle, antelope, and a handful of gritty ranches and small towns appear out of nowhere, only to disappear just as quickly, swallowed up in a Cinemascope landscape straight out of the movie *Giant*.

It's not just the country that's big. Folks walk a little taller, talk a little louder, dress a little brighter, and dream a little bigger in these parts. Beginning in the mid-1800s, Eddy, Chaves, De Baca and Lea Counties have seen their fair share of larger-than-life, Texas-style ranchers and oilmen. Texas cattle baron John Chisum blazed the first trail through the Pecos River Valley in the 1860s and amassed huge ranches south of Fort Sumner and Roswell on the strength of lucrative government contracts. The discovery of artesian water in the early 1900s ushered in the era of irrigation agriculture, allowing towns like Portales to capture the market on Valencia peanuts. Today's billionaires, men like Robert Anderson, have made (and lost) fortunes gambling on a different resource, oil, the "black gold" found beneath the ancient seabed of the Permian Basin.

Like the rough-hewn cowboys, miners and farmers who homesteaded here, southeastern New Mexico is a diamond-in-the-rough. Its best features are well concealed behind a homely exterior of pale, uninspiring desert that broils under 100°F (38°C) temperatures every summer. Take a closer look, though. There's more here than first meets the eye. Spectacular sunsets. Natural lakes, marshes and wildlife viewing. One of North America's most important archaeological sites. And, 750 ft (230 meters) below the surface of the desert, the ultimate hidden treasure: 30 miles (48km) of highly "decorated" caves preserved at Carlsbad Caverns National Park, New Mexico's top visitor attraction.

## Down under

Begin your tour in the town of **Carlsbad** ⓮, where the enjoyable **Living Desert Zoo and Gardens State Park** (505-887-5516; daily 9am–5pm, extended summer hours, admission), off US 285, is the perfect place to learn about the 200,000-sq-mile (520,000-sq-km) Chihuahuan Desert. A 1.3-mile (2-km) nature trail passes through several habitats, from sand hills along the nearby Pecos River to gypsum formations of the desert uplands and the pinyon-juniper zone of the hills. Living Desert cares for more than 200 species of animals that have been rescued and rehabilitated after injury in the wild. Look for black bear,

**PRECEDING PAGES:** Apache artist Albert Summa. **LEFT:** sunlight filters into Carlsbad Caverns. **BELOW:** Roswell shop window.

*Cowboy and companion keep an eye on the herd during a cattle drive near Roswell.*

bison, mountain lion, bobcat and numerous birds, from eagles to roadrunners. Of particular interest are endangered Mexican wolves, part of a captive breeding program designed to reintroduce wolves into the Southwest.

The immaculately laid-out gardens contain 300 species of desert plants, including signature Chihuahuan plants like lechuguilla, sotol and agave. If you're in Carlsbad the third weekend in May, don't miss the four-day Apache Mescal Roast held at the park, which includes arts and crafts, traditional dances and a chance to taste mescal, the cooked heart of the agave.

The Mescalero Apache gathered agave from all over this region, including the area now encompassed by **Carlsbad Caverns National Park ⓯** (3225 National Parks Highway, Carlsbad, NM 88220, 505-785-2232, www.nps.gov/cave; daily 8am–5.30pm, to 7pm in summer), where they left behind roasting pits and painted pictographs at the Natural Cave entrance. Neither the Apache nor later Spanish explorers like de Sosa had any idea of what lay below the dusty surface of the Chihuahuan Desert. Certainly not cowboy Jim White, who accidentally fell into the caves in the late 1800s while collecting bat guano for fertilizer. For years, no one would believe White's stories about the limestone fantasia beneath Carlsbad. Eventually, White and a photographer documented the caves, leading to their preservation as a national park in 1930.

## A twist of limestone

Like many caves, Carlsbad Caverns was formed in a thick bed of limestone, but with one significant difference. These caves are part of what was once a 400-mile (640-km), horseshoe-shaped reef growing on an offshore shelf of a shallow, inland sea in the Permian Period, some 250 million years ago. The reef was composed of lime precipitated from seawater and limy secretions from sponges and calcareous algae. Eventually, this ancient sea became landlocked and evaporated, causing the reef to be buried under a load of gypsum, salt and potash that are now mined in the area.

**BELOW:** calcite formations adorn the caves.

The caves did not appear until much later, after a period of geological uplift elevated the Guadalupe Mountains and erosion began to strip away the sediments covering the fossil reef. The young mountains were particularly vulnerable to the hydrogen sulfide gas that seeped up into the water table from the oil reserves in the Permian Basin just to the southeast. The mixture of gas and the oxygen-rich water formed a mild sulfuric acid that dissolved large chambers at the level of the water table. As the water table dropped, caves formed at greater depths. Eventually, groundwater moving down cracks in the rocks encountered drier air in the caves, dropped its carbon dioxide load, and evaporated. Left behind were crystalline formations of calcite known as speleotherms, which decorate the inner surfaces of the caverns.

In the **Hall of Giants**, formations like Twin Domes are actually enormous stalagmites growing up from the floor. In other places, stalactites hang from the ceiling in great numbers and, where stalactites and stalagmites meet, great columns have grown up. Smaller icicle-like stalactites called soda straws hang in curtains, while eccentric helictites seem to grow in all directions. Smooth flowstone covers sloping surfaces with marblelike deposits and, in places, slow-moving water has caused rimstone dams to form. Water is a constant in the steady 56°F (13°C) temperature below ground, forming pools and lakes that may eventually become obscured by calcite lily pads and nests of cave pearls. Rarely, one sees delicate, needlelike aragonite formations, a product of similar depositional processes but with a different crystalline structure.

Map on page 280

Carlsbad offers a full roster of self-guided and ranger-guided tours, from easy to technical. But all visitors start with a self-guided tour of the **Big Room**, one of the world's largest chambers and the centerpiece of Carlsbad Caverns. An elevator leads to the chamber, which offers easy viewing along a paved trail, an underground concession, seating for ranger talks, even restrooms. Most people will want to enter the caves via the steep, 1-mile (1.6-km) paved trail leading from the **Natural Entrance**. The trail passes the **Bat Cave** passageway, summer breeding ground for some 300,000 Mexican freetail bats, whose whirring exits at twilight and entrances at dawn can be witnessed between May and October.

For the fit, wild cave tours are an essential part of the Carlsbad experience. On the moderate, three-hour **Lower Cave** tour, you'll view evidence left behind by Jim White and a National Geographic Society exploratory party in 1924. The entertaining two-hour **Left Hand Tunnel** tour by candle lantern highlights Carlsbad's early history, geology, cave pools and Permian age fossils. Carlsbad's most popular off-trail tour is the 1¼-mile (2-km) **Slaughter Canyon Cave** tour, offered daily in summer, where highlights are the 89-ft-high (27-meter) Monarch, one of the world's largest limestone columns.

If the idea of staying in touristy **Whites City** sets your teeth on edge, consider basing yourself in the pleasant little campground in neighboring **Guadalupe Mountains National Park** ⓰ (HC 60, Box 400, Salt Flat, TX 79847, 915-828-3251, www.nps.gov/gumo; daily 8am–6pm; admission), where you can hike on the uplifted portion of the same Permian Reef you see below ground at Carlsbad Caverns. Eighty miles (130km) of trails crisscross the desert and lead into the high country to 8,749-ft (2,667-meter) **Guadalupe Peak**, Texas's highest mountain. If you're here in the fall (the best time of year to visit), make a beeline for **McKittrick Canyon**, where changing Texas madrone, oak and other deciduous trees offer eye-popping color and many photo ops. On this trail, you can also visit the pretty stone cabin built by oil geologist Wallace Pratt, who fell in love with the Guadalupes and helped establish the national park in 1972.

**BELOW:** the park offers a variety of caving tours.

## Desert lakes

No other attractions on this tour offer nearly as much natural beauty and outdoor recreation as these two national parks, but several state parks come close. **Brantley Lake State Park** ⓱ (505-457-2384), a reservoir on the Pecos River near Carlsbad, is popular with boaters, water skiers, windsurfers and swimmers. A recent addition to the state park system, it was created at the site of the 1880s Wild West ghost town of Seven Rivers, where recent forensic evidence has revealed that most of the inhabitants died violent deaths.

Some of the cowboys passing through Seven Rivers

*Roswell is the UFO mecca of the western United States.*

**BELOW:** the International UFO Museum chronicles the events of the "Roswell Incident."

may have been responsible for naming **Bottomless Lakes State Park** ⓲ (505-624-6058), just east of Roswell. In fact, these sinkhole lakes aren't bottomless. They range in depth from 17 to 90 ft (5–27 meters) and were formed, like Carlsbad Caverns, from dissolved limestone. In summer, Lea Lake is a popular local swimming hole and has a pleasant campground.

Come back in fall or winter to visit 25,000-acre (10,000-hectare) **Bitter Lake National Wildlife Refuge** (505-622-6755), when thousands of migratory geese, ducks and sandhill cranes set up a temporary home here. The refuge is also a haven for several species of dragonfly. A popular Dragonfly Festival is held in spring.

## Unexpected Roswell

Who would expect to find one of the state's best museums in **Roswell** ⓳, the UFO Capital of the World? The superb WPA-era **Roswell Museum and Art Center** (100 W. 11th St, 505-624-6744, www.roswellmuseum.org; Mon–Sat 9am–5pm, Sun 1pm–5pm; free) outclasses the cheesy **International UFO Museum** *(see panel below)* by a light year. It has 11 galleries displaying the amazing Aston Collection of Plains Indian, Pueblo, Spanish Colonial, and early American artifacts and a variety of regional New Mexican works, from traditional carved furniture to cutting-edge modern art. The museum holds the largest collection of works by Roswell native Peter Hurd and wife Henriette Wyeth, which are displayed in the original 1937 Founders Gallery. Taos and Santa Fe artists are well represented too, with works by John Marin, Marsden Hartley, Victor Higgins, Pablita Velarde, and a particularly fine Georgia O'Keeffe painting entitled *Ram's Skull with Brown Leaves*, a favorite of the artist herself.

The museum's central mission is to encourage the arts, in all their forms. An

## RENDEZVOUS AT ROSWELL

In July 1947, witnesses in and around the town of Roswell, New Mexico, reported that a strange aircraft crashed into the desert 35 miles (56km) north of town. Although the military establishment has long held that the vehicle was simply a high-altitude balloon, many others – civilian and military alike – believe that it was an alien spacecraft and that federal personnel recovered the bodies of the occupants.

The validity of such claims is debated daily at the **International UFO Museum and Research Center** (114 N. Main St, Roswell, NM 88207, 505-625-9495; daily 9am–5pm; free). There, visitors can see photos of the key players in the story, view videotapes, and hear lectures about the so-called Roswell Incident. They can also examine artifacts and other pieces of evidence relating to the alleged spaceship crash or, for the serious visitor, conduct research at the 3,000-volume library, including a database of sightings and alien encounters.

The museum, incorporated in 1991, has turned Roswell into a kind of UFO mecca. If you happen to be visiting in summer, hang around for the **Roswell UFO Festival**, a weeklong event in July, with presentations by investigators, alien abductees, authors and other UFOlogists.

Art Education Center offers art classes, a ceramics studio, a research library and a teacher resource center. And, since 1977, artists from all over the country have taken advantage of Roswell Museum's well-regarded artist-in-residence (AIR) program, which was founded by artist Donald Anderson, whose **Anderson Contemporary Art Museum** (505-623-5600), on College Road, is worth a visit.

Among the alumni of the AIR program are artists Robert Colescott, Elmer Schooley and Mexican-American sculptor Luis Jimenez. You won't miss Jimenez's playful, neon-lit fiberglass *End of the Trail with Electric Sunset* sculpture in these galleries. Nor the engaging *Apache Dolly*, a welded metal sculpture by Chiricahua Apache sculptor Bob Haozous, son of famed sculptor Allan Houser, a perfect expression of the artist's interest in combining his cultural background with an interest in nature, politics and art.

## Stone tools and rock history

When Europeans arrived in New Mexico in the 1500s, Apaches and Comanches had been living in this region for centuries, hunting buffalo and antelope on the eastern grasslands and alternately trading and warring with pueblos along the Rio Grande. Until the early 1900s, it was believed that people had been living in North America for about 2,000 years. In the 1930s, two discoveries in the eastern part of the state turned that theory on its ear. Finely worked arrowheads found lodged in an extinct bison at **Folsom**, New Mexico, led archaeologists to push back the date of arrival to 8000 BC. Not long after, even older arrowheads were found lodged in bones in an old gravel pit in between Portales and Clovis, pushing back the date still farther, to 9000 BC.

Anyone with even a minor interest in archaeology will want to pay a visit to the **Blackwater Draw Museum** (505-562-2202; Tues–Sat 10am–5pm, Sun noon–5pm, open Mon in summer; admission), off US 70 between Portales and Clovis, a recently opened research center and museum interpreting the Clovis culture. The small museum is run by Eastern New Mexico University in Portales, well known for its excellent archaeology programs. You can view several short films, dioramas, timelines and examples of Clovis points and bones, and visit the nearby excavation site. Camping and picnicking are available at nearby **Oasis State Park** (505-365-5331), which has shade trees and a lake.

Believe it or not, the unremarkable town of **Clovis ⑳** (pop. 33,000) has another claim to fame. It is home to the **Norman Petty Studios** (1313 W. 7th St; call 505-356-6422 for tours), which, in 1958, helped launch the career of an unknown Texas musician named Buddy Holly. Over one incredible year, like a gathering storm building on the prairie, Petty, Holly and the Crickets recorded legendary hits like "Peggy Sue" and "That'll Be the Day." Then, just as suddenly, Holly was killed in an air crash in 1959 and the storm broke. Petty went on to discover Roy Orbison, Buddy Knox and Roger Williams, and nurtured other new musicians who recorded with him in his Clovis studio until his death in 1984. His widow, Vi, now runs the business, which is located in new digs down the road. Tours of the old studios are available by appointment. ❏

**BELOW:** the Permian Basin is rich in oil reserves. **OVERLEAF:** Roswell shopkeepers do a brisk trade in UFO-related signs and souvenirs.

Map on page 280

# ✺ INSIGHT GUIDES
# Travel Tips

# CONTENTS

# Getting Acquainted

## The Place

New Mexico became a state in 1912. At 121,356 sq miles (314,310 sq km), it is the fifth biggest state in the U.S., occupying 3.4 percent of its land mass. Yet its 1.83 million population – fewer people than the number of Puerto Ricans in New York City – represents only 0.64 percent of the nation's population. One in four workers are employed by the Federal government. At its northwestern corner, New Mexico borders Arizona, Utah and Colorado, the only place in the nation where four states meet.

Officially it is a bilingual state and one in three families speaks Spanish at home. It has become increasingly urbanized, with many people moving to Albuquerque and surrounding Bernalillo county. The town of Gallup, which styles itself "Indian Capital of the World," is a trading center for more than 20 Indian groups.

The state's nickname is "Land of Enchantment" and its motto is *Crescit Eundo* (It Grows as it Goes). The state bird is the roadrunner, the state mammal is the black bear, and the state flower is the yucca.

With elevations from 2,800 to 13,000 ft (850–4,000 meters), New Mexico is the meeting place of the Great Plains, the southern Rockies, and the Range and Basin Province. A vast reservoir of water underlies the state, a world of caves and caverns that has not yet been thoroughly explored. There are fossil beds scattered throughout the state. It has only 258 sq miles (668 sq km) of water.

A quarter of New Mexico is forested, and it includes seven national forests. Its geography encompasses mesas, lava flows, extinct volcanoes and dramatic rock formations.It is rich in natural resources, and major industries include mining (copper, potash, silver, uranium), oil and natural gas.

The legislature comprises 42 members of the Senate, elected for four years, and 70 members of the House, elected for two years. Most of the 33 counties are run by an elected board of commissioners.

## Climate

New Mexico spans a wide range of climate and life zones, but by and large you will find sunny skies, low humidity and limited precipitation. Climate varies widely with elevation.

## Public Holidays

On public holidays, post offices, banks, most government offices and a large number of shops and restaurants are closed. Public transport usually runs less frequently.

**New Year's Day:** January 1
**Martin Luther King, Jr.'s Birthday:** The third Monday in January
**Presidents Day:** The third Monday in February
**Good Friday:** March/April – date varies
**Easter Sunday:** March/April – date varies
**El Cinco de Mayo:** May 5
**Memorial Day:** Last Monday in May
**Independence Day:** July 4
**Labor Day:** First Monday in September
**Columbus Day:** Second Monday in October
**Election Day:** The Tuesday in the first full week of November during presidential-election years
**Veterans Day:** November 11
**Thanksgiving Day:** Fourth Thursday in November
**Christmas Day:** December 25

## Let It Snow

In winter, snow falling in the lowlands frequently melts by midday, but ski areas maintain good bases from late November into mid-April. Average annual snowfall at ski areas around Taos (including Angel Fire, Red River and Taos) ranges from 210 to 312 inches (533–793cm). At Ski Santa Fe the average is 225 inches (572cm). At Ski Apache, in the Sacramento Mountains of southern New Mexico, the average is 183 inches (465cm).

Climbing 1,000 ft (300 meters) is equivalent to traveling 300 miles (500km) northwards. In temperature, traveling from the lowest to the highest points of New Mexico is like traveling from Mexico to the north of Hudson Bay in Canada.

New Mexico enjoys 300 days of sunshine annually in the northern region and 350 days in the south. Yearly precipitation ranges from 40 inches (100cm) in the Sangre de Cristo Mountains to less than 10 inches (25cm) in the southern deserts. Most rain falls in brief, intense thunderstorms during the summer "monsoon" season, when dry washes, arroyos and narrow canyons are prone to flash floods.

Average high temperatures in **Santa Fe** and **Taos** reach the mid-80s°F (29°C) in summer. Nights are warm and pleasant, usually ranging from 60°F (16°C) to 70°F (21°C). Winter is chilly but often sunny, with highs in the 40s°F (4–10°C), nighttime lows well below freezing, and occasional heavy snowfall. Spring and fall are mild and pleasant, with highs in the 60s°F (15 to 20°C) and lows in the 30s°F (–1 to 4°C). Santa Fe gets about 14 inches (36cm) of rain per year, Taos 11 inches (28 cm).

In **Albuquerque**, 55 miles (230km) to the south of Santa Fe and about 1,700 ft (520 meters) lower in elevation, temperatures range from 65°F to 95°F (18–37°C) in summer to around 25°F (-4°C) in winter. Annual precipitation in

Albuquerque averages 9 inches (23cm). Winter is cold but generally sunny, with occasional snowfall, though it rarely lasts.

The weather is warmer in the low-lying desert regions of southern New Mexico. At **Las Cruces** (elev. 3,896ft/1,186 meters), for example, summer temperatures routinely hit the mid-90s°F (35°C) and often soar over 100°F (38°C), though temperatures are much cooler in mountainous areas such as those around Ruidoso. The skiing season at nearby Ski Apache, atop 12,000-ft (3,660 meters) Sierra Blanca, usually runs from December to late March or early April. Nights in the desert can be chilly even in summer, and winds are often brisk, so bring a sweater or light jacket.

## Time Zones

The continental U.S. is divided into four time zones. From east to west, later to earlier, they are Eastern, Central, Mountain and Pacific, each separated by one hour. New Mexico is on Mountain Standard Time (MST), seven hours behind Greenwich Mean Time. On the second Sunday in March, New Mexicans set the clock ahead one hour in observation of Daylight Saving Time. On the first Sunday in November, the clock is moved back one hour to return to Standard Time.

Other states in the region – Colorado, Utah and Arizona – are on Mountain Standard Time. All but Arizona observe daylight savings time. (One peculiarity to keep in mind: the Navajo Nation observes daylight savings time but the rest of Arizona does not.) California is on Pacific Standard Time and observes daylight savings time. Mexico does not observe daylight savings time.

# Planning the Trip

## Clothing

Think cool and comfortable. With few exceptions, western dress is informal. A pair of jeans or slacks, a polo or button-down shirt, and boots or shoes are appropriate at all but the fanciest places and events. Shorts and light shirts are suitable for most situations in the warmer months, though it's always a good idea to have a sweater or jacket for evenings, high elevations, or overly air-conditioned shops and restaurants.

If you plan on doing a lot of walking or hiking, it's worth investing in a sturdy pair of hiking shoes or boots. A thin, inner polypropylene sock and a thick, outer sock will help keep your feet dry and comfortable. If blisters or sore spots develop, quickly cover them with moleskin or surgical tape, available at most pharmacies or camping supply stores.

A high-factor sunblock, wide-brimmed hat and sunglasses are advisable too, even if the day starts out cloudy. The sun is merciless, especially in the desert, where shade is scarce.

## Electricity

Standard electricity in North America is 110–115 volts, 60 cycles A.C. An adapter is necessary for most appliances from overseas, with the exception of Japan.

## Maps

Accurate maps are indispensable in New Mexico, especially when leaving primary roads. Highway maps can be found at bookstores,

convenience stores and gas stations. Free maps may be available by mail from state or regional tourism bureaus. Free city, state and regional maps as well as up-to-date road conditions and other valuable services are also available to members of the Automobile Association of America (AAA). If you are driving any distance, the service is well worth the membership fee.

Maps of national parks, forests and other natural areas are usually offered by the managing governmental agency. Good topographical maps of national parks are available from **Trails Illustrated**, PO Box 3610, Evergreen, CO 80439, tel: 303-670-3457 or toll-free 800-962-1643; these maps are often in bookstores. Extremely detailed topographical maps are available from the **U.S. Geological Survey**, PO Box 25286, Denver Federal Center, Denver, CO 80225, tel: 303-236-7477, www.usgs.gov/sales.html. Like maps from Trails Illustrated, USGS maps are often available in higher-end bookstores and shops that sell outdoor gear.

## Entry Regulations

### PASSPORTS & VISAS

A passport, visitor's visa and evidence of intent to leave the U.S. after your visit are required for entry into the U.S. by most foreign nationals. Visitors from the United Kingdom and several other countries staying less than 90 days may not need a visa if entering as tourists. All other nationals must obtain a visa from a U.S. consulate or embassy. An international vaccination certificate may be required depending on your country of origin.

Everyone, including US citizens, traveling by air between the US and Canada, Mexico, the Caribbean and Bermuda must present a current passport; a birth certificate and photo ID are no longer acceptable as valid proof.

Once in the U.S. foreigners may visit Canada or Mexico for up to 30 days and re-enter the U.S. without a new visa. For additional information, contact a U.S. consulate or embassy or the U.S. State Department, tel: 202-663-1225.

### Extensions of Stay

Visas are usually granted for six months. If you wish to remain in the country longer than six months, you must apply for an extension of stay at the **Bureau of Citizenship and Immigration Services**, Washington District Office, 4420 N. Fairfax Drive, Arlington, VA 22203; 800-375-5283; www.bcis.gov

## CUSTOMS

All people entering the country must go through U.S. Customs, often a time-consuming process. To speed things up, be prepared to open your luggage for inspection and keep the following restrictions in mind.

● You must declare cash in excess of $10,000.

● Anything for personal use may be brought in duty- and tax-free.

● Adults are allowed to bring in one liter of alcohol for personal use.

● You can bring in gifts worth less than $400 duty- and tax-free. Anything over the $400 limit is subject to duty charges and taxes.

● Agricultural products, meat and animals are subject to complex restrictions, especially if entering in California. Leave these items at home if at all possible.

For more details, contact a U.S. consulate or U.S. Customs, www.customs.gov/travel/travel.htm.

## Health

### PRECAUTIONS

**Insurance**: It's vital to have medical insurance when traveling. Though hospitals must provide emergency treatment to anyone who needs it whether or not they have insurance, you may have to prove you can pay for treatment of anything less than a life-threatening condition. Know what your policy covers and have proof of the policy with you at all times or be prepared to pay at the time service is rendered.

**Flash floods**: Sudden downpours – even those falling miles away from your location– can fill canyons and dry riverbeds with a roaring torrent of water and mud that will sweep away everything in its path. Travelers should be especially careful during the summer monsoon season. Avoid hiking or driving in arroyos or narrow canyons, and never try to wade or drive across a flooded stream. If rain begins to fall or you see rain clouds in the distance, move to higher ground. It's impossible to outrun or even outdrive a flash flood. Take action before water level begins to rise.

**Sunburn**: Even a couple of hours outdoors can result in sunburn, so protect yourself with a high-SPF sunscreen and polarized sunglasses. The elderly and the ill, small children and people with fair skin should be especially careful. Excessive pain, redness, blistering or numbness mean you need professional medical attention. Minor sunburn can be soothed by taking a cool bath.

**Dehydration**: Drink plenty of liquids and, if outdoors, carry bottles of water and something to eat. The rule of thumb is a gallon (4l) of water per person per day. Don't wait to get thirsty – start drinking as soon as you set out. Also avoid the sun at its hottest: 2–4pm.

**Drinking water**: All water from natural sources must be purified before drinking. *Giardia* is found throughout the West, even in crystal-clear water, and it can cause severe cramps and diarrhea. The most popular purification methods are tablets or filters (both available from camping supply stores) or by boiling water for at least three minutes. Drink only bottled water in Mexico, and avoid ice cubes.

**Cactus**: To avoid being pricked, stay on trails and wear long pants and sturdy boots. Some people may have allergies to the prickly varieties of these beautiful desert plants.

**Hypothermia**: This occurs when the core body temperature falls below 95°F (35°C). At altitude, combinations of alcohol, cold and thin air can produce hypothermia. Watch for drowsiness, disorientation

## Abandoned Mines

Exercise caution around old buildings and abandoned mines. Structures may be unstable and the ground may be littered with broken glass, nails and other debris. Mine shafts are particularly dangerous. Never enter a mine shaft or cave unless accompanied by a park ranger or other professional.

and sometimes increased urination. If possible get to a hospital, otherwise blankets and extra clothing should be piled on for warmth. Don't use hot water or electric heaters and don't rub the skin. The elderly should be especially careful in extremely cold weather.

**Frostbite**: Symptoms of frostbite, which occurs when living tissue freezes, include numbness, pain, blistering and whitening of the skin. The most immediate remedy is to put frostbitten skin against warm skin. Simply holding your hands for several minutes over another person's frostbitten cheeks or nose may suffice. Otherwise, immerse frostbitten skin in warm (not hot!) water. Refreezing will cause even more damage, so get the victim into a warm environment quickly.

**Altitude sickness**: This is not a serious consideration in most parts of the state, although people traveling from sea level may feel uncharacteristically winded at elevations as low as 6,000 or 7,000 ft (1,800–2,100 meters). The sensation usually passes after a few days. Symptoms, including nausea, headache, vomiting, extreme fatigue, light-headedness and shortness of breath, intensify over 10,000 ft (3,000 meters). Although the symptoms may be mild at first, they can develop into a serious illness. Move to a lower elevation and try to acclimatize gradually.

### INSECTS & ANIMALS

**Snakes**: New Mexico has two venomous snakes – rattlesnakes and coral snakes. Only about 3 percent of people bitten by a rattlesnake die, and these are mainly small children. Walk in the open, proceed with caution among rocks, avoid dark or overgrown places where snakes might lurk, shake out bedding or clothing that has been lying on the ground, and wear sturdy hiking boots. Snakes often lie on roads at night because of the residual heat radiating from the pavement, so use a flashlight if walking on a paved road after dark. Keep your hands and feet where you can see them, and don't let children poke under rocks or logs.

Snakebite kits are good psychological protection, but there is controversy over how effective they really are. If bitten, apply a tourniquet lightly above the bite toward the heart. Try to identify the species and go immediately to a doctor.

**Gila monsters**: North America's only venomous lizard looks menacing but is easily recognized and rarely encountered.

**Insects**: Bees are abundant, which should concern only those allergic to the sting. The kissing bug is an unusual looking black insect with an unpleasant bite. There are fire ants and some varieties of wasp. Their sting can be painful but isn't dangerous unless you're allergic to their venom.

The bite of a black widow spider and tarantula and the sting of a scorpion's tail can pack a punch but are rarely a serious health threat to adults. Scorpions are nocturnal, so use flashlights if you walk barefoot in the desert at night. They often hide in recesses, dark corners and old wood piles and like to crawl into protected places, so shake out clothes or sleeping bags that have been on the ground and check your shoes before slipping them on in the morning.

## Money Matters

### CURRENCY

The basic unit of American currency, the dollar ($1), is equal to 100 cents. There are four coins, each worth less than a dollar: a penny or 1 cent (1¢), a nickel or 5 cents (5¢), a dime or 10 cents (10¢) and a quarter or 25 cents (25¢).

There are several denominations of paper money: $1, $5, $10, $20, $50 and $100. Each bill is the same color, size and shape; be sure to check the dollar amount on the face of the bill.

It is advisable to arrive with at least $100 in cash (in small bills) to pay for ground transportation and other incidentals.

## AUTOMATIC TELLER MACHINES (ATMs)

ATMs are the most convenient way to access cash and are widely available throughout the state. They are usually found at banks, shopping malls, supermarkets, service stations, convenience stores, and hotels. ATM, or debit, cards may also be used at a growing number of grocery stores and gas stations, much as credit cards are.

## TRAVELER'S CHECKS

Foreign visitors are advised to take U.S. dollar traveler's checks since exchanging foreign currency – whether as cash or checks – can be problematic. A growing number of banks offer exchange facilities, but this practice is not universal.

Most shops, restaurants and other establishments accept traveler's checks in U.S. dollars and will give change in cash. Alternatively, checks can be converted into cash at the bank.

## CREDIT CARDS

These are very much part of daily life in the U.S. They can be used to pay for pretty much anything, and it is also common for car rental firms and hotels to take an imprint of your card as a deposit. Rental companies may oblige you to pay a large deposit in cash if you do not have a card.

You can also use your credit card to withdraw cash from ATMs. Before you leave home, make sure you know your PIN (personal identification number) and find out which ATM system will accept your card. The most widely accepted cards are Visa, MasterCard, American Express, Diners Club, and Discovery.

Money may be sent or received by wire at any **Western Union** office (tel: 800-325-6000) or **American Express Money Gram** office (tel: 800-543-4080).

## Insurance

Most visitors to the U.S. will have no health problems during their stay. Even so, you should never leave home without travel insurance to cover both yourself and your belongings. Your own insurance company or travel agent can advise you on policies, but shop around since rates vary. Make sure you are covered for accidental death, emergency medical care, trip cancellation and baggage or document loss.

## Getting There

### BY AIR

The following carriers serve Albuquerque International Airport or, as it is now known, "Sunport":

**America West**. Tel: 800-235-9292 Nonstop service to Phoenix and Las Vegas with connections across the country.

**American**. Tel: 800-433-7300 Nonstop service to Chicago and Dallas-Fort Worth, with connections around the nation and world.

**Continental**. Tel: 800-525-0280 Nonstop service to Newark and Houston, with connections to national and international destinations.

**Delta**. Tel: 800-221-1212 Nonstop service to Dallas-Fort Worth, Atlanta, Salt Lake City and Cincinnati with connections across the nation and world.

**Frontier**. Tel: 800-432-1359
Nonstop service to Denver with regional connections.

**Great Plains**. Tel: 866-929-8646
Nonstop service to Oklahoma City and Colorado Springs. Direct service to Tulsa and Nashville.

**Mesa** . Tel: 800-637-2247
Commuter airline with nonstop service to Colorado Springs and nonstop and direct service to many cities in New Mexico, including Hobbs, Clovis, Carlsbad, Roswell and Farmington.

**Northwest**. Tel: 800-225-2525
Nonstop service to Minneapolis-St. Paul and connections around North America and the world.

**Rio Grande**. Tel: 866-929-8646
Nonstop service to Durango, Alamogordo and Taos.

**Skywest**. Tel: 800-453-9417
Nonstop regional jet service to Salt Lake City, with connections at Delta's hub there.

**Southwest**. Tel: 800-435-9792
By far the largest carrier at the Sunport, offering nonstop service to Dallas, Phoenix, El Paso, Lubbock, Midland, Baltimore-Washington, Portland, Seattle, Salt Lake City, Las Vegas, Los Angeles, St. Louis, Chicago, Orlando and San Diego.

**United**. Tel: 800-241-6522
Frequent nonstop service to Denver with connections around the nation and world

**A note about security:** Stricter airport security is expected to continue indefinitely and will impose some constraints on passengers and visitors to the Sunport. Keep these guidelines in mind as you prepare for your flight.

Check directly with your airline before going to the airport. Make sure your flight has not been cancelled, rescheduled or delayed.

Allow plenty of time for check-in prior to your scheduled departure time. As much as two hours may be required. Anticipate longer lines at airline ticket counters, increased security screening and other potential delays. Your airline can advise you how much extra time to allow. Call your airline in advance

## Hitchhiking

Hitchhiking is illegal in many places and ill-advised everywhere. It's an inefficient and dangerous method of travel. Don't do it.

for a recommendation.

Picture ID (such as a driver's license or passport) is absolutely essential for flight check-in at the ticket counter and other locations prior to boarding your aircraft. Please be prepared to present your ID at the security checkpoint and at the gate area.

Only passengers with tickets or passengers who can produce airline-approved documentation will be allowed beyond the security checkpoint. If you are utilizing e-tickets or ticketless travel, please confirm with your airline what you will need at the checkpoint.

Exceptions to this rule may be made for special circumstances such as parents escorting children or a need to accompany an elderly individual to the gate. Check with your airline prior to reaching the security checkpoint for advice on how to best handle this situation so you avoid any unnecessary delays once you reach the checkpoint.

Anyone waiting on arriving passengers or accompanying departing passengers must stay outside the security checkpoint area – they are no longer allowed access to the gate areas.

Sharp objects of any description, composition or length are strictly prohibited beyond the security checkpoint. This includes knives and scissors of any kind. Cutting objects such as box cutters and straight razors are not allowed past the checkpoint. Metal nail files, corkscrews, ice picks, letter openers, nail clippers with a comb knife, and screwdrivers are among other restricted items.

If you happen to be carrying a restricted item and it is detected at the security checkpoint, you will be given the option of taking the item back to your vehicle or checking it at your airline ticket counter. If you

choose neither of these options, the item will be collected by security screening personnel and cannot be returned.

The Transportation Security Administration (TSA) is responsible for the passenger screening at the security checkpoint. For more information about screening policies, see www.tsa.dot.gov.

New carry-on baggage restrictions allow only one carry-on bag and one personal item such as a purse, briefcase or laptop computer per passenger. If you have more items than allowed, you will be asked to go back and check the extra items at the ticket counter.

The Sunport's parking garage and long-term surface lots are open. Expect some parking restrictions on the 3rd and 4th levels of the garage.

Unauthorized vehicles left unattended at the terminal curb on both the upper and lower level roadways will be cited and towed immediately. Loading and unloading of passengers and baggage at the curb is permitted. However, waiting at the curb – in or with your vehicle – is not allowed. Airport Police and traffic security personnel will ask individuals who park and wait to move along. If you are picking someone up, you are strongly encouraged to park in the Sunport's short-term parking garage if a wait of any length is anticipated.

## BY TRAIN

Amtrak offers more than 500 destinations across the U.S. The trains are comfortable and reliable, with lounges, dining cars, snack bars and, in some cases, movies and live entertainment. Most routes offer sleeper cars with private cabins in addition to regular seating.

Amtrak's **Southwest Chief** runs from Chicago to Los Angeles, with stops in Raton, Las Vegas, Lamy, Albuquerque and Gallup, New Mexico. The **Sunset Limited** runs from Orlando to Los Angeles and stops at Deming and Lordsburg, New Mexico, and El Paso, Texas.

Ask about two- or three-stopover discounts, senior citizens' and children's discounts, and Amtrak's package tours. International travelers can buy a USA Railpass, good for 15 to 30 days of unlimited travel on Amtrak throughout the United States.

Contact **Amtrak** (tel: 800-872-7245, www.amtrak.com) for detailed scheduling.

## BY BUS

One of the least expensive ways to travel in America is by interstate bus. The largest national bus company is **Greyhound**, tel: 800-231-2222. The company routinely offers discounts such as go-anywhere fares. An Ameripass offers unlimited travel for 7, 15, 30 or 60 days. Greyhound serves more than 40 towns and cities in New Mexico, including Albuquerque, Santa Fe, Taos, Española, Farmington, Gallup, Las Cruces, Las Vegas, Ruidoso, Lordsburg, Roswell, Alamogordo and Carlsbad. A rental car or other transport is necessary to reach remote locations.

## BY CAR

Driving is by far the most convenient way to travel in New Mexico, especially outside the major cities. Major roads are well-maintained, although some backcountry roads may be unpaved. If you plan on driving into remote areas or in heavy snow, mud or severe weather, it's a good idea to use a four-wheel-drive vehicle with high clearance.

### Maps & Information
Your greatest asset as a driver is a good road map. Maps can be obtained from state tourism offices, filling stations, supermarkets and convenience stores. Although roads are maintained even in remote areas, it is advisable to listen to local radio stations and to check with highway officials or police officers for the latest information

on weather and road conditions, especially in winter or if planning to leave paved roads.

### Driving in Remote Areas
If you plan to drive in uninhabited areas, carry a spare tire and extra water – at least 1 gallon (4l) per person per day. A cell phone is a good idea, too, though some areas may be out of range of the nearest communications tower.

Service stations can be few and far between in remote areas. Not every town will have one, and many close early. It's always better to have more fuel than you think you will need.

**A word of caution:** If your car breaks down on a back road, do not attempt to strike out on foot, even with water. A car is easier to spot than a person and provides shelter from the elements. If you don't have a cell phone or your phone doesn't work, sit tight and wait to be found.

## Vehicle Rental

### CAR RENTALS

Auto rental agencies are located at all airports, in cities and many large towns. In most places, you must be at least 21 years old (25 at some locations) to rent a car and you must have a valid driver's license and at least one major credit card. Drivers under 25 may have to pay an extra fee, as will additional

## AAA

If you intend to do a lot of driving, consider joining the American Automobile Association (AAA). Fees are reasonable and benefits many: emergency road service, maps, insurance, traveler's checks, bail bond protection and other services. AAA has reciprocity agreements with many foreign automobile associations.

**AAA**, 4100 E. Arkansas Drive, Denver CO 80222, tel: 800-222-4357; www.aaa.com

drivers. Foreign drivers must have an international driver's license. Be sure that you are properly insured for both collision and personal liability. Insurance won't be included in the base rental fee. Insurance cost varies depending on the car and the type of coverage, but it is usually $15–35 per day. You may already be covered by your own auto insurance or credit-card company, so check with them first.

Many companies offer unlimited mileage. If not, you may be charged an extra 10–25¢ or more per mile over a given maximum. Rental fees vary depending on the time of year, location, how far in advance you book your rental, and if you travel on weekdays or weekends. Inquire about discounts or benefits for which you may be eligible, including corporate, credit-card or frequent-flyer programs.

| | |
|---|---|
| Advantage | 505-247-1066 |
| Alamo | 800-327-9633 |
| Avis | 800-331-1212 |
| Budget | 800-527-0700 |
| Dollar | 800-800-4000 |
| Enterprise | 800-325-8007 |
| Hertz | 800-654-3131 |
| National | 800-227-7368 |
| Thrifty | 800-367-2277 |

## RV RENTALS

No special license is necessary to operate a motor home (or recreational vehicle – RV for short), but they aren't cheap. When you add up the cost of rental fees, insurance, gas and campsites, renting a car and staying in motels or camping may be less expensive.

Keep in mind, too, that RVs are large and slow and may be difficult to handle on narrow mountain roads. If parking space is tight, driving an RV may be extremely inconvenient. Still, RVs are very popular, and some travelers swear by them. For additional information about RV rentals, call the **Recreational Vehicle Rental Association**, tel: 800-336-0355; www.rvra.org.

# Practical Tips

## Newspapers

All cities and most large towns have a local newspaper. For national and international news, along with local and regional events, check the papers listed below. Also available are the *New York Times, Los Angeles Times, Washington Post, USA Today* and *Wall Street Journal.* Forget about finding overseas newspapers, except in a few big hotels and specialty bookstores.

**Albuquerque Journal**
7777 Jefferson NE, Albuquerque, NM 87109; tel: 505-823-3800; www.abqjournal.com

**Albuquerque Tribune**
7777 Jefferson NE, Albuquerque, NM 87109; tel: 505-823-7777; www.abqtrib.com

**Crosswinds**
3701 San Mateo Blvd NE, Suite J, Albuquerque, NM; tel: 505-883-4750. A progressive weekly.

**Gallup Independent**
500 N. 9th St, Gallup, NM 87305; tel: 505-863-6811; www.gallupindependent.com

**Las Cruces Sun-News**
256 W. Las Cruces Ave, Las Cruces, NM 88004; tel: 505-541-5400; www.lcsun-news.com

**Los Alamos Monitor**
256 D.P. Rd, Los Alamos, NM 87544; tel: 505-662-4185; www.lamonitor.com

**Navajo Times**
Highway 264 & Route 12, Window Rock, AZ 86515; tel: 928-871-6642; www.thenavajotimes.com

**Santa Fe New Mexican**
202 E. Marcy St, Santa Fe, NM 87501; tel: 505/983-3303; www.sfnewmexican.com
The Friday arts and entertainment section "Pasatiempo" is an invaluable source of information on music, film, theater, gallery shows, dining out and other events.

**Santa Fe Reporter**
132 E. Marcy St, Santa Fe NM 87501; tel: 505-988-5541; www.sfreporter.com
An alternative weekly.

**Santa Fe Times**
418 Cerrillos Rd, Suite 15, Santa Fe, N.M. 87501; tel: 505-982-0588; www.santafetimes.com
This is a useful online magazine.

**Taos News**
226 Albright St, Taos, NM 87571; tel: 505-758-2241; www.taosnews.com

**Weekly Alibi**
2118 Central Ave SE, #151, Albuquerque, NM 87106; tel: 505-346-0660; www.alibi.com
An alternative weekly with a strong countercultural flavor.

The following magazines feature profiles of interesting destinations and local people as well as restaurant listings and a calendar of events.

**El Palacio**
113 Lincoln Ave, Santa Fe, NM 87504; tel: 505-827-4361; www.museumofnewmexico.org
Magazine of the Museum of New Mexico.

**Focus/Santa Fe**
1441 S. St Francis Drive, Suite C, Santa Fe, NM 87505; tel: 505-982-8990.
A splashy arts bimonthly.

**La Herencia del Norte**
P.O. Box 22576, Santa Fe, NM 87502; www.herencia.com
A quarterly publication dedicated to New Mexico's Hispanic culture and history.

**New Mexico Magazine**
P.O. Box 12002, Santa Fe, NM 87504; tel: 505-827-7447; nmmagazine.com
A monthly magazine with feature articles and numerous color photos, published by the Department of Tourism.

**Out!**
P.O. Box 27237, Albuquerque, NM 87125; www.outmagazine.com
Monthly magazine for the gay and lesbian community

**Santa Fean**
444 Galisteo, Santa Fe, NM 87501; tel: 505-983-1444; www.santafean.com
Restaurant reviews, information on the arts, shopping, fashion and special events.

**The**
1208-A Mercantile Rd, Santa Fe 87507; tel: 505-424-7641; www.themagazineonline.com
A free arts monthly.

## Postal Services

Even the most remote towns are served by the U.S. Postal Service. Smaller post offices tend to be limited to business hours (Monday–Friday 9am–5pm), although central, big-city branches may have extended weekday and weekend hours.

Stamps are sold at all post offices. They are also sold at some convenience stores, filling stations, hotels and transportation terminals, usually from vending machines.

For reasonably quick delivery within the U.S. at a modest price, ask for priority mail, which usually reaches its destination within two or three day.

For overnight deliveries, try U.S. **Express Mail** or one of several domestic and international courier services:
**Fedex**, tel: 800-238-5355
**DHL**, tel: 800-345-2727
**United Parcel Service**, tel: 800-742-5877

## Tipping

Service workers in restaurants and hotels depend on tips for a significant portion of their income. With few exceptions, tipping is left to your discretion and gratuities are not automatically added to the bill. In most cases, 15–20 percent is typical for tipping waiters, taxi drivers, bartenders, barbers and hairdressers. Porters and bellmen usually get $1 per bag.

***Poste Restante***

## Foreign Embassies in the United States

**Australia:** 1601 Massachusetts Ave NW, Washington, DC 20036, tel: 202-797-3000.
**Belgium:** 3330 Garfield St NW, Washington, DC 20008, tel: 202-333-6900.
**Canada:** 501 Pennsylvania Ave NW, Washington, DC 20001, tel: 202-682-1740.
**Denmark:** 3200 Whitehaven St NW, Washington, DC 20008, tel: 202-234-4300.
**France:** 4101 Reservoir Road NW, Washington, DC 20007, tel: 202-944-6000.
**Germany:** 4645 Reservoir Road NW, Washington, DC 20007, tel: 202-298-4000.
**Great Britain:** 3100 Massachusetts Ave NW, Washington, DC 20008, tel: 202-462-1340.
**Greece:** 2221 Massachusetts Ave NW, Washington, DC 20008, tel: 202-667-3168
**India:** 2536 Massachusetts Ave NW, Washington, DC 20008, tel: 202-939-7000.
**Israel:** 3514 International Drive NW, Washington, DC 20008, tel: 202-364-5500.
**Italy:** 1601 Fuller St NW, Washington, DC 20009, tel: 202-328-5500.
**Japan:** 2520 Massachusetts Ave NW, Washington, DC 20008, tel: 202-939-6700.
**Mexico:** 1911 Pennsylvania Ave NW, Washington, DC 20006, tel: 202-728-1600.
**Netherlands:** 4200 Wisconsin Ave NW, Washington, DC 20016, tel: 202-244-5300.
**New Zealand:** 37 Observatory Circle NW, Washington, DC 20008, tel: 202-328-4800.
**Norway:** 2720 34th Street NW, Washington, DC 20008, tel: 202-333-6000.
**Portugal:** 2125 Kalorama Road NW, Washington, DC 20008, tel: 202-328-8610.
**Singapore:** 3501 International Place NW, Washington, DC 20008, tel: 202-537-3100.
**South Korea:** 2600 Virginia Ave NW, Washington, DC 20037, tel: 202-939-5600.
**Spain:** 2375 Pennsylvania Ave NW, Washington, DC 20037, tel: 202-452-0100.
**Taiwan:** 4201 Wisconsin Ave NW, Washington, DC 20016, tel: 202-895-1800.

Visitors can receive mail at post offices if it is addressed to them, care of "General Delivery," followed by the city name and (very important) the zip code. You must pick up this mail in person within a week or two of its arrival and will be asked to show a valid driver's license, passport or some other form of picture identification.

## Telephone, Telegram, and Internet Access

Public telephones are located at many highway rest areas, service stations, convenience stores, bars, motels and restaurants.

To call from **one area to another**, dial 1 before the three-digit area code, then the local seven-digit number. If you want to pay for the call with coins, a recorded voice will tell you how many to insert. Unless you have a calling card, your only other option is to call your party "collect" (reversing the charges) by dialing 0 before the number. Rates vary for long-distance calls, though you can often take advantage of lower long-distance rates on weekends and after 5pm on weekdays.

Prepaid calling cards are sold at convenience stores and some filling stations. Essentially, customers pay in advance for a specific number of minutes of calling time. Not all cards work for international calls. Be sure to inquire before purchasing.

Many businesses have **toll-free** (no charge) telephone numbers; these are always prefaced with 800, 866,888, 877 or 887 rather than an area code. Note that if you dial a toll-free number from abroad, you will be charged the normal international rate for the call.

The quickest way to get help is to dial 0 for the operator. Directory Assistance calls from pay telephones are free. However, to be connected to some of them you must first insert a coin, but as soon as you are connected with the operator it will be returned to you. To get the **information operator** dial 411, but to get an information operator in another city, dial 1-(area code of the city)-555-1212.

### Dialing Abroad

To dial abroad (Canada follows the U.S. system), first dial the international access code 011, then the country code. If using a U.S. phone credit card, dial the company's access number below, then 01, then the country code.
**Sprint,** tel: 10333
**AT&T,** tel: 10288.
**Country codes:**

| | |
|---|---|
| Australia | 61 |
| Austria | 43 |
| Belgium | 32 |
| Brazil | 55 |
| Denmark | 45 |
| France | 33 |
| Germany | 49 |
| Greece | 30 |
| Hong Kong | 852 |
| Israel | 972 |
| Italy | 39 |
| Japan | 81 |
| Korea | 82 |
| Netherlands | 31 |
| New Zealand | 64 |
| Norway | 47 |
| Singapore | 65 |
| South Africa | 27 |
| Spain | 34 |
| Sweden | 46 |
| Switzerland | 41 |
| United Kingdom | 44 |

**Western Union** (tel: 800-325-6000) can arrange money transfers and telegrams. Check the Web (www.westernunion.com) or phone directory or call information for local offices.

Fax machines are available at

most hotels and motels. Printers, copy shops, stationers and office-supply shops may also have them, as well as some convenience stores.

**Dataports** for laptop computers and Palm Pilots are available at most business hotels. **E-mail and Internet access** is also available at public libraries, Internet cafes and copy shops like Kinkos.

## Weights & Measures

Despite efforts to convert to metric, the U.S. still uses the Imperial System of weights and measures.

| | | |
|---|---|---|
| 1 inch | = | 2.54 cm |
| 1 foot | = | 30.48 cm |
| 1 yard | = | 0.9144 meter |
| 1 mile | = | 1.609 km |
| 1 pint | = | 0.473 liter |
| 1 quart | = | 0.946 liter |
| 1 ounce | = | 28.4 grams |
| 1 pound | = | 0.453 kg |
| 1 acre | = | 0.405 hectare |
| 1 sq mile | = | 259 hectares |
| 1 centimeter | = | 0.394 inch |
| 1 meter | = | 39.37 inches |
| 1 kilometer | = | 0.621 mile |
| 1 liter | = | 1.057 quarts |
| 1 gram | = | 0.035 ounce |
| 1 kilogram | = | 2.205 pounds |
| 1 hectare | = | 2.471 acres |
| 1 sq km | = | 0.386 sq. mile |

## Useful Addresses

### NEW MEXICO TOURISM OFFICES

**Alamogordo Chamber of Commerce**
1301 N. White Sands Blvd, Alamogordo, NM 88311; tel: 505-437-6120; www.alamogordo.com
**Albuquerque Convention & Visitors Bureau**
20 First Plaza, Suite 601, Albuquerque, NM 87102; tel: 800-284-2282; www.abqcvb.org
**Angel Fire Chamber of Commerce**
PO Box 547, Angel Fire, NM 87710; tel: 505-377-6661, 800-446-8117; www.angelfirechamber.org
**Aztec Chamber of Commerce**
110 N. Ash, Aztec, NM 87410; tel: 505-334-9551; www.aztecnm.com
**Bloomfield Chamber of Commerce**
224 N. Broadway, Bloomfield, NM 87413; tel: 505-632-0880

**Carlsbad Convention & Visitors Bureau**
PO Box 910, Carlsbad, NM 88220; tel: 505-887-6516; www.chamber.caverns.com
**Cimarron Chamber of Commerce**
104 N. Lincoln Ave, Cimarron, NM 87714; tel: 505-376-2417; ww.ccccok.org
**Cloudcroft Chamber of Commerce**
PO Box 1290, Cloudcroft , NM 88317; tel: 505-682-2733; www.cloudcroft.net
**Española Valley Chamber of Commerce**
417 Big Rock Center, Española, NM 87532; tel: 505-753-2831; www.espanola.com/chamber/
**Farmington Convention & Visitors Bureau**
3041 E. Main St, Farmington, NM 87402; tel: 505-326-7602, 800-448-1240; www.farmingtonnm.org
**Gallup Convention & Visitors Bureau**
701 Montoya Blvd, PO Box 600, Gallup, NM 87301; tel: 505-863-3841; www.gallupnm.org
**Las Cruces Convention & Visitors Bureau**
211 N. Water St, Las Cruces, NM 88001; tel: 505-541-2444; www.lascrucescvb.org
**Las Vegas/San Miguel County Chamber of Commerce**
PO Box 128, Las Vegas, NM 87701; tel: 505-425-8631; www.lasvegasnewmexico.com
**Lordsburg/Hidalgo County Chamber of Commerce**
117 E. 2nd St, Lordsburg, NM 88045; tel: 505-542-9864
**Los Alamos County Chamber of Commerce**
109 Central Park Square, Los

## Business Hours

Standard hours for business offices are Monday–Friday 9am–5pm. Many banks open a little earlier, usually 8.30am. A few open on Saturday morning. Post offices are usually open Monday–Friday 8am–5pm and Saturday 8am–noon. Most stores and shopping centers are open weekends and evenings.

Alamos, NM 87544; tel: 505-662-8105 or 800-444-0707; www.vla.com/chamber
**New Mexico Department of Tourism**
491 Old Santa Fe Trail, Santa Fe, NM 87501; tel: 505-827-7400; www.newmexico.org
**Roswell Visitors Bureau**
426 N. Main, Roswell, NM 88201; tel: 888-ROSWELL, 505-624-7704; www.roswellcvb.com
**Santa Fe Convention & Visitors Bureau**
P.O. Box 909, Santa Fe, NM 87504; tel: 984-6760, 800-777-2489; www.santafe.org
**Silver City/Grant County Chamber of Commerce**
201 N. Hudson, Silver City, NM 88061; tel: 505-538-3785, 800-548-9378; www.silvercity.org
**Taos County Chamber of Commerce**
PO Drawer I, Taos, NM 87571; tel: 505-758-3873, 800-732-8267; www.taoschamber.com
**Taos Ski Valley Visitor & Conference Bureau**
PO Box 91, Taos Ski Valley, NM 87525; tel: 800-992-7669; www.taoswebb.com/vtsv
**Turquoise Trail Association**
PO Box 1335, Cedar Crest, NM 87047; tel: 505-281-5233; www.turquoisetrail.org
**Ruidoso Chamber & Convention Center**
720 Sudderth Drive, P.O. Box 698, Ruidoso, NM 88355; tel: 505-257-7395; www.ruidoso.net/index.html

## NATIONAL PARKS & WILDERNESS AREAS

**Bureau of Land Management**
New Mexico Office, 1474 Rodeo Rd, Santa Fe, NM 87502; tel: 505-438-7400; www.publiclands.org
**National Park Service**
Southwest Region, PO Box 728, Santa Fe, NM 87504-0728; tel: 505-988-6016; www.nps.gov
**New Mexico Public Lands Information Center–Santa Fe**
1474 Rodeo Rd, Santa Fe, NM 87505; tel: 505-438-7542; www.publiclands.org

**New Mexico Public Lands Information Center–Roswell**
2909 W. Second St,Roswell, NM 88201; tel: 505-627-0210; www.publiclands.org
**New Mexico State Park and Recreation Division**
408 Galisteo St, Santa Fe, NM 87504; tel: 505-827-7173; www.emnrd.state.nm.us/nmparks
**U.S. Forest Service**
Southwest Regional Office, 517 Gold Ave SW, Albuquerque, NM 87102; tel: 505-842-3292; www.fs.fed.us

## Security & Crime

Emergency (police/fire): **911**

A few common-sense precautions will help keep you safe while traveling in New Mexico. For starters, know where you are and where you're going. Whether traveling on foot or by car, bring a map and plan your route in advance. Don't be shy about asking for directions. Most people are happy to help.

Don't carry large sums of cash or wear flashy or expensive jewelry. Lock unattended cars and keep your belongings in the trunk. If possible, travel with a companion, especially after dark.

If involved in a traffic accident, remain at the scene. It is illegal to leave the scene of an accident. Find a nearby telephone or ask a passing motorist to call the police, then wait for emergency vehicles to arrive.

Carry a cell phone. Few items are more useful if you're lost, in an accident, need to report an emergency, or your car has broken down.

Driving under the influence of alcohol carries stiff penalties, including fines and jail. Wearing seatbelts is required. Children under four must be in a child's safety seat.

# Where to Stay

## Price Guide

Price categories are based on the average cost of a double room per night.

| | |
|---|---|
| $ | $50 or less |
| $$ | $50–150 |
| $$$ | $150–250 |
| $$$$ | $250 or more |

## Choosing Lodging

New Mexico offers a great variety of accommodations, ranging from rustic cabins and modest adobes with little in the way of amenities to extravagant resorts with a myriad of special features. Some places – inexpensive chain motels, for example – are suitable for a single night on the road. Others such as golf resorts, spas and dude ranches are destinations in themselves and offer enough diversions to keep guests busy for a lengthy visit. It's always advisable to make reservations well in advance for the high season – winter in the southern deserts and summer in the high country. Santa Fe and Taos are especially busy in summer. Unless you book several months in advance, accommodations are virtually impossible to find in Santa Fe during the annual Indian Market in August and, to a slightly lesser extent, Spanish Market in July. Travelers in search of a bargain will find tempting off-season discounts.

**Chain motels.** Chains are reliable and convenient but tend to lack character. You can usually depend on a clean, comfortable room for a reasonable cost. In general, prices range from $50 to $150 depending on location and additional amenities such as a pool, exercise room and restaurant.

### Moderate to Expensive

| | |
|---|---|
| Best Western | 800-528-1234 |
| Hilton | 800-HILTONS |
| Holiday Inn | 800-HOLIDAY |
| Hyatt | 800-228-9000 |
| Sheraton | 800-325-3535 |
| La Quinta | 800-531-5900 |
| Marriott | 800-228-9290 |
| Radisson | 800-333-3333 |
| Ramada | 800-2-RAMADA |
| Westin | 800-228-3000 |

### Budget

| | |
|---|---|
| Comfort Inn | 800-228-5150 |
| Days Inn | 800-325-2525 |
| Econo Lodge | 800-553-2666 |
| Howard Johnson | 800-654-2000 |
| Motel 6 | 800-466-8356 |
| Quality Inn | 800-228-5151 |
| Red Lion Inn | 800-733-5466 |
| Super 8 | 800-800-8000 |
| Travelodge | 800-578-7878 |

**Hotels**. Larger and generally more comfortable than motels, hotels are designed for upscale business travelers and tourists, and are usually situated in a central area with easy access to attractions and public transportation. Nearly all have at least one restaurant and bar and such amenities as a pool, a fitness center, meeting facilities, room service, a gift shop and an extensive lobby. Some such as Embassy Suites or AmeriSuites offer one- or two-bedroom suites (some with kitchenettes) that are suited for long stays or families. Always look for new or newly renovated properties as these will be in the best condition and have the most up-to-date facilities.

**Resorts**. Luxury, relaxation and recreation are emphasized at resort properties, most of which have large, sumptuous rooms, suites or casitas (Southwestern-style cottages), fine dining, extensive grounds with manicured landscaping, and such recreational facilities as ski slopes, golf courses, tennis courts and elaborate pools as well as health and beauty spas. A minimum stay of two or three nights is sometimes required.

**Bed and breakfasts**. B&Bs tend to be more homey and personal than hotels. In many cases, you're a guest at the innkeeper's home. Some are historic houses or inns decorated with antiques, quilts, art and various period furnishings; others offer simple but comfortable accommodations. Before booking, ask if rooms have telephones or televisions and whether bathrooms are private or shared. Ask about breakfast, too. The meal is included in the price but may be anything from a few muffins to a multicourse feast. Guests may be served at a common table, a private table or in their rooms. For more information contact:
**New Mexico Bed and Breakfast Association**
Tel: 505-766-5380, 800-661-6649; www.nmbba.org
**Albuquerque Bed and Breakfast Association**
Tel: 505-898-4500; www.abqbandb.com
**Bed and Breakfast Inns of Taos**
Tel: 888-547-8226; www.taos-bandb-inns.com

**Guest ranches**. Guest, or dude, ranches range from working cattle operations with basic lodging to full-fledged "resorts with horses" that have swimming pools, tennis courts and other amenities. Most ranches offer horseback riding lessons, guided pack trips, entertainment like rodeos, square dances and storytellers, and plenty of hearty food. If traveling with a family, be sure to ask about a children's program. For more information and an extensive list of dude ranches contact:
**Dude Ranchers Association**
112 12th St, PO Box 2307, Cody, WY 82414, tel: 307-587-2339; www.duderanch.org
**Guest Ranches of North America**
P. O. Box 191625, Dallas, TX 75219; tel: 214-912-1100; www.guestranches.com

## Lodging by Area

Hotels are listed in alphabetical order by region.

## SANTA FE

**Adobe Abode**
202 Chapelle St, Santa Fe, NM 87501; tel: 505-983-3133; www.adobeabode.com
Built in 1907 as officers' quarters for Fort Marcy, this delightful adobe house is three blocks from the Plaza. The six rooms and suites are designed in a variety of styles, ranging from Adirondack, Provencal, Cowboy and English Garden. For extra privacy, ask for the courtyard rooms behind the main house. Amenities: full breakfast, private baths, cable television, free parking, complimentary sherry; some rooms with fireplace and patios. **$$$**
**Alexander's Inn**
529 E. Palace Ave, Santa Fe, NM 87501; tel: 505-986-1431 or 888-321-5123; www.alexanders-inn.com
Conveniently located between Canyon Road and the Plaza, this bed-and-breakfast harmoniously blends Southwestern and Craftsmen-style architecture. Ten units, including several nearby cottages and casitas, are impeccably appointed with brass or four-poster beds, Mexican tile and handmade furniture; some have fireplaces or wood-burning stoves, a kitchen, a porch and a separate sitting room. Amenities: Continental breakfast, all but two rooms with private bath, phone. **$$–$$$**
**Bishop's Lodge**
Bishop's Lodge Rd, Santa Fe, NM 87501; tel: 505-983-6377, 800-732-2240; www.bishopslodge.com

## Price Guide

Price categories are based on the average cost of a double room per night.

| | |
|---|---|
| **$** | $50 or less |
| **$$** | $50–150 |
| **$$$** | $150–250 |
| **$$$$** | $250 or more |

Originally established in 1851 as a retreat for Bishop Jean Baptiste Lamy, this luxury resort is set on 1,000 acres (400 hectares) in the foothills of the Sangre de Cristo Mountains about 3 miles (5km) from the Plaza. More than 100 rooms and suites are situated in 15 small lodges furnished in Pueblo or Spanish Colonial style. Deluxe accommodations have fireplaces and patios. Recreational activities include horseback riding on the ranch and in the adjacent Santa Fe National Forest, tennis, hiking on an extensive trail network, swimming and fishing. The ShaNah Spa offers massage, body treatments, facials and other services. A daily children's program includes pony rides, hiking, time on the playground, arts and crafts, cookouts, storytelling, lawn games and movies. Las Fuentes restaurant offers Nuevo Latino cuisine (a combination of Central and South American styles) in a refined yet easygoing atmosphere. The Bishop's original chapel is in the National Register of Historic Places. **$$$–$$$$**
**Eldorado Hotel**
309 W. San Francisco St, Santa Fe, NM 87501; tel: 505-988-4455 or 800-286-6755; www.eldoradohotel.com
A five-story luxury hotel near the Plaza, with a grand lobby, more than $1 million of original artwork on display, rooftop pool, health club and plush rooms, many with kiva fireplaces and/or balconies. The Old House restaurant offers gourmet dining in a refined Southwestern atmosphere. A favorite of celebrities and visiting dignitaries. **$$$–$$$$**
**Galisteo Inn**
HC 75 Box 4, Galisteo, NM 87540; tel: 505-466-8200; www.galisteoinn.com
It's worth the drive to stay in this old hacienda in Galisteo Village. The chef allows guests to pick their own veggies from the organic gardens. It's a great place to relax and explore the Galisteo Basin's rich history. **$$–$$$**

**Garrett's Desert Inn**
311 Old Santa Fe Trail, Santa Fe, NM 87501
tel. 505-982-1851 or 800-888-2145
www.garrettsdesertinn.com
This motel, two blocks from the Plaza, has the most affordable rates around. You won't find chi-chi Santa Fe Style touches here, but the 76 standard rooms are comfortable, and six suites have small living rooms and kitchens with microwave ovens and small refrigerators. Limited wheelchair access. Onsite Avis Rent-a-Car and Camelot World Travel. Adjoining restaurant and dance club. **$$**

**Hilton of Santa Fe**
100 Sandoval St, Santa Fe, NM 87501; tel: 800-336-3676 or 505-988-2811; www.hiltonofsantafe.com
Built around the 300-year-old estate of one of Santa Fe's founding families, the Hilton offers 157 guest rooms and 3 suites arranged around a central courtyard pool. In addition, three luxurious casitas within the original adobe walls offer extra space, with a living and dining area, kitchenette, kiva fireplace, hand-crafted furnishings, Jacuzzi tub and an outdoor patio. Other amenities include a health club and three restaurants, including the highly regarded Piñon Grill, specializing in entrees prepared on a wood-fired grill. **$$$–$$$$**

**Hotel Santa Fe**
1501 Paseo de Peralta, Santa Fe, NM 87501; tel: 800-825-9876 or 505-982-1200;
www.hotelsantafe.com
Owned partly by Picuris Pueblo, this attractive, three-story Pueblo-Revival-style hotel has 128 rooms and suites beautifully appointed in tasteful Southwestern style. Every unit has a microwave oven, stocked honor bar, phone modem, internet access, balcony or patio, and oversized king, double or hide-away beds. The Hacienda, a wing of luxury suites, was added in 2001. Special features include units with corner fireplaces, 10-ft (3-meter) ceilings, handcrafted furnishings, polished hardwood floors with Southwestern-style rugs, granite

bathrooms, 27-inch television sets, and the services of a butler. Lovely public spaces feature original works of art, including pieces by well-known American Indian sculptor Allan Houser. Picuris dancers and musicians occasionally perform on the patio. Lectures by historians and archaeologists are offered regularly. The hotel's restaurant, Amaya, serves a delectable selection of dishes influenced by Pueblo Indian and northern New Mexican cuisine, as well as regional foods from around the United States (see "Where to Eat"). For a special treat, ask to dine in the tepee. Other amenities include a heated outdoor pool and a courtesy shuttle to the Plaza, just a few minutes away. **$$–$$$$**

**Hotel St. Francis**
210 Don Gaspar Ave, Santa Fe, NM 87501; tel: 800-529-5700 or 505-983-5700; www.hotelstfrancis.com
Beautifully renovated in 1986 in the style of an elegant European hotel, the St. Francis – about a block from the Plaza – has more than 80 smartly appointed guest rooms, most with brass or iron beds and period hardwood furniture. Dine alfresco at The Club or enjoy a drink in the collegial, wood-paneled atmosphere of the Artist's Pub. Afternoon tea is served daily in the lobby or on the veranda, with an assortment of pastries, scones and finger sandwiches as well as port or champagne. **$$$**

**Inn at Loretto**
211 Old Santa Fe Trail, Santa Fe, NM 87501; tel: 505-988-5531 or 800-727-5531;
www.hotelloretto.com
Modeled after the terraced adobes of Taos Pueblo, the Loretto is a picturesque five-story structure about two blocks from the Plaza. Guest rooms are furnished in regional style with hand-carved furniture, woven rugs and Pueblo-style architectural details; some rooms have fireplaces and shared balconies. A full-service spa and restaurant serving fine Southwestern cuisine are contained within the complex. **$$$–$$$$**

**Inn of the Anasazi**
113 Washington Ave, Santa Fe, NM 87501; tel: 800-688-8100 or 505-988-3030;
www.innoftheanasazi.com
A half block from the Plaza is this extraordinary boutique hotel, designed in the style of the Anasazi, or Ancient Puebloan, ruins of the Four Corners area. Stone floors, vigas, latillas, oversized cacti and an abundance of local art set the scene in the public spaces and 59 guest rooms, all with gas kiva fireplaces, four-poster beds, hand-woven textiles, and organic linens, soaps and other toiletries. Massage and aromatherapy treatments are available upon request. The Anasazi Restaurant (see "Where To Eat") is one of the finest in town. **$$$$**

**Inn of the Turquoise Bear**
342 E. Buena Vista St, Santa Fe, NM 87501; tel: 505-983-0798;
www.turquoisebear.com
The former home of poet and essayist Witter Bynner is now a spacious adobe villa with 10 guest rooms, many with tile or plank floors, fireplaces and viga ceilings. Among the luminaries who have stayed here are Willa Cather, Ansel Adams, Igor Stravinsky, Edna St. Vincent Millay, Robert Frost, W. H. Auden and Georgia O'Keeffe. For extra privacy ask for the carriage house. Amenities: complimentary breakfast. **$$–$$$$**

**La Fonda**
100 E. San Francisco St, Santa Fe, NM 87501; tel: 505-982-5511 or 800-523-5002;
www.lafondasantafe.com
You'll get a glimpse of old Santa Fe at this Pueblo-style hotel on the southeast corner of the Plaza. Each of the 167 rooms has its own individual – sometimes quirky – decor, with hand-painted furniture, tile murals and other artsy touches. Some rooms have fireplaces and balconies. For an extra measure of luxury, ask for the rooftop suites of La Terraza. The dark and comfy lobby, La Fiesta Lounge and rooftop Bell Tower Bar have been favorite meeting places for decades. **$$$**

**La Posada de Santa Fe Resort and Spa**
330 E. Palace Ave, Santa Fe, NM 87501; tel: 800-727-5276 or 505-986-0000;
laposada.rockresorts.com
The 1882 Victorian home of merchant Abraham Staab and his young bride Julia forms the core of this gracious hotel, set on 6 grassy acres (2,4 hectares) about three blocks from the Plaza. Wood-beamed ceilings, antique furnishings and local art lend the guest rooms a rustic elegance. Guests interested in the para-normal may want to ask for the Victorian Room, where the shade of Julia Staab – one of Santa Fe's most celebrated ghosts – is said to reside. The Fuego Restaurant offers fine dining (ask for a patio table) laced with Southwestern flavors. Massage, aromatherapy, stone therapy, facials, mud wraps and other body treatments are available at the Avanyu Spa.
**$$$–$$$$**

**Water Street Inn**
427 W. Water St, Santa Fe, NM 87501; tel: 505-984-1193 or 800-646-6752; www.waterstreetinn.com
A comfortable, Southwestern-style bed-and-breakfast within walking distance of the Plaza. Twelve rooms and suites have brick floors, beamed ceilings, four-poster and antique beds, fireplaces, decks and patios. Amenities: Continental breakfast, evening happy hour, private baths, cable television with VCR, CD player, video library, air-conditioning, private voice mail.
**$$–$$$**

## LOS ALAMOS AND ENVIRONS

**Adobe Pines Bed & Breakfast**
2101 Loma Linda Drive, Los Alamos, NM 87544
tel. 505-661-8828 or
toll-free 866-661-8828
This attractive modern adobe home offers several quiet, comfortable rooms with spectacular panoramic views of the Pajarito Plateau. Amenities include free continental

breakfast, high-speed Internet access, in-room cable TV, private baths, and use of microwave and refrigerator. Completely nonsmoking. **$$**

**Best Western Hilltop House Hotel**
400 Trinity Dr, Los Alamos, NM 87544; tel: 800-462-0936; www.bestwestern.com
Situated in downtown Los Alamos about 10 miles (16km) from Bandelier National Monument, this newly renovated hotel is appealing to both business travelers and families. Amenities: indoor pool, exercise equipment, meeting facilities, Continental breakfast, restaurant. **$$**

**Canyon Inn Bed and Breakfast**
80 Canyon Rd, Los Alamos, NM 87544; tel: 505-662-9595 or 800-662-2565;
www.canyoninnbnb.com
Simple accommodations with the homey atmosphere typical of a bed-and-breakfast inn. Nothing particularly extravagant or precious here, just modest, comfortable lodging at a reasonable price. Amenities: complimentary Continental breakfast, private bath, laundry and kitchen facilities. **$$**

**Holiday Inn Express Los Alamos**
2455 Trinity Dr, Los Alamos, NM 87544; tel: 505-661-1110;
www.hiexpress.com
A modern, moderately-priced chain motel in the downtown area. Rather generic, but a reasonable value for a short stay. Amenities: complimentary Continental breakfast, fitness room. **$$**

## ABIQUIU, CHAMA AND ENVIRONS

**Abiquiu Inn**
PO Box 120, Abiquiu, NM 87510; tel: 505-685-4378 or 800-447-5621; www.abiquiuinn.com
Guests have their choice of casitas, rooms or suites with kitchens. Four rooms have access to a private patio courtyard with water fountain, flower beds and benches. Small casitas have private verandas with hammocks.

Large casitas accommodate up to four people and consist of a main room with a wood stove or fireplace, hand-tiled bath, eat-in kitchens, and separate bedrooms. Amenities: private bath, cable television, telephone. **$$**

**Casa del Rio Bed & Breakfast**
P.O. Box 702, Abiquiu, NM 87510; tel: 800-920-1495 or 505-753-2035; www.bbonline.com/nm/casadelrio
This contemporary hacienda is set in a secluded spot at the foot of the cliffs above the Rio Chama, more than a mile from the main road. La Casita, a little adobe cottage with a kiva fireplace and traditional wood ceiling, is especially cozy. Amenities: free breakfast, private bath. **$$**

**Chama Trails Inn**
2362 Hwy 17, Chama, NM 87520; tel: 505-756-2156 or 800-289-1421; www.chamatrailsinn.com
Well-kept and thoughtfully decorated, this roadside inn has more personality than most motels, with pine furniture, interesting artwork and a few rooms with gas fireplaces. The inn is a short drive from the Cumbres & Toltec Scenic Railroad. Amenities: private bath, television, refrigerator, sauna and hot tub. **$$**

**Gandy Dancer**
P.O. Box 810, 299 Maple Ave, Chama, NM 87520; tel: 505-756-2191 or 800-424-6702;
www.gandydancerbb.com
Seven rooms decorated in period style await travelers at this pretty Victorian bed-and-breakfast about a block from the Cumbres & Toltec Scenic Railroad. Fresh flowers, lace drapes and soft comforters give the guest rooms a homey feel. Amenities: full complimentary breakfast, private bath. **$$**

**Ghost Ranch Education and Retreat Center**
HC77, Box 11, Abiquiu, NM 87510; tel: 877-804-4678, 505-685-4333; www.ghostranch.org
Owned by the Presbyterian Church, Ghost Ranch offers no-frills lodging ranging from dormitory-style rooms to bare-bones casitas. In addition to the magnificent location, the big attraction here is

the schedule of seminars and workshops, including topics such as landscape photography, creative writing, silversmithing, painting, earth science and more. **$–$$**

**Ojo Caliente Spa and Resort**
50 Los Banos Dr, Ojo Caliente, NM 87549; tel: 800-222-9162; www.ojocalientespa.com
An old-fashioned inn at one of the oldest health resorts in North America. The 1916 Mission Revival hotel has charming, rustic rooms and a porch with rockers. There's more privacy and amenities in the separate guest cottages. Guests bathe in the bathhouse of the hot springs. A full service spa offers massages and treatments. The Artesian Restaurant offers light spa fare, as well as other cuisines. **$$–$$$**

**Parlor Car Bed and Breakfast**
311 Terrace Ave, Chama, NM 87520; tel: 505-756-1946 or 888-849-7800; www.parlorcar.com
Situated across the street from the Cumbres & Toltec Scenic Railroad, this pink Tudor-style house offers three meticulously furnished rooms reflecting the golden age of train travel. Amenities: private bath, complimentary breakfast, flower garden. **$$**

**Rancho de San Juan**
US 285, Ojo Caliente, NM; tel: 505-753-6818; www.ranchodesanjuan.com
Refined Southwestern style is evident in every corner of this hacienda-style compound, surrounded by more than 200 acres (80 acres) in the foothills of the Sangre de Cristo Mountains. Encompassed within the expansive grounds are 17 guest units ranging from elegant "standard" rooms, with kiva fireplaces, beamed ceilings and private portals, to spacious casitas, with full kitchens, fireplaces, whirlpool tubs and antique or designer furnishings. In-room massage is available with advanced notification. The restaurant (see "Where To Eat") is regarded as one of the finest in northern New Mexico. Amenities: complimentary full breakfast, private telephone, private bath,

## Price Guide

Price categories are based on the average cost of a double room per night.

| | |
|---|---|
| **$** | $50 or less |
| **$$** | $50–150 |
| **$$$** | $150–250 |
| **$$$$** | $250 or more |

some rooms with whirlpool tub. **$$$–$$$$**

**The Timbers at Chama**
HC 75, Box 136 (off NM 512), Chama, NM 87520; tel: 505-588-7950; www.thetimbersatchama.com
This former hunting lodge exudes outdoorsy Western charm. Set on 400 wildlife-rich acres (160 hectares) in the southern Rockies, the lodge has five rooms and a guest house wrapped in wood paneling and furnished in rustic western style. A great room features a cathedral ceiling and massive stone fireplace. The guest house is equipped with a kitchen, fireplace, satellite television and redwood deck. Amenities: full complimentary breakfast, private bath with Jacuzzi tub. **$$–$$$**

## GALLUP, CHACO CANYON AND NAVAJO COUNTRY

**Best Western Inn Grants**
1501 E. Santa Fe Ave, Grants, NM 87020; tel: 505-287-7901
Rooms are cheery and spacious at this large motel, featuring an indoor pool and room service during dinner hours. Amenities: restaurant, cable television, gift shop, fitness center. **$–$$**

**Cimarron Rose Bed-and-Breakfast**
689 Oso Ridge Rd, Grants, NM 87020; tel: 800-856-5776; www.cimarronrose.com
Set on a scenic byway near El Morro National Monument and the Ramah Navajo Reservation, this inn offers two suites decorated in rustic style with pine walls, wood and tile floors, beamed ceilings and fully equipped kitchens. One suite has an antique wood-burning stove in the bedroom; the other has a lovely private patio.

Amenities: complimentary free breakfast, private bath, VCR, CD player. **$$**

**El Rancho Hotel**
1000 E. Hwy 66, Gallup, NM 87301; tel: 800-543-6351 or 505-863-9311; www.elranchohotel.com
Listed in the National Register of Historic Places, El Rancho was built in 1937 by R. E. Griffith, brother of filmmaker D. W. Griffith and a director in his own right. The hotel was a favorite of Hollywood actors filming in the area, and the two-story, Western-style lobby, with heavy wood beams, stone fireplace and matching curved staircases, is lined with signed photos of such luminaries as Alan Ladd, Katharine Hepburn, Gene Autry, Henry Fonda, Ronald Reagan, John Wayne and Mae West. Guest rooms are named after the stars who stayed in them and furnished with heavy pine furniture. Amenities: cable television, outdoor pool, restaurant, lounge, gift shop. **$$**

**Holiday Inn Express Grants**
1496 E. Santa Fe Ave, Grants, NM 87020; tel: 505-285-4676
Basic comfort, a convenient location and good value are the attractions at this contemporary chain motel about 2 miles (3km) from downtown Grants. Amenities: complimentary Continental breakfast, indoor pool, cable television. **$–$$**

**Holiday Inn Gallup**
2915 W. 66 Hwy, Gallup, NM 87301; tel: 505-722-2201 or 800-432-2211
A comfortable modern motel popular with families and business travelers. Spacious rooms are a cut above most roadside inns. Amenities: two restaurants, lounge, complimentary breakfast, indoor pool, fitness center and game room. **$$**

**Kokopelli's Cave Bed & Breakfast**
3204 Crestridge Dr, Farmington, NM 87401; tel: 505-326-2461 or 505-325-7855
There's nothing quite like this 1,650-sq-ft (150-sq-meter) cave home excavated from a sandstone cliff 280 ft (85 meters) above the

La Plata River north of Farmington.
The cave has one bedroom, a den,
a fully stocked kitchen, and a
bathroom with a unique waterfall-
style shower. The cave is set in a
remote area outside of town.
Reaching the entrance involves
hiking down steps carved into the
cliff face. A one-of-a-kind experience
for travelers who crave adventure.
Amenities: VCR with video library,
stocked kitchen. **$$$**

**Navajo Nation Inn**
48 Hwy 264, Window Rock, AZ
86515; tel: 520-871-4108 or 800-
662-6189
Simple, comfortable motel located
in the capital of the Navajo Nation.
Indian tacos and other local fare
are served in the dining room.
Amenities: restaurant, air
conditioning, television. **$$**

**Silver River Spa Retreat and Adobe
Inn Bed & Breakfast**
3151 W. Main St, PO Box 3411,
Farmington, NM 87401; tel: 505-
325-8219 or 800-382-9251;
www.cyberport.com/silveradobe
Set on a bluff overlooking the San
Juan and La Plata Rivers, this
contemporary B&B is ideal for
nature lovers who want a closer
look at the countryside in northwestern New Mexico. Two guest
rooms and a guest house are
furnished in rustic style, with walls
and ceilings of exposed adobe and
rough sawn timbers, cozy beds with
down comforters, patios and private
tiled bathrooms. A gourmet breakfast with organic ingredients is
served each morning in the dining
room. A massage therapist is
available. Amenities: complimentary
full breakfast, private bath. **$$–$$$**

**Sky City Hotel**
PO Box 310 (I-40, exit 102), Acoma,
NM 87034; tel: 505-552-6123 or

888-759-2489;
www.skycityhotel.com
Acoma Pueblo owns this modern
hotel and casino complex, with 134
rooms and suites, and an airy atrium
lobby. Amenities: pool, weight room,
restaurant, gift shop featuring Indian
arts and crafts, meeting facilities,
adjacent casino. **$$**

## SANTA FE TRAIL

**Casa del Gavilan**
Hwy 21, PO Box 518, Cimarron, NM
87714; tel: 505-376-2246 or 800-
428-4526; www.casadelgavilan.com
Built in Pueblo Revival style about
1912, this adobe villa is set in the
foothills of the Sangre de Cristo
Mountains outside Cimarron. Four
bedrooms have 12-ft-high (4-meter)
ceilings, vigas and Western artwork.
A two-bedroom guest house is
across the courtyard from the main
building. Amenities: private bath,
one room with fireplace. **$$**

**Inn on the Santa Fe Trail**
1133 N. Grand Ave, Las Vegas, NM
87701; tel: 888-448-8438 or 505-
425-6791
All rooms are arranged around a
central courtyard at this well-
maintained older motel. Nice
touches include the handmade
furniture, armoires and wrought iron
light fixtures. Suites have a pullout
sofa and refrigerator. Amenities:
restaurant, outdoor pool, television
set. **$$**

**Microtel Raton**
1640 Cedar St, Raton, NM 87740;
tel: 505-445-9100;
www.microtelinn.com
A new budget hotel, with spacious
rooms, an attractive 24-hour lobby
and, if you need extra room, suites
with sleeper sofas and refrigerators.
Amenities: free Continental
breakfast, adjacent restaurant,
cable television, data port. **$$**

**Plaza Hotel**
230 Plaza, Las Vegas, NM 87701;
tel: 505-425-3591 or 800-328-
1882; www.plazahotel-nm.com
Built in 1882 and now fully
restored, the Plaza has 36 rooms of
various sizes, most furnished with
antiques and original architectural

details. Although not luxurious in
the modern sense, it exudes a
certain worn stateliness in keeping
with its frontier heritage. Amenities:
restaurant and saloon, free
Continental breakfast, room service
during dinner hours, cable
television, business center, in-
house massage. **$$**

**Star Hill Inn**
PO Box 707, Sapello, NM 87745;
tel: 505-425-5605;
www.starhillinn.com
Amateur astronomers will be in
heaven at this bed-and-breakfast
designed to meet the needs of
dedicated skywatchers. Situated on
200 wooded acres (80 hectares) in
the Sangre de Cristo Mountains 20
minutes northwest of Las Vegas,
the inn offers eight one-, two-, or
three-bedroom cottages, with
kitchen, fireplace, private bath,
handcrafted furnishings and porch.
Bring your own telescope or rent
one at the inn. **$$–$$$**

**St. James Hotel**
17th and Collinson Sts, Cimarron,
NM 87714; tel: 866-472-5019
The St. James was built in 1872 by
French immigrant Henri Lambert,
the personal chef to Napoleon
Bonaparte, Abraham Lincoln and
General Ulysses S. Grant. It's said
that 26 men were killed here and
some of their ghosts have been
hanging around ever since.
Notorious gunman Clay Allison
reputedly danced on the bar, once
part of the dining room, which still
has bullet holes in the pressed tin
ceiling. Other notables who stayed
at the St. James include train
robber Blackjack Ketchum, Buffalo
Bill Cody, Annie Oakley and author
Zane Grey, who wrote *Fighting
Caravans* here. Today the inn's 14
restored guest rooms have a
sparse frontier elegance, though
none have phones or televisions and
most bathrooms are quite small. An
annex has 10 fully equipped motel-
style rooms with none of the charm
of the original hotel, which rather
defeats the point of staying here.
But the hotel's Murder Mystery
weekends are very popular.
Amenities: restaurant, coffee shop,
gift shop. **$$**

## HIGH ROAD TO TAOS AND THE RIO GRANDE VALLEY

### Casa Escondida
PO Box 142, 64 County Road 0100, Chimayo, NM 87522; tel: 505-351-4805 or 800-643-7201; www.casaescondida.com
Built in Spanish Colonial style, with such architectural touches as wooden tongue-and-groove ceilings, saltillo tile floors and wooden vigas, the Casa is set on 6 acres (2.4 hectares) in the mountain village of Chimayo. The bed-and-breakfast has eight guest rooms, some with a fireplace or woodstove, private patio or oversized bathtub. Amenities: full complimentary breakfast, private bath, hot tub, laundry service. **$$**

### Comida de Campos
off NM 68, Embudo, NM 87531; tel: 877-552-4452, 505-852-0017; www.comidadecampos.com
Guests stay in casitas on this 20-acre (8-hectare) organic farm on the banks of the Rio Grande about 30 minutes south of Taos. Fully equipped kitchens are stocked with chile and other spices grown on the farm, and guests are invited to pick their own vegetables as needed. Owner Margaret Campos and a roster of guest chefs offer hands-on lessons in traditional New Mexican cooking in an open-air kitchen equipped with a pair of *hornos*, or beehive-shaped ovens. For a genuine experience of rural life in northern New Mexico, this place can't be beat. A warm, wonderful experience. **$$**

### Rancho Arriba
PO Box 338 (off NM 76), Truchas, NM; tel: 505-689-2374; www.ranchoarriba.com
This small hacienda-style bed-and-breakfast is situated on a working ranch bordering Carson National Forest. Accommodations in the guest wing are rustic, with viga and latilla ceilings, handmade furniture, and a kiva fireplace. All but one of the four units share bathrooms. Amenities: complimentary full breakfast cooked on a wood stove. **$–$$**

## TAOS AND ENVIRONS

### Adobe and Stars Bed and Breakfast Inn
584 SF Hwy 150, Taos, NM 87571; tel: 505-776-2776 or 800-211-7076; www.taosadobe.com
Situated between Taos and Taos Ski Valley, this new, Pueblo-style inn features eight guest rooms with a kiva fireplace, beamed ceiling, handcrafted Southwestern furniture, regional art, large windows with mountain views, and a Jacuzzi tub or double shower. Amenities: complimentary full breakfast, telephone, wi-fi access. **$$–$$$**

### Alma del Monte
PO Box 617, 372 Hondo Seco Rd, Taos, NM 87571; tel: 505-776-2721 or 800-273-7203; www.almaspirit.com
This new hacienda-style house outside Taos offers five guest bedrooms furnished in Southwestern style with antiques, sculptures and other artworks. Each room has a whirlpool tub and kiva fireplace, and opens to an inner courtyard. Amenities: complimentary full breakfast, private bath, sitting area, in-room CD player and telephone, patios, horse-boarding facilities. **$$$**

### Alpine Village Suites
PO Box 917, Taos NM 87571; tel: 505-776-8540 or 800-576-2666; www.alpine-suites.com
These one-bedroom suites at the base of the ski slope sleep up to four people. Each has a kitchenette; most have a sun deck and fireplace. Guests have access to a slopeside hot tub, sauna and ski lockers. The Alpine Village complex houses two full-service ski shops, a restaurant and bar. Amenities: television and VCR, full bathrooms, telephones; inquire about ski packages. **$$–$$$**

### Austing Haus
PO Box 8, State Route 150, Taos Ski Valley, NM 87525; tel: 505-776-2649 or 800-748-2932; taoswebb.com/hotel/austinghaus
One of the largest timber frame structures in North America is nestled in the forest 1½ miles (2.4km) from the ski area. All rooms have private baths; some have fireplaces and sleeping lofts. There's an indoor hot tub and a breakfast room overlooking the Sangre de Cristo Mountains. Amenities: complimentary Continental breakfast buffet, television, telephone, meeting facilities. **$$–$$$**

### Casa de las Chimeneas
405 Cordoba Rd, Taos, NM 87571; tel: 505-758-4777 or 877-758-4777; www.visittaos.com
Surrounded by 7-ft (2-meter) adobe walls and lavish flower gardens is this luxurious Pueblo-style inn, just two blocks from the historic Plaza. Eight impeccably designed guest rooms are decorated in contemporary Southwestern style, with beamed ceilings, high-quality bedding and linens, a mini-refrigerator stocked with complimentary juices and sodas, fireplaces and tiled bathrooms, some with a whirlpool tub. On-site spa and massage services are available for an extra fee. Amenities: complimentary breakfast and evening hors d'oeuvres, cable television, private telephone, concierge services. **$$$–$$$$**

### El Monte Sagrado
317 Kit Carson Road, Taos, NM 87571
tel. 800-828-8267
www.elmontesagrado.com
Opened in 2003, owner Tom Worrell's exotic eco-resort is nestled in a residential area just three blocks from downtown. Worrell set out to prove that good design, recycled materials, and an environmental ethos can go hand in hand with discreet luxury, and has succeeded admirably. The hotel occupies a small footprint but feels spacious. Its 37 elegant suites overlook a healing circle in the center of the property and define luxury, each decorated in a variety of international themes, from American Indian to Asian. Water – a scarcity in the desert – is omnipresent throughout the property, where it is purified and returned for use via a series of

channels, waterfalls, and koi ponds. Local organic produce and free-range bison and yak from Worrell's own ranch are served in an attractive, airy restaurant. The resort has a full-service spa. Healing workshops and cooking classes are held onsite. Twelve casitas in renovated historic adobes sleeping 2 – 8 are located nearby. **$$$$**

**Historic Taos Inn**
125 Paseo del Pueblo Norte, Taos, NM 87571; tel: 888-518-8267 or 505-758-2233; www.taosinn.com
Opened in 1936, the inn encompasses several 19th-century houses in a modern complex. Each of the rooms is different, though all are decorated in traditional Southwestern style, many with kiva fireplaces, viga ceilings, white plaster walls, tile floors and antique furniture. The Adobe Bar, described as "the living room of Taos," is a local favorite, with a full schedule of live jazz, flamenco, gospel, country and more. The complex also includes Doc Martin's (see "Where To Eat"), a highly regarded Taos eatery. Amenities: room service, VCR upon request, some rooms with fireplace (be sure to ask if it is functional) and/or sitting area. **$$–$$$**

**Mabel Dodge Luhan House**
240 Morada Lane, Taos, NM 87571; tel: 505-751-9686 or 800-846-2235; www.mabeldodgeluhan.com
This lovely bed-and-breakfast is the former home of Mabel Dodge Luhan, socialite and patron of the arts whose guests included D. H. Lawrence, Georgia O'Keeffe and Ansel Adams. Though not as plush as some of the newer inns, you can't beat the place for historic ambience. After all, how many b&bs can boast bathroom windows painted by D. H. Lawrence or offer the opportunity to stay in a guest room once occupied by Georgia O'Keeffe. Rooms in the main structure have viga ceilings, arched doorways, adobe walls and carved furniture. Accommodations in a new building feature fireplaces and private bathrooms. A nearby cottage

has a kitchenette, two bedrooms, a sitting area and three fireplaces. The inn has conference facilities and is host to a workshop series focusing on meditation, writing and the arts. Amenities: complimentary breakfast, hot tub, some rooms with fireplace, private and shared bathrooms. **$$–$$$**

---

## ALBUQUERQUE AND ENVIRONS

**Bóttger-Koch Mansion Bed-and-Breakfast**
110 San Felipe NW, Albuquerque, NM 87104; tel: 505-243-3639 or 800-758-3639; www.bottger.com
Travelers have a choice of seven comfortably appointed rooms at this pretty pink Victorian just a few steps from the Old Town Plaza. Designer linens, down-filled comforters, lace curtains, antique beds, pressed tin ceilings and period furnishings create a plush and relaxing atmosphere. Amenities: complimentary full breakfast, private baths, phones, cable television, air conditioning. **$$–$$$**

**Doubletree**
201 Marquette Ave NW, Albuquerque, NM 87102; tel: 505-247-3344 or 888-223-4113; www.doubletreealbuquerque.com
Comfortable, contemporary downtown hotel popular with business people and families. Amenities: air conditioning, cable television, data port, restaurant, bar, workout room, outdoor pool, laundry service, gift shop, meeting facilities, parking. **$$–$$$**

**Hyatt Regency**
330 Tijeras Ave, Albuquerque, NM 87102; tel: 505-842-1234 or 800-233-1234; albuquerque.hyatt.com
This elegant, high-rise hotel is adjacent to the Albuquerque Convention Center. Rooms are quite large and decorated in contemporary style with mahogany furniture, plush armchairs and large windows with views of the downtown area and surrounding mountains. Amenities: air conditioning, cable television, data port, outdoor pool, health club,

laundry service, room service, restaurant, bar, gift shop, conference rooms, parking. **$$–$$$**

**Hyatt Regency Tamaya Resort and Spa**
1300 Tuyuna Trail, Santa Ana Pueblo, NM 87004; tel: 800-55-HYATT; www.hyatt.com
Spectacular Tamaya Resort is New Mexico's first high-end destination resort on Indian land. Strong echoes of Chaco Canyon can be found in the 350-room hotel's Great Kiva-style layout and orientation to the cardinal directions. Rooms are plush and spacious in a soothing contemporary style. The resort has two championship golf courses, three swimming pools, a fitness center and full-service spa, two excellent restaurants, art-filled public spaces, and an onsite Santa Ana Pueblo museum. Cultural activities include dancing, nature walks along the Rio Grande, horseback riding on sacred lands, cooking classes, storytelling and more. Shuttles transport guests to the tribe's casino. The Corn Maiden restaurant offers gourmet dining in an adobe-style building. **$$$–$$$$**

**La Posada de Albuquerque**
125 Second St NW (at Copper Ave), Albuquerque, NM 87102; tel: 505-242-9090 or 800-777-5732; www.laposada-abq.com
Built in 1939 by New Mexico native Conrad Hilton and listed on the National Register of Historic Places, La Posada reconciles authentic Southwestern design with the needs of a large downtown hotel. An attractive two-story lobby features hand-painted murals, carved beams and balconies, tile floors, fountains and a series of white plaster archways. Guest rooms – some rather snug – are furnished with handcrafted beds and bureaus and cheery linens of Southwestern design. Amenities: air conditioning, cable television, data ports, room service, restaurant, two lounges, meeting facilities, laundry service, parking. **$$–$$$**

**La Quinta Inn Albuquerque West**
6101 Iliff Rd NW, Albuquerque, NM 87121; tel: 800-297-0144
You'll find good value at this

contemporary motel about 5 miles (8km) from downtown Albuquerque. Rooms are fairly large and simply but appealingly furnished. Amenities: complimentary Continental breakfast, cable television, data port, air conditioning, parking. **$$**

**Los Poblanos Inn**
4803 Rio Grande Blvd NW, Albuquerque, NM 87107; tel: 866-344-9297; www.lospoblanos.com
Housed in a beautiful 1930s John Gaw Meem hacienda, Los Poblanos sits on 25 acres (10-hectares) of farmland in the North Valley. Six rooms are arranged around a courtyard, and there is a separate guest house suitable for families. Innkeepers Penny and Armin Rembe are easy-going, well-informed hosts. Their huge collection of Southwest art fills every corner. **$$–$$$$**

**Mauger Estate Bed-and-Breakfast Inn**
701 Roma Ave NW, Albuquerque, NM 87102; tel: 505-242-8755 or 800-719-9189; www.maugerbb.com
Built in 1897 and now listed in the National Register of Historic Places, this elegant Queen Anne-style inn is beautifully decorated with period furnishings, original artwork and comfy sofas and bedding. For extra room or a long stay, ask for the fully equipped two-bedroom, two-bathroom townhouse next to the inn. Old Town and the Convention Center are both within walking distance. Amenities: complimentary buffet breakfast, private bath, stocked refrigerators, phones, data ports, satellite television, access to fitness center, gift shop, parking. **$$–$$$**

**The Potteries**
4100 Dietz Farm Circle NW, Albuquerque, NM 87107; tel: 505-344-3144 or 800-795-3144; www.collectorsguide.com/thepotteries
A guest room and a suite are available at this unusual bed-and-breakfast, which serves as both the home and pottery studio of proprietor Liz Anderson. The inn is within walking distance of the Rio Grande Nature Conservancy. Amenities: private bath, patio. **$$**

**Radisson Hotel Conference Center**

## Price Guide

Price categories are based on the average cost of a double room per night.

| | |
|---|---|
| **$** | $50 or less |
| **$$** | $50–150 |
| **$$$** | $150–250 |
| **$$$$** | $250 or more |

**Albuquerque**
2500 Carlisle Blvd NE, Albuquerque, NM 87110; tel: 505-888-3311 or 800-333-3333; www.radisson.com
A recent renovation at this stylish business hotel added tasteful Southwestern touches to the lobby and guest rooms. Accommodations are roomy, with contemporary furnishings and the high-tech extras (like high-speed Internet access) expected of a new hotel. Amenities: cable television, data ports, restaurant, lounge, pool, fitness center, airport shuttle. **$$**

**Sheraton Old Town Hotel**
800 Rio Grande Blvd NW, Albuquerque, NM 87104; tel: 505-843-6300 or 800-237-2133
Southwestern elements blend seamlessly with efficient high-rise design at this downtown hotel adjacent to Albuquerque's Old Town Plaza. Amenities: cable television, air conditioning, data ports, fitness center, outdoor pool, restaurant, cafe, lounge, laundry service, meeting facilities. **$$**

# SILVER CITY, LAS CRUCES AND THE SOUTHWEST CORNER

**Bear Mountain Lodge**
P.O. Box 1163, Silver City, NM 88062; tel. 505-538-2538 or toll-free 877-620-BEAR
www.bearmountainlodge.com
This attractive 1928 lodge in Silver City has at times been a ranch, boys school, country club, and dude ranch. It reopened in 2001 after a painstaking restoration by the Nature Conservancy of New Mexico. The lodge's resident naturalist offers daily talks and hikes through

two nearby bird preserves on the Gila River. Six rooms in the Lodge, four in Myra's Retreat, and the Wren's Nest guesthouse feature hand-carved ceiling vigas and 1920s Mission-style furnishings, with luxury extras, such as Jacuzzi tubs in some rooms. The kitchen produces delicious breakfasts using organic produce. Locally hand-carved Southwest-style beds, tables, chairs, and armoires made from small-diameter trees from a local forest restoration project are found in every room. Many birds are attracted to the pond behind Myra's Retreat, the guesthouse named for legendary proprietess and avid birder Myra B. McCormick, who donated Bear Mountain Lodge to The Nature Conservancy in 1999. **$$**

**Black Range Lodge**
Box 119 (off NM 152), Kingston, NM 88042; tel: 505-895-5652; www.zianet.com/blackrange/lodge
This rustic mountain lodge is situated in the old mining community of Kingston in the foothills of Gila National Forest. The massive stone walls and log-beamed ceilings were salvaged from the ruins of a notorious casino and saloon dating to the 1880s. The lodge has three suites and four double rooms with private baths; two rooms have balconies. A new luxury guest house is available, with Jacuzzi tub, full kitchen and room for four guests. Amenities: complimentary buffet breakfast, common kitchen in main lodge, game room. **$$**

**Casitas de Gila Guesthouses**
50 Casita Flats Road (off Hooker Loop), P.O. Box 325, Gila, NM 88038; tel: 505-535-4455 or 877-923-4827; www.casitasdegila.com
Set on a bluff overlooking Bear Creek about 30 minutes from Silver City is this secluded cluster of five adobe *casitas* surrounded by hundreds of acres of mountain wilderness. Each *casita* has a fully-equipped kitchen, a living/dining room, a kiva fireplace, ceiling beams, a private bathroom and either one or two bedrooms. Decor includes Mexican furniture,

antiques and crafts as well as artwork by the owners and other local artists. Amenities: complimentary Continental breakfast, private baths and telephones, hot tub, telescope. **$$–$$$**

**Hilton Las Cruces**
705 S. Telshor Blvd, Las Cruces, NM 88011; tel: 505-522-4300; www.hilton.com
This seven-story hotel on the outskirts of Las Cruces combines warm Mexican decor with the usual array of business lodging amenities. Ask for a room on one of the upper floors for great views of the city and Organ Mountains. Amenities: air conditioning, cable television, pool, exercise facility, laundry service, restaurant. **$$–$$$**

**Mesón de Mesilla**
1803 Avenida de Mesilla, Mesilla, NM 88046; tel: 800-732-6025 or 505-525-9212
About 10 minutes from historic Mesilla Plaza, this 1983 pueblo-style inn has an award-winning restaurant, 14 rooms with baths, and one suite with kiva fireplace. Free shuttle service from Las Cruces Airport, gourmet breakfasts, and picnic baskets are available. **$$–$$$**

## ALAMOGORDO AND ENVIRONS

**Best Western Desert Aire**
1021 S. White Sands Blvd, Alamogordo, NM 88310; tel: 505-437-2110 or 800-528-1234
You'll find comfortable, functional lodging and good value at this popular chain motel. For an extra measure of comfort, ask for a

## Price Guide

Price categories are based on the average cost of a double room per night.

| | |
|---|---|
| **$** | $50 or less |
| **$$** | $50–150 |
| **$$$** | $150–250 |
| **$$$$** | $250 or more |

suite, with kitchenette and Jacuzzi tub. **$$**

**Casa de Patrón**
Box 27, Lincoln, NM 88338; tel: 800-524-5202 or 505-653-4676; www.casapatron.com
This adobe, once the home of Lincoln County Clerk Juan Patrón, was used in 1878 to confine Billy the Kid. Three guest rooms have private baths, wood floors and both contemporary and antique furnishings. One- and two-bedroom *casitas* are also available. Amenities: complimentary breakfast, some units with fireplace, Jacuzzi tub, and kitchenette. **$$**

**Ellis Store and Country Inn**
Hwy 380, MM 98, Box 15, Lincoln, NM 88338; tel: 800-653-6460 or 505-653-4609; www.ellisstore.com
McSween loyalists once stayed in this 1850 adobe inn during the Lincoln County War, and Billy the Kid was held captive here for two weeks prior to his trial. Each guest room in the main house, built in the 1850s, has a wood-burning stove, antiques and hand-made quilts. The adjacent mill house dates to the 1880s and has a rustic Old West ambience. A new addition, Casa Nueva, has two suites. Breakfast and dinner are gourmet feasts here (see "Where To Eat"). **$$**

**Hurd Ranch Guest Houses**
PO Box 100, San Patricio, NM 88348; tel: 505-653-4331; www.wyethartists.com/homes
Travelers have a choice of five guest houses on the 2,500-acre (1,000-hectare) Sentinel Ranch about 20 miles (32km) east of Ruidoso. Also here is the Hurd La Rinconada Gallery, which features the work of Michael Hurd, his parents Henriette Wyeth and Peter Hurd, and relatives Andrew and N. C. Wyeth. The cottages have one or two bedrooms, living/dining areas, private bathrooms, a kitchen, fireplace and satellite television; some have sunrooms. Decor is quite elegant, with a combination of antiques and designer furniture as well as original art by the Hurd-Wyeth family. **$$–$$$$**

**Inn of the Mountain Gods Resort and Casino**
P.O. Box 269, 287 Carrizo Canyon Road, Mescalero, NM 88340
tel. 505-464-4100 or toll-free 800-545-6040
www.innofthemountaingods.com
A new resort and 38,000-square-foot casino with over 1,000 slots opened in 2005 on the site of the former hotel-casino owned by the Mescalero Apache Tribe. The new Lake Tahoe-style resort is lavish and takes full advantage of its lovely setting on a sparkling lake in the Sacramento Mountains in the heart of the Mescalero Indian Reservation near Ruidoso. Recreational facilities include an 18-hole golf course, tennis courts, volleyball courts, stables, a marina with fishing boats, a pool, and shuttles to Ski Apache, the tribe's famous ski resort. Amenities: 273 rooms with air conditioning, television, two restaurants, two bars, convention and meeting facilities, outdoor guides available for excursions into the mountains. **$$$**

**Lodge at Cloudcroft**
1 Corona Place, Box 497, Cloudcroft, NM 88317; tel: 800-395-6343 or 505-682-2566
This 61-room, Bavarian-style hotel in the Sacramento Mountains was constructed by the railroad in 1899 and still has the air of a grand old lady on the mountaintop. Guests have included Pancho Villa, Judy Garland, Clark Gable and every governor of New Mexico since statehood. The hotel offers 47 rooms, 11 guest suites and a four-bedroom cottage with kitchenette. All rooms in the main lodge are decorated in period style with Victorian antiques. Activities include golf, croquet, skiing and hiking on nearby forest trails. The award-winning restaurant, Rebecca's, is named for the red-headed chambermaid who haunts the hotel. Amenities: restaurant, shops, private telephones and television, outdoor pool, spa, in-room massage, nine-hole golf course, tennis courts; skiing and hiking are available. **$$–$$$**

## CARLSBAD CAVERNS AND THE SOUTHEAST CORNER

**Best Western Guadalupe Inn**
17 Carlsbad Hwy, Whites City, NM 88268; tel: 505-785-2291 or 800-228-3767; www.bestwestern.com
Situated near the entrance to Carlsbad Caverns National Park, this 63-room motel has three sections: Walnut Inn, Cavern Inn, and Guadalupe Inn. Guadalupe Inn is built around a courtyard and offers spacious rooms with ceiling beams and Southwestern furnishings. A small waterpark is a new addition at Cavern Inn. A large swimming pool, saloon and restaurant are on the premises, along with an RV park with restrooms, showers, laundry facilities and pool privileges. Amenities: air conditioning, cable television, gift shop, arcade, restaurant, pool, meeting facilities. **$$**

**Best Western Motel Stevens**
1829 S. Canal St, Carlsbad, NM 88220; tel: 505-887-2851 or 800-730-2851; www.bestwestern.com
This chain motel has 204 spacious rooms, some with microwaves and refrigerators. A pool and restaurant are on the premises. Shuttle service is provided from the airport. Amenities: restaurant, limited room service, pool, laundry service, cable television, air conditioning. **$$**

**Carlsbad Holiday Inn**
601 S. Canal St, P.O. Box 128, Carlsbad, NM 88220; tel: 800-465-4329 or 505-885-8500; www.ichotelsgroup.com
Set in downtown Carlsbad about 23 miles (37km) from the caverns, the hotel offers 100 rooms furnished in Southwestern style, some with whirlpool baths. A restaurant specializes in gourmet dining; casual fare is available in an adjoining bar and grill. Amenities: air conditioning, cable television, two restaurants, limited room service, outdoor pool, sauna, whirlpool, workout room, laundry facility, complimentary airport shuttle. **$$**

**Continental Inn**
3820 National Parks Hwy, Carlsbad, NM 88220; tel: 505-887-0341 or 877-887-0341
A good choice for those traveling on a budget, this two-story red-brick motel has 60 modest rooms with oak furniture and coffee makers. Suites have large sleeper sofas and can accommodate small groups. Amenities: air conditioning, cable television, outdoor pool. **$**

**Horseshoe Hacienda**
84 Means Rd, Carlsbad, NM 88220; tel: 505-785-2213 or 800-607-4600
This bed-and-breakfast, 4 miles (6.4km) from Carlsbad Caverns and 40 miles (64km) from Guadalupe Mountains National Park, has seven guest rooms, four with private baths. Hiking and horseback riding are available. Inquire about special chuck-wagon dinners and wagon rides. **$$**

## Camping

Most tent and RV sites in national and state parks and in national forests are available on a first-come, first-served basis, although increasingly campground space in popular parks is on a reservation basis. Campgrounds fill early during the summer season in the high country and winter in the southern deserts. Contact the parks for information on availability. Fees are usually charged for campsites. Backcountry permits may be required for wilderness camping.

# Where to Eat

## What to Eat

New Mexico cuisine is as varied and interesting as the state itself. A single dish may include a savory mix of red and green chile, yellow and blue cornmeal, a dark brown mound of beans with snowy sour cream, a pile of shredded lettuce, an improbably neon-green whip called guacamole with salty fried tortilla chips stuck in like banners, and a brightly colored salsa of red tomatoes, green chile, cilantro and white onions.

A couple of local customs to keep in mind: you may be asked by your waiter if you prefer red or green chile (green tends to be milder but it depends on the crop); and some traditional meals are served with sopaipillas, a puffy fried dough eaten with honey.

In addition to the native dishes, large towns like Santa Fe, Taos and Albuquerque offer everything from pasta parlors to sushi bars. Many of the most interesting restaurants have built their reputations on blending Southwestern flavors with a variety of international cuisine. Still, it's hard to go wrong with the traditional repertoire: enchiladas, tacos, burritos, flautas, chile rellenos, posole, guacamole and lots of red-hot chile.

## Restaurants by Area

### SANTA FE

**Amaya Restaurant at Hotel Santa Fe**
1501 Paseo de Peralta, Santa Fe, NM 87501; tel: 505-982-1200
This unique hotel restaurant is

majority-owned by Picuris Pueblo and serves innovative native cuisine. Chef Patrick Klein highlights fresh local produce and game, such as venison, antelope, game hen, and bison from the tribe's own herd near Taos. The signature Picuris Mixed Grill features elk tenderloin, orange-ginger duck breast, mint-crusted lamb chop, and fragrant bison sausage accompanied by tender young vegetables, mashed potatoes, and a pool of fragrant garlic-herb demi-glace sauce. An elegant vegetable Napoleon will satisfy the vegetarians in the group. You could also make a meal from several starters, such as a lovely roasted squash bisque with fried cotija cheese wonton and poussin with microgreens, leaving room for a decadent white chocolate and hazelnut warm bread pudding. Al fresco dining is available on a lovely patio. Ask about dining in the teepee for a special event. Prices are extremely reasonable for downtown Santa Fe, particularly lunchtime when soups, salads, salmon, buffalo burgers, and salads on delicious local Sage Bakehouse bread are all $10 and under. **$–$$**

**Anasazi Restaurant**
Inn of the Anasazi, 113 Washington Ave, Santa Fe, NM 87501; tel: 505-988-3236; www.innoftheanasazi.com
Chefs at this award-winning restaurant combine "foods of the earth from Native America, foods of the soul from northern New Mexico and foods of substance from the American Cowboy." Eclectic dishes such as buffalo carpaccio, Navajo flat bread with fire roasted peppers, chipotle mustard glazed chicken and venison osso bucco live up to a very high standard of taste and presentation. The atmosphere is romantic and contemporary, with architectural cues from Ancient Puebloan culture. Organic meats and vegetables are used whenever possible. **$$**

**Cafe Pasqual**
121 Don Gaspar St, Santa Fe, NM 87501; tel: 505-983-9340 or 800-722-7672; www.pasquals.com
The cuisine is inspired by Mexican, Asian and local traditions at this festive and cozy eatery, decorated with hand-painted Mexican tiles and murals by the renowned Mexican painter Leovigildo Martinez. Whether you choose Thai green curry with Japanese eggplant, tacos al diablo, grilled lamb chops with pomegranate glaze or one of a dozen other intriguing entrées, it's hard to go wrong here. Breakfast (served until 3pm) is equally appealing, with traditional Mexican belly busters like huevos rancheros, huevos motuleños and the chorizo burrito. **$$**

**Chocolate Maven Bakery & Cafe**
821 W San Mateo, Santa Fe, NM 87501; tel: 505-984-1980
There's something innately comforting about a good bakery, and this is one of the best in town. Stop by to stock up on such sweet indulgences as Belgian chocolate fudge brownies and green chile scones, or merely to watch the chefs at work behind the glassed-in kitchen. Better yet, take a seat at one of the pretty little tables for breakfast or lunch, when you can take your pick from a variety of egg dishes, fluffy pancakes or the justly celebrated red lentil soup. **$**

**Cowgirl Hall of Fame**
319 S. Guadalupe St, Santa Fe, NM 87501; tel: 505-982-2565; www.cowgirl-santafe.com
Tangy barbecue and grilled dishes like mesquite-smoked brisket, spare ribs and whiskey pork chops

## Price Guide

Price categories indicate the approximate cost of dinner for one, excluding beverages, tax and tip. The standard tip is 15 percent, more for exceptional service or a large party. In some cases, the gratuity may be included in the bill.

| | |
|---|---|
| **$** | $20 or less |
| **$$** | $20–40 |
| **$$$** | $40–60 |
| **$$$$** | $60 and up |

are the specialty at this fun Western-style restaurant bedecked with old cowgirl photos. The kitchen does a creditable job with New Mexican dishes like chile rellenos and chicken fajitas as well as a spicy Jamaican jerk chicken and an interesting salmon taco al carbon. The bar features live music almost every night. The outdoor patio has a children's play area that keeps kids happy while their parents enjoy a peaceful meal. **$**

**Coyote Cafe**
132 W. Water St, Santa Fe, NM 87501; tel: 505-983-1615; www.coyote-cafe.com
Celebrity chef and cookbook author Mark Miller helped put Santa Fe on the culinary map and continues to delight diners with his "nouvelle Southwestern" cuisine. The menu changes often, but a recent installment included chile-glazed beef short ribs, black truffle risotto, scallops a la vera cruzana and the venerable "cowboy cut" – an aged Angus beef ribeye. The rooftop Coyote Cantina is open in summer for lighter Cuban fare. **$$–$$$**

**Geronimo**
724 Canyon Rd, Santa Fe, NM 87501; tel: 505-982-1500
There's a warren of intimate dining rooms in this classic 1756 adobe building in Santa Fe's fashionable gallery district. While a bit pricey, most diners agree the fine "Global Fusion-Southwest" cuisine is worth every penny. Of particular note is a lobster appetizer served on a bed of angel hair pasta and, for the main course, grilled elk tenderloin. The lunch menu offers variations of many of the same dishes at a fraction of the cost. Dining under the *portal* on a warm summer evening is especially pleasant. **$$–$$$**

**Guadalupe Café**
422 Old Santa Fe Trail, Santa Fe, NM 87501; tel: 505-982-9762
Efficient service, a warm atmosphere and excellent New Mexican food are a winning combination at this popular, moderately-priced restaurant, just three blocks from the Plaza. Good choices include the seafood or

guacamole enchiladas, chalupas (a fried bowl-shaped corn tortilla stuffed with shredded chicken or beef, beans and a dollop of guacamole) and, for vegetarians, the fresh vegetable burrito plate. Breakfast is equally appealing, with freshly baked muffins and hearty fare like huevos rancheros. Don't pass on dessert. Luscious concoctions like the Heath bar and chocolate amaretto pies are worth the extra calories. The front patio has a great view of the tourist parade on the Old Santa Fe Trail. **$–$$**

**Pink Adobe**
406 Old Santa Fe Trail, Santa Fe, NM 87501; tel: 505-983-7712; www.thepinkadobe.com
This old standby has been pleasing residents and visitors alike for more than 50 years with such well-prepared Continental and Southwestern dishes as porc Napoleone, lamb curry, tamales, enchiladas and a charred New York strip called steak Dunigan. The building is said to be more than 300 years old. The Dragon Bar is a local favorite. **$–$$**

**Santacafé**
231 Washington Ave, Santa Fe, NM 87501; tel: 505-984-1788; www.santacafe.com
Understated elegance is the motif at this restored hacienda, built in the mid-1800s by the controversial priest and politician Padre Jose Manuel Gallegos. Southwestern and Asian flavors cohabit in the kitchen with mutually beneficial results. Santacafé has been praised by no less than the *New York Times* for its fresh and flavorful (but rarely flashy) menu, featuring such winning entrées as the "Southwestern" cassoulet, roasted poblano chile relleno and a variety of seafood specialties. **$$**

**Santa Fe Baking Company**
504 W. Cordova Rd, Santa Fe, NM 87501; tel: 505-988-4292.
Make a stop at this local hangout for the best inexpensive breakfast burritos in town and a mouth-watering selection of baked goods or to hobnob with the diverse clientele. A great place for a taste

of the real Santa Fe. **$**

**The Shed**
113½ E. Palace Ave, Santa Fe, NM 87501; tel: 505-982-9030
Housed in a 17th-century hacienda just off the Plaza, this local favorite has been serving hearty New Mexican fare for more than 50 years. Enchiladas – served in the "stacked" New Mexican style – are primo. The green chile stew and blue-corn tacos and burritos are good, too. Leave room for dessert – among the best in Santa Fe. **$–$$**

**Shohko-Cafe**
321 Johnson St, Santa Fe, NM 87501; tel: 505-983-7288
Sometimes only sushi will do. If that's the case, pull a chair up to the sushi bar at this Japanese restaurant for a wide array of expertly prepared raw seafood. In addition to a familiar selection of nigiri, sashimi and rolls, you'll find a local specialty made with green chile. Non-sushi-eaters have a good choice of yakitori, sukiyaki, teriyaki and tempura. **$$**

**Thai Café**
329 W. San Francisco St, Santa Fe, NM 87501; tel: 505-982-3886
Tired of heavy Mexican food? Try this Thai-inspired restaurant near the Plaza. Hints of lemongrass, basil, cilantro, coconut, peanuts and fiery chile are woven into traditional selections such as pad Thai, tom yum gai and red and green curry, though you can expect a few contemporary variations as well, including a nice mango chicken and spicy Balinese-style squid. **$**

**Tía Sophia's**
210 W. San Francisco St, Santa Fe, NM 87501; tel: 505-983-9880
There are no pretentions at this neighborhood spot, a favorite of government workers and a good spot for people watching. The chile is superb, and the breakfast burritos are rich, flavorful and filling enough to see you through a tough day of touring. **$**

**Tomasita's**
500 S. Guadalupe St, Santa Fe, NM 87501; tel: 505-983-5721
A former railroad station is the setting for this lively and informal

New Mexican restaurant – one of the most popular in town – where traditional dishes such as chile relleños, enchiladas, burritos and red and green chile are outstanding and the crowd is always spirited. Reservations are not accepted, so expect to wait for a table. **$**

## LOS ALAMOS AND ENVIRONS

**Hill Diner**
1315 Trinity Dr, Los Alamos, NM 87544; tel: 505-662-9745
Burgers, chicken-fried steak and other down-home comfort food are the bill of fare at this large diner. **$**

**Laughing Lizard Café**
PO Box 263; Jemez Springs, NM 87025; tel: 505-829-3108; www.thelaughinglizard.com
Excellent sandwiches, burritos, pizza and salads are featured at this friendly cafe, housed in a former mercantile center with hardwood floors, 11-ft-high (4-meter) pressed tin ceilings and 3-ft-thick (1-meter) adobe and stone walls. Boxing champ Jack Dempsey once fought here during his early days as a camp brawler. Homemade pies and fruit cobbler are a great way to cap a meal. **$**

**Los Ojos Restaurant & Saloon**
NM 4, Jemez Springs, NM 87025; tel: 505-829-3547
Burgers and beer are the attractions at this old-time roadhouse near Jemez State Monument. The weekend crowd is actually quite lively, and there's plenty of room in the saloon for performers and dancers. **$**

## ABIQUIU, CHAMA AND ENVIRONS

**Cafe Abiquiu**
PO Box 120 (US 84), Abiquiu, NM 87510; tel: 505-685-4378
Run by nearby Dar al-Islam, this pretty little adobe has Middle Eastern specialties as well as New Mexican enchiladas, fajitas and burritos. Pies and cobblers are made with fresh fruit in season. Box

lunches are available for travelers exploring the region. **$**

**High Country Restaurant**
Main St, Chama, NM 87520; tel: 505-756-2384.
The decor is nothing to write home about, but the burgers are juicy, the pork ribs succulent, the steaks thick, and the trout – a local specialty – nicely done. Add a side order of beans and potato salad and you have the makings of a first-class feed. The bar's fun, too – the kind of place where customers are encouraged to toss their peanut shells on the floor. **$**

**Rancho de San Juan**
US 285, Ojo Caliente, NM; tel: 505-753-6818;
www.ranchodesanjuan.com
A cozy fireside dining room is the setting for a beautifully presented, fixed-price, four-course meal at this elegant inn and restaurant in the sere foothills of the southern Rockies. The menu changes often, though recent selections have included grilled veal sirloin, grilled chipotle marinated tiger prawns with mango salsa, and roasted rack of lamb with Dijon-pepper crust. Desserts are veritable works of art. A precious island of elegance in northern New Mexico's backcountry. **$$$–$$$$**

**Viva Vera's Mexican Kitchen**
2202 NM 17, Chama, NM 87520; tel: 505-756-2557
Frozen Margaritas are just the thing to cool the red-hot chile liberally applied to enchiladas, burritos and other traditional fare at this unassuming place, which, according to its fans, serves the best Mexican food north of Albuquerque. Judge for yourself. The restaurant is in a big new building about a mile from the Cumbres & Toltec train station. **$**

## GALLUP, CHACO CANYON AND NAVAJO COUNTRY

**Earl's**
1400 E. 66 Ave, Gallup, NM 87301; tel: 505-863-4201
This old-time diner may be a little rough around the edges, but it's filled with local characters who come for decent New Mexican food and the usual selection of sandwiches, burgers and fries. Indian people sell jewelry and other wares from table to table. **$**

**Huwak'a Restaurant**
PO Box 310 (I-40, exit 102), Acoma, NM 87034; tel: 505-552-6123 or 888-759-2489;
www.skycityhotel.com
Owned by Acoma Pueblo, this new restaurant in the Sky City Hotel is open 24 hours. The Huwak'a buffet is a good deal for those with big appetites. Prime rib, seafood, sandwiches and burgers can also be ordered à la carte. **$**

**Jerry's Cafe**
406 W. Coal Ave, Gallup, NM 87301; tel: 505-722-6775
Popular with local folks, this little eatery may look a little dodgy from the outside, but the New Mexican food is quite good and there's certainly plenty of it. Customers squeeze into booths, while chowing down on big platters laden with enchiladas, burritos and other rib-sticking dishes loaded with chile and beans. **$**

**Navajo Nation Inn**
48 Highway 264, Window Rock, AZ 86515; tel: 928-871-4108
A favorite meeting place for locals and people visiting on business, the restaurant serves Navajo tacos and a few other local specialties as well as standard American diner food. **$**

**Rio Grande Coffee Company's Atomic Espresso Bistro**
122 N. Main Ave, Aztec, NM 87410; tel: 505-334-0109
This arty cafe is a little slice of Bohemia in the far northwest corner of New Mexico. Breakfast and lunch feature a variety of croissant and bagel sandwiches, pancakes, omelettes, egg dishes, quiche, soups and salads. Or just stop by for a strong cup of coffee and a yummy selection of pastries, cakes and cinnamon rolls. **$**

**Three Rivers Eatery & Brewhouse**
101 E. Main St, Farmington NM 87401; tel: 505-324-2187
A dozen hand-crafted beers are on tap at this brewpub, in a handsome brick building once occupied by the *Farmington Times Hustler* newspaper. The dinner menu is quite appealing, too, with a tasty selection of thick burgers, barbecued ribs, homemade soups, seafood and pasta. Kids will enjoy the hand-brewed root beer, apple cider and cherry cream soda. **$–$$**

## SANTA FE TRAIL

**Blackjack's Grill**
Inn on the Santa Fe Trail, 1133 N. Grand Ave, Las Vegas, NM 87701; tel: 505-425-6791
This hotel restaurant serves fine Continental cuisine and a few local specialties in a snug dining room or, on warm evenings, on a pleasant outdoor patio. All in all, it's a welcome change of pace from fast-food joints and Mexican restaurants. **$–$$**

**The Carson-Maxwell Dining Room at the St. James Hotel**
17th and Collinson Sts, Cimarron, NM 87714; tel: 866-472-5019;
stjamescimarron.com
Jesse James, Clay Allison and a who's who of other notorious gunmen stopped in for a drink and bite to eat at this historic Wild West bar and restaurant. At least 26 men were killed here, and customers can still see bullet holes in the dining room's pressed-tin ceiling. The atmosphere is much more peaceful these days, though customers still come for the Old West ambience and excellent food. Most dinners are built around a hefty serving of meat – bison pot roast, rib-eye steak, smoked pork chops and roasted chicken, although there's usually at least one seafood or pasta dish as well. Breakfast, lunch and dinner are

served in Vera's Cafe, which adjoins Lambert's Saloon. **$$**
**Del's Family Restaurant**
1202 E. Tucumcari Blvd, Tucumcari, NM 88401; tel: 505-461-1740; www.delsrestaurant.com
When you see a big cow standing atop a sign above Old Route 66, you know you've arrived at Del's, a diner-style restaurant with a reputation for large and tasty steaks. There's a variety of Mexican food, too, but it's not nearly as good as the sirloin, rib-eye or charbroiled chicken, all served with potatoes, vegetables, and a trip to the soup and salad bar. A great value for those with big appetites **$**
**Joseph's Bar & Grill**
865 Will Rogers Dr, Santa Rosa, NM 88435; tel: 505-472-3361; www.route66.com/Josephs
This old-fashioned diner has been feeding travelers on Old Route 66 since 1956. Fajitas, enchiladas, tamales, chile rellenos and other New Mexican specialties are the best choices, although it's hard to top the juicy burgers. The trout's pretty good, too. Leave room for a milkshake, a bowl of ice cream or a slice of pie. **$**

## HIGH ROAD TO TAOS AND THE RIO GRANDE VALLEY

**Embudo Station**
PO Box 154 (off NM 68), Embudo, NM 87531; tel: 505-852-4707 or 800-852-4707; www.embudostation.com
Housed in a 19th-century narrow-gauge railway station and set in a cottonwood grove on the banks of the Rio Grande, Embudo Station serves a delectable selection of barbecued ribs, charbroiled steaks, grilled chicken, oak-smoked rainbow trout and a variety of authentic New Mexican dishes as well as some excellent vegetarian fare. Wash it all down with a green chile ale or one of the other specialty beers brewed fresh on the premises. The main restaurant is closed in winter, but the smaller "bistro" is open for sandwiches and beer on a limited schedule. **$$**

**Léona's**
Next door to the Santuario de Chimayo is this taco stand where, according to some reviewers, you'll find the best tortillas and tamales in northern New Mexico. There are only a few tables and the lines are often long, but this may be your best bet if you don't have time for a real sit-down meal. **$**
**Rancho de Chimayo**
PO Box 11, Country Road 98, Chimayo, NM 87522; tel: 505-351-4444; www.ranchochimayo.com
Some critics say this old-fashioned hacienda-style restaurant is a victim of its own success. And when tour busses disgorge hordes of hungry tourists, one can see their point. While quality may have slipped a bit over the years, the food is still quite good, and there are few places more pleasant than the patio to enjoy a tangy Margarita and a heaping platter of enchiladas or carne adovada. Like the nearby Santuario de Chimayo, this place is worth a pilgrimage. **$**
**Trading Post Café**
4179 Paseo del Pueblo Sur, Ranchos de Taos, NM 87557; tel: 505-758-5089
There's fine art on the walls and a whirlwind of activity in the open kitchen at this lively gourmet restaurant, where diners have a choice of fine pasta dishes such as penne arrabbiata, escargot with crispy angel hair and fettuccine a la Carbonara. Meat eaters can tuck into lamb chops with tomato mint sauce, crispy garlic pork chops, rosemary chicken or a nicely done bistecca Fiorentina. On the lighter side is a magnificent Caesar salad. And for comfort food, you can't beat a giant bowl of chicken noodle soup or minestrone. **$–$$**

## TAOS AND ENVIRONS

**Apple Tree**
123 Bent Street, Taos, NM 87571; tel: 505-758-1900
Dishes like the tiger shrimp enchilada or mango chicken enchilada give Southwestern cuisine a creative twist at this

romantic adobe near the Plaza. Those with more traditional tastes may prefer carne adovada, chile rellenos or a straightforward rib-eye steak, all given gourmet treatment. The interior is divided into several snug dining rooms, but the best tables are under the eponymous apple tree in the outdoor courtyard. **$$**
**Bent Street Deli and Cafe**
120 Bent St, Taos, NM 87571; tel: 505-758-5787
Breakfast and lunch at this country-style cafe feature omelettes, fresh pastries, homemade soups, sandwiches and salads. The dinner menu is a bit more ambitious, with seafood Provençal, lasagna, curried pork, clams with pesto sauce and more. The heated patio is pleasant even on chilly nights. **$–$$**
**Bravo**
1353-A Paseo del Pueblo Sur, Taos, NM 87571; tel: 505-758-8100
You'll be surrounded by shelves stocked with fine wines and specialty beers at this restaurant and wine shop. Good for a light dinner, the menu includes salads, pasta, gourmet pizza and a few heartier choices like roast duck or chicken. Excellent sandwiches, including a tasty Cajun catfish sandwich, are served for lunch. Takeout is available, too. **$**
**Doc Martin's**
25 Paseo del Pueblo Norte, Taos, NM 87571; tel: 505-758-2233
Oenophiles will have a field day at this contemporary Southwestern restaurant, a multiple winner of *Wine Spectator* magazine's Award of Excellence, with more than 400 wines to choose from. The cuisine is quite special, too, with appetizers like maple-cured venison and ancho veal dumplings and beautifully presented entrées like seared salmon and roasted poblano peppers stuffed with duck confit and goat cheese. Breakfasts are big and tasty. Try the blue corn and blueberry hotcakes or, a traditional favorite, huevos rancheros. Lunch is served, too. **$$**
**Eske's Brew Pub & Eatery**
106 Des Georges Lane, Taos, NM 87571; tel: 505-758-1517

The beer is good, the crowd is boisterous, and the food is filling at this popular brew pub half a block from the Plaza. The menu isn't big but has several interesting items, including something called The Fatty (a tortilla filled with beans, mashed potatoes and cheese smothered in chile turkey stew), a bratwurst and sauerkraut sandwich, and a green chile burrito. There's sushi at least one night a week and an assortment of other special events, including a full schedule of live music. Wash it all down with a few home brews; seasonal specialties include a green chile beer, Irish stout, bok beer and English-style bitter. **$**

**Michael's Kitchen**
305 Paseo del Pueblo Norte, Taos, NM; tel: 505-758-4178
For those who like breakfast any time of day, there's this interesting little place, which serves a breakfast menu of omelettes, pancakes, biscuits and gravy, pork chops and eggs, huevos rancheros and more throughout the day. There's a lunch and dinner menu, too, with steak, burgers, fried chicken and a long list of New Mexican favorites. For health-conscious eaters, there's the "health food" special – a double order of fries smothered with chile and cheese – which you can top off with homemade donuts, eclairs and cream puffs from the on-site bakery. **$**

**Momentitos de la Vida**
PO Box 505, Arroyo Seco, NM 87514; tel: 505-776-3333
The cuisine is described as "New American" at this elegant spot north of Taos, where the eclectic menu ranges from a delicate smoked trout eclair and Louisiana blue crab cakes to pistachio-encrusted rack of lamb, plum-glazed duckling and saffron lobster risotto, all presented with an artistic flare. A little on the pricey side, but a welcome change for a romantic night out. **$$**

**Taos Pizza Out Back**
712 N. Pueblo Rd, Taos, NM 87571; tel: 505-758-3112
There's pizza and then there's Taos

Pizza Out Back. Funky, spirited and often crowded with mountain bikers, river runners and other outdoorsy types, this local institution turns out a thin-crusted pizza with a wide variety of gourmet toppings. The pizza primavera, for example, has mushrooms, artichoke hearts, olives, sun-dried, tomatoes, feta cheese and walnuts. On the pizza Vera Cruz is chicken marinated in a honey chipotle sauce, bell peppers, onions and melted mozzarella and smoked cheddar cheese. There are at least 15 other specialties and, of course, an option to "build yer own." Pasta, soups and salads are also on the menu, but it would be a shame to pass on the pizza. For dessert, don't miss the decadent Taos Yum – an enormous chocolate chip cookie with two scoops of ice cream, whipped cream and chocolate sauce. **$**

**Villa Fontana**
NM 522 (5 miles north of the Plaza), Taos, NM 87571; tel: 505-758-5800
Had enough chile and beans? Try this gourmet Northern Italian restaurant, the brainchild of Italian-born chef Carlo Gislimberti, who delights patrons with an ever-widening repertoire of classic dishes such as veal scaloppine, mushroom ravioli, roast pork, and beef tenderloin with brandy. If you like what you taste, ask about the chef's cooking school. **$$**

**Wild and Natural Cafe**
812 Paseo del Pueblo Norte, Taos, NM 87571; tel: 505-751-0480
A savory selection of vegetarian dishes, with Southwestern and Asian specialties. Finish off a three-course vegetarian dinner at the espresso and dessert bar. **$**

## ALBUQUERQUE AND ENVIRONS

**66 Diner**
1405 Central Ave NE, Albuquerque, NM; tel: 505-247-1421.
This spiffy neon-lit diner is a walk down memory lane for aficionados of Old Route 66. Located near the University of New Mexico. You'll find comfort food like chicken fried

steak, thick burgers, chicken pot pie, and malted milkshakes on the menu, and retro songsters like Bill Haley and Elvis Presley are on the jukebox. Good eats and a nostalgic treat. **$**

**Annapurna Ayurvedic Cuisine and Chai House**
2201 Silver SE, Albuquerque, NM tel. 505-262-CHAI
Annapurna (named for the goddess of nourishing food) serves carefully conceived organic, gluten- and wheat-free vegetarian/vegan dishes that are both tasty and promote health according to ancient Indian Ayurveda principles, as taught by Dr. Asant Lad, whose world-famous Ayurvedic Institute is in Albuquerque. Enjoy bowls of kitchari (a mixture of basmati rice, veggies, and spices), dal (pureed lentils), coconut soup, and a variety of hot, rolled breads with fillings served with chutney. The South Indian Sampler includes sag paneer (spinach with homemade cheese) and masala dosa, a delicious filled flatbread. Gluten-free desserts, such as scones, fruit pies, and dried fruit balls, are a tasty low-sugar meal in themselves with a cup of brewed chai. Two locations in Albuquerque and one now open in Santa Fe. Cooking classes, weekly live music, imported teas and Indian clothing for sale, wi-fi. Open for late breakfast, lunch, and dinner. Closed Sundays. **$$**

**Bob's Burgers**
5214 Menault Ave, Albuquerque, NM; tel: 505-875-9603
When only a hamburger will satisfy your hunger, come to this rather nondescript joint for a selection of plain and fancy burgers, including the volcano-hot Ranchero smothered in green chile sauce and a burger served in a taco shell. **$**

**Chow's Chinese Bistro**
1950 Juan Tabo NE, Albuquerque, NM 87112; tel: 505-298-3000
More creative than a typical Chinese restaurant and with a far better sense of humor, the bistro serves artfully prepared dishes with peculiar names (Old Lady Tofu, Nuts and Birds, Fish in a Garden) in a spare, modern setting. **$**

## Conrad's
La Posada de Albuquerque, 125 2nd St NW, Albuquerque, NM 87102; tel: 505-242-9090
The restaurant at this classic downtown hotel serves imaginative Southwestern fare in a casual but spiffy dining room with starched linen tablecloths and snappily attired waiters. **$**

## El Pinto
10500 4th St NW, Albuquerque, NM; tel: 505-898-1771; www.elpinto.com
El Pinto has been *the* choice for authentic New Mexican food in the Corrales area since 1962. A good place for breakfast after watching the mass ascension at the annual Balloon Fiesta. **$**

## Flying Star
Dietz Farm Plaza, 4026 Rio Grande Blvd NW, Albuquerque, NM; tel: 505-344-6714
With several locations in Albuquerque, Flying Star has something for everyone, from fabulous homemade soups, salads and pizza to sandwiches, espresso, ice cream and pastries. Browse a well-stocked magazine stand while dining and soak in the informal ambience. **$**

## Frontier Restaurant
2400 Central SE, Albuquerque, NM 87106; tel: 505-289-3130
Don't leave the University District without enjoying a huge breakfast burrito smothered in hot chile at the city's best bargain eatery, opposite the University of New Mexico's main entrance. The 24-hour diner is an Edward Hopper classic, with 1950s Googie architecture and servers in white hats. The restaurant claims to serve 4,600 breakfast burritos per week and more than 7,000 tortillas per day. **$**

## Price Guide

Price categories indicate the rough cost of dinner for one, excluding beverages, tax and tip.

| | |
|---|---|
| **$** | $20 or less |
| **$$** | $20–40 |
| **$$$** | $40–60 |
| **$$$$** | $60 and up |

## Garduno's of Mexico
8806 Fourth St NW, Albuquerque, NM 87110; tel: 505-898-2772
The key to Garduno's popularity is fresh and authentic Mexican food. You know the guacamole is fresh, because it's made by the waiters right at your table. Follow up with chimichangas (a grilled flour tortilla stuffed with beef, chicken, shrimp or crab, and topped with guacamole, sour cream and chile), chile relleno, posole and a variety of enchiladas. There are other locations in Santa Fe and Las Vegas. **$**

## Range Cafe Albuquerque
4200 Wyoming Blvd NE, Albuquerque, NM 87111; tel: 505-293-2633
The chefs at this good-natured restaurant treat such humble fare as chicken-fried steak, meatloaf, biscuits and gravy, chile stew and enchiladas with an attention to detail usually reserved for haute cuisine. The kitschy Western decor is a lot of fun. A second location is at 925 Camino Del Pueblo in Bernalillo; tel: 505-867-4755. **$–$$**

## Hurricane's Restaurant
4330 Lomas Blvd NE, Albuquerque, NM 87110; tel: 505-255-4248
One of America's greatest contributions to world cuisine – the drive-in burger joint – is alive and kicking. The decor is nothing to write home about, but you can't beat this place for big portions and down-home retro chic. **$**

## India Kitchen Restaurant
6910 Montgomery Blvd NE, Albuquerque, NM 87109; tel: 505-884-2333
The strip-mall setting is uninspiring, but the excellent Indian food is worth the trip, especially if you're a vegetarian in search of something more interesting than green salad and french fries. In fact, the menu lists nearly two dozen vegetarian dishes. **$**

## Monte Vista Fire Station
3201 Central Ave NE, Albuquerque, NM 87106; tel: 505-255-2424
Housed in a former fire station built in 1936, this Pueblo Revival-style building on Old Route 66 is home to a popular restaurant specializing in beautifully presented American cuisine. Start with flash fried shrimp and calamari drizzled with cilantro pesto or seared sesame-crusted ahi tuna, then move on to grilled Rocky Mountain lamb chops, blackened filet of beef or chile-rubbed ribeye steak. **$–$$**

## Mr. Powdrell's BBQ Restaurant
5209 4th St NW, Albuquerque, NM 87107; tel: 505-345-8086
Southern, hickory-smoked barbecue is the stock in trade at this down-home restaurant. Stop by for a platter heaped with ribs, sausage, brisket or tender catfish and satisfying side dishes like okra, cole slaw and corn on the cob. **$**

## Ragin' Shrimp
3619 Copper Ave NE, Albuquerque, NM 87108; tel: 505-254-1544
A modern gallery-like dining room is the setting for a selection of hot and spicy dishes. Shrimp, crawfish, beef tenderloin, pork, mussels and clams are served over rice or angel hair pasta with your choice of sauces – Cajun, Jamaican, Thai-style peanut, curry and green chile Alfredo. The sauces come in four heat levels: mild, medium, hot and extra-hot. Only seasoned devotees of the chile pepper should consider the latter two. Jambalaya, gumbo and a few other Cajun specialties are also on the menu. **$**

## Restaurant Antiquity
112 Romero St NW, Albuquerque, NM 87102; tel: 505-247-3545
A warren of romantic little dining rooms awaits diners at this adobe about a block from Old Town plaza. Continental cuisine is the order of the day – mainly steak and seafood with rich sauces – including chateaubriand for two, a nice shrimp scampi, and lobster tail. The wine list isn't extensive, but it's thoughtfully chosen. **$$**

## Sadie's Cocinita
6230 4th St NW, Albuquerque, NM 87107; tel: 505-345-5339
Residents and travelers alike flock to this casual eatery for authentic – and seriously hot – New Mexican food. The carne adovada is among the best in New Mexico. Burritos, enchiladas, tamales, guacamole salad and pork chops are big

winners, too. Expect to wait for a table, although service is friendly and efficient once seated. Pass the time in the cantina with a Margarita. **$**

**Scalo Northern Italian Grill**
3500 Central Ave SE, Albuquerque, NM 87106; tel: 505-255-8781
Diners can watch chefs at work in the show kitchen at this lively – often noisy – dining spot in the trendy Nob Hill district. Osso bucco, barbecued quail, salmon with dill sauce and tender calamari are a few of the highlights. If you like your pasta al dente, you will no doubt be pleased with the selection of pasta dishes here. The thin-crusted, brick-oven pizza is tasty, too, and a good choice for those with light appetites or small budgets. **$$**

---

## SILVER CITY, LAS CRUCES AND THE SOUTHWEST CORNER

**A.I.R. Espresso, Art, Ice Cream**
112 N. Hudson St, Silver City, NM 88061; tel: 505-388-5952
You'll find southwestern New Mexico's best cup of joe at this little cafe, a popular hangout for local artists, gallery-owners and other arty types. Coffee beans are roasted on the premises, giving the place a delicious aroma. Ice cream and a few pastries are also available. **$**

**Buckhorn Saloon & Opera House**
32 Main St, Pinos Altos, NM; tel: 505-538-9911
Though it looks a little rough around the edges on the outside, inside diners are greeted with white tablecloths and candlelight. Situated in tiny Pinos Altos, about 7 miles (11km) north of Silver City, the restaurant features homemade dishes such as prime rib, New York strip steak with green chile, fried shrimp and excellent salads. The saloon is an authentic slice of the Old West. There are live blues or folk singers several nights a week, and old-time melodramas in the adjacent Opera House on Friday and Saturday. **$–$$**

**Diane's Restaurant & Bakery**

510 N. Bullard St, Silver City, NM 88061; tel: 505-538-8722
Lace curtains, hardwood floors and starched white linens add a note of refinement to this otherwise casual restaurant, which is justly recognized as an oasis of fine dining in southwest New Mexico's often dreary culinary landscape. The menu ranges widely, from linguine with a hearty meat sauce and Thai-style seafood with coconut curry to rack of lamb and juicy ribeye steak. For lunch, try a salad, quiche, spanokopita (spinach, mushrooms and feta cheese in a flaky crust), or a thick sandwich made with bread baked on the premises. In fact, all the baked goods are excellent. **$–$$**

**Double Eagle**
2355 Calle de Guadalupe, Mesilla, NM; tel: 505-523-6700
A beautifully restored 19th-century mansion with gold leaf ceilings, crystal chandeliers, gilt mirrors and period art set the scene for elegant dining at this landmark building on Old Mesilla Plaza. The menu features Continental and several Southwestern dishes, including tournedos Maximillian (filet mignon medallions sautéed tableside in butter and garlic), bourbon-glazed strip steak, chicken Mesilla (grilled chicken breast with sautéed Mesilla green chile and Mennonite cheese) and several pasta dishes. The Sunday buffet brunch is a treat. **$$**

**Jalisco's Cafe**
100 S. Bullard St, Silver City, NM 88061; tel: 505-388-2060
This family-owned restaurant serves platters laden with such homemade Mexican specialties as chile rellenos, enchiladas and excellent sopaipillas, airy pillows of fried dough drizzled

with honey. The burgers are quite good, too. **$**

**Mesón de Mesilla**
1803 Avenida de Mesilla, Mesilla, NM 88046; tel: 800-732-6025 or 505-525-9212
Expect fine dining at this Pueblo-style inn and restaurant near Old Mesilla Plaza. A team of Cordon Bleu chefs turn out artfully presented American and Continental cuisine. Filet mignon, chateaubriand, rack of lamb and cedar-planked salmon are a few favorites. The wine list is exceptional. **$$–$$$**

---

## ALAMOGORDO, RUIDOSO AND ENVIRONS

**Cafe Rio**
2547 Sudderth Dr, Ruidoso, NM 88345; 505-257-7746
First-rate, thick-crusted pizza is made from scratch at this friendly pizzeria/restaurant. Don't expect the usual gooey cheese, sweet sauce and canned topping. The Hawaiian combo has pineapple and Canadian bacon heaped on top, and the "Connoisseur" has parmesan and ricotta cheese, garlic sausage and red onions. Of course, you can custom-design yours any way you like. If pizza and calzone aren't your thing, try the Portuguese green soup (with sausage, kale and potatoes) or the shrimp jambalaya. Desserts are homemade, too. The double layer chocolate cake with chocolate espresso frosting is worth the extra calories. **$**

**Greenhouse Cafe**
103. S. Lincoln, Capitan, NM 88316; tel: 505-354-0373
Located in tiny Capitan, across from Smokey Bear Historical Park, the Greenhouse is a real find. Housed in the former Hotel Chango restaurant – the passion of artist/chef Jerrold Flores, who still lives next door – the Greenhouse offers delicious, natural foods raised in the owners' hydroponic greenhouses. Signature dishes include blackened tilapia, Polynesian-style grilled chicken, and the popular Pacific Rim double

noodle soup. Sunday brunch, lunch and dinner. **$–$$**

**Isaac's Table**
Ellis Store and Country Inn, Hwy 380, MM 98, Box 15, Lincoln, NM 88338; tel: 800-653-6460 or 505-653-4609; www.ellisstore.com
The "Regulators" (as the McSween gang was known) took refuge here during the Lincoln County War, and Billy the Kid was later held captive in the building while waiting for a pardon from Governor Lew Wallace. Now travelers and residents repair to the inn's restaurant for gourmet dining in a refined, country setting. The style is Continental, with a special emphasis on French cuisine. Breakfast, available to guests at the inn, is a treat worth spending the night for. **$$**

**Sundance**
2523 Sudderth Dr, Ruidoso, NM 88345; tel: 505-257-2954
www.sundancesteakandseafood.com
Candlelight and earth-toned decor add a romantic touch to this unexpected island of fine regional cuisine in Ruidoso. The repertoire isn't particularly extensive or innovative, but what the chefs do – including chateaubriand, duck à l'orange and veal chops – they do well. **$$**

**Rebecca's**
The Lodge at Cloudcroft, 1 Corona Place, Box 497, Cloudcroft, NM 88317; tel: 800-395-6343 or 505-682-2566
Named after the resident ghost, Rebecca's serves fine Southwestern and Continental cuisine in a sunny and elegant dining room in the grand Lodge at Cloudcroft. **$$**

---

### CARLSBAD CAVERNS AND THE SOUTHEAST CORNER

**Lucy's Mexicali Restaurant**
701 S. Canal St, Carlsbad, NM 88220; tel: 505-887-7714
If you like your food hot and spicy, stop at this friendly little cantina, where traditional New Mexican dishes are laced with potent local chile. Excellent Margaritas and a

good selection of specialty beers are on hand to put out the fire in your mouth. **$**

**Red Chimney Pit Barbeque**
817 N. Canal St, Carlsbad, NM 88220; tel: 505-885-8744
Fans of Southern-style barbecue won't be disappointed at this little family-run place, where just about everything – chicken, pork ribs, turkey, brisket, ham – is slathered with a sweet and spicy sauce that's been a closely guarded secret for decades. **$**

**Velvet Garter Steakhouse and Saloon**
26 Carlsbad Cavern Hwy, Whites City, NM; tel: 505-785-2291
Prime rib, steak, fried shrimp and a pretty decent selection of Italian food like spinach lasagna and eggplant Parmesan are on the menu at this family-friendly restaurant a short drive from the entrance to Carlsbad Caverns National Park. **$–$$**

# Culture

## Performing Arts

### ALBUQUERQUE

**Adobe Theater**
9813 Fourth St NW, Albuquerque NM; tel: 505-898-9222
New and established comedies, dramas and musicals are offered nearly every month.

**Albuquerque Little Theater**
224 San Pasquale SW, Albuquerque, NM 87104; tel: 505-242-4750
Community theater near Old Town presenting popular comedies, dramas and musicals as well as children's theater.

**KiMo Theatre**
423 Central Ave NW, Albuquerque, NM 87102; tel: 505-768-3544
This landmark 1927 Pueblo/Art Deco palace features a wide variety of live shows, ranging from musical groups of every style to classical theater, comedy troupes, even body-building shows. Any event is worth attending, if only to get a closer look at the theater's magnificent interior.

**New Mexico Ballet Company**
PO Box 21518, Albuquerque, NM 87154; tel: 505-292-4245
Touring companies and original ballet are presented at Popejoy Hall, the KiMo Theatre and other venues.

**New Mexico Jazz Workshop**
3205 Central Ave NE, Ste 104/106, Albuquerque, NM 87106; tel: 505-255-9798
This jazz appreciation organization presents guest artists at venues around the city, jazz and salsa concerts at the Albuquerque Museum Sculpture Garden, and the Madrid Blues Festival in the tiny

town of Madrid on the Turquoise Trail.

**Musical Theater Southwest**
4804 Central SE, Albuquerque NM 87108; tel: 505-262-9301
The area's largest community theater company presents musicals at the Hiland Theater and Popejoy Hall.

**New Mexico Symphony Orchestra**
3301 Menaul Blvd NE, Albuquerque, NM 87190; tel: 505-881-8999 or 800-251-6676
The state's premier symphony presents classical, pops and chamber music at Popejoy Hall and other venues, and is host to a variety of distinguished guest performers.

**Popejoy Hall**
University of New Mexico, Center for the Arts, Albuquerque, NM 87131; tel: 505-277-3824
New Mexico's largest multi-use theater is home to the New Mexico Symphony Orchestra, Musical Theatre Southwest and The Ovation Series, which brings touring Broadway shows, ballet and modern dance companies and other cultural programs to New Mexico.

**Vortex Theater**
2004½ Central Ave SE, Albuquerque, NM 87106; tel: 505-247-8600
A community-run organization that provides a venue for classic, contemporary and experimental theater.

## SANTA FE

**Aspen Santa Fe Ballet**
550-B St. Michael's Dr, Santa Fe, NM 87505; tel: 505-983-5591
A classical and contemporary repertoire is presented at the Lensic Performing Arts Center.

**Camel Rock Casino**
Highway 84/285, Santa Fe, NM 87506; tel: 505-984-8414
Pop stars and comedians appear at this casino about 10 minutes north of Santa Fe. A few recent acts include the Smothers Brothers, Neil Sedaka and Peter, Paul & Mary.

**Lensic Performing Arts Center**
211 W. San Francisco St, Santa Fe, NM 87501; tel: 505-988-1234

This beautifully restored movie palace is now a 850-seat performance center, featuring the Santa Fe Symphony Orchestra and a variety of concerts, lectures, films and theater.

**Maria Benitez Teatro Flamenco**
Radisson Santa Fe, 750 N. San Francisco Dr, Santa Fe, NM 87501; tel: 505-955-8562
One of the world's best flamenco companies rivets audiences with its virtuosity. The company performs late June through August at an intimate nightclub-style theater in the Radisson hotel.

**Santa Fe Chamber Music Festival**
P.O. Box 2227, Santa Fe, NM 87504; tel: 505-983-2075
A summer series of resident and guest performers takes place at the Lensic, Museum of Fine Arts and St. Francis Auditorium.

**Santa Fe Desert Chorale**
PO Box 2813, Santa Fe, NM 87504; tel: 505-988-7505
This chamber choir's repertoire encompasses works in a wide variety of styles from medieval to avant-garde and many world premieres. Performances are staged at the Lensic, St. Francis Cathedral and venues throughout the state.

**Santa Fe Opera**
Hwy 285/84, Santa Fe, NM; tel: 505-986-5900 or 800-280-4654
Classics and new works are performed by renowned artists at this dramatic amphitheater 7 miles (11km) north of Santa Fe. The season runs from late June through August.

**Santa Fe Playhouse**
142 E. DeVargas St, Santa Fe, NM 87504; tel: 505-983-4262
Founded in 1922, the Playhouse is

## Tickets

Tickets for most sport and cultural events can be purchased by phone from ETM Ticketing/Dillard's (800-638-4253), Ticketmaster (480-784-4444) or directly from the box offices (see individual listings).

the oldest continuously running theater company west of the Mississippi. The program includes comedies, musicals, dramas, new work by local playwrights, and the annual *Fiesta Melodrama* satirizing the Santa Fe scene.

**Santa Fe Pro Musica**
PO Box 2091, Santa Fe, NM 87504; tel: 505-988-4640 or 800-960-6680
A series of baroque and classical music featuring well-known guest performers is presented at the Lensic, St. Francis Auditorium and other venues in Santa Fe and Albuquerque. The season runs from September to April.

**Santa Fe Symphony**
P.O. Box 9692, Santa Fe, NM 87504; tel: 505-983-3530
The symphony performs at the Lensic, October to May.

**Theater Grottesco**
Various venues; tel. 505-474-8400 www.theatergrottesco.org
Founded in Paris in 1983, Theater Grottesco began as a touring company and moved to Santa Fe in 1996. Off-beat and decidedly fresh in its outlook, the company focuses on homegrown talent in terms of writers, actors, and designers. During its May through June season, the company performs original full-length and short pieces at various performance spaces around town.

**Theaterwork**
1336 Rufina Circle; tel. 505-471-1799. www.theaterwork.org
This nonprofit theater company has produced more than 70 full-length productions ranging from the classics and operas to original new works by local playwrights. Company members offer classes in acting, design, play writing, and story collecting for adults and children. The season runs September through June. Tickets are very reasonable.

**Wise Fool Puppet Theater**
2778 Agua Fria, Unit BB; tel. 505-992-2588
www.wisefoolnm.org
Founded in 1993, Wise Fool New Mexico continues a long folk tradition of using storytelling,

puppetry, circus arts, and public spectacle to shake up its audiences and get them to view the world around them differently. Performances are participatory, and the public is encouraged to attend hands-on workshops to learn such popular activities as stilt walking and trapeze. A unique experience.

## TAOS

**Music from Angel Fire**
PO Box 502, Angel Fire, NM 87710; tel: 505-377-3233
Classical and jazz series presented at Angel Fire Community Center, Taos Center for the Arts and the Ilfeld Auditorium in Las Vegas.
**Taos Chamber Music Festival**
Box 1879, Taos, NM 87571; tel: 505-776-2388
Associated with the acclaimed Taos School of Music, the series presents performances by world-class musicians at the Taos Community Auditorium.
**Taos Center for the Arts**
133 Paseo del Pueblo Norte, Taos, NM 87571; tel: 505-758-2052
A wide variety of events, from classical music, Chinese acrobats, comedy troupes and local theater to art exhibitions, is presented at this facility near the Plaza.

## Native American Cultures

Cultural sensitivity is vital in Indian Country. Because some Indian people may feel uncomfortable or ambivalent about the presence of outsiders, it is very important to be on your best behavior. Below are a few "dos" and "don'ts" to keep in mind.
● Don't use racist terms. Referring to an Indian as chief, redskin, squaw, buck, Pocahontas, Hiawatha or other off-color terms is highly offensive.
● Abide by all rules and regulations while on Indian land and at Indian events. These may include prohibitions on photography, sketching, taking notes, video and audio recording. In some cases a photo-

graphy fee may be required. If you wish to take an individual's picture, you must ask permission first (a gratuity may be requested).
● Respect all restricted areas. These are usually posted, but ask permission before hiking into wilderness or archaeological areas, driving on back roads, wandering around villages, entering ceremonial structures, or attending events.
● Try to be unobtrusive. Remember that you are a guest at Indian communities and events. Be polite and accommodating. In general, it is better to be too formal than too casual.
● Don't ask intrusive questions or interrupt during Indian ceremonies or dances. Even if an Indian event is not explicitly religious (such as a powwow), it may have a spiritual component. Show the same respect at Indian ceremonies that you would at any other religious service. At all events, try to maintain a low profile. Do not talk loudly, push to the front of a crowd, block other people's view, or sit in chairs that do not belong to you.
● Keep in mind that ceremonies and Pueblo dances aren't performances scheduled for public viewing. You may hear jokes about "Indian time." Prepare for long delays before ceremonies, powwows and other events.

**Acoma Pueblo**
PO Box 309, Acoma, NM 87034; tel: 505-552-6604
**Cochiti Pueblo**
PO Box 70, Cochiti, NM 87072; tel: 505-465-2244
**Isleta Pueblo**
PO Box 1270, Isleta, NM 87022; tel: 505-869-3111
**Jemez Pueblo**
PO Box 100, Jemez Pueblo, NM 87024; tel: 505-834-7359
**Jicarilla Apache Tribe**
PO Box 507, Dulce, NM 87528; tel: 505-759-3242
**Laguna Pueblo**
PO Box 194, Laguna, NM 87026; tel: 505-552-6654
**Mescalero Apache Tribe**
PO Box 176, Mescalero, NM

88340; tel: 505-671-4494
**Nambe Pueblo**
Route 1, Box 117-BB, Santa Fe, NM 87501; tel: 505-455-2036
**Navajo Nation**
PO Box 308, Window Rock, AZ 86515; tel: 928-871-6436
**Picuris Pueblo**
PO Box 127, Penasco, NM 87553; tel: 505-587-2519
**Pojoaque Pueblo**
Route 11, Box 71, Santa Fe, NM 87501; tel: 505-455-2278
**Sandia Pueblo**
PO Box 6008, Bernalillo, NM 87004; tel: 505-867-3317
**San Felipe Pueblo**
PO Box 4339, San Felipe, NM 87001; tel: 505-867-3381
**San Ildefonso Pueblo**
Route 5, Box 315-A, Santa Fe, NM 87501; tel: 505-455-2273
**San Juan Pueblo**
PO Box 1099 ,San Juan Pueblo, NM 87566; tel: 505-852-4400
**Santa Ana Pueblo**
2 Dove Rd, Bernalillo, NM 87004; tel: 505-867-3301
**Santa Clara Pueblo**
PO Box 580, Española, NM 87532; tel: 505-753-7330
**Santo Domingo Pueblo**
PO Box 99, Santo Domingo, NM 87052; tel: 505-465-2214
**Taos Pueblo**
PO Box 1846, Taos, NM 87571; tel: 505-758-9593
**Tesuque Pueblo**
Route 5, Box 360-T, Santa Fe, NM 87501; tel: 505-983-2667
**Zia Pueblo**
135 Capitol Square Dr, Zia Pueblo, NM 87053; tel: 505-867-3304
**Zuni Pueblo**
PO Box 339, Zuni, NM 87327; tel: 505-782-7238

## Indian Casinos

A compact signed by the governor in 1993 allows the state's Indian tribes to establish casinos on their reservations. In addition to gambling, many casinos offer lodging, dining and live entertainment.

**Apache Nugget Casino**
Cuba, NM; tel: 505-759-3242

**Casino Sandia**
I-25 & Tramway Rd, Albuquerque,
NM 87184; tel: 800-526-9366
**Isleta Casino & Resort**
11000 Broadway Blvd SE,
Albuquerque, NM 87105; tel: 877-
747-5382
**Santa Ana Star Casino**
54 Jemez Canyon Dam Rd,
Bernalillo, NM 87004; tel: 505-867-
0000
**Casino Hollywood**
25 Hagan Rd, San Felipe, NM
87001; tel: 877-529-2946
**Oh Kay Casino Resort**
Hwy 68, San Juan Pueblo, NM
87566; tel: 877-829-2865
**Camel Rock Casino**
US 84/285, Santa Fe, NM; tel:
800-462-2635
**Cities of Gold Casino**
10-B Cities of Gold Rd, Santa Fe,
NM 87501; tel: 877-455-3313

## Calendar of Events

*January*
**King's Day Celebration**
Dances at Picuris Pueblo; tel: 505-
587-2519
**Mesilla Valley Balloon Rally**
Las Cruces; tel: 505-523-9206
**Nambe Pueblo Dances**
Buffalo, deer and antelope dances,
Nambe Pueblo; tel: 505-455-2036
**San Ildefonso Feast Day**
Buffalo, deer and comanche
dances, San Ildefonso Pueblo; tel:
505-455-2273
**Taos Pueblo Dances**
Turtle, buffalo or deer dance, Taos
Pueblo; tel: 505-758-1028
**Winter Wine Festival**
Taos Ski Valley; tel: 505-776-2233

*February*
**Candelaria Day Celebration**
Dances at Picuris Pueblo; tel: 505-
587-2519
**Cuchillo Pecan Festival**
Truth or Consequences; tel: 505-
743-3201
**Deer Dances**
San Juan Pueblo; tel: 505-852-
4400
**Gathering of Quilts**
Truth or Consequences; tel: 505-
744-5472
**Winefest**

Tastings from local wineries and
breweries paired with food from
Santa Fe's top restaurants to
benefit Santa e Pro Musica. Silent
auction; tel. 505-988-4640

*March*
**Albuquerque Antiquarian Book Fair**
UNM Conference Center; tel: 505-
291-9653
**Baca Rodeo**
One of the Southwest's largest
rough stock rodeos, Belen; tel: 505-
287-9534
**Rio Grande Arts and Crafts Festival**
State Fairgrounds, Albuquerque; tel:
505-292-7457
**Rockhound Roundup**
Southwest New Mexico State
Fairgrounds, Deming; tel: 505-544-
8643
**St. Joseph's Feast Day**
Harvest and various other dances,
Laguna Pueblo; tel: 505-552-6654

*April*
**Easter Celebrations**
Dances at most Indian pueblos; tel:
505-246-2261
**Gathering of Nations Powwow**
University Arena, Albuquerque; tel:
505-836-2810
**Rattlesnake Round-up**
Otero County Fairgrounds,
Alamogordo; tel: 505-434-0788

*May*
**Cinco de Mayo**
Festivals are held throughout the
state celebrating Mexican liberation
from French occupation.
**Farmington Invitational Balloon Festival**
Farmington; tel: 800-448-1240
**Jemez Red Rocks Arts & Crafts Show**
Jemez Pueblo; tel: 505-834-7235
**New Mexico Wine and Chile Wars**
Doña Ana County Fairgrounds, Las
Cruces; tel: 505-646-4543
**PRCA Rodeo**
Alamogordo; tel: 505-434-0788
**Santa Cruz Feast Day**
Blessings of the Field and Corn
Dance, Taos Pueblo; tel: 505-758-
1028
**Santa Maria Feast Day**
Acoma Pueblo; tel: 800-747-0181

**St. Phillip's Feast Day**
San Felipe Pueblo; tel: 505-867-
3381
**Silver City Blues Festival**
Silver City; tel: 888-758-7289
**Taos Spring Arts Festival**
Art exhibits, musical events,
theatrical performances, film
festivals and readings are held at
venues throughout Taos; tel: 505-
758-3873.

*June*
**Blessings of the Field**
Corn dance, Tesque Pueblo; tel: 505-
983-2667
**Corn Dances**
Santa Ana Pueblo; tel; 505-867-3301
**New Mexico Arts and Crafts Fair**
More than 200 artists and
craftspeople exhibit their work at the
New Mexico State Fairgrounds,
Albuquerque; tel: 505-884-9043
**Pioneer Days Rodeo**
Clovis; tel: 505-763-3435
**Rodeo de Santa Fe**
Santa Fe Rodeo Grounds; tel: 505-
471-4300
**San Antonio Feast Day and Comanche Dance**
Santa Clara Pueblo; tel: 505-753-
7326
**San Juan Pueblo Feast Day**
Buffalo, corn and comanche dances,
Taos Pueblo; tel: 505-852-4400
**Santa Fe Trail Rendezvous**
Raton; tel: 505-327-2029
**St. Anthony's Feast Day**
San Ildefonso Pueblo; tel: 505-455-
2273
**Taos Poetry Circus and World Championship Poetry Bout**
Taos; tel: 505-758-1800
**Wild, Wild West Pro Rodeo**
Silver City; tel: 505-538-3785

*July*
**Annual Art Festival**
Ruidoso; tel: 877-784-3676
**Eight Northern Indian Pueblos Arts & Crafts Fair**
San Ildefonso Pueblo; tel: 505-747-
1593
**Jicarilla Apache Little Beaver Roundup and Rodeo**
Dulce; tel: 505-843-7270
**Mescalero Apache Ceremonial Dances**
Dances, powwow, Native American

food, parade and rodeo, Mescalero Apache Reservation; tel: 505-671-4494

**San Buenaventura Feast Day**
Santo Domingo Pueblo; tel: 505-465-2214

**Santa Ana Feast Day**
Laguna Pueblo; tel: 505-552-6654
Taos Pueblo; tel: 505-758-1028

**Santa Fe International Folk Art Market**
Museum Hill. Worldwide folk artists converge on Milner Plaza for two-day event; tel: 505-476-1203

**Santa Fe Wine Festival**
El Rancho de las Golondrinas, Santa Fe; tel: 505-471-2261

**Santiago Feast Day**
Corn dance, Taos Pueblo; tel: 505-758-1028

**Taos Powwow**
Taos Pueblo; tel: 505-758-1028

**Traditional Spanish Market**
Features the work of more than 300 Hispanic artists and crafts-people in the historic Plaza; tel: 505-982-2226

**Wild Thing Championship Bull Riding**
Red Rock State Park, Gallup; tel: 505-863-5402

*August*
**Antique Old West and Country Show**
Sweeney Center, Santa Fe; tel: 505-992-8929

**Bat Flight Breakfast**
Outdoor breakfast at Carlsbad Caverns as thousands of bats return to the caves, Carlsbad Caverns National Park; tel: 505-785-2232

**Inter-Tribal Indian Ceremonial**
A huge powwow at Red Rock State Park near Gallup, with arts and crafts shows, parades, rodeo and more; tel: 505-722-3829

**Old Lincoln Days**
Lincoln; tel: 505-653-4372

**San Lorenzo Feast Day**
Acoma Pueblo; tel: 505-252-1139
Cochiti Pueblo; tel: 505-465-2244

**Santa Clara Feast Day**
Buffalo, harvest or corn dance, Santa Clara Pueblo; tel: 505-753-7330

**Santa Fe Indian Market**
Santa Fe's Plaza becomes an open-air market at the country's largest exhibition of American Indian arts

and crafts. Book hotels well in advance; tel: 505-983-5220

**Santo Domingo Pueblo Feast Day**
Corn Dance, Santo Domingo Pueblo; tel: 505-465-2214

**Zuni Tribal Fair**
Zuni Pueblo; tel: 505-782-4481

*September*
**Annual Navajo Nation Fair**
Huge event. Rodeo, carnival, parades, intertribal powwow, Miss Navajo Nation pageant, food, concerts; tel: 928-871-6478

**Harvest Dances**
San Juan Pueblo; tel: 505-852-4400

**Hatch Chile Festival**
Hatch; tel: 505-267-4468

**International Bat Festival**
Carlsbad; tel: 505-887-6516

**New Mexico State Fair**
One of the largest fairs in the nation with PRCA rodeo and western recording stars, Albuquerque; tel: 505-265-1791

**New Mexico Wine Festival**
Bernalillo; tel: 505-867-3311

**San Estevan Feast Day and Harvest Dance**
Acoma Pueblo; tel: 505-252-1139

**San Geronimo Feast**
Sunset dance, foot race, pole climbing, social dances and trade fair, Taos Pueblo; tel: 505-758-1028

**Socorro County Fair and Rodeo**
Socorro; tel: 505-835-0424

**Stone Lake Fiesta**
Jicarilla Apache dances, Dulce; tel: 505-843-7270

**Taos Fall Arts Festival**
Concerts, gallery openings, dances, theater. Venues throughout the Taos area; tel: 800-732-8267

**Taos Trade Fair**
Costumed interpreters bring the Spanish colonial and mountain man period to life. La Hacienda de los Martinez; tel: 505-758-4270

*October*
**Albuquerque International Balloon Fiesta**
The world's largest gathering of hot-air balloons is staged over a nine-day festival with a great variety of events; tel: 888-422-7277

**Cowboy Days**
Cowboy music and poetry, chuck-wagon food, dancing, and ranching

demonstrations, New Mexico Farm & Ranch Heritage Museum, Las Cruces; tel: 505-522-4100

**Fall Chile Festival**
Grants; tel: 800-748-2142

**Lincoln County Cowboy Symposium**
Cowboy poets, musicians, chuck wagons and artisans. Ruidoso Downs; tel: 505-653-4372

**Northern Navajo Nation Fair**
Shiprock Fairgrounds; tel: 505-368-1089

**Ruidoso Oktoberfest**
Ruidoso; tel: 877-877-9322

**Southern New Mexico State Fair**
Doña Ana County Fair Grounds Las Cruces; tel: 505-524-8602

**St. Clair Wine Fest**
Deming; tel: 505-546-2674

*November*
**Festival of the Cranes**
Bosque del Apache, Socorro; tel: 505-835-2077

**San Diego Feast Day**
Buffalo, corn, Comanche and deer dances, Tesque Pueblo; tel: 505-983-2667

**Weems Artfest**
More than 250 artists show their work at the State Fairgrounds in Albuquerque; tel: 505-293-6133

*December*
**Canyon Road Farolito Walk**
Farolitos illuminate the streets and houses of Canyon Road, crowded with strollers, musicians and carolers; tel: 505-983-7317

**Christmas Celebrations**
Acoma Pueblo; tel: 505-552-6604
San Idlefonso Pueblo; tel: 505-455-3549
Tesque Pueblo; tel: 505-983-2667
Santa Clara Pueblo; tel: 505-753-7326
Nambe Pueblo; tel: 505-455-2036
Laguna Pueblo; tel: 505-552-6654
San Juan Pueblo; tel: 505-852-4400
Taos Pueblo; tel: 505-758-1028
Zia Pueblo; tel: 505-867-3304
Picuris Pueblo; tel: 505-587-2519

**Winter Spanish Market**
Spanish colonial arts and crafts, as well as modern interpretations, are exhibited at the winter version of this popular arts fair. Sweeney Convention Center, Santa Fe; tel: 505-922-2226

# The Great Outdoors

## NORTHERN NEW MEXICO

**Aztec Ruins National Monument**
84 County Road 2900, Aztec, NM 87410; tel: 505-334-6174

**Bandelier National Monument**
HCR 1, Box 1, Suite 15, Los Alamos, NM 87544; tel: 505-672-3861 (x517) or 505-672-0343

**Capulin Volcano National Monument**
PO Box 40, Capulin, NM 88414; tel: 505-278-2201

**Chaco Culture National Historical Park**
PO Box 220, Nageezi, NM 87037; tel: 505-786-7014

**Clayton Lake State Park**
3 Mountain View Road, Clayton, NM 88415; tel. 505-374-0243

**Cimarron Canyon State Park**
PO Box 185, Eagle Nest, NM 87718; tel: 505-377-6271

**Coyote Creek State Park**
PO Box 477, Guadalupita, NM 87722; tel: 505-387-2328

**El Vado State Park**
PO Box 367, NM 87575; tel: 505-588-7247

**Fenton Lake State Park**
455 Fenton Lake Rd, Jemez Springs, NM 87025; tel: 505-829-3630

**Fort Union National Monument**
PO Box 127, Watrous, NM 87753; tel: 505-425-8025

**Heron Lake State Park**
PO Box 159, Los Ojos, NM 87551; tel: 505-588-7470

**Hyde Memorial State Park**
740 Hyde Park Rd, Santa Fe, NM 87501; tel: 505-983-7175

**Morphy Lake**
PO Box 477, Guadalupita, NM 87722; tel: 505-387-2328

**Navajo Lake State Park**
1448 NM 511 #1, Navajo Dam, NM 87419; tel: 505-632-2278

**Pecos National Historical Park**
PO Box 418, Pecos, NM 87552; tel: 505-757-6414

**Storrie Lake State Park**
HC33, Box 109, Las Vegas, NM 87701; tel: 505-425-7278

**Sugarite Canyon State Park**
HCR 63, Box 386, Raton, NM 87740; tel: 505-445-5607

## CENTRAL NEW MEXICO

**Bluewater Lake State Park**
PO Box 3419, Prewitt, NM 87045; tel: 505-876-2391

**Conchas Lake State Park**
PO Box 976, Conchas Dam, NM 88416; tel: 505-868-2270

**El Malpais National Monument**
P.O. Box 939, Grants, NM 87020; tel: 505-285-4641

**El Morro National Monument**
Route 2, Box 43, Ramah, NM 87321; tel: 505-783-4226

**Manzano Mountains State Park**
HC-66, Box 202, Mountainair, NM 87036; tel: 505-344-7240

**Oasis State Park**
1891 Oasis Rd, Portales, NM 88130; tel: 505-356-5331

**Petroglyph National Monument**
6001 Unser Blvd NW, Albuquerque, NM 87120; tel: 505-899-0205

**Salinas Pueblo Missions National Monument**
P.O. Box 517, Mountainair, NM 87036; tel: Abo, (505) 847-2400; Gran Quivira, (505) 847-2770; Quarai, (505) 847-2290

**Santa Rosa Lake State Park**
PO Box 384, Santa Rosa, NM 88433; tel: 505-472-3110

**Sumner Lake State Park**
HC 64, Box 125, Fort Sumner, NM 88119; tel: 505-355-2541

**Ute Lake State Park**
PO Box 52, Logan, NM 88426; tel: 505-487-2284

**Villanueva State Park**
PO Box 40, Villanueva, NM 87583; tel: 505-421-2957

## SOUTHERN NEW MEXICO

**Bottomless Lakes State Park**
HC 12, Box 1200, Roswell, NM 88201; tel: 505-624-6058

**Brantley Lake State Park**
PO Box 2288, Carlsbad, NM 88221; tel: 505-457-2384

**Caballo Lake State Park**
PO Box 32, Caballo, NM 8793; tel: 505-743-3942

**Carlsbad Caverns National Park**
3225 National Parks Highway, Carlsbad, NM 87747; tel: 505-785-2232

**City of Rocks State Park**
PO Box 50, Faywood, NM 88034; tel: 505-536-2800

**Elephant Butte Lake State Park**
PO Box 13, Elephant Butte, NM 87935; tel: 505-744-5923

**Gila Cliff Dwellings National Monument**
HC 68 Box 100, Silver City, NM 88061; tel: 505-536-9461

**Environmental Ethics**

Remember the old saying: "Take nothing but pictures, leave nothing but footprints." The goal of low-impact/no-impact backpacking is to leave the area in the same condition as you found it, if not better. If you're camping in the backcountry, don't break branches, level the ground or alter the landscape in any way. Make fires in designated places only. Otherwise, use a portable camping stove. When nature calls, answer with a trowel: dig a hole 6 inches (15cm) deep and at least 200 ft (60 meters) from water, campsites and trails. Take away all trash, including toilet paper.

### Wildlife

Never approach wild animals. Use binoculars, a spotting scope or a camera with telephoto lens to get a good look. Don't try to feed or touch wildlife, not even the "cute" ones like chipmunks, squirrels and prairie dogs (they may carry diseases). Don't try to move animals into a better position by calling or herding them.

## National Park Passes

If you plan to visit several parks on your vacation, consider buying a 12-month **National Park Pass**. The pass costs $50 and covers entrance fees to all National Park Service areas but does not cover camping fees or other use fees, such as cave tours.

The **Golden Age Passport** is available to U.S. citizens who are age 62 or older. There is a one-time charge of $10, but the pass is good for life. It provides free entrance to most federal recreation areas and provides a 50% discount on use fees, such as camping fees.

The **Golden Access Passport** is available to U.S. citizens who have a permanent disability. The pass is free and is good for life. It provides free entrance to most federal recreation areas and provides a 50% discount on use fees.

Passes are available at parks that charge an entrance fee.

**Leasburg Dam State Park**
PO Box 6, Radium Springs, NM 88054; tel: 505-524-4068
**Living Desert Zoo and Gardens**
PO Box 100, Carlsbad, NM 88221; tel: 505-887-5516
**Oliver Lee Memorial State Park**
409 Dog Canyon, Alamogordo, NM 88310; tel: 505-437-8284
**Pancho Villa State Park**
PO Box 450, Columbus, NM 88029; tel: 505-531-2711
**Percha Dam State Park**
PO Box 32, Caballo, NM 87931; tel: 505-743-3942
**Rio Grande Nature Center State Park**
2901 Candelaria Road NW, Albuquerque, NM 87107; tel. 505-344-7240
**Rockhound State Park**
PO Box 1064, Deming, NM 88030; tel: 505-546-6182
**White Sands National Monument**
PO Box 1086, Holloman AFB, NM 87747; tel: 505-679-2599 or 505-479-6124

# Tours and Outfitters

## Tour Operators

**Access Santa Fe/Aboot About Santa Fe**
624 Galisteo #32, Santa Fe, NM 87501; tel: 505-988-2774; www.accesssantafe.com. Walking tours of Santa Fe.
**Destination Southwest**
20 First Plaza Galeria NW, Ste 212, Albuquerque, NM 87102; tel: 505-766-9068 or 800-999-3109; www.destinationsouthwest.com. Guided multiday tours of New Mexico and the Southwest.
**Far Horizons Archaeological & Cultural Trips**
PO Box 2546, San Anselmo, CA 94979; tel: 415-482-8400; www.farhorizon.com. Archaeological tours of Chaco Canyon and northern New Mexico.
**Great Southwest Adventures**
PO Box 31151, Santa Fe, NM 87594; tel: 505-455-2700; www.swadventures.com. Guided tours of northern New Mexico.
**Largo Navajoland Tours**
PO Box 3244, Gallup, NM 87305; tel: 505-863-0050 or 888-726-9084; www.navajolandtours.com
**Outback Tours**
PO Box 32774, Santa Fe, NM 87594; tel: 888-772-3274; www.outbacktours.com. Half-, full-or multiple-day Jeep "safaris."
**Pathways Customized Tours**
161F Calle Ojo Feliz, Santa Fe, NM 87505; tel: 505-982-5382; www.santafepathways.com. Tours of cliff dwellings and Indian pueblos, Taos, Georgia O'Keeffe Country and Santa Fe.
**Royal Road Tours**
826 Camino del Monte Rey, Ste A-3, Santa Fe, NM 87505; tel: 505-982-

4512; www.royalroadtours.com. Southwest tours and education programs.
**Rojo Tours**
PO Box 15744, Santa Fe, NM 87505; tel: 505-474-8333; www.rojotours.com. Customized tours of New Mexico.

## Hot-air Ballooning

**Castle Dawn Ballooning**
12213 Modesto NE, Albuquerque, NM 87122; tel: 505-280-0849
**Sweet Escape Hot Air Balloon Rides**
216 Dogwood Trail SE, Rio Rancho, NM 87124; tel: 505-891-7634 or 800-385-4453
**Braden's Beautiful Balloons**
PO Box 30584, Albuquerque, NM 87190; tel: 505-261-8249 or 800-367-6625
**Hot Alternatives & Outdoor Balloons**
3103 May Circle, Rio Rancho, NM 87124; tel: 505-269-1174 or 800-322-2262
**Rainbow Ryders**
11520 San Bernardino NE, Albuquerque, NM 87124; tel: 505-823-1111 or 800-725-2477
**Skyspan Adventures Balloon Rides**
tel: 505-250-2300
**World Balloon**
4800 Eubank NE, Albuquerque, NM 87111; tel: 505-293-6800

## Outdoor Adventure

**Big River Raft Trips**
Box 16-D, Pilar, NM 87531; tel: 505-758-9711 or 800-748-3746 Whitewater rafting through the Rio Grande Gorge.

## Backcountry Permits

Backcountry travel on public lands may require a permit, and there may be quotas on the number of visitors. To find out if permits are necessary, inquire at state or national parks well in advance of your arrival. For trips on National Forest or BLM land, contact the New Mexico Public Lands Information Center, 1474 Rodeo Rd, Santa Fe, NM 87505; tel: 505-438-7542.

**Embudo Station**
PO Box 154, Embudo, NM 87531; tel; 505-852-4707 or 800-852-4707. Pleasant day trips on the Rio Grande.

**Enchanted Lands Enterprise**
PO Box 1222, Los Alamos, NM 87544; tel: 505-661-8687. Mountain biking tour of the Enchanted Circle in the Sangre de Cristo Mountains north of Taos.

**Far Flung Adventures**
PO Box 707, El Prado, NM 87529; tel: 800-359-2627. Half-day and overnight trips on the Rio Grande and Rio Chama.

**Known World**
tel: 800-983-7756. Guided white-water rafting, mountain biking, fly fishing and hiking adventures.

**Kokopelli Rafting Adventures**
541 W. Cordova Rd, Santa Fe, NM 87501; tel: 800-879-9035. Half-day to eight-day expeditions on the Rio Grande and Rio Chama.

**Los Rios River Runners**
PO Box 2734, Taos NM 87571; tel: 505-776-8854 or 800-544-1181. Rio Grande raft trips in Taos Box and the lower gorge on the Rio Grande and on the Rio Chama.

**Native Sons Adventures**
1033-A Paseo del Pueblo Sur, Taos, NM 87571; tel: 505-758-9342 or 800-753-7559. Rafting on the Rio Grande as well as mountain biking and snowmobiling in the Sangre de Cristo Mountains.

**New Mexico Mountain Bike Adventures**
PO Box 443, Cerillos, NM 87010; tel: 505-474-0074; www.bikefun.com. One-day and overnight biking trips in the Santa Fe area and throughout the state.

**Rio Grande River Tours**
PO Box 2769, Ranchos de Taos, NM 87557; tel: 505-758-0762 or 800-525-4966. Trips in Taos Box, Rio Grande Gorge and "the Racecourse" from three hours to a full day.

**Roadrunner Tours**
PO Box 274 (Hwy 434), Angel Fire, NM 87710; tel: 800-377-6416; www.rtours.com. Horseback riding tours of Santa Fe County, the Abiquiu area, the Sangre de Cristo Mountains and the Jemez Mountains.

**Southwest Safaris**
PO Box 945, Santa Fe, NM 87504; tel: 505-988-4246 or 800-842-4246. Scenic air and land adventures in New Mexico and the Southwest.

**U-Trail**
PO Box 66 (Hwy 180 ), Glenwood, NM 88039; tel: 505-539-2426 or 800-887-2453. Pack trips in the Gila Wilderness.

**Wild Earth Llama Adventures**
54 Ron's Rd, Santa Fe, NM 87505; tel: 800-758-5262. Day hikes and guided multi-day wilderness treks for all ages and fitness levels.

**WingsWest Birding Tours**
2599 Camino Chueco, Santa Fe, NM 87505; tel: 800-583-6928. Customized birding adventures year-round throughout New Mexico.

**Wolf Whitewater**
4626 Palo Alto SE, Albuquerque NM 87108; tel: 505-262-1099. Canoe and kayak lessons as well as guided raft trips on the Rio Grande.

## Historic Railways

**Cumbres & Toltec Scenic Railroad**
Hwy 17, Chama, NM 87520; tel: 800-724-5451

**Denver & Rio Grande Western Railroad**
Española Valley Chamber of Commerce, 417 Big Rock Center, Española, NM 87532; tel: 505-753-2831

**Sante Fe Southern Railroad**
410 S. Guadalupe St, Santa Fe, NM 87501; tel: 888-989-8600

# Sport

## Spectator Sports

### BASEBALL

The AAA **Albuquerque Isotopes** (1601 Avenida Cesar Chavez SE, Albuquerque, NM 87106; tel: 505-924-2255) play at newly renovated Isotopes Park.

### UNM LOBOS

The other big name in sports is the **University of New Mexico Lobos**. The Lobos play **baseball** at Isotopes Park or University Stadium, **basketball** at the University Arena (better known as "The Pit") and **football** at University Stadium. Call 505-925-5627 for information and tickets.

### HOCKEY

The New Mexico **Scorpions** of the Central Hockey League play at Tingley Coliseum (New Mexico State Fairgrounds, Central Ave and Louisiana Blvd, Albuquerque). Call 505-881-7825 for information and tickets.

### AUTO RACING

**Aztec Speedway**
Hwy 544, Aztec, NM; tel: 505-334-2023 or 505-327-6314; www.aztecspeedway.com

**Cardinal Motor Speedway**
1 Mile North of Eunice on Loop 18, Eunice, NM 88231; www.cardinalmotorspeedway.com

**Duke City Raceway**
301 Murry Rd SE, Albuquerque, NM 87105; www.dukecity raceway.com

**Southern New Mexico Speedway**
11 miles west of Las Cruces at exit
132 off I-10; tel: 505-524-7913 or
800-658-9650;
www.snmspeedway.com
**Sandia Motorsports**
PO Box 66150, Albuquerque, NM
87193-6150; tel: 505-352-8888;
www.sandiamotorsports.com
**Sertoma Speedway**
PO Box 4126, Alamogordo, NM
88310; tel: 505-585-8662;
www.sertomaspeedway.com

## HORSE AND DOG RACING

Horse racing is held at **Downs at
Albuquerque** (201 California St NE,
Albuquerque; tel: 505-266-5555);
**Sunland Park** (101 Futurity Dr,
Sunland Park; tel: 505-589-1131);
**Sunray Park and Casino** (39 Rd
5568, Farmington; tel: 505-566-
1200); **Ruidoso Downs** (US 70,
Ruidoso; tel: 505-378-4431)

## Participant Sports

### BICYCLING

Opportunities abound for mountain
and road biking in New Mexico.
Several organizations provide
information on trails, races, group
tours and other events. The **New
Mexico Bicycle Coalition**
(www.bikenm.org) promotes cycling
throughout the state and sponsors a
variety of events. Regional cycling
clubs include the **Taos Cycle Club**
(www.taoscycleclub.com); **Los
Alamos County Cyclist's Coalition**
(www.labikes.org); **Mesilla Valley
Bicycle Coalition** (www.hipnt.com);
and **Road Runners Cycling Club**
(www.tourdela.home.mindspring.com).

### FISHING

Fishing licenses are required and
can be obtained from the **New
Mexico Department of Game and
Fish** (408 Galisteo Street, Santa
Fe, NM 87501; tel. 505-827-7911
or toll-free 800-862-9310;
www.gmfsh.state.nm.us). Fishing on
Indian reservations requires tribal
permits.

## GOLF

There are scores of public and
private golf courses as well as full-
fledged golf resorts throughout the
state. Some of the better courses
are listed below.

### NORTHERN NEW MEXICO
**Angel Fire Country Club**, Angel Fire;
tel: 505-377-6401. 18 holes, par
72
**Hidden Valley Country Club**, Aztec;
tel: 505-334-3248. 18 holes
**Las Campanas de Santa Fe**, 218
Camino la Tierra, Santa Fe; tel:
505-992-6420. 18 holes, par 72
**Los Alamos Golf Course**, 4250
Diamond Dr, Los Alamos; tel: 505-
662-8139. 18 holes, par 72
**Marty Sanchez Links de Santa Fe**,
Caja del Rio Rd, Santa Fe; tel: 505-
955-4470. 18 holes, par 72
**Piñon Hills Golf Course**, 2101
Sunrise Pkwy, Farmington; tel: 505-
326-6066. 18 holes, par 72
**San Juan Country Club**, 5775
Country Club Dr, Farmington; tel:
505-327-4451. 18 holes, par 70
**Santa Fe Country Club**, Airport Rd,
Santa Fe; tel: 505-471-0601. 18
holes, par 72
**Taos Country Club**, 54 Golf Course
Dr, Ranchos de Taos; tel: 505-758-
7300. 18 holes, par 72
**Towa Golf Resort**, 17746 US Hwy
84/285; tel: 505-455-9000. 18-
hole, par 72

### CENTRAL NEW MEXICO
**Albuquerque Country Club**, 601
Laguna Blvd SW, Albuquerque; tel:
505-243-7156. 18 holes, par 70
**Arroyo del Oso Golf Course**, 7001
Osuna Rd NE, Albuquerque. 18
holes, par 72
**Championship Course at University
of New Mexico**, 3601 University
Blvd SE, Albuquerque; tel: 505-277-
4546. 27 holes
**Coyote del Malpais Golf Course**,
2001 Golf Course Rd, Grants; tel:
505-285-5544. 18 holes, par 72
**Four Hills Country Club**, 911 Four
Hills Rd, Albuquerque; tel: 505-299-
9555. 18 holes, par 72
**Gallup Municipal Golf Course**,
1109 Susan St, Gallup: tel: 505-
863-9224. 18 holes, par 72

**Isleta Eagle**, 4001 NM 47,
Albuquerque; tel: 505-869-0950.
27 holes
**Ladera Golf Course**, 3401 Ladera
Dr NW, Albuquerque; tel: 505-836-
4449. 18 holes, par 72
**Los Altos Golf Course**, 9717
Copper Ave NE, Albuquerque; tel:
505-298-1897. 27 holes, par 71
**Paradise Hills Golf Club**, 10035
Country Club Ln NW, Albuquerque;
tel: 505-898-7001. 18 holes, par 72
**Pueblo de Cochiti Golf Course**,
1399 Cochiti Hwy, Cochiti Lake; tel:
505-465-2239. 18 holes, par 72
**Rio Rancho Golf/Country Club**, 500
Country Club Dr SE, Rio Rancho; tel:
505-892-8440. 27 holes
**Santa Ana Golf Course**, 288 Prairie
Star Rd, Bernalillo. 27 holes

### SOUTHERN NEW MEXICO
**Alto Lakes Country Club**, Country
Club Dr, Alto; tel: 505-336-4231.
18 holes, par 71
**Cree Meadows Country Club**, 310
Country Club Dr, Ruidoso; tel: 505-
257-5815. 18 holes, par 71
**Desert Lakes Golf Course**, 2351
Hamilton Rd, Alamogordo; tel: 505-
437-0290. 18 holes, par 72
**Hobbs Country Club**, Carlsbad Hwy
West, Hobbs; tel: 505-393-5212.
18 holes, par 72
**Inn of the Mountain Gods Golf
Course**, Mescalero; tel: 505-257-
5141. 18 holes
**Lake Carlsbad Golf Course**, 901
Muscatel Ave, Carlsbad; tel: 505-
885-5444. 18 holes, par 72
**Las Cruces Country Club**, 2700 N.
Main St, Las Cruces; tel: 505-526-
8731. 18 holes, par 72
**Links of Sierra Blanca**, 105 Sierra
Blanca Dr, Ruidoso; tel: 505-258-
5330. 18 holes, par 72
**The Lodge at Cloudcroft Golf
Course**, 1 Corona Pl, Cloudcroft;
tel: 505-682-2098. 9 holes, par 34
**Lovington Country Club**, E. Star
Route, Lovington; tel: 505-396-
6619. 18 holes, par 70
**Ocotillo Park Golf Course**, N.
Lovington Hwy, Hobbs; tel: 505-397-
9297. 18 holes, par 72
**Picacho Hills Country Club**, 6861
Via Campestre, Las Cruces; tel:
505-523-2556. 18 holes, par 72
**Riverside Country Club**, 1700 W.

Orchard Ln, Carlsbad; tel: 505-885-4253. 18 holes
**Scott Park Memorial Municipal Golf Course**, Silver City; tel: 505-538-5041. 18 holes, par 72
**Sonoma Ranch Golf Course**, 1274 Golf Course Rd, Las Cruces; tel: 505-521-1818. 18 holes, par 72
**Spring River Golf Course**, 1612 W. Eighth St, Roswell; tel: 505-622-9506. 18 holes, par 71

## TENNIS

Public tennis courts are available in just about every city and large town in New Mexico, although avid players may find it more convenient to stay at a hotel with courts. Contact the city or county Parks and Recreation Department for locations and hours. For information on tournaments, lessons and leagues, contact the **U.S. Tennis Association Southwest Section** (602-956-6855; www.southwest.usta.com).

## KAYAKING, CANOEING AND RAFTING

New Mexico offers an abundance of both whitewater and flatwater paddling. For information on routes and conditions, consult the agency that manages the river or lake. Other sources of information are paddling clubs and outdoor-gear retailers. For more information, contact the **Adobe Whitewater Club** (PO Box 3835, Albuquerque, NM, 87190; www.adobeww.org),

## SKIING

New Mexico has six downhill skiing areas:
**Angel Fire**
PO Drawer B, Angel Fire, NM 87710; tel: 800-633-7463; www.angelfireresort.com
**Ski Rio**
Costilla, NM 87524; tel: 505-758-7707; www.skirio.com
**Ski Santa Fe**
2209 Brothers Rd, Santa Fe, NM 87505; tel: 505-982-4429; www.skisantafe.com
**Red River**

PO Box 900, Red River, NM 87558; tel: 505-754-2223; www.redriverskiarea.com
**Sipapu**
HC 65, Route Box 29, Vadito, NM 87579; tel: 800-587-2240; www.sipapunm.com
**Ski Apache**
P.O. Box 220, Ruidoso, NM 88355; tel: snow 505-257-9001, accommodations 800-253-2255, disabled skiers 505-336-4416; www.skiapache.com
**Taos Ski Valley**
P.O. Box 90, Taos Ski Valley, NM 87525; tel: 505-776-2291; skitaos.org

### NORDIC SKIING
**Enchanted Forest** (417 W. Main St, Red River, NM 87558; tel: 505-754-2374; www.enchantedforestxc.com) offers more than 30 groomed cross-country trails on 1,400 acres (566 hectares) as well as ski instruction and equipment rentals.

# Further Reading

## Nonfiction

**HISTORY**
*Anasazi America: 17 Centuries on the Road from Center Place*, by David E. Stuart. Albuquerque: University of New Mexico Press, 2000.
*Ancient Ruins of the Southwest: An Archaeological Guide*, by David Grant Noble. Flagstaff: Northland Publishing, 2000.
*The Architecture of the Southwest*, by Trent Elwood Sanford. Tucson: University of Arizona Press, 1997.
*Art of the Golden West*, by Alan Axelrod. New York: Abbeville Press, 1990.
*Billy the Kid: A Short and Violent Life*, by Robert M. Utley. Lincoln: University of Nebraska Press, 1991.
*The Chaco Meridian: Centers of Political Power in the American Southwest*, by Stephen Lekson. Walnut Creek: Altamira Press, 1999.
*The Book of the Navajo*, by Raymond Friday Locke. Los Angeles: Mankind Publishing, 1976.
*A Convenient Spy: Wen Ho Lee and the Politics of Nuclear Espionage*, by Dan Stober and Ian Hoffman. New York: Simon & Schuster, 2002.
*Down the Santa Fe Trail and into Mexico*, by Susan Shelby Magoffin. New Haven: Yale University Press, 1926.
*Great River: The Rio Grande in North American History*, by Paul Horgan. New York: Harcourt Brace Co, 1971.
*A History of the Jews in New Mexico*, by Henry J. Tobias. Albuquerque: University of New Mexico Press, 1992.
*An Illustrated History of New Mexico*, by Thomas E. Chavez. Albuquerque: University of New Mexico Press, 1992.
*Indian Rock Art of the Southwest*, by Polly Shaafsma. University of

New Mexico Press, 1986.
***The Making of the Atomic Bomb***,
by Richard Rhodes. New York:
Simon & Schuster, 1995.
***Mythmakers of the West: Shaping
America's Imagination***, by John A.
Murray. Flagstaff: Northland
Publishing, 2001.
***New Mexico: An Interpretive
History***, by Marc Simmons.
Albuquerque: University of New
Mexico Press, 1988.
***Pueblos, Villages, Forts, and Trails:
A Guide to New Mexico's Past***, by
David Grant Noble. Albuquerque:
University of New Mexico Press.
1994.
***Reopening the American West***, by
Hal K. Rothman, ed. Tucson:
University of Arizona, 1998.
***Turn Left at the Sleeping Dog:
Scripting the Santa Fe Legend
from 1920-1955***, by John Pen La
Farge. Albuquerque: University of
New Mexico Press, 2001.

## CULTURE

***Artists of the Canyons and
Caminos: Santa Fe, the Early
Years***, by Sarah Nestor and Edna
Robertson. Santa Fe: Ancient City
Press, 1976.
***The House at Otowi Bridge: The
Story of Edith Warner and Los
Alamos***, by Peggy Pond Church.
Albuquerque: University of New
Mexico Press, 1979.
***Café Pasqual's Cookbook: Spirited
Recipes from Santa Fe***, by
Katherine Kagel. San Francisco:
Chronicle Books, 1993.
***Cinema Southwest: An Illustrated
Guide to the Movies and Their
Locations***, by John A. Murray.
Flagstaff: Northland Publishing,
2000.
***Dancing Gods***, by Erna Ferguson.
Albuquerque: University of New
Mexico, 1931.
***Edge of Taos Desert: An Escape to
Reality***, by Mabel Dodge Luhan.
Albuquerque: University of New
Mexico Press, 1987.
***From the Faraway Nearby: Georgia
O'Keeffe as Icon***, edited by Ellen
Bradbury and Christopher Merrill.
Albuquerque: University of New
Mexico Press, 1998.
***From This Earth: The Ancient Art***

***of Pueblo Pottery***, by Stewart
Peckham. Santa Fe: Museum of
New Mexico Press, 1992.
***Heaven's Window: A Journey
Through Northern New Mexico***, by
Michael Wallis and Jack Parsons.
Portland: Graphic Arts Center
Publishing Co., 2001.
***The Legacy of Maria Martinez***, by
Richard L. Spivey. Santa Fe:
Museum of New Mexico Press,
2003.
***Low 'n Slow: Lowriding in New
Mexico***, by Jack Parsons and
Carmella Padilla. Santa Fe:
Museum of New Mexico Press,
1999.
***Masked Gods***, by Frank Waters.
Athens: Swallow Press, 1950.
***The People: Indians of the
American Southwest***, by Stephen
Trimble. Santa Fe: School of
American Research Press, 1993.
***Utopian Vistas: The Mabel Dodge
Luhan House and American
Counterculture***, by Lois P. Rudnick.
Albuquerque: University of New
Mexico Press, 1998.

## ESSAYS

***America, New Mexico***, by Robert
Leonard Reid. Tucson: University of
Arizona Press, 1998.
***Benigna's Chimayo: Cuentos from
the Old Plaza***, by Don J. Usner.
Santa Fe: Museum of New Mexico
Press, 2001.
***Best of the West: An Anthology of
Classic Writing from the American
West***, edited by Tony Hillerman.
New York, Harper Collins, 1991.
***Dancing to Pay the Light Bill:
Essays on New Mexico and the
Southwest***, by Jim Sagel. Santa Fe:
Red Crane Books, 1991.
***Edge of Taos Desert: An Escape to
Reality***, by Mabel Dodge Luhan.
Albuquerque: University of New
Mexico Press, 1987.
***A Garlic Testament***, by Stanley
Crawford. New York: HarperCollins,
1992.
***Getting Over the Color Green:
Contemporary Environmental
Literature of the Southwest***, Scott
Slovic, ed. Tucson: University of
Arizona Press, 2001.
***New Mexico, Rio Grande and other
Essays***, by Tony Hillerman. New

York: HarperPerennial, 1993.
***A Sand County Almanac and
Sketches Here and There***, by Aldo
Leopold. New York: Oxford
University Press, 1949.
***Songs of the Fluteplayer: Seasons
of Life in the Southwest***, by
Sharman Apt Russell. New York:
Addison Wesley, 1991.
***The West: A Treasury of Art and
Literature***, edited by T.H. Watkins
and Joan Watkins. New York: Hugh
Lauter Levin Associates, 1994.

## TRAVEL

***From Santa Fe to O'Keeffe
Country: A Journey Through the
Soul of New Mexico***, by Rhoda
Barkan and Peter Sinclaire. Santa
Fe: Ocean Tree Books/Adventure
Roads Travel, 2003.
***Ghost Towns of the American
West***, by Bill O'Neal. Lincolnwood,
IL: Publications International, 1995.
***The Guide to National Parks of the
Southwest***, by Nicky Leach. Tucson:
Southwest Parks & Monuments
Association, 1992.
***The Hiker's Guide to New Mexico***,
by Laurence Parent. Helena, MT:
Falcon Press, 1991.
***The Mysterious Lands: A Naturalist
Explores the Four Great Deserts of
the Southwest***, by Ann H. Zwinger.
Tucson: University of Arizona, 1989.
***New Mexico's Best***, by Richard
Mahler. Golden, CO: Fulcrum
Publishing, 1996.
***New Mexico's Wilderness Areas***,
by Bob Julyan. Englewood, CO:
Westcliffe Publishers, 1998.
***Only in Santa Fe***, by Susan Hazen-
Hammond. Stillwater, MN: Voyageur
Press, 1992.
***A Sense of Mission: Historic
Churches of the Southwest***, by
David Wakely and Thomas A. Drain.
San Francisco: Chronicle Books,
1994.
***The Roadside Geology of New
Mexico***, by Halka Chronic. Missoula,
MT: Mountain Press, 1987.
***The Roadside History of New
Mexico***, by Francis L. Fugate and
Roberta B. Fugate. Missoula, MT:
Mountain Press, 1989.

## Fiction & Poetry

**Bless Me, Ultima,** by Rudolfo Anaya. New York: Warner Editions, 1995.

**Ceremony,** by Leslie Marmon Silko. New York: Penguin Books, 1988.

**The Dance Hall of the Dead**, by Tony Hillerman. New York: Harper & Row, 1973.

**The Dark Wind**, by Tony Hillerman. New York: Harper & Row, 1982.

**Death Comes for the Archbishop,** by Willa Cather. New York: Knopf, Inc., 1927.

**The Delight Makers: A Novel of Prehistoric Pueblo Indians,** by Adolph Bandelier. New York: Harcourt Brace Jovanovich, 1890.

**House Made of Dawn,** by N. Scott Momaday. New York: Perennial Books, 1999.

**Loving Pedro Infante,** by Denise Chavez. New York: Farrar Strauss Giroux, 2000.

**The Man Who Killed the Deer,** by Frank Waters. Athens, OH: Swallow Press, 1971.

**The Milagro Beanfield War,** by John Nichols. New York: Ballantine Books, 1976.

**Red Earth: Poems of New Mexico,** edited by Alice Corbin, Lois Rudnick and Ellen Zieselman. Santa Fe: Museum of New Mexico Press, 2003.

**Red Sky at Morning,** by Richard Bradford. Philadelphia: Lippincott, 1968.

**Skinwalkers,** by Tony Hillerman. New York: Harper & Row, 1987.

**A Thief of Time,** by Tony Hillerman. New York: Harper & Row. 1988.

**Woven Stone,** by Simon Ortiz. Tucson: University of Arizona, 1992.

## Movies/Videos

**All the Pretty Horses**, 1999. Billy Bob Thornton uses the area around Las Vegas as the backdrop for this adaptation of Cormac McCarthy's dark Western epic.

**Butch Cassidy and the Sundance Kid**, 1968. Paul Newman and Robert Redford play lovable outlaws in this sweet buddy film, shot partly in Taos and Chama.

**Contact**, 1997. Jodie Foster plays an astronomer who detects a message from aliens at the Very Large Array in this adaptation of a Carl Sagan novel.

**Easy Rider**, 1969. Anti-heroes Peter Fonda and Dennis Hopper rumble through Santa Fe and Taos in this counterculture classic.

**Indian Day School**, 1898. Thomas Alva Edison was responsible for the first movie made in New Mexico, a brief glimpse of Indian school-children at Isleta Pueblo.

**Lonesome Dove**, 1989. Locations throughout the state, including Angel Fire, Bonanza Creek Ranch, Cook Ranch, San Ildefonso Pueblo and Santa Fe, appear in this television miniseries, an adaptation of Larry McMurtry's epic novel, starring Robert Duvall and Tommy Lee Jones.

**The Milagro Beanfield War**, 1988. Robert Redford produced this film, based on a John Nichols novel and shot in Truchas. Gorgeous scenery, evocative cinematography and a captivating story capture the spirit of northern New Mexico's hispanic culture.

**Natural Born Killers**, 1994. Woody Harrelson and Juliette Lewis are the killers in question in Oliver Stone's deranged road picture, with location shots at Albuquerque, Gallup, Shiprock and the Rio Grande Gorge Bridge in Taos.

**Silverado**, 1985. This wry Western send-up starring Kevin Kline, Kevin Costner, John Cleese and Brian Dennehy was filmed at two "movie ranches," the Cook and Eaves Ranches, in northern New Mexico.

**White Sands**, 1992. The snowy dunes of White Sands National Monument provide a beguiling backdrop to this murder mystery, featuring Willem Dafoe.

**Wild Wild West**, 1999 . Will Smith and Kevin Kline try to breathe life into an old television series in this Western fantasy. Much of the Cook Ranch movie set was destroyed by explosions during the filming.

## Other Insight Guides

Nearly 200 companion titles to this volume cover every continent. More than 40 of the titles are devoted to the US and include:

**Insight Guide: Arizona and the Grand Canyon** covers every corner of the state, from the canyon country of the north to the urban pleasures of Phoenix and the Valley of the Sun.

**Insight Guide: Colorado** covers America's alpine wonderland, with its world-class ski resorts, picturesque mountain towns, and wilderness parks, plus Denver, the Mile High City.

**Insight Guide: American Southwest** provides a stunningly illustrated overview of Arizona, New Mexico, Utah and Las Vegas, and includes features on the region's history, culture, flora and fauna.

**Insight Guide: US National Parks West**, written by park rangers and other experts, ranges from Texas to North Dakota, from California to Colorado, and then on to the national parks of Alaska and Hawaii. It includes top nature photography.

# ART & PHOTO CREDITS

**Steve Bruno** 50
**Richard Cummins** 81, 135, 136B, 153B, 233, 234B, 293, 294BR
**Kevin Downey** 111, 118–119, 301
**Ken Gallard** 58, 104–105, 106, 107, 109, 110, 112, 200–201, 212, 223
**John Gattuso** 258T, 286T
**George H.H. Huey** 4L, 18, 19, 20, 22, 24, 36–37, 90L, 92, 94L, 95, 97, 98, 100, 101, 116–117, 120, 148, 168–169, 170, 174, 181, 187, 195B, 237L, 242, 288–289
**Kerrick James** 86–87, 145, 207, 210–211, 216, 226, 231, 291, 298
**Catherine Karnow** 32, 66, 74, 75, 243, 292B
**Bob Krist** 124–125, 128–129, 224–225
**Library of Congress** 16, 26, 28, 41, 42, 44, 45, 64–65, 90R, 189
**Los Alamos Historical Society** 46, 47, 48, 49
**Museum of New Mexico** 14–15 (neg no 5324), 17 (Henry A. Schmidt, neg no 12653), 29, 33 (T. Harmon Parkhurst, neg no 9973), 34 (neg no 88121), 35 (J.R. Riddle, neg no 38211), 38 (Edward Kemp, neg no 151373), 39 (neg no 65116), 43 (Bennett & Burrall, neg no 14264), 56–57 (T. Harmon Parkhurst, neg no 3895), 161 (John Candelario, neg no 165660), 163 (T. Harmon Parkhurst, neg no 3860), 218B (neg no 40406), 258B (Edward S. Curtis, neg no 143715), 281B (neg no 30769), 287 (R.W. Russell, neg no 15893)
**Richard Nowitz** 2, 3B, 4B, 4–5, 5B, 10–11, 21, 30, 51, 54, 55, 59, 60, 61, 62, 67, 68, 71, 73, 76, 77, 78, 79, 82, 83, 91, 99, 108, 113, 114–115, 130, 132T, 134T, 134B, 136T, 137, 138T, 138L, 138R, 139, 140T, 140B, 142T, 142B, 143T, 143B, 144T, 144B, 149, 152T, 152B, 153T, 154T, 154B, 155, 156T, 164T, 166T, 177, 186T, 195T, 196T, 197, 198B, 206T, 208T, 208B, 213, 214T, 214B, 215T, 215B, 216T, 217, 218T, 219L, 219R, 220T, 220–221, 221T, 222T, 228–229, 230, 232T, 234T, 235, 236T, 236B, 237R, 238T, 238B, 239, 240–241, 244T, 245, 246T, 246B, 247, 248T, 248B, 250–251, 253, 254T, 257, 262, 264–265, 269T, 269B, 270T, 271, 272T, 272B, 273, 274T, 274L, 274R, 275T, 275B, 276–277, 278, 281T, 282T, 282B, 283, 284T, 284B, 285T, 285B, 286BL, 286BR, 292T, 294T, 294BL, 295, 296–297, 299, 300T, 300B, 302T, 302B, 303, 304
**Jack Parsons** 8–9, 12, 40, 53, 63, 69, 70, 84, 94R, 131, 133, 141, 156B, 158–159, 160, 164B, 166B, 176, 183, 185, 190–191, 192, 193, 196B, 198T, 199, 202, 203, 204T, 204B, 205, 206B, 209, 222B, 244B, 249, 255, 266, 267, 279
**Santa Fe Convention & Visitors Bureau** 72, 80, 151
**Smithsonian Institution** 25, 184T
**Tom Till** 27, 88, 89, 93, 96, 102, 157, 172–173, 178–179, 256, 259, 260–261
**Stephen Trimble** 6–7, 146–147, 150, 165, 167, 171, 175, 180, 182, 184B, 188, 252
**Wiley/Wales** 52, 103, 126, 186B, 270B, 290

**Map Production** Laura Morris

# Index

*Numbers in italics refer to photographs*

# TRULY ADVENTUROUS

# TRULY ASIA

In the heart of Asia lies a land of many cultures, wonders and attractions. Especially for the adventure seeker to whom fear is not a factor. There are hundreds of thrills to experience. Mount Kinabalu. Mulu Caves. Taman Negara. These are just a few places where you'll always find that rewarding adrenaline rush. Where is this land, so challenging and exhilarating? It can only be Malaysia, Truly Asia.

*Malaysia*
*Truly Asia*